THE AESTHETICS OF NOSTALGIA:
HISTORICAL REPRESENTATION IN OLD ENGLISH VERSE

RENÉE R. TRILLING

The Aesthetics of Nostalgia:

Historical Representation
in Old English Verse

UNIVERSITY OF TORONTO PRESS
Toronto Buffalo London

©University of Toronto Press Incorporated 2009
Toronto   Buffalo   London
www.utppublishing.com
Printed in Canada

ISBN 978-0-8020-9971-6

Printed on acid-free, 100% post-consumer recycled paper with vegetable-based inks.

Library and Archives Canada Cataloguing in Publication

Trilling, Renée R.
   The aesthetics of nostalgia: historical representation in Old English
verse / Renée R. Trilling.

(Toronto Anglo-Saxon series)
Includes bibliographical references and index.
ISBN 978-0-8020-9971-6

1. English poetry – Old English, ca. 450–1100 – History and criticism.
2. Literature and history – England.   3. Nostalgia in literature.   4. History
in literature.   I. Title.   II. Series: Toronto Anglo-Saxon series

PR1764.B58 2009   829'.1009   C2009-902077-7

The author gratefully acknowledges the University of Exeter Press for permission to quote excerpts from the following: 'The Ruin,' in *Three Old English Elegies*, ed. R.F. Leslie (Exeter: University of Exeter Press, 1988), pp. 51–2 (ISBN 978-0-85989-184-4); 'Deor,' in *The Exeter Anthology of Old English Poetry*, ed. Bernard J. Muir, rev. 2nd ed. (Exeter: University of Exeter Press, 2000), pp. 281–3 (ISBN 978-0-85989-629-0); and 'Widsith,' in *The Exeter Anthology of Old English Poetry*, ed. Bernard J. Muir, rev. 2nd ed. (Exeter: University of Exeter Press, 2000), pp. 238–43 (ISBN 978-0-85989-629-0).

University of Toronto Press gratefully acknowledges the financial assistance of the Centre for Medieval Studies, University of Toronto, in the publication of this book.

University of Toronto Press acknowledges the financial assistance to its publishing program of the Canada Council for the Arts and the Ontario Arts Council.

University of Toronto Press acknowledges the financial support for its publishing activities of the Government of Canada through the Book Publishing Industry Development Program (BPIDP).

For Jim and Rowan

Contents

Acknowledgments

It is a tremendous pleasure to be able, finally, to thank the many people whose support, both intellectual and personal, has sustained the creation of this book. Like most academic work, it is largely the fruit of conferences, seminars, workshops, reading groups, colloquia, and informal conversations too numerous to mention. Many people whose offhand remarks made me think differently go unnamed here, as do the scholars before me whose work enabled me to undertake this project in the first place, but I want to acknowledge their contributions.

My first and greatest debt is to my former dissertation director, Katherine O'Brien O'Keeffe, whose guidance has helped me to develop as a scholar and to avoid many professional pitfalls. Her intellectual rigour and generosity set a very high standard indeed, and it has been an honour to have her as a teacher and mentor. I am also grateful to the members of my dissertation committee at the University of Notre Dame, Gerald Bruns, Jill Mann, and Michael Lapidge, for their criticism as well as their encouragement. I learned a great deal from them and from other members of the Notre Dame faculty, especially Kathleen Biddick, Dolores Warwick Frese, Maura Nolan, and Ewa Plonowska Ziarek. They were kind yet exacting teachers, and I was extremely fortunate to begin my research career under such tutelage. My graduate colleagues also made Notre Dame an inspiring place to think and learn, and I am thankful for the camaraderie of Siobhain Bly Calkin, Sara Crosby, Anne Enenbach, Erich Hertz, Paul Patterson, Scott Smith, and Kathleen Tonry.

The University of Illinois has been a wonderful place in which to bring this project to completion, and I am grateful for this truly remarkable intellectual community. Charlie Wright has been guide, editor, coach, and cheerleader over the past few years, and I feel very lucky to have landed in his department. Dennis Baron, Jon Ebel, Jed Esty, Lori Garner, Stephen Jaeger, Jim Hurt, Marcus Keller, Curtis Perry, Nora Stoppino, Carol Symes, Joe Valente, Julia Walker, and Brian Walsh all read and commented on portions of the project at various stages in its development, and many conversations with Karen Fresco, Andrea Goulet, Catharine Gray, Matt Hart, Anne D. Hedeman, Lilya Kaganovsky, Marianne Kalinke, Zachary Lesser, William Maxwell, Erin Murphy, Michael Rothberg, Rob Rushing, Yasemin Yildiz, and the graduate students in my Fall 2006 seminar helped me to think through new approaches to the material. My department head, Martin Camargo, was a voice of support and reassurance at every stage of this process, and the University has provided generous support in the form of research and travel grants.

My debts extend far beyond Notre Dame and Illinois, however, and it has been my privilege to be a part of a warm and welcoming community of medieval scholars. I am especially grateful to Chris Abram, Tom Bredehoft, Warren Brown, Scott Bruce, Sam Collins, Tracey-Anne Cooper, Abe Delnore, Nick Doane, Martin Foys, Jason Glenn, Bruce Holsinger, Ethan Knapp, Anna Trumbore Jones, Anne Lester, Roy Liuzza, Laura Morreale, Andrew Rabin, Theo Riches, Alice Sheppard, Kathleen Stewart, Paul Szarmach, and Emily Thornbury for serving as interlocutors on many occasions and for reminding me how extraordinary this profession can be. I owe more than I can express to Rebecca Stephenson and Jacqueline Stodnick, who read every word of this book, including many that, thanks to them, are no longer in it. Their humour, honesty, and friendship have been among the greatest rewards of a career in academia.

From the first draft, I dreamed of this book as a Toronto book, and seeing it published by the University of Toronto Press is gratifying indeed. I am very grateful to the editors, Suzanne Rancourt and Barb Porter, who have shepherded me expertly through the publication process, and to the UTP production staff, particularly Theresa Griffin, who have saved me from many errors. I would also like to thank the anonymous readers, whose insightful comments, thoughtful criticism, and enthusiastic evaluations have made the final product a much better book than the one I originally sent them. Their professionalism has been a model for me, and their efficiency has allowed the book to see the light of day sooner than I expected.

My parents, Neil and Becky Trilling, always encouraged me to read as much as I wanted to, little knowing where it would lead. Their unflagging support has seen me through the ups and downs of both my work and my life. I am grateful to my daughter, Rowan Trilling-Hansen, for reminding me how important stories are and for the hugs, cuddles, and laughter that have sustained me for the past six years. My husband, Jim Hansen, has been a support to me since before I began the project, and is the only one who really knows what it has meant to me. Without him the book would not exist, and it is one of many things for which I owe him thanks.

An earlier version of chapter 1 appeared as 'Ruins in the Realm of Thoughts: Reading as Constellation in Anglo-Saxon Poetry' in *The Journal of English and Germanic Philology*. Copyright 2009 by the Board of Trustees of the University of Illinois. Used with permission of the University of Illinois Press.

Abbreviations

AN&Q	*American Notes & Queries*
ASE	*Anglo-Saxon England*
ASNSL	*Archiv für das Studium der neueren Sprachen und Literaturen*
ASPR	*Anglo-Saxon Poetic Records*
CCSL	Corpus christianorum, series latina
CSEL	Corpus scriptorum ecclesiasticorum latinorum
EEMF	Early English Manuscripts in Facsimile
EETS	Early English Text Society
EHD	English Historical Documents
EHR	*English Historical Review*
ELH	*English Literary History*
ES	*English Studies*
fol., fols	folio, folios
JEGP	*Journal of English and Germanic Philology*
JMEMS	*Journal of Medieval and Early Modern Studies*
JMH	*Journal of Medieval History*
MGH	Monumenta Germaniae historica
MLN	*Modern Language Notes*
MLQ	*Modern Language Quarterly*
MLR	*Modern Language Review*
MP	*Modern Philology*
MS, MSS	manuscript, manuscripts
N&Q	*Notes & Queries*
NM	*Neuphilologische Mitteilungen*
PBA	*Proceedings of the British Academy*
PIMS	Pontifical Institute of Mediaeval Studies
PQ	*Philological Quarterly*

RES	*Review of English Studies*
s.a.	*sub anno*, under the year
SELIM	*SELIM: Journal of the Spanish Society for Medieval English Language and Literature*
SM	*Studi Medievali*
SP	*Studies in Philology*
SPCK	Society for Promoting Christian Knowledge
TRHS	*Transactions of the Royal Historical Society*

THE AESTHETICS OF NOSTALGIA:
HISTORICAL REPRESENTATION IN OLD ENGLISH VERSE

Introduction:
The Form of History

Creative nostalgia reveals the fantasies of the age, and it is in those fantasies
and potentialities that the future is born. One is nostalgic not for the past the
way it was, but for the past the way it could have been. It is this past perfect
that one strives to realize in the future.

Svetlana Boym, *The Future of Nostalgia*

The image of the Germanic lord, seated at the head of the mead-hall and
calling for the scop to sing the history of his ancestors, is an iconic, if anachronistic, cultural artefact, yet it continues to inform many readings of
Anglo-Saxon poetic texts. Certainly the first Anglo-Saxonists approached
the poetry by picking apart texts like *Beowulf* and *Widsith* for historical
information about the pre-Migration Germanic peoples, searching for the
site of the Battle of Brunanburh, and mapping the narrative of *The Battle
of Maldon* onto the terrain of Essex. As J.R.R. Tolkien reminded everyone
in 1936, however, *Beowulf* is poetry first, and history only in a secondary,
ancillary sense.[1] Furthermore, the heroic 'tradition' is a product not of
generations of Germanic storytelling but of poems committed to manuscript in the tenth and eleventh centuries and providing our only evidence
of such a tradition. That these poems lay claim to the representation of
history by situating themselves alongside the legendary tales of the Anglo-
Saxons' pagan ancestors only complicates the picture, for the heroic world
of pre-Migration Germania bears little resemblance to the world of late
Anglo-Saxon England. The Germanic lord was as anachronistic then as he
is now, and heroic Old English verse accordingly is coloured by a profound

---

1 J.R.R. Tolkien, '*Beowulf*: The Monsters and the Critics,' *PBA* 22 (1936): 245–95.

sense of nostalgia. Nostalgia, which paradoxically affirms the past (and very often a fictional past at that) by reconstituting the story of its passing, is primarily concerned with the present; and in the very excesses of nostalgic longing, Slavoj Žižek and J.M. Fritzman locate the foundations of representation and the possibility of ideology.[2] Literary nostalgia is thus, as Fredric Jameson has noted, principally an aesthetic project that makes use of pre-existing forms (Jameson calls them stereotypes) in order to distance the reader from the present.[3] From this perspective, Old English historical poetry, with its aesthetics of nostalgia, becomes a medium in which Anglo-Saxon England works out its collective relationship to the present through the poetic representation of a heroic past.

Nostalgia encompasses the collective longing of a cultural unconscious that can be traced through its literary remains. The traditional elements that poetry draws on for its ideological force are products of literary discourse; they are fictive constructs endowed with meaning by being projected into an imagined past. Yet the world invoked by Anglo-Saxon poetry is not one of pure fiction, and the heroic ethos that underscores it has identifiable sources, despite the fact that its existence in tenth century Anglo-Saxon England is a literary construct. Heroic history does not create a world out of whole cloth, but stitches together a patchwork of ideas, myths, and relics of the past to create a coherent picture of historicity in the present. Because they can never be fully reconstructed as they originally existed (in large part because they never did), these fragments of the past will always exceed attempts to represent them, and for that reason serve as the perfect vehicle for an ideology generated at the nexus of aesthetics and desire.[4] Like the crumbling walls of *The Ruin*, the fragments of

---

2 Slavoj Žižek, *The Sublime Object of Ideology* (London: Verso, 1989); J.M. Fritzman, 'The Future of Nostalgia and the Time of the Sublime,' *Clio* 23 (1994): 167–89.

3 Fredric Jameson, 'Nostalgia for the Present,' in *Postmodernism, or, The Cultural Logic of Late Capitalism*, 279–96 (Durham: Duke University Press, 1991). I use 'aesthetic' in the sense developed by Kant and Hegel, to indicate the mediation performed by the work of art between the particular and the universal; see Immanuel Kant, *Critique of Judgement*, trans. and introd. J.H. Bernard (New York: Hafner, 1951); and G.W.F. Hegel, *Introductory Lectures on Aesthetics*, trans. Bernard Bosanquet, ed. and introd. Michael Inwood (London: Penguin, 1993).

4 As per Žižek's definition of ideology: 'a kind of reality which is possible only on condition that the individuals partaking in it are *not* aware of its proper logic; that is, a kind of reality *whose very ontological consistency implies a certain non-knowledge of its participants*' (*Sublime Object*, 21; emphasis in original). For Žižek, 'the Sublime is therefore the paradox of an object which, in the very field of representation, provides a view, in a negative way, of the dimension of what is unrepresentable' (203). For heroic

the heroic tradition can be reused to construct a new edifice thoroughly imbued with the aura of history.

Writing about popular conceptions of the decade we call 'the fifties,' Jameson explains that 'the list [of traits that define "the fifties"] is not a list of facts or historical realities (although its items are not invented and are in some sense "authentic"), but rather a list of stereotypes, of ideas of facts and historical realities.'[5] The trappings of heroic life that decorate poems like *The Battle of Maldon* and *The Battle of Brunanburh* are similarly the conventionally recognized relics of an earlier age, invoked in a new context to provide contemporary life with shape and meaning. It is this connection to the idea of a 'tradition' that makes nostalgia such a powerful vehicle for group, and even national, identity: the richness of a tradition purporting to extend backwards through history into the mists of the group's mythic origin provides a solid ideological foundation for the construction of present unity. Jameson sees this kind of aesthetic exploration as evidence of a collective unconscious working out its relationship to its own present; in this sense, historical poetry is not really concerned with representing the past, but rather with recording the present moment. Accordingly, 'historicity is, in fact, neither a representation of the past nor a representation of the future (although its various forms *use* such representations): it can first and foremost be defined as a perception of the present as history; that is, as a relationship to the present which somehow defamiliarizes it and allows us that distance from immediacy which is at length characterized as a historical perspective.'[6] Through the invocation of historicity, the present takes on the aura of the past, and the operation of historical discourse distances readers from the event at the same time that the aesthetic operation allows readers to experience it more immediately. Nostalgia, then, must be understood in a dialectical relationship to history: as it attempts to reconstruct the lost past in the present moment, its manipulation of material events into aesthetic objects turns the present into history, thereby reifying the separation between present and past.[7]

history, nostalgia operates in that negative space to point toward the unrepresentable past of its own narrative construction.

5 Jameson, 'Nostalgia,' 279.
6 Jameson, 'Nostalgia,' 284; emphasis in original.
7 Susan Stewart connects the desire that drives nostalgia with the desire that drives narrative, and separates both from what she calls 'lived experience': 'Nostalgia is a sadness without an object, a sadness which creates a longing that of necessity is inauthentic because it does not take part in lived experience. Rather, it remains behind and before that experience. Nostalgia, like any form of narrative, is always ideological:

The production of Anglo-Saxon historical verse, like any history-writing, is a project rooted very much in the ideology of its own historical present, but it artfully disguises that ideology behind a mask of 'tradition,' glossing over the fact that 'tradition' itself is a product of present writings and rewritings. The strength of that tradition, however, and its ideological power to shape our understanding of what Anglo-Saxon England really was, is evinced not only by a sizeable corpus of heroic poetry, both secular and religious and spanning at least four centuries of production, but also by the tenacity with which literary criticism clings to the image of the Anglo-Saxon warrior as an icon of English values. Anglo-Saxon vernacular literature is thus haunted by the spectre of a heroic past that is always absent, a tradition that has been created by the poets and that is continually mourned by the poetry.[8] Yet this, as Susan Stewart suggests, is precisely what nostalgia does: it mourns a past that never existed by creating it through narrative.[9] Certainly this is what the Old English poets who take history as the subject of their verse do; but it is also, perhaps paradoxically, what scholars of the Anglo-Saxon period do, gazing at the objects of their study with the interests of the present very much in mind.

The purpose of this book is to illuminate the role of this nostalgia for the past in Old English literature by exploring the relationship between poetic form and historical consciousness in early English vernacular verse.[10] I take as my starting point the current trend in literary studies toward reconsideration of aesthetics and formalism, but I do so with the explicit intention of thinking historically about both aesthetics and form; as Seth Lerer has put it, 'formalist analysis in medieval literary study needs

---

the past it seeks has never existed except as narrative, and hence, always absent, that past continually threatens to reproduce itself as a felt lack' (23). The lack of the past becomes the object of desire, and the longing for what is missing drives the narrative of nostalgic history. Significantly, what is lacking is not simply the lost past, but a sense of meaning in the present; nostalgia addresses this lack through the narrative creation of a past that will help the present make sense. See Stewart, *On Longing: Narratives of the Miniature, the Gigantic, the Souvenir, the Collection* (Durham: Duke University Press, 1993).

8 Svetlana Boym, for example, differentiates between customs, which are long-standing practices carried more or less intact through time, and traditions, which are created retrospectively in order to serve a present need. See Boym, *The Future of Nostalgia* (New York: Basic, 2001), 42–3.

9 Stewart, *On Longing*, 22–7.

10 I borrow this idea from the historical mediation of aesthetics and hermeneutics outlined by Hans-Georg Gadamer: 'art is never simply past but is able to overcome temporal distance by virtue of its own meaningful presence' (*Truth and Method*, 2nd rev. ed., rev. trans. Joel Weinsheimer and Donald G. Marshall [New York: Continuum, 1995], 165).

to be reclaimed from its New Critical close reading, but it also needs to be seen as the place where aesthetics and ideology may come together.'[11] In recent decades, the role of literature in the construction of Anglo-Saxon values, beliefs, and community identity has received considerable attention. Nicholas Howe, for example, has examined the length and breadth of the literary tradition, and pointed to the repeated emergence of a 'myth of migration' that articulates the Anglo-Saxons' relationship to their continental past and becomes a point of common identification.[12] Other scholars, such as Kathleen Davis, emphasize the importance of this communal history: the 'recollection of a national history in the form of an appeal to an ideal past not only posits the nation as a preexisting, homogeneous entity, but also authorizes the contemporary nation in terms of *apparently* intrinsic, timeless charateristics.'[13] One of those 'apparently timeless characteristics' is the heroism of the Germanic warrior tradition, and heroic poetry played no small role in the formation and articulation of English identity.[14] Thinking about the formation of English identity in literary terms makes

---

11 Seth Lerer, 'The Endurance of Formalism in Middle English Studies,' *Literature Compass* 1 (2003): 1–15 at 1, http://www.blackwellsynergy.com/doi/full/10.1111/j.1741-4113 .2004.00006.x. For an overview (and critique) of 'new formalism,' see Marjorie Levinson, 'What Is New Formalism?' *PMLA* 122 (2007): 558–69; a longer version of the essay is available at http://sitemaker.umich.edu/pmla_article. But see also Jim Hansen, who argues that a re-evaluation of the aesthetic offers new opportunities for apprehending the historicity of texts in 'Formalism and Its Malcontents: Benjamin and de Man on the Function of Allegory,' *New Literary History* 35 (2004): 663–83.

12 Howe's work not only established the 'migration myth' as a key term in the study of Anglo-Saxon literature; it also offered a methodology for apprehending the power of literary works to function ideologically, as a lens through which their readers, both medieval and modern, might perceive the historical conditions of Anglo-Saxon England (Howe, *Migration and Mythmaking in Anglo-Saxon England* [New Haven: Yale University Press, 1989; repr. Notre Dame: University of Notre Dame Press, 2001]).

13 Kathleen Davis, 'National Writing in the Ninth Century: A Reminder for Postcolonial Thinking about the Nation,' *JMEMS* 28 (1998): 611–37 at 622; emphasis in original.

14 Jennifer Neville, for example, has explored how the Germanic tradition served as a myth of origins for both Carolingian and Anglo-Saxon nationalism; in her analysis, *Beowulf* becomes both an aesthetic and an ideological archetype; and texts like the Chronicle poems mirror the Latin panegyrics composed for Charlemagne to celebrate monarchical heroism and national identity as consubstantial. See Neville, 'History, Poetry, and "National" Identity in Anglo-Saxon England and the Carolingian Empire,' in *Germanic Texts and Latin Models: Medieval Reconstructions*, ed. K.E. Olsen, A. Harbus, and T. Hofstra, 107–26 (Leuven: Peeters, 2001). See also Thorlac Turville-Petre, *England the Nation: Language, Literature, and National Identity, 1290–1340* (Oxford: Clarendon, 1996); and Peter R. Richardson, 'Making Thanes: Literature, Rhetoric, and State Formation in Anglo-Saxon England,' *PQ* 78 (1999): 215–32.

use of what Brian Stock has called 'textual communities' and recognizes the importance of literature's mediation of history, both as a reflection of contemporary modes of thought and as a tool for shaping a reader's perception of the world.[15] But such thinking does not necessarily explore how that shaping proceeds from the aesthetic form that distinguishes the literary work in the first place; and in the midst of this focus on historical context, the crucial fact that heroic poetry is a work of art as well as a vehicle for ideology has frequently been overlooked. The aesthetics of nostalgia that give Old English historical poetry its distinctive colouring proceed as much from the formal qualities of the verse as from the longing and desires of the poets and their audiences.

This is not to say that a poem like *Beowulf* has been ignored by formalists; far from it. Metrics, source studies, oral traditional poetics, and structural patterns such as interlace and envelope have been deployed in myriad ways to illuminate the poem for modern readers, and no half-line has been left unturned. The culmination of these formalist exercises is Fred Robinson's 1985 Beowulf *and the Appositive Style*, which argues that the characteristic features of Old English poetry – at the grammatical level, apposition, and at the level of the poem, digression and repetition – create a 'syntactically open poem' that allows the *Beowulf* poet to explore the complexities of the Christian Anglo-Saxons' relationship to their pagan heritage.[16] Apposition presents audiences with a range of semantic possibilities, and each apposition likewise has multiple meanings with both Christian and pagan colouring. Robinson argues that 'in *Beowulf* the poet is concerned with confronting his Christian nation with the heroic age of their heathen ancestors ... [and] to achieve this confrontation (and ultimately reconciliation) he exploits in a unique way the paratactic, juxtapositional character of Old English poetic style.'[17] The polyvalence of the heroic lexicon in the post-conversion era means that individual words can bear both pagan and Christian meanings simultaneously, and this 'semantic stratification of Old English poetic diction' makes a place for the heroic

---

15 Stock's 'textual communities' are comprised of both literate readers of texts and illiterate hearers of texts read or performed aloud. Stock thus extends the influence of textuality on medieval 'modes of thought' beyond conventional literacy to include a much wider scope of audiences (Brian Stock, *The Implications of Literacy: Written Language and Models of Interpretation in the Eleventh and Twelfth Centuries* [Princeton: Princeton University Press, 1983], especially 1–10 and 30–87).

16 Fred C. Robinson, Beowulf *and the Appositive Style* (Knoxville: University of Tennessee Press, 1985), 15–16.

17 Robinson, *Appositive Style*, 27.

past in Christian Anglo-Saxon England: 'By restricting his names for the higher being(s) to words which have two possible referents, Christian and pre-Christian, and then placing these words in a poem in which simultaneous Christian and pre-Christian contexts are pervasively present, he has solved in a way that is seriously meaningful the problem that is central to his theme of cultural reconciliation.'[18] Robinson finds ultimately that the poet uses the open syntax of the appositive style, its digressions and repetitions, and the semantic simultaneity it allows to gently nudge the poem's readers toward a Christian reconciliation with their pagan past. The meaning of the poem, in both its literal and its symbolic aspects, is embedded in its form; it is in fact the very structure of the bipartite alliterative long line, and the replication of its formal patterns at the level of structure as well as syntax, that allows the poet to accomplish this. In this reading, form and content are inseparable; Robinson has made a profound statement about the relation between aesthetics and meaning in Old English verse.

For Robinson, Anglo-Saxon poetic form is essential to the poet's project of reconciliation between pagan past and Christian present because it synthesizes the seemingly opposing meanings of individual words and episodes through apposition and juxtaposition. But this synthesizing does not necessarily lead to a smooth transition from pagan past to Christian present. As Roy Liuzza has put it, '*Beowulf* offers instead a deeply conflicted reflection on the uses of history, the inaccessibility of the past, and the deceptive and ambivalent roles played by memory and literature in the creation of culture.'[19] The nostalgia that underwrites that reflection surfaces again and again from the appositives and disjunctions that characterize Old English poetic style, ultimately emerging as a fundamental aesthetic in the poetry itself at the level of both the line and the narrative. The significance of poetic form in the formation of historical consciousness goes far beyond the synthesis of a Christian identity; the alliterative long line, its appositive style, and its obsession with the past produce a dialectical notion of history that ultimately resists the totalization of a single perspective, whether Christian or pagan. For *Beowulf* does not, in fact, suppress the pagan past through the possible Christian valances of its lexicon; that past remains present through the very ambiguity that Robinson identifies as formally fundamental. The Christian meaning of individual

18 Robinson, *Appositive Style*, 57, 40.

19 Roy M. Liuzza, '*Beowulf*: Monuments, Memory, History,' in *Readings in Medieval Texts: Interpreting Old and Middle English Literature*, ed. David F. Johnson and Elaine Treharne, 91–108 (Oxford: Oxford University Press, 2005), 106–7.

words and episodes is certainly available to the reader who is a believer, as Robinson argues, but semantic polyvalence preserves the words' and episodes' pagan meanings alongside the Christian ones. *Beowulf*'s relationship to the past and to the workings of memory is far too complicated for it to be said that the poem represents the eventual triumph of Christianity over pagan belief, and the poem does not offer a single vision, either of the heroic age it channels or the late Anglo-Saxon age of its transcription.

Both within the poem and in its transmission, then, *Beowulf* reminds readers of the fragile and complex link between history and memory. The poem both re-creates the ancient world of the heroic age and, at the same time, mourns its passing. Just as the alliterative long line fragments grammar and creates meaning through the accumulation of appositive detail, *Beowulf* presents history as fragments, disjunctive, and, most of all, accretive. When Beowulf emerges victorious from his struggle with Grendel, the first public act of the grateful Danes is to offer a song in his honour:

> Hwilum cyninges þegn,
> guma gilphlæden,   gidda gemyndig,
> se ðe ealfela   ealdgesegena
> worn gemunde,   word oþer fand
> soðe gebunden;   secg eft ongan
> sið Beowulfes   snyttrum styrian,
> ond on sped wrecan   spel gerade,
> wordum wrixlan …[20]
>
> (867b–874a)

In one of the poem's famous digressions, the scop recounts Beowulf's deeds alongside the exploits of the legendary Sigemund, placing the newly minted hero on a par with one of the greatest figures of Germanic tradition (874b–897). The significance of this expression of honour is not lost on Beowulf, nor on readers of the poem; the magnitude of Beowulf's achievement is directly proportional to the speed with which it is commemorated in verse, and immortality and glory are thereby secured for as long as the poem survives. The juxtaposition with a hero from legend is

---

20 *Beowulf*, ed. Friedrich Klaeber, 3rd ed. (Lexington, MA: D.C. Heath, 1950). 'At that time, the king's thane, the boastful man, mindful of songs, he who ardently kept in mind a great many of the old verses, found new words bound with truth; the man then cleverly began to rehearse Beowulf's adventure and skillfully fashion a direct account of the tale, intermingling words.' All quotations of poetry are cited by line number, and all translations, unless otherwise noted, are my own.

indeed a form of honour, but not an unqualified one. The poet's verses on Beowulf blend smoothly into a story about Sigemund and the dragon, a stylistic move that highlights Beowulf's victory, but also foreshadows the dragon battle that will end his life. The invocation of Heremod's exile in lines 898–915 further qualifies Beowulf's victory and raises questions about the transience of fame: will Beowulf ultimately earn the lasting renown of a Sigemund, or will he share in Heremod's ignominious fate?[21] The four separate figures, lifted from their chronological contexts, form what Walter Benjamin would call a 'constellation'[22] and share space in a reflective moment that invokes them all. In this constellation, the historical distance between the Sigemund and Heremod of the ancient past, the Beowulf of the present moment, and the dragon yet to come collapses.[23] The juxtaposition of Beowulf, Sigemund, Heremod, and the dragon presents not a simple comparison or contrast, but a dialectic. The meaning of Beowulf's deed is not commensurate with either victory or defeat; neither term represents the fullness of its significance, which is contingent on its placement within a historically mediated structure of similar events. At the moment of victory, the poet celebrates Beowulf's triumph in terms of legendary glory, but he also presages future defeat. This narrative strategy reminds the audience that Beowulf's deeds have meaning not in isolation, but as part of a larger constellation of events that considers the victory over Grendel alongside Beowulf's other deeds, both successful and unsuccessful, as well as alongside the deeds of other men of history and legend. The juxtaposition of multiple events allows for their simultaneous comparison and differentiation in a single narrative moment that resists a totalizing reading in a historical sense. Understanding the significance of Beowulf's fight with Grendel, then, requires meditation upon a series of interrelated historical events, including – but not limited to – the history

---

21 See R.E. Kaske, 'The Sigemund-Heremod and Hama-Hygelac Passages in *Beowulf*,' *PMLA* 74 (1959): 489–94.

22 Benjamin uses the image of the constellation to express a critical methodology in which concepts are drawn into a relation so that their arrangement allows the observer to apprehend a larger meaning or idea, just as the arrangement of stars in a constellation allows the viewer to apprehend the image of Andromeda or Orion. See Walter Benjamin, *The Origin of German Tragic Drama*, trans. John Osborne (London: Verso, 1998), 34. For a fuller discussion, see pp. 30–42 below.

23 Scholars generally agree that the majority of the poem's audience would already be familiar with the story; as Liuzza remarks, 'Whatever else *Beowulf* intends to be, it is evident from the outset that is does not intend to be a surprise' ('Monuments, Memory, History,' 92).

of Grendel's depredations among the Danes, the story of Sigemund's exploits, the cautionary tale of Heremod's loss of reputation, and the deeds that Beowulf has yet to accomplish; even then, such understanding does not exhaust the possibilities of meaning present in this highly charged narrative moment.

Through the aesthetics of nostalgia, a poem like *Beowulf* can mediate between a longing for communion with ancient heroes and the recognition that their antiquity sets them apart. The dead, like Sigemund, Hygelac, and Beowulf himself, are repeatedly resurrected and then reburied through the aesthetic process of the heroic poem. This historical juxtaposition is replicated by the form of the poetry itself, which balances forward motion, through a strict rhythmical metre that binds together the two sides of the caesura, with alliteration and appositives that refer backward and forward to other half-lines. In the passage just quoted, for example, alliteration joins pairs of half-lines into alliterative long lines and emphasizes their poetic integrity: 'guma gilphlæden, gidda gemyndig ...' (line 868). Yet each half-line is not necessarily complete in itself, and the reader is often forced to cross a line break in order to get the full sense of the phrase: 'se ðe ealfela ealdgesegena / worn gemunde ...' (869–870a). In line 870, alliteration crosses the caesura to join the end of one phrase, *worn gemunde*, to the beginning of another, *word oþer fand*, which demands that the reader then continue past another line break to get the full meaning of the phrase: 'word oþer fand / soðe gebunden' (870b–871a). Sometimes the alliteration spills over and joins half-lines that belong, metrically, to separate long lines, as in the alliteration on 's' in lines 871–3. The integrity of the long line is thus susceptible to disruption by semantics and poetics alike, and the simultaneous assertion and disruption of wholeness is the very fabric of the Anglo-Saxon poetic form. The form of Anglo-Saxon poetry thus embodies both a steady movement forward, in its metre, and repeated movements of recursion, in its use of alliteration, appositives, and enjambment, just as the passage honouring Beowulf's victory both advances the narrative and pauses to reflect on its historical connections to both past and future.[24] Put together, the stylistic movement forward and backward within a narrative that likewise moves forward and backward in time generates an aesthetics of nostalgia, which looks to the past as something that is simultaneously separate from and embodied in the present.

Reading the commemoration of Beowulf's victory in this way prompts reflections about the imbrication of poetry, memory, and history in a larger

---

24 Klaeber refers to this as the poem's 'lack of steady advance' (*Beowulf*, lvii–lviii).

sense; an audience trained to reflect on narrative in this manner will doubt-less bring these skills and tastes to the interpretation of other kinds of stories. The songs and stories that memorialize important people and events not only reflect the values and beliefs of their authors and audi-ences, but also have the power to shape readers' interpretations of history and to inform their representations of their own present. The singer's spontaneous account of *sið Beowulfes* and its evocation of a dialectical re-lation between various pasts and presents is only one example of the many ways in which *Beowulf* resists a unified reading.[25] The poet locates his story in a web of interrelated narrative, where historical figures like Hygelac exist alongside mythical ones like Sigemund, and the line between history and myth is deliberately blurred. As the arresting opening lines indicate, the poem sets Beowulf's deeds against the history of the *Gar-Dena* who are not Beowulf's own people, but who instantly evoke a sense of heroism and glory:

> HWÆT, WE GAR-DEna   in geardagum,
> þeodcyninga   þrym gefrunon,
> hu ða æþelingas   ellen fremedon![26]   (1–3)

These lines are one example of the ways in which, as Roberta Frank has shown, the *Beowulf* poet's 'sense of history' leads him to strive for histor-ical verisimilitude; he is interested in these sixth century Danes because, 'by the 890s at least, Heremod, Scyld, Healfdene, and the rest, were taken to be the common ancestors both of the Anglo-Saxon royal family and of the ninth-century Danish immigrants.'[27] The poem is able to bring together ancient past and aesthetic present, thereby bridging the gap both between periods in time and between history and legend. From this perspective, the speculative historicism of *Beowulf* fulfils a very real need not only at the moment of its composition, but at the time the poem was copied into

---

25 Juxtaposition, digression, and interlace have long been recognized as characterizing the poem's style. See John Leyerle, 'The Interlace Structure of *Beowulf,' University of Toronto Quarterly* 37 (1967): 1–17; Robinson, *Appositive Style*; and Ward Parks, 'Ring Structure and Narrative Embedding in Homer and *Beowulf,' NM* 89 (1988): 237–51.
26 'Listen. We have heard of the glory of the kings of the Spear-Danes in days gone by, how those princes performed brave deeds.'
27 Roberta Frank, 'The *Beowulf* Poet's Sense of History,' in *The Wisdom of Poetry: Essays in Early English Literature in Honor of Morton W. Bloomfield*, ed. Larry D. Benson and Siegfried Wenzel, 53–65 and 217–77 (Kalamazoo, MI: Medieval Institute Publica-tions, 1982), 63.

the Nowell Codex and in its subsequent readings and rereadings. *Beowulf*'s accretive, allusive, temporally fragmented verse narrative holds itself together by the themes that run through its many, oft-referenced tangents. The poem's chronology moves from Beowulf's youthful exploits to his death as an aged king, but along the way the narrative twists and turns through flashback and foreshadowing, gesturing toward characters and events outside the poem but within the mythic tradition and allowing historical detail to accumulate so that Beowulf's death, when it finally occurs, has meaning beyond the mere events of the poem.

What precisely that meaning is has been the topic of much scholarly debate ever since Tolkien argued that the poem is literature rather than history, from Dorothy Whitelock's argument that the poem was meant to honour the eighth-century King Offa of Mercia to Frank's suggestion that it was intended to smooth over Anglo-Scandinavian relations in the late tenth century – or even, as Kevin Kiernan has suggested, to compliment the Danish monarchs of the early eleventh.[28] In spite of frequent disagreement about date, origin, and purpose, scholars generally concur that the poem's digressions – its manner of narrating events both forward and backward in time, and both directly and allusively – are a central feature of *Beowulf*'s art, and are therefore a key to understanding the poem as a whole. Indeed, it is these very digressions, and the 'world of tragedy' to which they gesture, that create a sense of history for the reader.[29] Stanley Greenfield has commented that 'it is precisely in the accretion of historical material ... that we are made epically aware'; and Leonard Tennenhouse remarks that 'with each recounting of history we are literally taken farther back in time ... In the process of extending the public memory, the poet makes mythology into history by creating and emphasizing the sense of the past.'[30] This 'sense of the past' is profoundly nostalgic, gazing backward to a heroic past from which the present poet or reader is separated in both time and space. Yet the same nostalgia that longs for the past is able, by means of the aesthetic experience, to re-create that lost heroic age, and the poem's structure thus embodies the paradox of nostalgia, which longs for communion with a past that it helps to establish as separate from the

28 Tolkien, 'Monsters and Critics'; Dorothy Whitelock, *The Audience of* Beowulf (Oxford: Clarendon, 1951); Frank, 'Sense of History'; Kevin Kiernan, Beowulf *and the* Beowulf *Manuscript*, rev. ed. (Ann Arbor: University of Michigan Press, 1997).

29 W.P. Ker, qtd in Tolkien, 'Monsters and Critics,' 251.

30 Stanley B. Greenfield, 'Geatish History: Poetic Art and Epic Quality in *Beowulf*,' *Neophilologus* 47 (1963): 211–17 at 216; Leonard Tennenhouse, '*Beowulf* and the Sense of History,' *Bucknell Review* 19 (1971): 137–46 at 145.

present. With its allusions, the poem sketches the outlines of a whole world of the past and, through their accretion, gives the reader a historical consciousness that makes that world meaningful in the present, whether as a heroic precursor to the newly Christian English aristocracy,[31] or as a fragmentary and damned pre-Christian existence on which a Christian audience can look with horror and pity – or both.[32] In either case, the poem's aesthetic both depends upon and helps to perpetuate a nostalgic longing that recapitulates the ambiguity of the appositive style; the past, as shaped by the Old English alliterative long line and its aesthetics of nostalgia, is both a foreign country and an ancestral home.

Beowulf serves as a predictable starting point for examining the relationship between historical understanding and poetic form in large part because of its status in the English literary canon: it is a well-known and well-studied poem that explicitly locates the origin of English literature in the narration of ancient history. Yet if historians, both early and late, have perceived *Beowulf*'s historical priorities to be confused, in that the poem focuses on the tale of a single, otherwise unknown (and probably fictional) hero at the expense of more general historical detail, that is perhaps because the poem's historical methodology differs so markedly from that of traditional medieval historiography. The 'medieval consciousness of history,' as Hans-Werner Goetz describes it, consisted of 'a divine process of a history of salvation in which every past (and present) were integrated,' and in which 'historiography was a kind of "historical theology", a kind of (literary) exegesis of historical events.'[33] Rosamond McKitterick also describes medieval historiography, even when concerned with world or universal history, as focused on 'the steady progression towards the Christian people' that the salvation narrative dictates.[34] National histories, following

---

31 Patrick Wormald, 'Bede, Beowulf, and the Conversion of the Anglo-Saxon Aristocracy,' in *Bede and Anglo-Saxon England: Papers in Honour of the 1300th Anniversary of the Birth of Bede, Given at Cornell University in 1973 and 1974*, ed. Robert T. Farrell, 32–95 (London: British Archaeological Reports, 1978).

32 Robert W. Hanning, '*Beowulf* as Heroic History,' *Medievalia et Humanistica*, n.s., 5 (1974): 77–102.

33 Hans-Werner Goetz, 'Historical Consciousness and Institutional Concern in European Medieval Historiography (Eleventh and Twelfth Centuries),' in *Making Sense of Global History: The 19th International Congress of the Historical Sciences Oslo 2000 Commemorative Volume*, ed. Sølvi Sogner, 350–65 (Oslo: Universitetsforlaget, 2001), 351. See also Goetz, *Geschichtsschreibung und Geschichtsbewußtsein im hohen Mittelalter* (Berlin: Akademie Verlag, 1999).

34 Rosamond McKitterick, *Perceptions of the Past in the Early Middle Ages* (Notre Dame: University of Notre Dame Press, 2006), 19.

the models of Eusebius and Orosius, tell the story of a nation's rise to Christian virtue; political triumphs and military successes figure as a measure of God's favour rather than as evidence of individual valour. Certainly this is the narrative sketched by Bede's *Historia ecclesiastica gentis Anglorum*, which charts the rise of the Anglo-Saxons from pagan Germanic invaders to a people chosen by God to occupy the promised land of Britain. The work has long been understood as early evidence for the ideology of the *gens Anglorum* as a people with a unified identity, and it too draws on representations of the past to serve the needs of a present community of readers.[35] But the *Historia ecclesiastica* also serves as a point of reference for the disparity between Goetz's standard 'medieval consciousness of history' and the historical consciousness generated by heroic verse like *Beowulf*. The topic of this history is the same: Bede, like the *Beowulf* poet, is deeply interested in the Germanic peoples who conquered England and eventually became the Anglo-Saxons, and he presents them in an idealized rhetorical light.[36] Also like *Beowulf*, Bede's text is governed by aesthetic concerns that impart a particular kind of understanding to the events it recounts.[37] Unlike the poets of the heroic tradition, however, Bede is not interested in reactivating an ancient sense of honour and glory; instead, he regards the migratory peoples as one link in the chain of progress that culminates in the Anglo-Saxons' dominion over England as an explicitly Christian nation. His relationship to the past may be complex, but it is decidedly not ambiguous.

The *Historia ecclesiastica gentis Anglorum* is, quite literally, 'grounded' in the island; it opens with a long descriptive passage detailing not only the island's location, from the point of view of Rome, but also the range and variety of natural resources to be found there: 'BRITANNIA Oceani insula, cui

---

35 Patrick Wormald, 'Bede, the *Bretwaldas* and the Origins of the *gens Anglorum*,' in *Ideal and Reality in Frankish and Anglo-Saxon Society: Studies Presented to J.M. Wallace-Hadrill*, ed. Patrick Wormald, Donald Bullough, and Roger Collins, 99–129 (Oxford: Basil Blackwell, 1983), and '*Engla Lond*: The Making of an Allegiance,' *Journal of Historical Sociology* 7 (1994): 1–24; Sarah Foot, 'The Making of *Angelcynn*: English Identity before the Norman Conquest,' *TRHS*, 6th ser., 6 (1996): 25–49. But see also Steven Fanning, who argues that the evidence for a unified identity in Bede has been overstated; Fanning, 'Bede, *Imperium*, and the Bretwaldas,' *Speculum* 66 (1991): 1–26.

36 On the disparity between Anglo-Saxon England in the seventh and eighth centuries and the pious and unified version depicted by Bede, see Walter Goffart, 'Bede's History in a Harsher Climate,' in *Innovation and Tradition in the Writings of the Venerable Bede*, ed. Scott DeGregorio, 203–26 (Morgantown: West Virginia University Press, 2006).

37 Traditional historical discourses, like more self-consciously literary texts, are subject to their own aesthetic mandates; see Hayden White, *The Content of the Form: Narrative Discourse and Historical Representation* (Baltimore: Johns Hopkins University Press, 1987).

quondam Albion nomen fuit, inter septentrionem et occidentem locata est … Opima frugibus atque arboribus insula, et alendis apta pecoribus ac iumentis, uineas etiam quibusdam in locis germinans, sed et auium ferax terra marique generis diuersi, fluuiis quoque multum piscosis ac fontibus praeclara copiosis; et quidem praecipue issicio abundat et anguilla.'[38] In Bede's hands, the island becomes a promised land, and the Anglo-Saxons eventually settle there not because of their military superiority to the Christian Britons, but because they were chosen by God both to punish the Britons for falling away from the faith and to make the island a more properly Christian nation, in the fullness of time and through the efforts of various apostles and saints. The story told by the *Historia ecclesiastica* is the story of their inevitable conversion – how they gradually but steadily became different from the heroic pagans who began to dominate the island in the fifth and sixth centuries. Book I tells how Christianity first came to the island under the Romans and how the Britons squandered God's favour, thereby bringing God's wrath down on themselves in the form of a pagan Germanic invasion. After the Anglo-Saxons conquer, they are evangelized in short order by both the Augustinian mission and the Irish, thus fulfilling their destiny to become not only a Christian people but a people chosen by God to inhabit this land of milk and honey. Books II–III detail the spread of Christianity more widely throughout the island, and Books IV–V show the English themselves setting out as missionaries to the Continent; these four books are peppered liberally with miracles and stories of divine intervention that demonstrate repeatedly and with great clarity the worthiness of the Anglo-Saxons as God's chosen people. The memorable anecdotes of Gregory spotting the slave boys in the market and remarking punningly on their angelic appearance, of Æthelthryth preserving her virginity, of dirt from the spot where Oswald fell performing miracles, and of Cædmon receiving the divine gift of song are only a handful of the people, places, and events through which Bede charts the course of God's plan for the English and locates it firmly in the people, the culture, and the very soil of Anglo-Saxon England. Bede walks his audience through the conversion of the English, taking them from beholding the pagan invaders of a promised land to recognizing a people chosen by God, with their own saints and missionaries

---

38 *Bede's Ecclesiastical History of the English People*, ed. and trans. Bertram Colgrave and R.A.B. Mynors (Oxford: Clarendon, 1969), 1.1; henceforth *HE*. 'Britain, once called Albion, is an island of the ocean and lies to the north-west … The island is rich in crops and in trees, and has good pasturage for cattle and beasts of burden. It also produces vines in certain districts, and has plenty of both land- and waterfowl of various kinds. It is remarkable too for its rivers, which abound in fish, particularly salmon and eels, and for copious springs' (translation from Colgrave and Mynors).

spreading the faith from their island home. The smooth arc of this narrative, and its careful presentation in five well-ordered books of Latin prose history, exemplifies a conventional medieval historical consciousness in both form and content; aesthetics, once again, condition understanding. Unlike the oscillating and ambiguous aesthetics of heroic verse, however, Bede's Latin text moves steadily forward to chart its progressive movement toward a glorious Christian present and future.

Throughout, Bede is concerned not only to record the people and events that are significant for Anglo-Saxon history, but also to show how that particular history is bound up with the universal history of Christian redemption; his use of a system of chronology dating from the birth of Christ – Bede is the first historian to use such a system – is no small part of this project. The *Historia ecclesiastica* is thus also the story of how Bede's contemporaries came to find their own exalted place in the salvation drama and in the larger world of Christendom: how the English move inexorably toward the telos of salvation. The story is not without its occasional regressions; there is apostasy and backsliding aplenty, and the closing chapters of the *Historia ecclesiastica* betray uncertainty about future prosperity, with a hint of nostalgia for the heady religious fervour of the golden age.[39] Yet even this longing backward gaze ultimately returns readers' focus to future salvation. As Scott DeGregorio notes, Bede counters his anxiety about abuses of monasticism by means of the exegesis of biblical historical examples that allow him to urge reform in texts such as the Letter to Ecgbert and his commentary on Ezra.[40] In these cases, when the present state of Christianity

---

39 In *HE* 5.23, Bede describes comets portending disaster in 729 AD and worries about instability in Northumbria under Ceolwulf, 'cuius regni et principia et processus tot ac tantis redundauere rerum aduersantium motibus ut, quid de his scribi debeat quemue habitura sint finem singula, necdum sciri ualeat' [Both the beginning and the course of his reign have been filled with so many and such serious commotions and setbacks that it is as yet impossible to know what to say about them or to guess what the outcome will be]. He also seems to fear a lack of military readiness, and perhaps also abuses of monasticism, during this time of relative peace: 'Qua adridente pace ac serenitate temporum, plures in gente Nordanhymbrorum, tam nobiles quam priuati, se suosque liberos depositis armis satagunt magis, accepta tonsura, monasterialibus adscribere uotis quam bellicis exercere studiis. Quae res quem sit habitura finem, posterior aetas uidebit' [In these favourable times of peace and prosperity, many of the Northumbrian race, both noble and simple, have laid aside their weapons and taken the tonsure, preferring that they and their children should take monastic vows rather than train themselves in the art of war. What the result will be, a later generation will discover]. See also Colgrave and Mynors, 560 n1.

40 Scott DeGregorio, 'Footsteps of His Own: Bede's Commentary on Ezra-Nehemiah,' in *Innovation and Tradition*, ed. DeGregorio, 143–68 at 155–65.

compares poorly with a more pious Christian past, nostalgia serves as a tool to realign the people with their salvation destiny. As Jan Davidse reminds us, Bede's historical method is inseparable from the Christian exegetical framework of his religious belief; for Bede, as for other medieval historians, history has meaning primarily in so far as it reveals God's plan for humankind in salvation. 'The task of the historian,' Davidse writes, 'was to establish what happened in a reliable manner and in the proper sequence ... But the description of history had no significance in itself. It was important because the facts had a meaning in the eyes of the believer who was alive at the moment and at a later time and who read what had been written down ... To the believer, knowledge of the past could open the door to salvation.'[41] Knowledge of the past is therefore directed not toward understanding the present, as in the case of Old English heroic poetry, but rather toward achieving the future.

The overall structure of the *Historia ecclesiastica* supports this claim, in moving from the inheritance of a promised land through conversion to stature as a Christian nation strong enough in its faith to send out its own missionaries to its Germanic cousins on the Continent. But like *Beowulf*'s, the *Historia*'s sources of historical understanding extend beyond narrative structure to the level of form as well. Bede's debt to salvation history is rhetorical as well as thematic; Roger Ray has shown how his reliance on certain literary models affects the form, and consequently the content, of his text.[42] In modelling his own work on the rhetoric of patristic exegesis found in, for example, Augustine's *De consensu Evangelistarum*, Bede employs the *narratio veri similis* in order to emphasize the workings of the *vera lex historiae*; his concern is not with the details of the event so much as with the truth of the Christian meaning the event reveals. Like the appositive style, exegetical rhetoric carries within it a certain historical consciousness, which views the past as evidence of a divine plan for a people. Bede, like the Church Fathers themselves, reflected consciously on the use of classical rhetoric for scriptural exegesis. This was not simply one way of writing history; it was the only way to write history properly. Ray shows how Bede's consciousness of biblical style helps him convey the salvific dimension of English history by arranging it according to the same conventions that inspired not only the

---

41 Jan Davidse, 'The Sense of History in the Works of the Venerable Bede,' *SM* 23 (1982): 647–95 at 656.

42 Roger D. Ray, 'Bede, the Exegete, as Historian,' in *Famulus Christi: Essays in Commemoration of the Thirteenth Centenary of the Birth of the Venerable Bede*, ed. Gerald Bonner, 125–40 (London: SPCK, 1976).

patristic commentaries on scripture, but the writing of scripture itself. 'Perhaps,' he writes, 'Bede imposed on his own account of Christian beginnings in England the same pattern by which he thought Moses had shaped the earliest history of all religion.'[43] By employing a biblical aesthetic, Bede turns English history into biblical history; it follows the shape, and consequently the meaning, of its exegetical predecessors in documenting 'the steady progression towards the Christian people.' Like the appositive style of the *Beowulf* poet and other Old English poets, Bede's formal choices shape the kind of historical consciousness his text embodies, and the *Historia ecclesiastica* views the past accordingly: as prologue to the triumph of present virtue and future salvation, with the memory of pagan ancestors safely tucked away on the far side of an immutable temporal boundary. In place of *Beowulf*'s ambiguity about the meanings of history and its continually fluctuating relation to the present, the *Historia ecclesiastica* offers a secure vision of the Anglo-Saxons as the embodiment of a Christian people moving confidently on the road to salvation. This vision had powerful ideological implications as well, and the concept of a *gens Anglorum* – the idea that the English were one people who have been chosen by God – was an ideological construct that later writers and rulers were able to exploit.[44] Bede's vision, of course, draws on the normative forms for Christian history, and becomes normative in its turn; the teleological lines of salvation history govern the bulk of official historiographical production in Anglo-Saxon England, both in Latin and in the vernacular. Old English poetry, even when it recounts verifiable historical events, does not generally rate as reliable history for modern scholars.

It would be imprudent, and indeed unnecessary, to suggest that Bede's *Historia ecclesiastica* and *Beowulf* are antagonistic in their differing approaches to history; they also have a great deal in common.[45] As founding moments in the English literary tradition, both texts enjoy considerable popularity. Bede is rightly regarded as the father of English historiography, and the *Historia ecclesiastica* circulated in hundreds of manuscripts

---

43 Ray, 'Bede, the Exegete,' 134. Alan Thacker takes this idea a step further, suggesting that all Bede's written work was intended, from the level of grammar to that of allegoresis, to organize Christian knowledge in a particular way for his students; see 'Bede and the Ordering of Understanding,' in DeGregorio, *Innovation and Tradition*, 37–63.

44 As in Wormald, 'Bede, the *Bretwaldas*'; and Foot, 'Making of *Angelcynn*.'

45 Andrew Scheil has recently argued that *Beowulf*'s vision of history in fact owes a great deal to late antique and early medieval conventions of historiography; see 'The Historiographic Dimensions of *Beowulf*,' *JEGP* 107 (2008): 281–302.

throughout the Middle Ages. *Beowulf* is a staple of English literature surveys and often the only Anglo-Saxon text that people outside the field
have read. Both texts accordingly have been seen as foundational to the
development of English political and social identity. As Maurice Halbwachs
has noted, and as most historians would agree, the shared memory of a
common past is a powerful tool for social cohesion, and texts like *Beowulf*
and the *Historia ecclesiastica* both work to draw their audiences into the
memory of a common past.[46] But the two texts take up alternative, if not
necessarily opposing, theoretical positions on the construction of historical understanding: there is *Beowulf*'s allusive ambiguity on the one hand,
and Bede's unidirectional narrative of progress on the other. It may be useful, then, to position *Beowulf* and Bede at opposite ends of the spectrum
of historiographic possibilities in Anglo-Saxon England. The divide in
some ways (and not surprisingly) replicates our own modern disciplinary
divide between literature and history, but at its root are the very real and
powerful formal differences in the kinds of historical consciousness – the
relationships between present and past – that each text engenders. Simply
put, alliterative heroic poetry invites readers to think about the past in
ways very different from those promoted by the linear, teleological view
of history that governs Latin medieval historiography. Bede may be the
father of English historiography, but his is a particular brand of history,
and, as a wide array of work on folklore and oral poetics has demonstrated, it was not the only kind of history-writing current in Anglo-Saxon
culture.[47] The function of historical writing – how it works on its audience, and the kinds of meaning it is capable of producing – varies as much
according to form as it does according to authorial intention or date and
place of composition. Though not necessarily competing with each other,
these two visions of history reveal political investments as widely divergent

---

46 Maurice Halbwachs, *Les cadres sociaux de la mémoire* (Paris: Presses Universitaires de
    France, 1952), English trans. *On Collective Memory*, ed. and trans. Lewis A. Coser
    (Chicago: University of Chicago Press, 1992); and *La mémoire collective* (Paris: Presses
    Universitaires de France, 1950), English trans. *The Collective Memory*, trans. Francis J.
    Ditter, Jr, and Vida Yazdi Ditter (New York: Harper and Row, 1980). See also James
    Fentress and Chris Wickham, *Social Memory* (Oxford: Blackwell, 1992); and the essays
    collected in *The Uses of the Past in the Early Middle Ages*, ed. Yitzhak Hen and
    Matthew Innes (Cambridge: Cambridge University Press, 2000).
47 See, for example, John Miles Foley, *Immanent Art: From Structure to Meaning in
    Traditional Oral Epic* (Bloomington: Indiana University Press, 1991); and Joseph
    Harris, 'A Nativist Approach to *Beowulf*: The Case of Germanic Elegy,' in *Companion
    to Old English Poetry*, ed. Henk Aertsen and Rolf H. Bremmer, Jr, 45–62 (Amsterdam:
    VU University Press, 1994).

as the texts' formal characteristics. Bede's teleological vision of history moves inexorably forward, whereas the historical consciousness of a Beowulfian aesthetic is marked by its nostalgia, a mode better suited to mediating a dialectic of past and present. Recovering fragments of history and expounding their significance for the present moment, the aesthetics of nostalgia simultaneously encompass a past that is always present, and a present that mourns its irrevocable loss. This ambiguity may be less adaptable, by virtue of its formal requirements, to the needs of a progressive notion of history, but it accounts for a significant portion of Anglo-Saxon textual production and demands reconsideration. My goal, then, is to attempt a better understanding of how the aesthetics of nostalgia function to produce a historical consciousness that works precisely against the demands of a linear teleology. What purpose did this kind of history serve for its Anglo-Saxon readers, and how can it help us better understand the people and the culture that produced it? Can it perhaps help us think differently about our own relationship to the medieval past?

The connection between poetic aesthetics and the historicity of Anglo-Saxon literature has been studied explicitly, to some degree, in recent decades. Pauline Head, for example, notes the diglossia produced by digression and juxtaposition in Old English poetry, particularly in terms of its appropriation of history: 'This poetry does not draw from the past as if from something distinct from itself; rather it carries its past with it.'[48] Probing as it is, however, Head's analysis remains at the level of narrative structure and its relation to social and historical contexts. Elizabeth Tyler, on the other hand, investigates how the conventional language of Old English poetry becomes a source for poets in the later Anglo-Saxon period – what Tyler calls 'the aesthetics of the familiar.' In a poem like *The Battle of Maldon*, she argues, poetic convention functions at the verbal level to critique the present. Although she suggests that the nostalgia implied by the aesthetics of the familiar indicates little hope for the future, she does not explore the implications of those aesthetics for understanding the event, the Battle of Maldon itself, as history, nor for the historical consciousness of Old English historical poetry more generally.[49] Situated at the intersection of form and content, Anglo-Saxon historical poetry is also a nexus for a variety of interrelated binaries and the ideological processes that emerge from them: Latin and

---

48   Pauline E. Head, *Representation and Design: Tracing a Hermeneutics of Old English Poetry* (Albany: State University of New York Press, 1997), 112.
49   Elizabeth M. Tyler, *Old English Poetics: The Aesthetics of the Familiar in Anglo-Saxon England* (York: York Medieval, 2006), 159–71.

English, prose and poetry, history and legend, Christian and Germanic, sacred and secular life, and reality and representation.

The *Aesthetics of Nostalgia* takes up these binaries to frame the investigation of Anglo-Saxon historical consciousness. The following chapters examine the dichotomy between the ways in which texts like *Beowulf* and the *Historia ecclesiastica* think about the relation between past and present, and they consider explicitly how that dichotomy is embedded in aesthetic aspects of the texts. Most important, each chapter explores how different formal conventions have produced different, and sometimes competing, kinds of historical consciousness for readers of the texts, both medieval and modern. The first half of the book traces the development of the two strains of historiography exemplified by Bede and *Beowulf* – teleological and constellative – in Anglo-Saxon literature generally, in contexts where the line between representation and reality has been deliberately blurred through aesthetic fashioning. In chapter 1, I build upon Benjamin's concept of the constellation as the figure for historical consciousness to argue that the formal aesthetic of Anglo-Saxon poetry, which works through accretion, parallelism, and the balance of opposing elements, embodies this dialectical structure. In Benjamin's terms, poetry 'redeems' the past by locating and recognizing fragments of it within the present. By invoking fragments of legendary history and removing them from their original narrative context, Anglo-Saxon vernacular poetry forges thematic links between people and events of the past and those of the present, resulting in a view of history as a constitutive element of the present rather than as a prelude to it. The Anglo-Saxon poems *Deor* and *The Ruin* reveal this unorthodox vision of history through their manipulation of both heroic legend and alliterative poetic technique. Instead of a linear narrative progression, these poems organize history by relating individual events to the present moment. *Deor* consciously manages the juxtaposition of characters and events from the heroic tradition to affirm the meaning of history; for Deor, the sufferer's reflection upon the past offers philosophical consolation. *The Ruin*, meanwhile, posits its Anglo-Saxon audience as inhabiting the continuing presence of the past, not as succeeding or supplanting it. The underlying philosophy of Anglo-Saxon vernacular historiography thus differs significantly from the Christian teleology of salvation history that characterizes mainstream medieval history-writing. In the progressive narrative, redemption is not an ongoing process; it is the final moment, the telos, of all history. Benjamin's notion of redemption, incidentally, has kinship with the work of medievalists, who bring together fragments of the past as their objects of study, collecting them from the random events of manuscript compilation, transmission, rebinding, loss, discovery, and editing. The survival of these texts, and the forms they take, is generally the result not of careful planning, but of historical vicissitude. The critical model of the constellation may thus prove more practical, in some ways, than a progressive model of literary history.

In chapter 2, the stakes of redemption become even clearer in vernacular biblical verse. At the same time that the Germanic tradition had a tremendous impact on the historical consciousness of early English writers, biblical history maintained its strong influence over the interpretation and representation of the past. I explore the intersections of these two strands of influence in one of the four great Anglo-Saxon poetic codices, the Junius Manuscript (Oxford, Bodleian Library MS Junius 11). *Genesis A*, *Genesis B*, and *Exodus* show Anglo-Saxon poets co-opting the structures of Germanic verse to reconstitute the ancient past for contemporary audiences, thereby effectively collapsing the distances (both temporal and cultural) between Old Testament narratives and heroic forms. Like their legendary counterparts, these biblical poems teach readers how to approach the past through the repeated confluence and conjunction of events and ideals normally separated in time and space. In *Christ and Satan*, the manuscript's final poem, past, present, and future collide in the space of a lyrical reflection on sin and redemption that grants a God-like perspective on human temporality. As objects located at the intersection of Christian and Germanic traditions, the Junius poems embody the hybridity of Anglo-Saxon culture. The contrast between these poems and the telos-driven narratives of both the Latin Vulgate and Ælfric's Old English translations is striking indeed. Read side by side with their prose counterparts, the poetic treatments of Genesis and Exodus begin to undercut the theological and temporal imperatives of biblical history. As Ælfric's prefaces to his translations make clear, the possibility of salvation depends on the absolute separation of past and present in order to grasp the course of history as the figuration and fulfilment of the salvation narrative. In the Junius poems, however, past and present are anything but separate, and the narrative focus shifts from future salvation to a present relationship between the audience and God. The poetry's vision of history and its significance for the present thus places it at odds with more orthodox scriptural interpretation. The stakes of historical representation, then, have everything to do with constructing an idea of the present.

What happens, then, when these literary models are used to shape the representation of contemporary events in the later Anglo-Saxon period? In chapter 3, I turn from the redaction of legendary and biblical history to the representations of contemporary historical events in vernacular verse. The practical and literary implications of the non-teleological historical temporality of *Beowulf*, *The Ruin*, *Genesis*, and *Exodus* materialize in the juxtaposition of texts written at the turn of the millennium, including the Anglo-Saxon Chronicle, the homilies of Wulfstan, and *The Battle of Maldon*. In these texts, writers take the models of historical understanding they have learned from reading legendary and biblical history and create a discourse of the present modelled on those same techniques. As a result, the texts reveal distinct ideological purposes. Not surprisingly, a writer of telos-driven prose narratives interprets Viking attacks and English defeats quite differently than does a poet whose inspiration comes from verses about legendary heroes. Prose narratives seek to recount events in terms of cause and effect. Wulfstan's homilies, for example, detailing the Anglo-Saxons' failings in Christian terms, interpret political decline as the wages of sin. Wulfstan posits rampant moral decay as the proximate cause of the Viking attacks; repentance and contrition, therefore, are the best remedy. The Anglo-Saxon Chronicle, meanwhile, finds its own explanation in successive failures of political leadership; its unremitting narrative of cowardice and repeated emphasis on leaders who run away and armies that scatter charts the eventual Danish conquest as a natural consequence of English weakness. *The Battle of Maldon*, however, takes a different tack entirely, in aggrandizing the heroes who stand firm against the Vikings and blaming contemporary political figures for failing to live up to the heroic code. When Wulfmær pulls a spear from his lord's body and hurls it back to strike the enemy, and when Byrhtnoth's men, one by one, declare their intention to die rather than surrender, political expedience seems to give way to patriotism. The nostalgia generated by what Robert Hanning has called 'heroic history' provides a firm foundation for the construction of English cultural identity at a moment when the nation faces the grave threat of defeat and ultimate conquest.[50] In witnessing the transformation of current events into historical discourse, we can see how poetic form conditions the ideological content of historical representation.

The same profound nostalgia for a heroic past underscores verse memorials in other venues of the late Anglo-Saxon period, and the final two chapters examine the verse of the Anglo-Saxon Chronicle. With its multiple and diverse manuscript witnesses, the Anglo-Saxon Chronicle provides evidence for historiographic practices at times and places ranging from the ninth to the twelfth centuries and from Winchester and Canterbury to Worcester

---

50 Hanning, '*Beowulf* as Heroic History,' 77.

and York. Along with geographic and chronological diversity, the Chronicle shows generic diversity in incorporating both verse and prose annals in almost all manuscripts. It thus becomes possible to chart the relationship between form and ideology across the considerable range of Chronicle manuscripts. In chapter 4, close readings of the canonical Chronicle poetry show that the heroic history so clearly articulated in *Maldon* emerges as an ideological product of Wessex hegemony that can be located quite clearly in the early Chronicle manuscripts that were produced in or near centres of Wessex power. These poems rely heavily on nostalgia for the heroic past, as embodied in traditional verse forms, to create metrical memorials to the real-life events recorded in the late tenth and early eleventh century annals. *The Battle of Brunanburh*, like *Maldon*, offers history in an aestheticized mode, and both poems draw their inspiration from the equally ornamented, if less verifiable, examples of the heroic canon. They impart a particular kind of historicity to the events and people they describe, in which historical significance depends on a relation not to future salvation but to past glory. In this respect, they run counter to more traditional modes of historiography, in which historical consciousness is governed almost exclusively by linear narrative forms that point unerringly toward the telos of salvation. In the tenth century, the heroic exploits of Athelstan, Edmund, and their descendants expand the borders of Anglo-Saxon dominion and link English identity firmly to the warrior ethos that is the product of the literary imagination, as well as to the dynasty of Alfred. The end of that dynasty is signalled in the final canonical poem, *The Death of Edward*, as a convenient terminus for both poetic form and cultural identity reinforcing the idea that nation and ruling family are conjoined by history, tradition, and ideology. Yet this heroic ideology is closely tied to the traditional poetic forms of canonical verse. The significance of these observations becomes clearer when we examine the non-traditional Chronicle verse, most of which is found in later manuscripts written further from the sphere of Wessex influence.

Literary conventions are not static, and as poetic form changes, the historical consciousness it engenders changes too. As Angus McIntosh first pointed out in 1949, Anglo-Saxon literary form is better understood as a continuum than as a binary. In place of 'verse' and 'prose,' McIntosh suggests a range of formal possibilities, and this approach allows for far more creative and productive readings of medieval texts.[51] Scholars have identified various kinds of non-traditional verse among the Chronicle's annals,

---

51 Angus McIntosh, 'Wulfstan's Prose,' Sir Israel Gollancz Memorial Lecture 1948, *PBA* 35 (1949): 109–42.

and as these passages distinguish themselves from straightforward prose annals, they demand aesthetic and formal analysis. In chapter 5, such analysis reveals a bifurcation in the uses of verse as historical representation in late Anglo-Saxon England. Unlike their traditional heroic counterparts in the earlier southern manuscripts, the poems of the northern manuscripts do not evoke nostalgia for the heroic age. Instead, they opt to represent historical events within a salvation teleology, thereby giving rise to changes in poetic form. Rhythmical and rhyming verses on distinctly non-heroic events, such as the accession and death of Edgar and the martyrdoms of Edward and Alfred, work not to memorialize rulers in heroic form, but to remind a sinful population that their punishment is the loss of good Christian rulers. Functioning as apostrophes rather than cenotaphs, the poems produce textual space for reflection and commentary on the providential meaning of events, not verse memorials for fallen heroes. As a result, the rise of non-traditional verse forms (which many scholars still discount altogether as poetry) and their use of salvation models accentuate the formal link between heroic history and traditional alliterative aesthetics. The contrast between the traditional verse of the southern manuscripts and the rhythmical and rhyming verse of the northern recension brilliantly illustrates the interdependence of form and content and the use of poetry as both a tool of hegemonic discourse and a vehicle for dissent. In addition to clarifying the operation of nostalgia in dynastic propaganda, therefore, a closer look at the aesthetics of the Anglo-Saxon Chronicle actually forces us to rethink where we draw the line between poetry and prose.

Using vernacular historical poetry as a focal point, then, I want to reaffirm the centrality of poetic aesthetics to the construction of specific vernacular models of historical understanding at various key points in the early medieval period. Because poetic forms of historical investment are often at odds with the dominant forms of Christian historiography from the same time and place, Anglo-Saxon historical poetry can offer an alternative window on how the Anglo-Saxons thought about themselves in relation to the past. In their poetry, the Anglo-Saxons locate themselves as the heirs to two great cultural traditions, and consequently the poems are really as much about the Anglo-Saxon present as they are about either a heroic German or an ancient biblical past. If *Beowulf* tells us little about the history of early medieval Scandinavia, and even less about the history of Anglo-Saxon England, it does tell us a great deal about an Anglo-Saxon historical consciousness, about a mode of understanding that recognizes the past as past, but seeks for meaning in the past's relationship to the present.

1 Art and History in Old English Heroic Poetry

The truth content of artworks is the objective solution of the enigma posed by each and every one. By demanding its solution, the enigma points to its truth content. It can only be achieved by philosophical reflection. This alone is the justification of aesthetics.

Theodor Adorno, *Aesthetic Theory*

Wrætlic is þes wealstan,   wyrde gebræcon;
burgstede burston;   brosnað enta geweorc.[1]

The Ruin

The refrain of *Deor* has long been an interpretive crux for Anglo-Saxon scholars. Rare enough as a device in Old English poetry, this refrain – *Þæs ofereode, þisses swa mæg* [that passed away, so can this] – is semantically as well as formally obscure.[2] The phrase lacks a clear nominative, and the subject of the singular third person verbs *ofereode* [passed away] and *mæg*

---

1 'Wondrous is this wall of stone, shattered by fate; the buildings have fallen apart; the work of giants decays' (1–2) (*The Ruin*, ed. R.F. Leslie, in *Three Old English Elegies*, rev. ed. [Exeter: University of Exeter, 1988]).

2 The repeated phrase 'Ungelic is us' [It is different for us] in *Wulf and Eadwacer*, which follows *Deor* in the Exeter Book, could also be considered a refrain, but it appears only twice in the poem, as compared to *Deor*'s sixfold repetition. There are no other examples of a refrain in Old English poetry. For a comprehensive overview of the sources of the refrain and its relationship to various traditions of consolation proverbs, see Joseph Harris, '"Deor" and Its Refrain: Preliminaries to an Interpretation,' *Traditio* 43 (1987): 23–53. On its grammatical function, see Juan Camilo Conde Silvestre, 'The Spaces of Medieval Intertextuality: *Deor* as a Palimpsest,' *SELIM* 5 (1995): 63–77 at 64 n1.

[can] might be 'it,' or perhaps 'he' or 'she,' but that subject remains un-expressed. The genitives *þæs* and *þisses* likewise point to an unidentified substantive; literally translated, the refrain must read something like 'With respect to that [it] passed away, with respect to this [it] likewise can.' It is possible, but not necessary, to understand 'with respect to that' as refer-ring to the fragment of legend that precedes the refrain; 'with respect to this' can be taken to reference Deor's current situation, which is the im-petus for his reflections. Still, the unexpressed subject remains vague; is it the subjective experience of suffering, or perhaps the meaning one con-structs for it? Finally, the verb *mæg* itself is problematic; the modal aux-iliary *magan* [to be able to] expresses only the possibility that 'it' will *ofer-gan*, or pass away. The meaning of this short passage, repeated six times in the forty-two-line poem, is ambiguous in the extreme. *Deor*'s refrain, meant to offer consolation, tenders possibility, but not certainty. In the end, that seems small consolation indeed.

The ambiguity of *Deor*'s refrain is one particularly lucid example of the uncertainties that often challenge modern readers of medieval literature. Since Fred Robinson's definition of the 'appositive style' in Anglo-Saxon poetry, ambiguity has been seen as a hallmark of the form.[3] Yet Robinson's theory has its own teleology, one in which pagan meanings are ultimately supplanted by a 'correct' Christian reading,[4] and it has not gone un-questioned. More recent critical engagements with Anglo-Saxon poetry have focused on how their particular form of signification 'affirms ambi-guity and escapes simple binary definition,' as Gillian Overing puts it.[5] The historicity of the texts and their afterlives in the modern period like-wise inform Allen Frantzen's critical practice; and Pauline Head asserts 'the unavoidable value of subjective reading' for the modern reader ap-proaching a medieval text.[6] This should hardly come as a surprise, even to

---

3 Fred C. Robinson, Beowulf *and the Appositive Style* (Knoxville: University of Tennessee Press, 1985).

4 As Patricia Dailey notes in 'Questions of Dwelling in Anglo-Saxon Poetry and Medieval Mysticism: Inhabiting Landscape, Body, and Mind,' *New Medieval Literatures* 8 (2006): 175–214 at 208.

5 Gillian R. Overing, *Language, Sign, and Gender in* Beowulf (Carbondale: Southern Illinois University Press, 1990), xxiv.

6 Allen J. Frantzen, *Desire for Origins: New Language, Old English, and Teaching the Tradition* (New Brunswick: Rutgers University Press, 1990); Pauline E. Head, *Represen-tation and Design: Tracing a Hermeneutics of Old English Poetry* (Albany: State University of New York Press, 1997).

medievalists; most of the literature we deem worthy of the name receives that attention precisely because it presents itself as endlessly rereadable, always subject to new interpretation.

If this observation sounds irredeemably postmodern, it is worth noting that the German Romantics made the same claims about poetry more than two hundred years ago. In the age of the Enlightenment, art revealed its ineffability through criticism's best attempts to define the category of the aesthetic; in the wake of poststructuralism and Marxist historicism, by contrast, such totalization is anathema. In both contexts, however, the notion of the work of art derives precisely from what is unrepresentable about it. In the eighteenth century, this ineffability was defined as moral truth, and it grounded the work of literary criticism. In the mid-twentieth century, by contrast, ineffability became indeterminability, and truth was surrendered to the play of the text. Although both kinds of analysis can tell us a great deal about how texts work, neither an idealist Kantian aesthetics nor a radically affirmative postmodern scepticism offers a way of dealing with the problem of history. Medievalists cannot forget about history; its material reality is ever-present in the crumbling pages of our manuscripts and in the marginal traces left by scribes, readers, and previous scholarship. As Hans Robert Jauss has written, 'a literary work is not an object that stands by itself and that offers the same view to each reader in each period. It is not a monument that monologically reveals its timeless essence.'[7] And though literary study in recent decades has faced no shortage of historicism, the recent turn toward new formalism raises a set of unique challenges for medievalists: how to balance our aesthetic and our historical impulses.[8] What medievalists need, and what Jauss offers, is a methodology that affirms both the aesthetic character of the literary work and its passage through human history. Yet fifty years before Jauss tried to solve this problem by a marriage of Marxist historicism and Russian Formalism, Walter Benjamin had found a similar way in which to articulate

---

7 Hans Robert Jauss, *Toward an Aesthetic of Reception*, trans. Timothy Bahti, Theory and History of Literature 2 (Minneapolis: University of Minnesota Press, 1982), 21.

8 This, it seems to me, has been the goal of the self-described new formalists. See the special issue, edited by Susan B. Wolfson and Marshall Brown, of *MLQ* 61 (2000). See also Marjorie Levinson, 'What Is New Formalism?' *PMLA* 122 (2007): 558–69; a longer version of the essay is available online at http://sitemaker.umich.edu/pmla_article/home. For the context of new formalism in medieval studies, see Seth Lerer, 'The Endurance of Formalism in Middle English Studies,' *Literature Compass* 1 (2003): 1–15, http://www.blackwellsynergy.com/doi/full/10.1111/j.1741-4113.2004.00006.x.

the aesthetic character of the work of art in its historical contingency; two of his major critical concepts – the constellation and the ruin – may prove equally fertile ground for medievalists.[9]

In a constellation, the image takes its shape from the relative position of the stars that form it from the perspective of the stargazer; its meaning derives from the position of the stargazer who sees the pattern and names it, often drawing on traditional narratives to do so. Hence the familiar patterns of Orion and Andromeda in the night sky, held together by gravitational forces but made meaningful through interpretation. In the critical constellation that Benjamin describes, concepts, rather than stars, appear to the critic in such a way that their relative arrangement is suddenly perceived as meaningful and becomes an image, or idea. Developing a predominantly visual and even spatial metaphor for the critical process opens up a number of intellectual possibilities. First and foremost, the constellation's engagement with concepts is not linear; it allows the critic to avoid assigning hierarchies of privilege or precedence. It skirts traditional binaries such as cause-effect or thesis-antithesis, preferring the simultaneous apprehension of multiple concepts that give rise fortuitously to the intimation of what Benjamin calls an 'idea.' Unlike Plato's Ideas, however, Benjamin's concepts are fundamentally material, and that is where his critical theory demands a return to history. The critical constellation honours a commitment to the idea of aesthetic sensibility while simultaneously demanding a more materialist treatment of the work of art as historical artefact. And as historical artefact, the work of art reminds us of the passage of time; it does not present itself to the viewer or reader in the pristine condition of its original conception, but rather with the accumulation of years, perhaps centuries, of wear and tear, transmission and reception, damage and reconstruction. Benjamin's figure for the material character of the artwork is the ruin – an image that both manages to embody the appearance of the artwork's original wholeness and connects the past moment of its creation to the present moment of its reception by means of the dialectical mediation of two temporally separated contexts. As a ruin, the work of art is being

---

9 Benjamin has found a small but dedicated audience among Anglo-Saxonists, especially in the work of Nicholas Howe (see 'Historicist Approaches,' in *Reading Old English Texts*, ed. Katherine O'Brien O'Keeffe, 79–100 [Cambridge: Cambridge University Press, 1997], and 'Rome: Capital of Anglo-Saxon England,' *JMEMS* 34 [2004]: 147–72). Head (*Representation and Design*) has also been influenced by Benjamin, as has Dailey ('Questions of Dwelling'); and a recent dissertation by Eileen A. Joy takes the Benjaminian motif of the wreckage of history as a metaphor for *Beowulf* studies ('*Beowulf* and the Floating Wreck of History' [PhD diss., University of Tennessee, Knoxville, 2001]).

continually rewritten; with each emergence into critical consciousness, the work must be read anew, but it retains the accumulated meaning of its historical pre-existence, and the reader must therefore confront not only the historical reality of the text and the moment of its creation, but also the historicity of his own present moment. In the constellation and the ruin, then, Benjamin offers a way of thinking through the aesthetic realization of historically contingent truths as they are embodied in the work of art and as they are intertwined with the workings of human history.

In what follows, not only do Benjamin's concepts of the constellation and the ruin serve as formal principles through which to approach Anglo-Saxon poetry that is itself concerned explicitly with the aestheticization of history; they also help to clarify the juxtaposition of conceptual and experiential elements that inheres in their distinctive poetic form. I do not attempt to connect elements of the Anglo-Saxon poetic tradition with one another – or with Benjamin, for that matter – in terms of a progression of literary technique, or in a relationship of genealogical causality. Rather, I want to suggest that Anglo-Saxon poetry itself posits history through the constellation and the ruin, implicitly if not explicitly. That is not to say that Anglo-Saxon poetry somehow foreshadows Benjamin's thinking, a millennium later, but rather that the mode of historical consciousness articulated in Benjamin's work found expression in the art of an earlier age and can illuminate our understanding of its aesthetic function.

The three poems I have chosen to examine here – *Deor*, *The Ruin*, and *Widsith* – are solely articulated through an atemporal arrangement of disparate elements, and this has important consequences for their mediation of temporality.[10] What interests me about these texts is twofold. First, I want to examine the way in which a poem can gather disparate elements, such as philosophical concepts or fragments of tradition, into a formal array that structures their interpretation, rather than implementing a linear teleology such as narrative. Second, I want to consider the model of understanding that such an array encourages, focused as it is on thinking through non- or anti-teleological connections to suggest a meaning both specific to

---

10 All three poems are found in the Exeter Book: Exeter, Cathedral Library MS 3501, fols 8–130, dated to c. 975 AD. See *The Exeter Book*, ed. George Philip Krapp and Elliott van Kirk Dobbie, ASPR 3 (New York: Columbia University Press, 1936); *The Exeter Anthology of Old English Poetry: An Edition of Exeter Dean and Chapter MS 3501*, ed. Bernard J. Muir, rev. 2nd ed. (Exeter: University of Exeter Press, 2000); and Donald Scragg, 'Exeter Book,' in *The Blackwell Encyclopaedia of Anglo-Saxon England*, ed. Michael Lapidge, John Blair, Simon Keynes, and Donald Scragg, 177–8 (Oxford: Blackwell, 1999).

the poem and greater than the sum of its parts. My readings of these texts therefore reveal the utility of the constellation as a critical model for literary scholars, particularly medievalists, whose attempts to trace a genealogical narrative of literary history are frequently frustrated by the fragmentary – or ruinous – state of the canon. Although we face a significant dearth of the information necessary for making historical or biographical arguments about texts, we can respect the historicity of this literature and find meaning in its generally lamented lack of coherence using a methodology that reveals the wealth of possibility inherent in the fragmentary remnants of the medieval past as such. The constellation is not just a way in which an artist like the *Beowulf* poet offers a moment of reflection on the relationship of past, present, and future, although it certainly is that. It is also a means by which modern readers might begin to apprehend meanings in individual texts, not in a necessarily vague historical context or through medieval mentalities that we cannot re-create, but rather as constellations of aesthetic fragments that afford an opportunity for creative and philosophical reflection, and that embody in their ruinous state the accumulation of cultural and critical history up to and including the present.

I. Benjamin and the Critical Constellations of Anglo-Saxon Verse

Benjamin's criticism offers us a way of thinking about works of art, in particular literature, as mediating between antinomies such as aesthetics and historicism because it posits the work as, by its very nature, a site of multiple dialectical tensions. The work is firmly rooted in its historical moment while also transcending human history as part of the history of objects. Although its meaning is immanent in its material form from its inception, that meaning is also subject to the transience of historical time. These dialectics of immanence and transcendence, stasis and transience, lead Benjamin to articulate the notion of the critical constellation. By visualizing the artwork's meaning as a constellation, Benjamin is able to account for, and hold in balance, a variety of often contradictory but nevertheless crucial elements. The constellation does not necessitate resolution; antinomies need not be reconciled, because the tension between them affords the constellation its very shape. Accordingly, the constellation allows the reader to acknowledge moments that other critics have neglected, either because they did not fit with a specific critical model, or because they contradicted other, more desirable moments of interpretation. Benjamin's desire to recuperate the neglected fragments of the past constitutes a driving force in his later work – it is a desire that literary scholars know all too well.

Throughout his work, Benjamin anticipates many of the problems familiar to us in the wake of new historicism: How can we attend to the aesthetic elements of a text while acknowledging its relation to history? How can we forge an interpretation that respects historical alterity but remains meaningful for modern readers? In other words, how can we negotiate the distances (temporal, geographical, ideological, linguistic, etc.) between ourselves and the objects of our study? These, the fundamental crises of literary criticism in any period, form a central problematic of Benjamin's thought:

> What has been preoccupying me is the question of the relationship of works of art to historical life ... The attempt to place the work of art in the context of historical life does not open up perspectives that lead us to its innermost core as, for example, the same attempt undertaken with regard to peoples leads us to see them from the perspective of generations and other essential strata ... Works of art have nothing that could connect them in a way that is comprehensive and fundamental at the same time, while such a comprehensive and fundamental connection in the history of a nation is the genealogical relationship among the generations.[11]

The causal, genealogical, and generally progressive mode of temporality that underwrites political and social history will not do for the history of art. To reduce artworks to the expression of an age or an individual talent is to strip them down; it equates meaning with intentionality. Put another way, the meaning of a literary text is not limited to the beliefs and concerns of its moment of creation. Benjamin argues that art exceeds mere subjective expression; the Hegelian 'spirit' of the artwork is not controlled by its human creator or by its human audience. 'Art,' he writes elsewhere, 'posits man's physical and spiritual existence, but in none of its works is it concerned with his response.'[12] Art constitutes a category outside human history, in what Benjamin will call the history of objects – artworks, he says, have a history of their own and are 'not merely the setting for history.'[13] This allows the work of art to stand apart from human history, to function not merely as a record of human thoughts and desires, but also

---

11   Benjamin to Florens Christian Rang, 9 December 1923, in *The Correspondence of Walter Benjamin, 1910–1940*, ed. Gershom Scholem and Theodor W. Adorno, trans. Manfred R. Jacobson and Evelyn M. Jacobson (Chicago: University of Chicago Press, 1994), 223–4.

12   'The Task of the Translator,' in *Illuminations*, ed. Hannah Arendt, trans. Harry Zohn (New York: Schocken, 1968), 69–82 at 69.

13   'Translator,' 71.

as an object with a meaning – and a history – in its own terms. Works of art are not windows into the creator's (or consumer's) soul. They are human creations, but their potential meanings exceed both the intentions of their creators and the desires of their consumers. Anglo-Saxon poetry has not, as a rule, been read as the expression of an individual poet's innermost thoughts and feelings; in this respect, it has always stood at one remove from the history of its creators, for the simple reason that we do not, for the most part, know who they were. Although the moment of their origin may be unknown to us, however, the texts themselves have survived, whereas their creators have not. But that does not make them autonomous; just as individual poems are embedded in manuscript contexts that may contain a wide range of other texts – homilies, law codes, recipes, chronicles, prayers, and the like – and emerge from a range of historical contexts – including royal courts, monastic scriptoria, and aristocratic patronage – so too is literary production embedded in the context of textual and·cultural production more generally.

The meaning of a work of art, then, emerges not from its representation of an individual's will, but from its relative position among other objects. Benjamin writes: 'There remains an intense relationship among works of art ... It is true as well that the specific historicity of works of art is the kind that can be revealed not in "art history" but only in interpretation. For in interpretation, relationships among works of art appear that are timeless yet not without historical relevance.'[14] For Benjamin, interpretation becomes the key to unlocking the artwork's meaning, and the goal of interpretation is, somewhat paradoxically, to apprehend the historicity that is not a part of historical life. While interpretation is indeed a human activity, the aesthetic experience – the moment at which the observer confronts, and is confronted by, the work of art – functions as a dialectic between individual and artefact. Interpretation takes place in the continuous oscillation between the individual's realm of human history and the artefact's place in the history of objects; meaning emerges from the space between the two, marked out by the event of interpretation. For Benjamin, this allows artworks to remain outside the teleology that drives human history; in consequence, the meaning of artworks can become 'timeless yet not without historical relevance.'[15] More specifically, it is the 'relationships

---

14 Benjamin to Rang, 224.
15 It would be a mistake to equate Benjamin's use of 'timeless' with 'unchanging'; rather, artworks-as-objects remain separate from, and can thus offer critiques of, the telos-driven ideologies of changelessness or progression that inform much human history.

among works of art' that become both evident and meaningful through interpretation, and these relationships – to historical context, to aesthetic precedents, to genre, to ideology, even transcendentally to some generalized 'artistic tradition' – become the focus of Benjamin's critical method. In the 'Epistemo-Critical Prologue' to *The Origin of German Tragic Drama*, Benjamin's study of the German *Trauerspiel*, these relationships resolve into the image of the constellation.[16] The array of individual elements that makes up a constellation does not determine its meaning; rather, the idea or constellation itself gives shape to the relationship among its elements.[17] 'Idea' becomes a technical term, corresponding to the principle that governs the relationships among concepts – ultimately, the idea is that which the phenomena, as a group, suggest. In terms of literary history, this

---

Art refuses the conformity of idealist or positivist modes of thinking; it calls the faculties of critical comprehension into question by repeatedly staging the incommensurable dialectics inherent in the work itself. Theodor W. Adorno more fully elaborates the potential of Benjamin's understanding of the history of objects than Benjamin himself did; for Adorno, art's critical function is its primary purpose, in which aesthetic form and historical content join together to embody a politics of critique. See *Aesthetic Theory*, ed. Gretel Adorno and Rolf Tiedemann, trans. Robert Hullot-Kentor, Theory and History of Literature 88 (Minneapolis: University of Minnesota Press, 1997), especially 175–99.

16 Benjamin, *The Origin of German Tragic Drama*, trans. John Osborne (London: Verso, 1998). Both Benjamin and Adorno employed the constellation as a critical model; for an overview, see Susan Buck-Morss, *The Origin of Negative Dialectics: Theodor W. Adorno, Walter Benjamin, and the Frankfurt Institute* (New York: Free Press, 1977), 90–110; and Steven Helmling, 'Constellation and Critique: Adorno's Constellation, Benjamin's Dialectical Image,' *Postmodern Culture* 14, no. 1 (2003), http://muse.jhu.edu/journals/pmc/v014/14.1helmling.html. On the *Trauerspiel* book in particular, see Charles Rosen, 'The Ruins of Walter Benjamin,' *New York Review of Books* 24, no. 17 (27 October 1977): 31–40, and 'The Origins of Walter Benjamin,' *New York Review of Books* 24, no. 18 (10 November 1977): 30–8; and Beatrice Hanssen, *Walter Benjamin's Other History: Of Stones, Animals, Human Beings, and Angels* (Berkeley: University of California Press, 1998). In the *Trauerspiel* book, Benjamin's goal, at least in part, is to separate criticism from the problems that plague a philosophy rooted in subject-object relations; in short, to remove art and art criticism from the realm of human history and recognize their place in the world of objects. Toward this end, he reassesses the critical function as an inversion of Platonic idealism; Plato's Ideas become, for Benjamin, the 'objective, virtual arrangement' of phenomena; 'Ideas are to objects as constellations are to stars' (*Origin*, 34).

17 'Whereas phenomena determine the scope and content of the concepts which encompass them, by their existence, by what they have in common, and by their differences, their relationship to ideas is the opposite of this inasmuch as the idea, the objective interpretation of phenomena – or rather their elements – determines their relationship to each other' (*Origin*, 34).

means that the meaning critics seek – what Benjamin would designate as truth – takes shape not through the interpretation of individual works, but through recognition of the interrelation of a group of works – or phenomena – that considers both their similarities and their differences. Truth thus resides not in the work itself, but in the constellation; more to the point, truth resides in the tension between the similarities and differences, extremes and averages, that comprise the constellation – as such, it is not quite knowable and never unitary.

As the opening example from *Beowulf* in the Introduction demonstrated, and as criticism has long recognized, understanding Anglo-Saxon poetry demands the recognition of the poem's contextual and intertextual relationships. The *Beowulf* poet invokes Sigemund, but does not explain who he is or why he is referenced at the moment of Beowulf's victory over Grendel. The audience is expected to draw on their familiarity with the larger canon of Germanic tradition to understand the meaning of the allusion and how its invocation contributes to the meaning of the poem.[18] What are commonly referred to as the 'traditional' elements of Anglo-Saxon verse, such as formulaic phrases and structures of accretion and repetition, cue audiences to make connections to a much larger interpretive framework based on the common knowledge of a wider tradition. As John Miles Foley has said, and as Benjamin would certainly agree, 'poetic

---

18 The idealized view of Anglo-Saxon poetry as the written remnants of a grand but now lost oral tradition commemorating its Germanic heritage has been more or less discounted by contemporary scholarship. Scholarly consensus has reached a useful compromise position of regarding this poetry as 'oral-derived,' a category that acknowledges the vast source material in Germanic legend and oral tradition without discounting the undeniable effects of literate, and consequently Christian, influences on the production of any medieval text. The terms of the more recent discussion are framed by the ground-breaking work of M.T. Clanchy, *From Memory to Written Record: England, 1066–1307*, 2nd ed. (Oxford: Basil Blackwell, 1993); and Brian Stock, *The Implications of Literacy: Written Language and Models of Interpretation in the Eleventh and Twelfth Centuries* (Princeton: Princeton University Press, 1983). It is vital to note that neither of these important studies considers the early medieval period in any detail except as the precursor to the period about which each makes a very convincing argument. For an exploration of the problems involved in pitting orality against literacy in the Anglo-Saxon period, see Howe, 'The Cultural Construction of Reading in Anglo-Saxon England,' in *The Ethnography of Reading*, ed. Jonathan Boyarin, 58–79 (Berkeley: University of California Press, 1993). On the compromise designation of 'oral-derived,' see Joseph Harris, 'A Nativist Approach to *Beowulf*: The Case of Germanic Elegy,' in *Companion to Old English Poetry*, ed. Henk Aertsen and Rolf H. Bremmer, Jr, 45–62 (Amsterdam: VU University Press, 1994).

meaning depends fundamentally on poetic structure.'[19] An audience's ability to make sense of a text depends largely on how carefully and artfully that text is structured according, or in response, to traditional conventions, so that meaning is inextricably bound to form. Moreover, the meaning of such a work is derived in large part from its metonymic connection to that larger tradition. Instead of depending upon the smooth lines of a narrative arc that moves from beginning through middle to end, oral and oral-derived texts create meaning through the synchronic connections between the story being told and the other stories it alludes to; events derive significance vertically, through relation to other events outside the story, as well as horizontally, in relation to other events within the story. Not only is the reader a key player in how the poem, as artistic experience, takes shape, but the thought process that goes into understanding the poem must work in several directions and on multiple levels at once.[20]

The kind of reading these texts demand moves quickly in the direction of allegory, in which parts of the poem derive their meaning not as individual units in a single storyline but as metonymic representations of a much larger meaning that is revealed through the process of interpretation. This metonymic structure further demands a reconsideration of the traditional dichotomy of form and content, which cannot be separated in these poems. Rather, form and content work together with the reader through an allegorical mechanism to create a meaning that is not merely literary or historical, but philosophical as well. Thus, as Foley writes, 'when we "read" any traditional performance or text with attention to the inherent meaning it necessarily summons, we are, in effect, recontextualizing that work, reaffirming contiguity with other performances or texts, or, better, with the ever-immanent tradition itself.'[21] Whether that 'contiguity' is total, and whether the text's 'inherent meaning' is ever fully available to the reader/audience, seems less certain. As John D. Niles has suggested, 'meaning in traditional art is not something that can be declared by fiat in some absolute realm beyond time and place. It is something that is contested with every act of reception. It is best approached in the plural.'[22]

---

19 *Immanent Art: From Structure to Meaning in Traditional Oral Epic* (Bloomington: Indiana University Press, 1991), 14.

20 Foley, *Immanent Art*, with special reference to Anglo-Saxon oral-derived poetry at 29–33 and 190–242; and 'Oral Traditional Aesthetics and Old English Poetry,' in *Medialität und mittelalterliche insulare Literatur*, ed. Hildegard L.C. Tristram, 80–103 (Tübingen: G. Narr, 1992).

21 Foley, *Immanent Art*, 9.

22 John D. Niles, '*Widsith* and the Anthropology of the Past,' *PQ* 78 (1999): 171–213 at 180.

This is the commonly accepted model of interpretation for Anglo-Saxon poetry, and its fundamental concepts align quite comfortably with Benjamin's early explication of the constellation as an array of disparate elements in the interpretation of which the observer plays a crucial role. But Anglo-Saxonists have yet to recognize the potential of this model – indeed, the need to invoke it – to solve the problem of aesthetics and history by incorporating contemporary readers into the constellation of meaning. Finding a role for the modern reader has long been a desideratum of Anglo-Saxon studies.[23] The insights of new historicism encourage us to acknowledge our own historicity as we approach the objects of our study; as Nicholas Howe writes, 'one must scrutinize the premises of one's own work and ... recognize the subtle and inescapable interactions between the historical moment at which one writes as a critic and the historical moment about which one writes.'[24] Yet acknowledging multiple contexts – even on the rare occasions when such acknowledgment extends, as it does in Howe's work, to multiple sites of reception throughout literary history – does not answer the question of how this poetry functions, as art, to produce aesthetic effects. Texts and readers alike are implicated in the act of interpretation;[25] one is not privileged over another, and the aesthetic experience opens the audience to the possibility of transformation. Both poetic meanings and historical truths are in a constant process of becoming as they are embodied in aesthetic form; the audience plays a key role in creating them, by means of the act of criticism that is inherent but never fully realized in the aesthetic experience. As a result, the 'commonly accepted model of interpretation' requires some nuancing: specifically, it demands the recognition that the 'poetic tradition' to which we often refer is not merely a human concept or creation, but also a historical artefact with a material existence independent of the history, desires, and intentions of the humans who created or consume it. The constellation restructures the mechanisms for apprehending meaning within a poetic text by

---

23 In 1990, Frantzen called for the revitalization of Anglo-Saxon studies by acknowledging its present political relevance, not just its role as intellectual origin, for contemporary literary studies; see *Desire for Origins*, especially 1–26 and 201–26. See also Howe, 'The New Millennium,' in *A Companion to Anglo-Saxon Literature*, ed. Phillip Pulsiano and Elaine Treharne, 496–505 (Oxford: Blackwell, 2001); and Clare Lees, 'Actually Existing Anglo-Saxon Studies,' *New Medieval Literatures* 7 (2005): 223–52.
24 Howe, 'Historicist Approaches,' 80.
25 Seth Lerer acknowledges this when he writes that *Beowulf* 'shows us that to read the legends of the past is to read by ourselves' (*Literacy and Power in Anglo-Saxon Literature* [Lincoln: University of Nebraska Press, 1991], 194).

acknowledging its independence even as it insists on its unalterable association in relationships with other material objects. Interpretation, then,
takes place somewhere between the critic and the objects that form a given
constellation from the critic's perspective.

The relationship between interpretation and historicity takes on an even
greater materiality and specificity in Benjamin's late (and posthumously
published) work *Theses on the Philosophy of History*,[26] in which the constellation joins with the more concrete dialectical image to formulate
Benjamin's theory of historical materialism and its attendant critical practice. The dialectical image is the figure for history because of the very
problematic that spawned the idea of the constellation to begin with: the
irreconcilable tension between past and present.

> It is not that what is past casts its light on what is present, or what is present
> its light on what is past; rather, image is that wherein what has been comes
> together in a flash with the now to form a constellation. In other words: im-
> age is dialectics at a standstill. For while the relation of the present to the past
> is purely temporal, the relation of what-has-been to the now is dialectical: not
> temporal in nature but figural <*bildlich*>. Only dialectical images are genu-
> inely historical – that is, not archaic – images.[27]

In Benjamin's historico-philosophical criticism, working through the dialectic does not resolve the tension between opposing elements, but creates
a third term: Benjamin's truth, or a redeemed past.[28] Like Erich Auerbach's
figura, the dialectical image links two historical moments through their
co-creation of interpretive meaning.[29] Unlike the *figura*, however, the

---

26 *Theses on the Philosophy of History*, in *Illuminations*, 253–64.

27 *The Arcades Project*, ed. Rolf Tiedemann, trans. Howard Eiland and Kevin McLaughlin
    (Cambridge, MA: Harvard University Press, 1999), 463.

28 Benjamin writes: 'The past carries with it a temporal index by which it is referred to
    redemption … Only a redeemed mankind receives the fullness of its past – which is to
    say, only for a redeemed mankind has its past become citable in all its moments'
    (*Theses*, 254). Historical materialism thus participates in the project of redemption by
    seizing fragments of the past and preventing them from being lost to history. See also
    the notion of the 'heterological historian' in Edith Wyschogrod, *An Ethics of Remem-
    bering: History, Heterology, and the Nameless Others* (Chicago: University of Chicago
    Press, 1998).

29 Auerbach writes: 'Figural prophecy implies the interpretation of one worldly event
    through another; the first signifies the second, the second fulfills the first. Both remain
    historical events; yet both, looked at in this way, have something provisional and
    incomplete about them; they point to one another and both point to something in the

dialectical image does not confirm a teleological view of history.[30] Arising from the history of objects rather than from human history, the dialectical image strives to shatter totality. The redemption of the past allows it to articulate its meaning from outside the teleologies of human history.[31] The opposition of this method to telos is crucial, and Benjamin's horror of teleological historicism is encapsulated in one of the most indelible images in his vast corpus, that of the Angel of History. 'Where we perceive a chain of events,' Benjamin writes, 'he sees one single catastrophe which keeps piling wreckage upon wreckage and hurls it in front of his feet.'[32]

When the critic then sets about contemplating these artefacts, not as 'beads of a rosary'[33] but as phenomena arrayed in a constellation, and as a process made up of moments of stasis, the truth the interpretation strives for is neither universal nor contingent; it resides within the dialectic of immanence and transcendence that circumscribes the work of interpretation.[34] The same holds true for the reader of Anglo-Saxon poetry, in terms both of literary history and of individual readings and rereadings. The moments at which these poems 'flash up' throughout literary history – in manuscripts, in editions, in scholarly criticism, and in classrooms – augment the poem's

future, something still to come, which will be the actual, real, and definitive event' ('Figura,' in *Scenes from the Drama of European Literature*, 11–76 [New York: Meridian, 1959], 58).

30 'In the figural system the interpretation is always sought from above; events are considered not in their unbroken relation to one another, but torn apart, individually, each in relation to something other that is promised and not yet present ... In the figural interpretation the fact is subordinated to an interpretation which is fully secured to begin with: the event is enacted according to an ideal model' (Auerbach, 'Figura,' 59).

31 Gerhard Richter writes, 'To articulate the past historically means to activate the historicity of our objects of study in a way that places them on the far side of the teleology of progress and the grand claims of conventional historicism' ('History's Flight, Anselm Kiefer's Angels,' *Connecticut Review* 24 [2002]: 113–36 at 120).

32 *Theses*, 257. The Angel of History is based on a Paul Klee painting, 'Angelus Novus,' currently held by the Israel Museum in Jerusalem.

33 Benjamin writes: 'Historicism contents itself with establishing a causal connection between various moments in history. But no fact that is a cause is for that very reason historical. It became historical posthumously, as it were, through events that may be separated from it by thousands of years. A historian who takes this as his point of departure stops telling the sequence of events like the beads of a rosary. Instead, he grasps the constellation which his own era has formed with a definite earlier one' (*Theses*, 263).

34 This dialectic is fundamental to Benjamin's thinking on art and history; for an analysis, see Jim Hansen, 'Formalism and Its Malcontents: Benjamin and de Man on the Function of Allegory,' *New Literary History* 35 (2004): 663–83.

meaning as it passes through time: at each moment of contact with human history, the poem accumulates meanings that then become a part of its history as object. The same is true for the process of reading the poem. From moment to moment, meaning shifts as different elements in the constellation flash before the reader 'at a moment of danger':[35] allusions to 'the tradition,' verbal echoes of other texts, references to human history, foreshadowing of the present or the future. This apprehension of constellations does follow a linear path, however, in the temporality of reading, as the reader encounters new concepts that change the shape of the constellation. Criticism requires, once more, a balance between the stasis of apprehending the individual constellation and the transience of shifting constellations as the reader moves through the poem. Read in this way, Anglo-Saxon poetry appears deeply aware of its connections both to other verse traditions and to more or less contemporaneous works, but not necessarily bound by the logics of causality or chronology. This awareness manifests itself in what might be considered the poetry's historical consciousness – the deliberate and intentional invocation of a history of objects that constitutes the Germanic tradition and that forms a constellation with the moment of the poem's composition, as well as with the various moments of its reception. And when we consider the poetic array as a constellation, the present moment of reading is interpolated into that historical consciousness as well; the poem itself becomes a fragment from the past that flashes up and demands recognition. The poetic constellation's deep-rooted historicism suggests, quite strongly, that Anglo-Saxon culture had more than one way of thinking about the past and its relation to the present; not all historical consciousness was governed exclusively by an orthodox Christian teleology.

II. Constellation as Poetics: *Deor*

The invocation of the history of objects emerges as the foundation for philosophical meditation in the Anglo-Saxon poem *Deor*. In the poem, the character of Deor mourns his fate as a displaced scop seeking a new position. Turning toward the distant Germanic past, Deor attempts to find consola-

---

35 Balancing the standstill of the monad with the ongoing flow of historical time is the challenge for the critic, who has only a moment in which to recognize the image of the past before it is gone forever: 'The past can be seized only as an image which flashes up at the instant when it can be recognized and is never seen again ... To articulate the past historically ... means to seize hold of a memory as it flashes up at a moment of danger' (Benjamin, *Theses*, 255).

tion for his present sorrow in exempla of suffering drawn from Germanic tradition.[36] Two prominent and largely original features of *Deor* invite special attention: its copious reference to Germanic legend and its use of a stanza-refrain structure.[37] The structure of the poem initiates a pattern of allusion and recursion that presents narrative fragments to the reader and then stages their interpretation – not in terms of the stories they are taken from, but in relation to the other fragments and to the moment of Deor's poetic utterance. Juan Camilo Conde Silvestre has argued that the poem's intertextuality, and thus its dependence on the recognition of a larger tradition, gives rise to its 'aesthetic appeal' and reminds us that 'these puzzling documents can be sorted out only by stepping from text to text.'[38] Intertextuality alone, however, accounts for only one context of the poem's reception. As Jauss is forced to remind us, a poem's original audience is not its only audience; the poem's own passage through time to the present must enter into our analysis as well.[39] The figure of the constellation thus illuminates and refracts the poem's formal elements, giving shape to meaning and anchoring that meaning by means of the repeated philosophical refrain; deep ruminative currents run below its carefully constructed surface, constellating a meditation on transience from a series of individual examples of suffering.

The poem consists of a series of six stanzas, each followed by a refrain. Five of these stanzas refer elliptically to stories from Germanic legend; the refrain, 'Þæs ofereode, þisses swa mæg' [that passed away, so can this], seems meant to remind Deor that the sufferings of those who came before are now in the past, as his own suffering will be some day – although the tragedies of Germanic legend are rather more epic than the situation of an unemployed scop. The opening stanzas refer to the captivity of Welund by Niðhad and to the sorrow caused by Welund's subsequent revenge in killing Niðhad's sons and raping and impregnating his daughter:

---

36 References to the Boethian overtones of Deor's consolation are standard in criticism of the poem; see Murray F. Markland, 'Boethius, Alfred, and *Deor*,' *MP* 66 (1968): 1–4; Leslie Whitbread, 'The Pattern of Misfortune in *Deor* and Other Old English Poems,' *Neophilologus* 54 (1970): 167–83; Kevin S. Kiernan, '*Deor*: The Consolations of an Anglo-Saxon Boethius,' *NM* 79 (1978): 333–40; and, more recently, Anne L. Klinck, *The Old English Elegies: A Critical Edition and Genre Study* (Montreal: McGill-Queens University Press, 1992), 43–6.

37 *Deor* has long been praised for its complex structure of stanza and refrain, unique among Anglo-Saxon lyrics; see, for example, Morton W. Bloomfield, 'The Form of *Deor*,' *PMLA* 79 (1964): 534–41; and Thomas T. Tuggle, 'The Structure of *Deor*,' *SP* 74 (1977): 229–42.

38 Silvestre, '*Deor* as a Palimpsest,' 74.

39 *Aesthetic of Reception*, 25–45.

Welund him be wurman   wræces cunnade,
anhydig eorl   earfoþa dreag,
hæfde him to gesiþþe   sorge ond longaþ,
wintercealde wræce;   wean oft onfond,
siþþan hine Niðhad on   nede legde,
swoncre seonobende   on syllan monn.
Þæs ofereode,   þisses swa mæg.

Beadohilde ne wæs   hyre broþra deaþ
on sefan swa sar   swa hyre sylfre þing –
þæt heo gearolice   ongieten hæfde
þæt heo eacen wæs;   æfre ne meahte
þriste geþencan,   hu ymb þæt sceolde.
Þæs ofereode,   þisses swa mæg.[40]   (1–13)

The perspective in these lines is a personal one; the reader is not meant to glean the details of a story (it is deliberately a well-known one, drawing on the metonymic function of the tradition)[41] but rather to grasp the emotional state of the characters so that he or she identifies with the sufferers, first Welund and then Beadohild. Through this identification, the reader is drawn into the philosophical world of the poem; each successive instance of suffering adds to the array, constellating an image or idea of suffering and consolation of which the reader's own present moment is an equally significant element. The form also works to keep the reader's thoughts in motion: each line moves forward through alliterative metre that defines the long line and emphasizes the nouns, verbs, and adjectives describing individuals and their suffering. The refrain, however, catches the reader off guard, both formally and semantically. It interrupts the flow of the poem's

---

40 'Weland knew suffering among the serpents, the single-minded man endured troubles, he had as his companions sorrow and longing, winter-cold misery; he often experienced woes, after Niðhad placed him under constraints, supple sinew-bonds on the better man. That passed away, so can this. For Beadohild, the death of her brothers was not as hard on her spirit as her own situation, that she had clearly realized that she was pregnant; she was never able to determine with confidence what she should do about that. That passed away, so can this.' Citations are taken from *Exeter Anthology*, ed. Muir, and are cited by line number. All translations are my own.
41 So well known, in fact, that even modern scholars have been able to track down the sources and analogues for *Deor*'s allusive invocations. This task comprises a considerable segment of scholarship on *Deor*; for a comprehensive overview of the analogues and their critical reception, see Kemp Malone, ed., *Deor*, rev. ed. (Exeter: University of Exeter, 1977), 4–14; Klinck, *Elegies*, 158–68; and R.D. Fulk and Christopher M. Cain, *A History of Old English Literature* (Malden, MA: Blackwell, 2003), 216–17.

narrative and disrupts the poem's regular metre, by placing alliterative and metrical weight on demonstratives. The refrain thus acts as a break, a moment at which the flow of thoughts stops and offers an opportunity for crystallization into a monad, thereby prompting reflection and meditation on the part of the reader.[42]

The rest of the poem follows this pattern both formally and thematically, although the opening allusion, to the legend of Welund, is both the longest and the most narrative. The other three allusions are shorter references to more obscure moments from the Germanic tradition: the romance of Mæðhild and Geat (lines 14–17) and the reigns of Theodoric and Eormanric (lines 18–27). Modern readers may have difficulty recognizing the allusions, but their emotional elements are clear; each is characterized by adjectives of sorrow, longing, and suffering, from Geat's 'sorglufu' [sorrowful love] (16a) to Eormanric's men 'sorgum gebunden' [bound in sorrows] (24b). Each stanza adds to the emotional burden of sorrow and despair, drawing its readers into an experience of longing for the same consolation that eludes the characters of the poem, including its speaker. Each stanza also ends with the refrain 'Þæs ofereode, þisses swa mæg,' returning the reader again and again to the 'þis' of Deor's present moment and perhaps the reader's own, as well as to the previous examples in the poem itself.

In its formal rigour, *Deor* carries out what Benjamin sees as the task of poetry: to engage the emotional commitments of the reader through confrontation with the conceptual thematics sedimented in the work of art. Through the first five stanzas, the poem builds its elegiac tone by means of the accretion of examples from history and legend. The mention of any one of these stories would suggest the appropriate emotional state to the reader; instead, however, the poem increases the narrative tension by piling suffering upon suffering, creating an effect not unlike the horror witnessed

---

42 Grasping the array requires the contemplative calm that Benjamin evoked in his earlier reference to monasticism: 'Thinking involves not only the flow of thoughts, but their arrest as well. Where thinking suddenly stops in a configuration pregnant with tensions, it gives that configuration a shock, by which it crystallizes into a monad. A historical materialist approaches a historical subject only where he encounters it as a monad' (*Theses*, 262–3). Benjamin borrows the idea of the monad from Leibniz, whose *Monadology* (trans. Paul Schrecker and Anne Martin Schrecker [Indianapolis: Bobbs-Merrill, 1965]) sets out a theory of the transcendence of rational understanding in its apperception of the divine. Adorno once again nuances this formulation by focusing on the moment of interpretation as one in which the monad crystallizes, but only for the moment. His emphasis on the ontology of art as a process of becoming rather than a stasis emphasizes the fluidity and flexibility of the constellation (*Aesthetic Theory*, 175–80).

by Benjamin's Angel of History. The 'wreckage' of history is equated with a legacy of suffering at repeated and otherwise unconnected moments in the Germanic past; as each of these moments flashes up before Deor, he seizes onto it by placing it in a constellation with the others, where they crystallize into a monad alongside Deor's own suffering in the present moment. By juxtaposing episodes with similar themes, *Deor* not only creates the desired emotional expression of sorrow and longing, but also makes a statement about his purpose in invoking these events. The episodes are not narrative, but emotive; their meaning for Deor, as for the poem's readers, is not established by the time line of their stories, but by their placement in relation to other non-narrative, emotive episodes. As a result, events have meaning in *Deor* not because of their place in a linear progression from past to present, but because of their associative connections and relations to other events from other places on the chronological spectrum. The legendary examples do not lead to or point toward Deor's current situation, but they allow him to construe it as meaningful. Once drawn in by the affective power of these examples, the reader, like Deor, confronts the philosophical problem of human suffering and meditates upon it, so that the reader too becomes an element of the constellation, part of the meaning of the poem. For each reader, and in every present moment, the elements of the constellation will present a unique array, necessitating an endless recursion to the act of critical mediation – interpretation. For Deor, the constellation allows him to juxtapose Germanic legend and Christian consolation without contradiction; for the reader, the poem's form dislodges it from its own historical moment and allows it to transcend the millennium or more between its original creation and present reading. Yet neither the poem nor its reader is liberated from the effects of history, and the refrain continues to draw attention to the passing of time; with each *Þæs ofereode, þisses swa mæg*, the poem records another instance of the accumulation of history as events pile up before the reader, carrying the detritus of the poetic tradition and its transmission through the ages.

The purpose of these juxtapositions – the idea, in the Benjaminian sense, to which their constellation gives shape – is made clear in the poem's final stanza, in which the constellation of examples allows the poem to mediate between the universality of a category such as 'human suffering' and the irreducible particularity of its individual instantiations:

Siteð sorgcearig,   sælum bidæled,
on sefan sweorceð,   sylfum þinceð
þæt sy endeleas   earfoða dæl;

mæg þonne geþencan   þæt geond þas woruld
witig dryhten   wendeþ geneahhe,
eorle monegum   are gesceawað
wislicne blæd,   sumum weana dæl.[43]   (28–34)

From the particular events of Germanic legends, and from the perspective of the *sorgcearig* individual who reflects on his own sorrowful state, the poem moves out to *eorle monegum*, describing the condition of sorrow and loneliness as a universal one that can afflict any person at any time and place – an existential truth as apparent to the modern reader as it is to Deor. In this passage, the self-pity of the *sorgcearig* occurs in a moment of stasis and gives rise in the subsequent moment to reflection on a critical constellation that points to the universal idea of human suffering. The examples from legend and history offer models of the transience and uncertainty of human life; those who find themselves suffering under the misfortune that is an inevitable phase of divine providence, like those whose sadness stems from the all-too-frequent change of heart of a ruler, can find plentiful examples of similar suffering through the course of human history. The examples themselves, however, are separable from that history; Beadohild need not remain in the context of the Welund legend in order for her suffering to signify for the poem's readers. But history is not merely, as Jorge Luis Bueno Alonso would have it, the 'background subject to a higher thematic aim.'[44] The poem neither needs nor attempts to equate Beadohild's suffering with Welund's, or to suggest that all suffering is somehow the same. Quite the contrary; the nature of the array allows Deor to resist passing judgments of value ('better' or 'worse,' 'greater' or 'lesser') on each instance of suffering and, eventually, to equate all human suffering with his own.

This becomes especially evident at the poem's close, where epic history finds itself on equal footing with the more mundane concerns of the unemployed poet. As the final piece of evidence for the ubiquity of human suffering, Deor offers his own experience, deliberately held back until the final lines of the poem:

---

43 'The sorrowful man sits, deprived of happiness; he becomes dark in spirit, and thinks to himself that this share of hardships will be endless. He may then think that throughout this world a wise lord causes change often enough; he shows many a man honour, and certain glory; to some, he shows a portion of woes.'

44 Jorge Luis Bueno Alonso, '"Less Epic Than It Seems": *Deor*'s Historical Approach as a Narrative Device for Psychological Expression,' *Revista Canaria de Estudios Ingleses* 46 (2003): 161–72 at 162.

Þæt ic bi me sylfum   secgan wille,
þæt ic hwile wæs   Heodeninga scop,
dryhtne dyre –   me wæs Deor noma.
ahte ic fela wintra   folgað tilne,
holdne hlaford,   oþþæt Heorrenda nu,
leoðcræftig monn,   londryht geþah
þæt me eorla hleo   ær gesealde.
Þæs ofereode,   þisses swa mæg.[45]

(35–42)

His displacement by another scop causes a loss of status and of identity;
Deor seems to be reasserting his role as a scop through the practice of his
art and the invocation of tradition it entails. His elegiac poem gathers up
fragments of Germanic legend without necessary narrative connections
(except for the examples of Welund and Beadohild, in which the suffering
of the former is the narrative impetus for the suffering of the latter) and
connects them by means of the theme of consolation and the transience of
suffering.[46] The constellation of these legendary fragments, along with
Deor's own story, takes on a distinctive shape: that of the image of suffering
as a component of human experience. For Deor, the array offers the com-
forting image of epic suffering transcended; for the reader, the incongru-
ities in degree of suffering indicate the depths of Deor's pain as well as his
self-aggrandizement. The constellation thus enables the poem to encompass a range of differences: legendary versus historical suffering, the trauma
of women versus the trauma of men, epic tragedies of the past on a national scale versus the less dramatic personal tragedy of Deor's displacement, the personal perspective of the speaker versus the detached perspective of the reader. They all point to a common theme, from which Deor
extracts the reassuring message that nothing lasts forever, even pain, but
from which the reader may well derive the message that pain is a continuing presence in human life.

As a result, the meaning that emerges from Deor's literary precedents is
not necessarily the universal or totalizing meaning he would seek. The
refrain, at each recurrence, brings the reader back to Deor's present, but
also reinforces the ambiguity of the poem's message. Past sufferings have,

---

45 'Of myself I wish to say that once I was scop to the Heodenings, dear to my lord; Deor
was my name. For many winters I had a good office, and a true lord, until now
Heorrenda, a man skilled in song, received the land-right that the protector of men
earlier gave to me. That passed away, so can this.'
46 See n36 above.

by definition, passed, but they have not necessarily left the sufferers in a state of happiness or even contentment.[47] Suffering may end only in death – a consolation that is ambiguous at best. Indeed, the very grammatical structure of the refrain underscores its philosophical ambiguity. The refrain recapitulates the resistance to totalization implied by the poem's constellative structure. Deor's desire for the consolation of a totalizing meaning remains unfulfilled; the reader, likewise, finds difficulty in extracting a single final lesson from the poem's ambiguous refrain.[48] But the frustration of both Deor's and the reader's desires stems from a plenitude, rather than a paucity, of meaning in the poem's constellation; the promise of inexhaustible possibility is the final consolation the poem affords, even if it is not precisely the consolation that is sought.

III. Material Dialectics of Past and Present: *The Ruin*

Deor performs something like a Benjaminian reading of its tradition; it sees individual instances apart from their originary contexts, arrayed against one another to create an image with a recognizable shape that changes depending on whether it is viewed from the perspective of the speaker or of the reader. In *The Ruin*, the image of the constellation once again illuminates the relationship between past and present, this time with the more explicitly materialist focus that Benjamin demanded; *The Ruin*, and its eponymous subject, returns us to the fundamental relation of aesthetics to the history of objects through what Eileen Joy has called 'a kaleidoscope of images of power and waste, bright buildings and crumbled stone.'[49] Like most former Roman colonies, Anglo-Saxon England was dotted with the physical remnants of ancient occupation, and the existence of such ruins was a material reminder of the past on a scale very different from that of the reminders of heroic poetry. In a context where such relics were literally a part of the landscape, it is hardly surprising to discover a profound interest in the past in the Anglo-Saxons' textual legacy – the continued

---

47 As Harris has noted, none of *Deor*'s legendary excerpts provides the example of a happy ending ('"Deor" and Its Refrain,' 44).

48 But see also Niles, who argues that the refrain's *mæg* becomes a first person singular verb in the final stanza, referring clearly to Deor's troubles and defining the scope of the refrain's reference retrospectively through the poem ('Excursus: The Refrain in *Deor*,' in *Old English Heroic Poems and the Social Life of Texts* [Turnhout: Brepols, 2007], 189–93).

49 Eileen Joy, 'On the Hither Side of Time: Tony Kushner's *Homebody/Kabul* and the Old English *Ruin*,' *Medieval Perspectives* 19 (2005): 175–205 at 190.

existence of their own relics. Their fascination with ancient objects and stories extended equally to biblical, Roman, and Germanic artefacts. As Michael Hunter notes, the Anglo-Saxons did not see the need to distinguish between different historical traditions: 'The artist of the Franks Casket saw nothing incongruous in combining on a small box scenes from Germanic heroic legend, from Roman history, and from the bible, while on one panel he depicted side by side the adoration of the magi and one of the more barbaric scenes of Germanic mythology, the vengeance of Weland on King Nithad.'[50] The Franks Casket can be read as another kind of constellation, as an object that embodies the juxtaposition of cultural artefacts in material form, presenting disparate elements in a visual array that calls for the viewer's critical mediation. The individual scenes exist and create meaning quite apart from their original contexts. On the casket, narrative fragments take material form as a part of the history of objects, pointing to, among other things, the heterogeneity of Anglo-Saxon tradition.[51]

A poem reflecting on the ancient heroic glory of ruins that were most likely Roman rather than Germanic is therefore not a contradiction, but an astute expression of a similar heterogeneity.[52] In *The Ruin*, Anglo-Saxon poetics attempts to express an explicitly material representation of space and time; the speaker, gazing upon a ruined city, alternately describes the sight and imagines what it must have looked like before the devastation. The ruin depicted so vividly in the poem would surely have evoked, for its Anglo-Saxon audience, the image of those crumbling walls so commonly associated with the work of giants – just as it evokes, for us, the image of the ruins left behind by a long-dead medieval civilization. Indeed, one of the poem's most compelling features is how deftly its musings mediate the question of temporality for speaker and reader alike.[53] Roy

---

50 Michael Hunter, 'Germanic and Roman Antiquity and the Sense of the Past in Anglo-Saxon England,' *ASE* 3 (1974): 29–50 at 46.

51 This heterogeneity, or hybridity, also emerges in literary works such as the Junius poems; see chap. 2 below.

52 As might be expected in a poem dealing with so concrete a subject, a fair amount of *The Ruin*'s critical history consists of debates about the location of the actual ruins that served as the poet's inspiration; references to hot baths (at 40b–41a) seem to tip the scales in favour of Roman Bath, if indeed the poem describes real ruins at all; these debates are summarized in Karl P. Wentersdorf, 'Observations on *The Ruin*,' *Medium Ævum* 46 (1977): 171–80. Ann Thompson Lee rightly reminds us, however, that 'the actual location of the poem is at best peripheral to our understanding of it;' see '*The Ruin*: Bath or Babylon? A Non-Archaeological Investigation,' *NM* 74 (1973): 443–55 at 443–4.

53 Daniel G. Calder links the use of 'shifting tenses' to the construction of the reader's perspective of temporality through the speaker's train of thought ('Perspective and Movement in *The Ruin*,' *NM* 72 [1971]: 442–5 at 443). Lee notes, 'The poet sees the city

Liuzza has argued that *The Ruin* and its parallel images of decay in *Genesis A* and *The Wanderer* embody a 'nostalgia for a past that is unbroken, inhabitable, articulate, and contiguous as well as a reminder of the speaker's own present state of brokenness, isolation, fallenness, and silence.'[54] But Benjamin's ruin, as dialectical image, does not give itself over wholly to nostalgia, and neither does *The Ruin*. The structure of the poem adumbrates a theory of history rooted in a specific notion of temporality that stands against more traditional formulations of medieval views of history, such as figural typology, genealogies, and cyclical nostalgia.[55] In *The Ruin*, the emphasis is on simultaneity rather than linearity; the past may be something separate and foreign, but it is something that constitutes a part of the present as well. Ruins are particularly well suited to signifying this complex and paradoxical understanding of temporality; their visible and undeniable decay indicates the passage of time, but their equally visible and undeniable existence in spite of their ruinous state asserts the continued presence, as a ruin, of the past. As objects, ruins embody the dialectic of past and present without ever demanding or allowing its reconciliation. The poem balances a series of dialectical tensions – present/past, death/birth, decay/wholeness, inside/outside, material/ideal – without privileging one over the other. Instead, the tensions of these multiple antinomies subsist to drive the poem and to give energy to the meditations it occasions. The dialectical structure of each element demands the recognition, but not the assimilation, of its opposite, most especially in the dialectic of temporality. The structure of the poem moves appropriately back and forth between past and present, following the speaker's thoughts, which by their very nature cannot be represented in a linear sequence. Reading the poem through the figure of the constellation, then, can bring

---

simultaneously in past and present: he sees the ruins as they now exist in his imagination or in reality, and at the same time he sees the process of decay actually taking place at some past time. His vision has a timeless quality which brings the city of the past as close or closer than the present one' ('Bath or Babylon,' 451). James F. Doubleday summarized the significance of the poem's approach to temporality more than three decades ago: 'Implicit in *The Ruin* is a philosophy of history, a way of looking at historical events' ('*The Ruin*: Structure and Theme,' *JEGP* 71 [1972]: 369–81 at 370).

54 Liuzza, 'The Tower of Babel: *The Wanderer* and the Ruins of History,' *Studies in the Literary Imagination* 36, no. 1 (Spring 2003): 1–35 at 16.

55 See, for example, Auerbach, 'Figura'; Nancy Partner, *Serious Entertainments: The Writing of History in Twelfth-Century England* (Chicago: University of Chicago Press, 1977); Gabrielle Spiegel, *Romancing the Past: The Rise of Vernacular Prose Historiography in Thirteenth-Century France* (Berkeley: University of California Press, 1993); and Lee Patterson, *Negotiating the Past: The Historical Understanding of Medieval Literature* (Madison: University of Wisconsin Press, 1987).

us closer to the problems and concerns of the Anglo-Saxons without sub-suming them into purely modern categories of analysis.

In *The Ruin*, the speaker meditates on a scene of destruction and decay over time:

> Hrofas sind gehrorene,   hreorge torras,
> hr[un]geat berofen,   hrim on lime,
> scearde scurbeorge   scorene gedrorene
> ælde undereotone.[56]   (3–6a)

Traditional Anglo-Saxon poetics give the passage its forward momentum; alliteration on 'hr-' links half-lines across caesuras and line breaks alike. The rhymes *hrim on lime* and *scorene gedrorene*, on the other hand, circle back on themselves, interrupting the poem's movement with moments of recursion. The poetic technique rests on building a similar series of contra-dictions: tall towers and roofs brought low, sturdy gates and halls demol-ished, all by the constant wearing-down of time. It is the juxtaposition of these contradictions – their simultaneous existence without the one ele-ment erasing or superseding the other – that replicates the work of the constellation. In *The Ruin*, the arrayed elements are not simply disparate, as in *Deor* or on the Franks Casket; they are in fact the embodiment of opposing forces, in irreconcilable tension with each other. Yet within the aesthetic space of the poem, these tensions require no reconciliation, and *The Ruin*, like the ruin it describes, comes to embody the paradox of his-torical temporality – the continuing presence of the absent past, and the recursion of memory within the forward motion of time.

The speaker's thoughts are not limited to the edifice he contemplates; included in his ruminations are the long-dead people who constructed it:

> Eorðgrap hafað
> waldendwyrhtan,   forweorone geleorene,
> heard gripe hrusan,   oþ hund cnea
> werþeoda gewitan.[57]   (6b–9a)

---

56 'Roofs have fallen apart; towers stand in ruins, bereft of their gate, and limed with frost; the gaping shelter from storms is rent, collapsed, undermined by age.' Citations are taken from *The Ruin*, ed. Leslie, and are cited by line number. All translations are my own.

57 'The grip of the earth, the hard grip of the ground, holds the master builders who have perished and passed away, until a hundred generations of the nation have departed.'

People and place are intertwined in the speaker's imagination; the ruined wall calls up its departed builders, and their legacy survives in the wall's enduring presence. The rhyming of *gehrorene, scorene, gedrorene, forweorone,* and *geleorene* in lines 3, 5, and 7 emphasize death, decay, and destruction as dominant themes of the poem while their rhymes embody, at the level of the aural, the relentless repetition and recursion that characterize the poem's philosophical reflection. Such formal recursion is all the more striking given the scarcity of rhyme as a poetic device in Old English,[58] and it works to stunning effect. Once again, the steady rhythm of the alliterative metre drives the poem relentlessly forward across each caesura and, in some cases, across line breaks, while rhyme reaches back to lines now past to disrupt a purely linear aesthetic. Rhyme and alliteration circle one another in a constant and extremely productive tension. In both their form and their content, these opening lines construct a notion of the passage of time, measured simultaneously in the decay of buildings and bodies and in the creation and subsequent departure of a hundred generations. Gazing back over the 'wreckage' once more, like the Angel of History, the speaker glimpses these figures briefly and gropes toward their significance. The dead are gone, but the present ruins bear witness to their passing and keep them from being lost to history, even as the linear temporality of genealogical time marches inexorably forward.

The Ruin struggles against the inexorability of linear time by striving for the moment of stasis, the 'flash' in which the past could be seized and redeemed; indeed, Nicholas Howe has written that '*The Ruin* may well be the most static poem in Old English.'[59] Howe describes beautifully the sedimentation of history in the poem's details, from the red stain on the lichen-covered wall to the marvel of stone ruins for a culture that builds in wood. But Howe, like Liuzza, finally comes down on the side of nostalgia, 'a hint of some lost golden age.'[60] Yet the poem itself does not, as these readings would suggest, end in nostalgia; as Patricia Dailey notes, 'this kind of reading (which presupposes a teleology as well as a theology) fails

---

58 For an overview of rhyme in Old English, see E.G. Stanley, 'Rhymes in English Medieval Verse: From Old English to Middle English,' in *Medieval English Studies Presented to George Kane*, ed. Edward Donald Kennedy, Ronald Waldron, and Joseph S. Wittig, 19–54 (Wolfeboro, NH: D.S. Brewer, 1988).

59 Howe, 'The Landscape of Anglo-Saxon England: Inherited, Invented, Imagined,' in *Inventing Medieval Landscapes: Senses of Place in Western Europe*, ed. John Howe and Michael Wolfe, 91–112 (Gainesville: University Press of Florida, 2002), 95.

60 Howe, 'Landscape,' 98.

to hear the strangely uplifting tone that persists throughout the poem and dominates the second half.'[61] In addition to acknowledging the continued presence (in both the temporal and the spatial senses of the word) of the past, the poem takes the further step of resurrecting that past in its awed re-creation of the ruin's former glory. The speaker marvels at the 'orþonc, ærsceaft' [monument of skill, ancient building] (line 16) that confounds contemporary engineering and notes with awe that

> Oft þæs wag gebad,
> ræghar ond readfah,   rice æfter oþrum,
> ofstonden under stormum.[62]
>   (9b–11a)

The speaker's sense of wonder reconstructs the now-toppled edifice before the reader's eyes: the wall capable of withstanding the strongest storms, which yet lies crumbling. The opposing forces of strength and weakness, glory and decay, life and death, continually circle around each other, re-enacting the dialectical image in an attempt to figure historical meaning. Throughout the poem, magnificent past and ruined present are juxtaposed in this manner. Beauty and joy prompt recognition of the death that finally destroyed them:

> Beorht wæron burgræced,   burnsele monige,
> heah horngestreon,   heresweg micel,
> meodoheall monig   mondreama full,
> oþþæt þæt onwende   wyrd seo swiþe.
> Crungon walo wide,   cwoman woldagas,
> swylt eall fornom   secgrof[ra] wera;
> wurdon hyra wigsteal   westenstaþolas.[63]
>   (21–7)

---

61 Dailey, 'Questions of Dwelling,' 185. Dailey, too, turns to Benjamin to read *The Ruin*, and concludes that '*The Ruin* offers itself as an allegory for the relatedness of poem to its own present and to its own interpretive act, drawing upon fragmented pasts reassembled for other ends' (192).

62 'For a long time this wall, grey with lichen and red-hued, endured; one kingdom after another, it remained standing through storms.'

63 'Bright were the city halls, many a bathhouse, high many-gabled roofs, a great martial sound, many a mead-hall filled with revelry, until powerful fate changed it all. Dead bodies fell far and wide, and the days of pestilence came; death took all of the brave troop of men; their ramparts became wastelands.'

With a single but ominous 'oþþæt,'[64] the great city of the imagination reverts to its present ruined state, brought low not by war or as the wages of sin, but by the simple passage of time – which is the fate of all temporal things. Death and pestilence replace life and strength, and the ramparts denoting a proud civilization turn instead to a wasteland. But the ruin is not the end of the story; at the thought of fallen glory, the speaker once again imagines how it used to be:

> Hryre wong gecrong,
> gebrocen to beorgum,   þær iu beorn monig,
> glædmod ond goldbeorht,   gleoma gefrætwe[d],
> wlonc ond wingal,   wighyrstum scan;
> seah on sinc, on sylfor,   on searogimmas,
> on ead, on æht,   on eorcanstan,
> on þas beorhtan burg   bradan rices.[65]
>
> (31b–37)

The poem doubles and emphasizes the sense of the destruction with another rhyming phrase, *wong gecrong*, and then immediately counters that sense with a long series of alliterative phrases highlighting the joy and vitality of the once-bright hall full of treasures and celebrating warriors. Oscillating continually between present and past, the speaker's (and, by extension, the reader's) thoughts do not belong to a particular historical moment. They break free from temporality, refusing to privilege the present over the past (or vice versa) but striving after the meaning that exceeds both present and past. The poem leaves its readers, by default of its fragmentary state, with an image of these people richly endowed with all the pleasures of human existence, savouring the trappings of their luxurious lives. As the piece stands, its final image is not one of destruction, decay, or ruin, but rather of the very full lives of the people who once inhabited this spot: it ends not in nostalgia but in redemption. *The Ruin* fills in the lacunae caused by time and decay to reconstruct an image of wholeness and beauty, long gone but far from forgotten. Speaker and reader

---

64 Michael Lapidge has noted the use of 'oþþæt' in signalling a reversal of fortune (*'Beowulf* and Perception,' lecture, University of Notre Dame, Notre Dame, IN, 17 February 1998; published as *'Beowulf* and Perception,' Sir Israel Gollancz Memorial Lecture 2000, *PBA* 111 (2001): 61–97.

65 'The ruin fell to the ground, broken into mounds of stone, where formerly many a man, joyous and bright with gold, was adorned in splendour, proud and flushed with wine; he shone with war trappings; he gazed on treasure, on silver, on precious stones, on wealth, on possessions, on jewellery, on this bright city of the wide kingdom.'

alike share the space of the poem with those ancient people whose works are now in ruins, but whose legacy lives on through the physical remnants of both the wall and the poem itself. *The Ruin* presents a series of Benjaminian images – a series of 'dialectics at a standstill' – that follow one another in quick succession, balancing the stasis of the moment of critical insight with the transience of the experience of reading.

The idea of the ruin thus becomes a locus for the simultaneous existence of past and present, and the poem posits reflection on the past as an experience in which the past is brought into a dialectical relationship with the reader's present – and, implicitly, future.[66] The speaker's gaze upon the ruined wall is suffused with a nostalgic melancholy, made all the more intense for the modern reader, who recognizes (as the speaker does not) that the departed generations are not Germanic heroes, but Roman conquerors. The pleasure of that sadness, engendered by the experience of aesthetic contemplation, underscores the dialectic of past and present that the ruin embodies. It recognizes a necessary distinction between the two, but it also acknowledges their continued interaction. That is most certainly the task of readers who approach the ruins of the Anglo-Saxon poetic corpus.[67] The fragmentary and damaged state of many early manuscripts prevents us from experiencing poems in their entirety, and the texts extant today likely represent only a fraction of the literary production of the period. Understanding Anglo-Saxon England thus demands the same work of imaginative reconstruction that the ruin asks of its observer. At the same time, however, it is incumbent upon us to honour the fragments themselves. It is impossible, and perhaps inadvisable, to attempt to fill in the gaps and lacunae – some material, such as damage to the manuscripts, and some literary, in the form of texts now lost – with our own inventions. The nature of the corpus itself seems to require us to consider what it means for a literary text to be a ruin, and to think about the history that

---

66 Dailey writes, 'While the poem speaks of its time, that is, while it is a product of its historical conditioning and speaks of its history, it is able to free itself from this temporal anchoring only because of an economy that works both ways' ('Questions of Dwelling,' 193).

67 The oft-noted parallel between the ruins in the texts and the ruins of the texts is the ground for Emily V. Thornbury's revealing exploration of aesthetics and editorial theory in the early history of modern Old English studies; see 'Admiring the Ruined Text: the Picturesque in Editions of Old English Verse,' *New Medieval Literatures* 8 (2006): 215–44, especially 217–25.

the text itself embodies.[68] In this, Benjamin has anticipated us, by declaring that works of art are, indeed, ruins themselves: 'The word "history" stands written on the countenance of nature in the characters of transience. The allegorical physiognomy of the nature-history [*Naturgeschichte*], which is put on stage in the *Trauerspiel*, is present in reality in the form of a ruin.'[69]

Here Benjamin seizes upon the image of the ruin, the fragment, to allegorize the significance of cultural production. 'In the ruin history has physically merged into the setting. And in this guise history does not assume the form of the process of an eternal life so much as that of irresistible decay.'[70] The ruin is the remnant of human activity – culture – impressed upon the materiality of objects; and the life within them, which the critic seeks to reanimate, is always already moving toward death:

> Mortification of the works: not then – as the romantics have it – awakening of the consciousness in living works, but the settlement of knowledge in dead ones ... In the last analysis structure and detail are always historically charged. The object of philosophical criticism is to show that the function of artistic form is as follows: to make historical content, such as provides the basis of every important work of art, into a philosophical truth. This transformation of material content into truth content makes the decrease in effectiveness, whereby the attraction of earlier charms diminishes decade by decade, into the basis for a rebirth, in which all ephemeral beauty is completely stripped off, and the work stands as a ruin.[71]

Aesthetics, then, is not simply beauty, which is a historically contingent category whose definitions change with the passage of time, but rather the dialectic of form and truth-content [*Wahrheitsgehalt*] that is a constant and continuing presence within the work of art. History and artefact merge through the process of mortification; truth and art intertwine to reveal the past in a way quite different from that employed by the narrative forms of historiography and art history. The apprehension of that

---

68 Caroline Walker Bynum famously reads 'the notion of digested and regurgitated fragments' in medieval visions of resurrection as 'a metaphor of the historian's subject matter'; see 'In Praise of Fragments: History in the Comic Mode,' in *Fragmentation and Redemption: Essays on Gender and the Human Body in Medieval Religion* (New York: Zone, 1992), 11–26 at 26.

69 *Origin*, 177.

70 *Origin*, 177–8.

71 *Origin*, 182.

truth is likened to the allegorical process: meaning is grasped not instantan-eously but through time, and the temporal element contributes to truth's ultimate elusiveness; by the time the reader reaches the end point of inter-pretation, the place where truth was, it has already become something else.

The image of the ruin serves two important purposes for Benjamin's reading of the *Trauerspiel*, and of literary history in general: first, it repre-sents the relationship between the human activity of aesthetic production and the material objects that it creates, always already ossified fragments of artistic truth; and second, it allegorizes the process of what Benjamin terms *Naturgeschichte*, or 'natural history,' in which the decay of objects takes place independently of, but not in isolation from, human history. The ruin, then, embodies a dialectic of stasis and transience that points, for Benjamin, toward theology, and the goal of criticism is the redemption of ideas through the process of interpretation. Benjamin's insights into the necessary excess of meaning and nonlinear temporality of the ruin proceed from the context of modern philosophical discourse, but his work is rife with images of the medieval – from the consideration of medieval drama and undated ruins in the *Trauerspiel* book to the 'beads of a rosary' and monastic contemplation of the *Theses on the Philosophy of History*. All that is to say that reading Benjamin as an Anglo-Saxonist is not simply the imposition of a modern mentality on medieval poems; rather, the forego-ing suggests that within medieval poetry itself, the heterogeneous, the antiteleological, and the fragmentary found space to speak to readers, then and now. Certainly the redemption of ideas is what these two Anglo-Saxon poems have attempted, as well as what we have attempted in read-ing them. *Deor* redeems past suffering in an attempt at consolation for present sufferers, and *The Ruin* redeems a long-dead civilization whose remnants continue to have meaning, as medieval poetry does, to readers who must imagine what the creators were like.

These examples are by no means rare in Anglo-Saxon poetry, in which past and present are often collapsed into narrative moments and formal elements. In *Beowulf*, the description of the magnificent hall of Heorot is intertwined with a description of its eventual destruction in fire (lines 74–85); and Beowulf himself foretells the failure of Freawaru's marriage to Ingeld at the same time that he describes the planned peace-pledge (2020–69a). The speaker of *The Wanderer* calls to mind the vanished hall-companions of former days, in contrast to the isolation and despair of his present. In *Widsith*, another displaced scop gathers together the fragments of legendary history in a tour de force demonstrating his poetic art. In a more material sense, editors and codicologists attempt to piece together the fragments of old manuscripts, supplying missing letters, words, and phrases where the depredations of time and the elements have rendered text illegible. Yet these imaginative reconstructions are always carefully marked, so that readers can dialectically perceive both the original lacuna and the 'complete' text that is the editorial creation; and as digital editions become more commonplace, readers will have more and more opportunity to experience the medieval text as a dialectical image. These attempts, and the desire to bridge historical distance that underwrites them, are evidence of the continuing relevance of medieval literature for modern readers. We seize these texts as they flash before us in a moment of recognition; we see them arrayed alongside diverse contemporaneous works, within a variety of literary traditions and genres, emerging from assorted historical and geographical contexts, and resonating with our own particular themes and concerns. Yet, like all the best art, they continue to elude our comprehension. The remnants of the medieval past lie scattered among the ruins of literary history, but we return to them again and again, generation after generation, sifting through the wreckage to piece together fragments of understanding, to contemplate the possibilities of meaning that emerge from their various constellations, and to recognize that they will forever call into question our attempts to apprehend them.

IV. Heroic History and the Presence of the Past

The marriage of form and historical consciousness in Anglo-Saxon poetry is not limited to *Deor* and *The Ruin*, and the methodology of juxtaposition and contemplation to which Old English alliterative verse is so well suited gives rise to a singularly Anglo-Saxon way of thinking about the past. For Anglo-Saxon heroic verse, the past is not a foreign country; although separated in time, the people, places, and artefacts of earlier generations remain a fully real and present part of contemporary culture. The movement that recuperates these fragments of the past is not one of simple reflective nostalgia; it is not merely a question of looking back longingly to earlier times, but rather of resurrecting that lost past and salvaging its meaning.[72] Deor makes no distinction between himself and the figures of Germanic legend; to him, they are connected by their shared suffering,

---

72 Svetlana Boym distinguishes between reflective nostalgia, which simply looks back longingly at the past and meditates on the passage of time, and restorative nostalgia, which seeks to recuperate and re-energize aspects of that lost past. See Boym, *The Future of Nostalgia* (New York: Basic, 2001), 41–55, and pp. 131–2 below.

and the reader too participates in this connection. The speaker of *The Ruin* likewise connects past and present, moving continually back and forth across the temporal divide both to mourn the loss of an ancient world and to re-experience it through the aesthetic process. If the building and burning of Heorot can occupy the same narrative space, then so too can Beowulf and Sigemund – or Beowulf, Sigemund, and an Anglo-Saxon audience, for that matter. History takes on a very different dimension through this aesthetic of nostalgia; far from being a record of past events, it is a portrait of the present, displaying in stunning detail the beliefs, needs, and desires of Anglo-Saxon society and how it imagined itself in the image of its forebears. Anglo-Saxon historical poetry, then, posits its Anglo-Saxon audience as inhabiting the continuing presence of the past, not as succeeding or supplanting it.

Deor and *The Ruin* articulate this historical relation at the level of the individual speaker, but a poem like *Widsith* offers a glimpse at how the relation comes into play for a reading or listening community as whole.[73] The poem presents itself as spoken by a scop named Widsith, who tells readers of his ability to recount the mixed history and legends of the wider Germanic peoples, offering what Howe has described as a catalogue of the essential texts of the Germanic tradition.[74] The absence of narrative emphasizes that the poem does not seek to tell the stories of these ancient kings, as Widsith claims to do. It does not detail the histories and characteristics of successful kings for a potential Anglo-Saxon patron. Rather, the poem seeks to bring together an encyclopaedia of Anglo-Saxon cultural heritage, by bridging gaps in time and place to assemble a wide range of peoples and places in the single enclosed space of a heroic poem. Widsith, as his name implies, has travelled widely among many different peoples, yet the catalogue of his travels becomes increasingly dubious; he claims to

---

73 Kemp Malone acknowledges the poet's artistry in his 1936 edition: 'the *Widsith* poet was a literary artist of considerable skill in composition. Certainly he produced a poem remarkable alike for its complexity and for the balance and proportion of its parts' (*Widsith*, ed. Malone [London: Methuen, 1936], 3). In the early years of *Widsith* criticism, scholars devoted their energies to identifying the kings and tribes listed in the poem; see, for example, Malone, 'Introduction,' in *Widsith*, 1–58, and '*Widsith* and the Critic,' *ELH* 5 (1938): 49–66. In more recent decades, criticism has turned toward the implications, particularly those of form, for understanding both the individual subjectivity of a poetic speaker and his relationship to Anglo-Saxon society; see, for example, Ray Brown, 'The Begging Scop and the Generous King in *Widsith*,' *Neophilologus* 73 (1989): 281–92.

74 Howe, *The Old English Catalogue Poems*, Anglistica 23 (Copenhagen: Rosenkilde and Bagger, 1985), 172–91.

have visited dozens of Germanic tribes as well the far-flung regions of the Romans, Greeks, Assyrians, and Indians. Separated by vast distances in both space and time, the tribes that appear in *Widsith*'s catalogue cannot represent a literal itinerary of an individual's travels, nor are they meant to. Rather, they offer a testament of poetry's power to commemorate and to bridge the distances in time and space that no single person could ever hope to cross. *Widsith*, then, is an example of how the aesthetic apprehension of the past operates at a collective level, of how an entire society can position itself vis-à-vis a cultural heritage drawn from various and sundry times and places.[75]

Read in this way, the poem takes on the weight of history that is immanent, as Benjamin would say, in all art, and reading the poem provides Anglo-Saxons with secure perceptions of both past and present. Indeed, its structure as an index of allusions that call to mind the larger tradition would force medieval readers to participate in the creation of the text's meaning, as Foley argues; and for modern readers, *Widsith* offers insight into how the Anglo-Saxons' literature subtly shaped the contours of their place in history. The poem's speaker, Widsith, becomes an allegory for an Anglo-Saxon culture that collects fragments from the myths and legends of the past, both to keep them from vanishing forever and to complete its own image of itself. This is the task of the Anglo-Saxon scop and Benjamin's critic alike. Assembling these fragments as a constellation in the poem, *Widsith* establishes a relationship between its various presents (the moments of its composition, copying, reading, etc.) and the past it seeks to contain. Instead of teaching about the past, the poem teaches readers how to approach the past. History, in *Widsith*, functions as a compilation or inventory of people and events, organized according to varying principles at different times and for assorted purposes. In fact, Niles sees *Widsith* as a major player in the formation of Anglo-Saxon national identity:

> When read in conjunction with other Anglo-Saxon historical writings that can plausibly be dated to the hundred-year period extending from the 880s (or the middle years of the reign of King Alfred, who reigned from 871 to 899) to about the year 980 (the approximate date when the Exeter Book was written out), the poem reveals how the English-speaking people who were living in Britain during this crucially formative period of state-formation –

---

75 David A. Rollman explores this very possibility when he calls *Widsith* 'an Anglo-Saxon defense of poetry'; see '*Widsith* as an Anglo-Saxon Defense of Poetry,' *Neophilologus* 66 (1982): 431–9.

the *Angelþeod*, as they called themselves – were constructing their historical present, with its various ethnic constituencies, out of a series of gestures toward the past.[76]

It is not the Anglo-Saxons' only cultural heritage; it is not even the only kind of cultural heritage to be found in the Exeter Book. But it grounds a particular mode of historiography in the heroic legends of the ancient past; it links the vernacular poetic tradition with the preservation of that past; and it emphasizes the role of poetry as the appropriate medium for the commemoration of the past.

Perhaps most important, *Widsith* affirms the value of history in a temporal and worldly, rather than a salvific, context, for the names preserved in poetry are recollected by the living. The poem itself closes on that note, with a sweeping statement about poets and their enduring legacies:

Swa scriþende   gesceapum hweorfað
gleomen gumena   geond grunda fela,
þearfe secgað,   þoncword sprecaþ;
simle suð oþþe norð   sumne gemetað
gydda gleawne,   geofum unhneawne,
se þe fore duguþe wile   dom aræran,
eorlscipe æfnan,   oþþæt eal scæceð,
leoht ond lif somod;   lof se gewyrceð,
hafað under heofonum   heahfæstne dom.[77]   (135–43)

Widsith argues that poetry, which can significantly outlive individuals, offers immortality through imagination, and that the permanence of art endows its subjects with similar longevity. Reading such a poem a thousand years later, it is difficult to contest this argument; after all, the energy with which scholars have pursued the identification of obscure tribes and places gives them life once again, and the obvious importance of this kind of history to an Anglo-Saxon audience allows their historical consciousness to make itself felt by modern readers.

---

76 Niles, 'Anthropology,' 173.
77 'Thus the minstrels of men go wandering with the fates through many lands, they announce their need and speak words of thanks, always, north and south, they find someone appreciative of songs and unstinting with gifts, he who wishes to raise up glory before his troops, to achieve nobility, until everything departs, light and life together; he secures praise, has a lasting glory under heaven.' Citation is taken from *Exeter Anthology*, ed. Muir, and is cited by line number. Translation is my own.

The underlying philosophy of Anglo-Saxon vernacular historiography thus differs significantly from the Christian teleology of salvation history characteristic of mainstream medieval history-writing. In the salvation narrative, redemption is not an ongoing process; it is the end point, the telos, of all history. Yet Benjamin's philosophical focus is on the redemption of the present, of reunifying the fragments of history into an image of wholeness, fleeting though that may be. As we shall see in the following chapters, the historical poetry of Anglo-Saxon England is heavily invested in constructing a coherent image out of fragments from the past. Both heroic and biblical history play an important role in the formation of Anglo-Saxon subjectivity; as a Christian nation but one with strong historical ties to the values of a war-band culture, Anglo-Saxon England tells itself stories about its past that draw on both traditions to create something unique. Nowhere is this more evident than in the Old English redactions of biblical literature, and the majestic Junius 11 offers a collection of historical poetry very different from the Exeter Book. Far from being a collection of fragments assembled by chance rather than by design, Junius 11 is a carefully planned *de luxe* manuscript, complete with illustrations and executed by master craftsmen. Its planning, design, and production all indicate an energetic investment in the transmission and dissemination of biblical narrative in an explicitly Anglo-Saxon format. Yet that format brings with it a particular mode of thinking about history and about the relation between past and present. If that historical mode is nonlinear and antiteleological, what is to become of the narrative arc of salvation history?

2 In Principio: Origins of the Present in Anglo-Saxon Biblical Verse

In huius monasterio abbatissae fuit frater quidam diuina gratia specialiter insignis, quia carmina religioni et pietati apta facere solebat, ita ut, quicquid ex diuinis litteris per interpretes disceret, hoc ipse post pusillum uerbis poeticis maxima suauitate et conpunctione conpositis in sua, id est Anglorum, lingua proferret. Cuius carminibus multorum saepe animi ad contemtum saeculi et appetitum sunt uitae caelestis accensi. Et quidem et alii post illum in gente Anglorum religiosa poemata facere temtabant, sed nullus eum aequiperare potuit. Namque ipse non ab hominibus neque per hominem institutus canendi artem didicit, sed diuinitus adiutus gratis canendi donum accepit.

Bede, *Historia ecclesiastica*[1]

For the substance of a poem is not merely an expression of individual impulses and experiences. Those become a matter of art only when they come to participate in something universal by virtue of the specificity they acquire in being given aesthetic form.

Theodor Adorno, *On Lyric Poetry and Society*

---

1 *Bede's Ecclesiastical History of the English People*, ed. and trans. Bertram Colgrave and R.A.B. Mynors (Oxford: Clarendon, 1969), 4.24; henceforth *HE*. Translations are also taken from this edition. 'In the monastery of this abbess there was a certain brother who was specially marked out by the grace of God, so that he used to compose godly and religious songs; thus, whatever he learned from the holy Scriptures by means of interpreters, he quickly turned into extremely delightful and moving poetry, in English, which was his own tongue. By his songs the minds of many were often inspired to despise the world and to long for the heavenly life. It is true that after him other Englishmen attempted to compose religious poems, but none could compare with him. For he did not learn the art of poetry from men nor through a man but he received the gift of song freely by the grace of God.'

The miracle of Cædmon's gift of song has often been read as the origin of Anglo-Saxon vernacular poetry, and with good reason. Few moments in Bede's *Historia ecclesiastica* are so frequently cited, perhaps because the story resonates with both pathos and triumph: an illiterate cowherd hides in shame from his turn at the harp, until he is given the divine ability to compose religious verse unequalled before or since.[2] With this divine gift, Cædmon becomes an Anglo-Saxon prophet, instructing his people in the history and doctrine of their faith.[3] For Bede, the story also fittingly extends the story he tells throughout the *Historia ecclesiastica*, that of the gradual naturalization of Christianity among the Anglo-Saxons. From the beginning of the English mission, Gregory instructs Augustine to sanctify the pagan shrines of the English in order to make the new religion more palatable to them: 'aqua benedicta fiat, in eisdem fanis aspergatur, altaria construantur, reliquiae ponantur. Quia, si fana eadem bene constructa sunt, necesse est ut a cultu daemonum in obsequio ueri Dei debeant commutari, ut dum gens ipsa eadem fana sua non uidet destrui, de corde errorem deponat, et Deum uerum cognoscens ac adorans, ad loca quae consueuit familiarius concurrat.'[4] By removing the idols from the shrines and replacing them with Christian relics, Augustine will be able to maintain the 'well-built' spaces in which the English are comfortable. Likewise, in the shifting of the slaughter of cattle to saints' feast days, traditional rituals are preserved and directed toward more spiritually suitable ends. The recognizable forms of worship are thus emptied of their pagan meaning and refilled with Christian content, from the conversion of ancient shrines to the deployment, in Book V, of a veritable fleet of native English saints and martyrs. The story of Cædmon is a logical continuation and fulfilment of this renovation project. Having transformed the spaces and practices of religious worship, the Christianization of the English continues into cultural

---

2 *HE* 4.24.
3 G. Shepherd, 'The Prophetic Cædmon,' *RES*, n.s., 5 (1954): 113–22. A.P.McD. Orchard illustrates the blending of Christian and Anglo-Saxon traditions about poetic inspiration in 'Poetic Inspiration and Prosaic Translation,' in *Studies in English Language and Literature: 'Doubt Wisely': Papers in Honour of E.G. Stanley*, ed. M.J. Toswell and E.M. Tyler, 402–22 (London: Routledge, 1996). See also Daniel Paul O'Donnell, *Cædmon's Hymn: A Multi-media Study, Edition, and Archive* (Woodbridge: D.S. Brewer, 2005).
4 *HE* 1.30. 'Take holy water and sprinkle it in these shrines, build altars and place relics in them. For if the shrines are well built, it is essential that they should be changed from the worship of devils to the service of the true God. When this people see that their shrines are not destroyed they will be able to banish error from their hearts and be more ready to come to the places they are familiar with, but now recognizing and worshipping the true God.'

transformation, filling the Germanic forms of alliterative verse with scriptural content. Like Augustine, who brought his flock into old, familiar spaces to hear the truth of the new religion, Bede uses Cædmon as an example of how to turn popular entertainment toward spiritual ends, of how to make familiar the unfamiliar language of scripture; and if we follow William of Malmesbury, Aldhelm does the same, by reciting heroic poems in order to gather an audience for his preaching.[5] As a beginning, then, for both Cædmon's divine work and the Old English poetic tradition, Cædmon's *Hymn* is a compelling object.

Bede tells us that Cædmon went on to compose songs about the entire span of biblical history, songs covering the Old Testament stories of Genesis and Exodus 'de aliis plurimis sacrae scripturae historiis' as well as the Passion, the Resurrection, and visions of heaven and hell.[6] In the early years of Anglo-Saxon studies, this catalogue was thought to refer to the contents of Oxford, Bodleian Library MS Junius 11, which contains Old English verse versions of the stories of Genesis, Exodus, and Daniel, along with a poem about the torments of hell and the promise of salvation known as *Christ and Satan*.[7] Although its contents are not Cædmon's work, and are in fact the work of multiple poets, Junius 11 remains an example of the kind of work that Cædmon set out to do: to cast Christian content in the familiar forms of heroic verse in order to deliver it to an English audience. But this project of cultural translation is not simply a matter of putting new wine into old bottles; just as pagan temples and shrines retained some of their old meaning, so too does the form of heroic verse retain its familiar associations. When Christian content meets Anglo-Saxon form, it does not simply supplant its pagan predecessor. Instead, a hybrid form results,

---

5 William of Malmesbury, *Gesta pontificum Anglorum: The History of the English Bishops*, ed. and trans. Michael Winterbottom, vol. 1 (Oxford: Clarendon, 2007), 5.190.4.

6 *HE* 4.24. 'and of many other of the stories taken from the sacred Scriptures.'

7 For a description of the manuscript, see N.R. Ker, *Catalogue of Manuscripts Containing Anglo-Saxon* (Oxford: Clarendon, 1957), no. 334. The manuscript was owned by Franciscus Junius, who produced the first edition of it in 1665 under the title *Caedmonis monachi paraphrasis poetica Genesios ac praecipuarum sacrae pagina historiarum* (Amsterdam, 1655); repr. and ed. Peter J. Lucas (Amsterdam: Rodopi, 2000). Complete facsimiles are available in *The Cædmon Manuscript of Anglo-Saxon Biblical Poetry, Junius XI in the Bodleian Library*, ed. Israel Gollancz (London: Oxford University Press, 1927); and *A Digital Facsimile of Oxford, Bodleian Library MS Junius 11*, ed. Bernard J. Muir, Bodleian Library Digital Texts 1 (Oxford: Bodleian Library, 2004). Ker, *Catalogue*, dates the manuscript to (s. x/xi, xi), but Leslie Lockett has recently argued for an earlier date, between c. 960 and c. 990; see 'An Integrated Re-examination of the Dating of Oxford, Bodleian Library, Junius 11,' *ASE* 31 (2002): 141–73.

with elements both similar to and different from the traditions that spawned it. As Homi Bhabha writes,

> the hybrid object ... retains the actual semblance of the authoritative symbol but revalues its presence by resisting it as the signifier of *Entstellung* – *after the intervention of difference*. It is the power of this strange metonymy of presence to so disturb the systematic (and systemic) construction of discriminatory knowledges that the cultural, once recognized as the medium of authority, becomes virtually unrecognizable. Culture, as a colonial space of intervention and agonism ... can be transformed by the unpredictable and partial desire of hybridity.[8]

What Bhabha sees happening with a dominant cultural tradition (in his example, English Christianity) when it is translated into a local, and supposedly inferior, language is equally true of the translation of the Christian tradition into English in the first place. The process of linguistic translation (which is simultaneously cultural translation) destabilizes the language of authority and disrupts the hierarchy (British/Indian or Latin/Anglo-Saxon) on which that authority is grounded. What begins as the imposition of authoritative discourses of colonial power gradually becomes a site of reassertion for those supposedly inferior subjects. Cædmon's poetry begins as a marginal gloss, subordinate in every way to the Latin tradition it translates; but the process of translation alters it, 'suauiusque resonando doctores suos uicissim auditores sui faciebat.'[9] Bede himself grants the vernacular verse primacy by refusing to present it in a Latin verse translation, opting instead for a prose paraphrase.[10] Hybridity thus

---

8 Homi K. Bhabha, *The Location of Culture* (London: Routledge Classics, 2004), 164; emphasis in original.

9 *HE* 4.24. 'and it sounded so sweet as he recited it that his teachers became in turn his audience.'

10 'Neque enim possunt carmina, quamuis optime conposita, ex alia in aliam linguam ad uerbum sine detrimento sui decoris ac dignitatis transferri' [For it is not possible to translate verse, however well composed, literally from one language to another without some loss of beauty and dignity] (*HE* 4.24). Katherine O'Brien O'Keeffe charts the development of the Old English gloss into literary text in the context of both Latin and Old English manuscripts containing the *Hymn*; see 'Orality and the Developing Text of Cædmon's *Hymn*,' *Speculum* 62 (1987): 1–20. Kevin Kiernan explores the relative authority of Latin text and Old English gloss in 'Reading Cædmon's "Hymn" with Someone Else's Glosses,' in *Old English Literature: Critical Essays*, ed. R.M. Liuzza, 103–24 (New Haven: Yale University Press, 2002); originally pub. in *Representations* 32 (1990): 157–74.

disrupts Latin's dominance over the vernacular, and Anglo-Saxon poetry produces its own authority – so successfully that, in later colonial contexts, English Christianity will come to play the same role in the colonial period that Latin Christianity had in the early Middle Ages.[11]

Such cultural hybridity has long been noted in Old English religious poetry, where expanded battle scenes enliven the versifications of Genesis and Exodus, saints talk like heroes, and Christ and his apostles become a Germanic warlord and his loyal retainers. But, as we have seen, the heroic aesthetic brings with it its own particular mode of historical consciousness – the bridging of historical gaps through the constellation of related events – which likewise works to familiarize contemporary audiences with the distant biblical past. In the same way that Germanic tradition places past and present alongside each other in a constellation in order to establish relationships of meaning between them, Anglo-Saxon biblical verse juxtaposes characters like Adam, Noah, and Abraham with one another and with the poetry's readers, thereby bringing its audience into the presence of biblical people and events. In this respect, vernacular poetry bears certain comparison with the liturgy, which also sought to collapse the distance between present and past through affective rituals and to bring communicants into the Real Presence of New Testament historical events.[12] Cædmon's goal may have been to Christianize the Anglo-Saxons, but in the process he also anglicized biblical history. In addition to granting authority to the vernacular, however, the creation of a hybrid object such as Anglo-Saxon biblical verse opens the door to unorthodox forms of interpretation:

> Hybridity represents that ambivalent 'turn' of the discriminated subject into the terrifying, exorbitant object of paranoid classification – a disturbing questioning of the images and presences of authority … It is not a third term that resolves the tension between two cultures … in a dialectical play of 'recognition'. The displacement from symbol to sign creates a crisis for any concept of authority based on a system of recognition: colonial specularity, doubly

---

11 As Kathleen Biddick notes in 'Bede's Blush: Postcards from Bali, Bombay, Palo Alto,' in *The Shock of Medievalism* (Durham: Duke University Press, 1998), 83–101 at 98–101.

12 See, for example, O.B. Hardison, *Christian Rite and Christian Drama in the Middle Ages: Essays in the Origin and Early History of Modern Drama* (Baltimore: Johns Hopkins University Press, 1965); and Gregory Dix, *The Shape of the Liturgy* (London: A and C Black, 1945). For the Anglo-Saxon context in particular, see M. Bradford Bedingfield, *The Dramatic Liturgy of Anglo-Saxon England* (Woodbridge: Boydell, 2002).

inscribed, does not produce a mirror where the self apprehends itself; it is always the split screen of the self and its doubling, the hybrid.[13]

Hybridity destabilizes the simple binary opposition between colonizer and colonized and refutes identity at either pole. It becomes a site for the reformulation of power, and the hybrid reflects back to authority its own ideological ambivalences. As a result, Anglo-Saxon biblical verse is able to envision biblical history, and its significance to readers, very differently from the way it is envisioned in the historical consciousness of the exegetical tradition.[14] The contrasts are stark indeed when a poem like *Genesis* is read alongside the prose translation of Genesis by Ælfric of Eynsham, and the differences centre precisely on competing ideas about how to think about history – more specifically, about how to consider the past in relation to the present when the stakes are salvation, and how those differences can be expressed formally.

In thinking about this verse historically – as historical discourse – rather than exclusively theologically, we can posit Old English biblical verse as a nexus for a variety of concerns expressed through dichotomy, those of form versus content, Christian versus pagan, Latin versus vernacular, history versus theology, and present versus past, to name a few. Within the scope of this chapter, I want to limit my investigation to a few key questions on the Old English verse adaptations of the Old Testament and their unique aesthetic mediation of biblical history. First, in what ways do the Junius poems help their vernacular audience to work through their relation to an origin? Just as the story of Cædmon serves as the origin of Anglo-Saxon vernacular verse, so it also helps to articulate the relationship of the Anglo-Saxon people to the origins of human history in the Christian tradition. Cædmon's *Hymn* serves as a site of convergence for native cultural origins and a foreign religious origin; it brings together the beginning of Anglo-Saxon poetry, the beginnings of the Anglo-Saxon church, and the beginning of the world. The biblical verse helps to continue this work by presenting Anglo-Saxon Christianity to its practitioners as a hybrid form that incorporates and builds on both cultural traditions. Second, how

---

13 Bhabha, *Location of Culture*, 162.
14 Although I use the term 'readers,' I recognize that much of the poems' audience would have experienced them aurally. 'Readers' thus indicates all members of the textual community, in Brian Stock's sense of the term; see *The Implications of Literacy: Written Language and Models of Interpretation in the Eleventh and Twelfth Centuries* (Princeton: Princeton University Press, 1983).

do these poems shape the presentation of narrative moments for their audience's understanding of biblical history? Much of this shaping is de facto; the jarring interpolations of *Genesis B* and of the patriarchal digressions in *Exodus* are quite likely due to the vicissitudes of textual transmission rather than to the plan of a knowing author. But they nevertheless give a distinct shape to the narratives of the poems as readers have received them, and that shape raises a number of intriguing possibilities. If we think about them as primarily historical rather than primarily theological, they fit quite comfortably with the kinds of historical consciousness we saw generated in *Deor*, *The Ruin*, and *Widsith*. The Junius poems move from the epic chronological sweep of *Genesis* and *Exodus* to the more lyric expressions of faith as a function of history in *Daniel* and *Christ and Satan*; in the end, lyric poetry grants its audience a communion with the divine that values salvation as much as, if very differently from, a Jerome or an Ælfric does.[15] As hybrid objects, then, these poems challenge the teleology of salvation history by transforming a future telos into a present idea apprehended through the constellation. Finally, what can these poems, as poems, tell us about how Anglo-Saxon culture attempted to mediate among its various cultural influences? As adaptations of biblical material, they articulate a strikingly different set of concerns from those underlying prose translations and homiletic treatments of the same materials, and a closing comparison of their vision of Christian history to that of Ælfric's biblical translations makes this difference manifest.

I. Reading the Anglo-Saxons or Reading Like an Anglo-Saxon?

Even where scholars have been attentive to questions of form in Anglo-Saxon biblical verse, they generally seek to bring the texts into line with traditional medieval allegoresis. As A.N. Doane notes in his edition of *Genesis A*, 'the problem which *Genesis A* presents, a sacred subject rendered into what was recently "pagan" verse form, goes to the very core of Christian poetry.'[16] Doane finds ultimately that, like Cædmon, 'the better

---

15 Theodor Adorno assigns to lyric poetry the capacity to express the individual voice and work out its relationship to a social totality; in lyric poetry, the tensions between the particular and the universal play themselves out in language, which is bounded historically. See 'On Lyric Poetry and Society,' in *Notes to Literature I*, ed. Rolf Tiedemann, trans. Shierry Weber Nicholson, 37–54 (New York: Columbia University Press, 1991).

16 *Genesis A: A New Edition*, ed. A.N. Doane (Madison: University of Wisconsin Press, 1978), 44.

of these poets are attempting to create verbal structures which will elicit by familiar means (formulaic poetry) spiritual or doctrinal responses deemed similar to those which the sacred texts are supposed to elicit from trained audiences.'[17] He insists that heroic form is not inimical to Christian content, and that a focus on the biblical and exegetical traditions 'helps us to open out the poem, to understand its "digressions," "variations" and "expansions," which on their face are of the nature of Old English heroic poetry, but which in content conform to the requirements of scriptural knowledge.'[18] Like Doane, George Hardin Brown finds in the formal aspects of Anglo-Saxon alliterative verse an ideal vehicle for the seeming contradictions and paradoxes of Christian theology.[19] For both Doane and Brown, the form of the poetry not only allows but actually generates a reader's understanding of complex, contradictory, even paradoxical information about salvation history. The alliterative half-line and its ability to hold disparate elements in balance with one another allows for a kind of mediation that is accomplished far less efficiently in prose. As we saw in chapter 1, in the poetry of Germanic myth and legend this mediation allowed for a reconciliation of the present with the past that haunts it; and Fred Robinson long ago argued that the dialectical balance of alliterative metre can also allow for a similar reconciliation of the Anglo-Saxons' pagan past with their Christian present.[20]

We would do well to heed Bhabha's caveat, however, that the translation of belief from one culture to another alters both, and to remember that the Christianity translated into popular verse form will necessarily take on new aspects drawn from Anglo-Saxon culture. To put it in literary terms, the formal structures of Anglo-Saxon verse are indeed well suited to the expression of paradox, but they also mediate that paradox for the reader – meaning does not simply pass transparently from source through poetry to audience, and the result may be less a reconciliation than a reformulation. Both Doane and Brown take form and content as static and separate categories, when in fact, as we saw in *Deor* and *The Ruin*, they are mutually dependent elements of a dynamic and inherently unstable dialectic.

---

17 Doane, *Genesis A*, 49.
18 Doane, *Genesis A*, 56.
19 George Hardin Brown, 'Old English Verse as a Medium for Christian Theology,' in *Modes of Interpretation in Old English Literature: Essays in Honour of Stanley B. Greenfield*, ed. Phyllis Rugg Brown, Georgia Ronan Crampton, and Fred C. Robinson, 15–28 (Toronto: University of Toronto Press, 1986).
20 Fred C. Robinson, Beowulf *and the Appositive Style* (Knoxville: University of Tennessee Press, 1985).

Yet they do not account for the fundamental contradiction of the form and content they examine: the metonymic structure of oral traditional verse does not operate according to a telos, but salvation history cannot function without one. The heroic constellation generates a proliferation of meaning that a teleological narrative would find difficult to tolerate; although it is possible, and even desirable, for events and figures in heroic history to reconfigure historical meaning in random and sometimes contradictory ways, the teleology of salvation will always construe historical events to point toward the same, constant meaning; as Frank Kermode puts it, everything exists 'under the shadow of the end,' and 'events derive their significance from a unitary system, not from their correspondence with events in other cycles.'[21] It seems imprudent, therefore, to consider the interpretation of these poems solely in the context of salvation doctrine and without taking into account the exigencies of poetic form and the changes it will have wrought on the interpretation of biblical narrative in the hybrid Anglo-Christian poems.

Doane and Brown are not alone in their assumptions, however. The Junius poems are generally held to be the product of extremely erudite authors, well schooled in patristic allegoresis and liturgical formulae.[22] Much ink has been spilled in the past century and a half over the precise extrabiblical sources, allegorical inferences, liturgical influences, and typologies of the Junius poems, with the result that we now have a great appreciation of the breadth and sophistication of the cultural context that was able to produce them.[23] The focus on sourcing has, I think, encouraged scholars to bring this wealth of background material to bear on their readings of the poems, thereby generating skilful interpretations with respect to both the biblical and the Germanic elements. In recent years the theological context has dominated the critical conversation, and reached a pinnacle in Paul Remley's comprehensive treatment of the patristic and

---

21 Frank Kermode, *The Sense of an Ending: Studies in the Theory of Fiction with a New Epilogue* (Oxford: Oxford University Press, 2000), 5.

22 See, for example, Michael Lapidge, 'Versifying the Bible in the Middle Ages,' in *The Text in the Community: Essays on Medieval Works, Manuscripts, Authors, and Readers,* ed. Jill Mann and Maura Nolan, 11–40 (Notre Dame: University of Notre Dame Press, 2006).

23 See J.M. Evans, '*Genesis B* and Its Background,' pts I and II, *RES,* n.s., 14 (1963): 1–16 and 113–23; Aaron Mirsky, 'On the Sources of the Anglo-Saxon *Genesis* and *Exodus,*' *ES* 48 (1967): 385–97; and Paul G. Remley, 'The Latin Textual Basis of *Genesis A,*' *ASE* 17 (1988): 163–89.

liturgical backgrounds of the Old Testament poems.[24] Many scholars, following Bernard Huppé,[25] adopted Augustine's allegorical method in order to make sense of Old English poetry in explicitly, and exclusively, Christian terms.[26] Indeed, a driving critical tendency has been to assert unity by assimilating the events of the Junius poems to the framework of salvation history, and the poems have often been considered under the rubric of 'Christian epic.'[27] Almost a century ago, James Bright noted some correspondence between the Junius poems and the liturgy of the Easter Vigil.[28] Virginia Day subsequently related the poems specifically to the catechetical *narratio* specified by Augustine in *De catechizandis rudibus*, sketching the general outlines of the Creation, Fall, Advent, Crucifixion, and Judgment.[29] J.R. Hall, following Day, has argued for reading the poems as an 'Old English epic of redemption' and suggested that they are patterned on a traditional understanding of 'the course of sacred history'; and Joyce Hill finds that 'they present their particular events in the context of an understanding of God's plan for mankind.'[30] Unfortunately, the poems themselves do not demand or even encourage this kind of reading. They make no reference to New Testament events as prefigured by the Old Testament events they narrate, and they do not explicitly prompt allegorical

---

24 Remley, *Old English Biblical Verse: Studies in Genesis, Exodus, and Daniel* (Cambridge: Cambridge University Press, 1996).

25 Bernard F. Huppé, *Doctrine and Poetry: Augustine's Influence on Old English Poetry* (New York: State University of New York Press, 1959).

26 On the two major strains of criticism, see Joyce Hill, 'Confronting *Germania Latina*: Changing Responses to Old English Biblical Verse,' in *The Poems of MS Junius 11: Basic Readings*, ed. R.M. Liuzza, 1–19 (New York: Routledge, 2002), 3–5; originally pub. in *Latin Culture and Medieval Germanic Europe. Proceedings of the First Germania Latina Conference held at the University of Groningen, 26 May 1989*, ed. Richard North and Tette Hofstra, 71–88 (Groningen: E. Forsten, 1992).

27 Ivan Herbison, 'The Idea of the "Christian Epic": Towards a History of an Old English Poetic Genre,' in Toswell and Tyler, *'Doubt Wisely'*, 342–61.

28 J.W. Bright, 'The Relation of the Cædmonian *Exodus* to the Liturgy,' *MLN* 27 (1912): 97–103. Phyllis Portnoy uses the liturgical lections for Holy Saturday to explain the presence of the anomalous *Daniel* and *Christ and Satan* in Junius 11, in '"Remnant" and Ritual: The Place of *Daniel* and *Christ and Satan* in the Junius Epic,' *ES* 75 (1994): 408–22.

29 Virginia Day, 'The Influence of the Catechetical *narratio* on Old English and Some Other Medieval Literature,' *ASE* 3 (1974): 51–61.

30 J.R. Hall, 'The Old English Epic of Redemption: The Theological Unity of MS Junius 11,' in Liuzza, *MS Junius 11*, 20–52 at 24–5; originally pub. in *Traditio* 32 (1976): 185–208, and 'The Old English Epic of Redemption: Twenty-Five Year Retrospective,' in Liuzza, *MS Junius 11*, 53–68; J. Hill, 'Confronting *Germania Latina*,' 10.

or typological associations. So a question is raised as to why complex allegoresis would be presented to a learned audience in the form of traditional vernacular heroic verse.

Although the authors of the Junius poems were undoubtedly familiar with much of the patristic and exegetical material uncovered by these and other critics, the same cannot necessarily be said of their audience, whose theological education may not have extended beyond the catechetical *narratio*. In shifting the critical focus from authors and sources to multiple possible audiences, we can consider what historical meanings these poems might have had for a popular audience. As Nina Boyd has pointed out, 'too great a willingness to explain that which is strange or seemingly obscure in Old English poetry as "figural" or "allegorical" ignores the possibility that individual poems often speak clearly and originally for themselves about the nature of a society undergoing profound cultural change'; and Phillip Rollinson has likewise remarked, 'That an author could have discussed the crossing of the Red Sea in terms of baptism ... does not mean that he has had to.'[31] Peter Lucas has suggested that scribal markings in Junius 11 indicate that the poems may have been intended for oral performance, and Laurel Amtower shows how sectional divisions heighten the effect of oral delivery for an audience of lay Christians.[32] The illustrations in the manuscript also indicate a possibly lay audience.[33] Like the fellow *rudes* to whom Cædmon sang his songs (or, for that matter, for whom Ælfric composed many of his sermons), the audience of the Junius poems may have been well short of familiarity with the complexities of theological paradox and patristic tradition. Cædmon, after all, was no exegete, yet his poetry became the archetypal bridge over which the *rudes* of Anglo-Saxon England might cross to salvation, and his story assumes a very different audience for this kind of poetry than the one implied by much of the scholarship on the Junius poems.

It seems worthwhile, therefore, to consider how the poems themselves might have instructed readers to think about biblical history, especially in

---

31 Nina Boyd, 'Doctrine and Criticism: A Revaluation of "Genesis A",' *NM* 83 (1982): 230–8 at 238; Phillip B. Rollinson, 'The Influence of Christian Doctrine and Exegesis on Old English Poetry: An Estimate of the Current State of Scholarship,' *ASE* 2 (1973): 271–84 at 282.

32 Peter J. Lucas, ed., *Exodus* (London: Methuen, 1977), 8–12 and 18; and Laurel Amtower, 'Some Codicological Considerations in the Interpretation of the Junius Poems,' *ELN* 30, no. 4 (1993): 1–10.

33 See Barbara Raw, 'The Probable Derivation of Most of the Illustrations in Junius 11 from an Illustrated Old Saxon *Genesis*,' *ASE* 5 (1976): 133–48.

terms of the heroic diction, themes, tropes, and forms they employ. Judith Garde has argued that the purpose of this poetry was to instruct the unlettered, and that literary criticism mistakes its object when it focuses on the exegetical rather than the educational context; '*history*, not allegory or typology, is central to the Christian proclamation of the faith.'[34] But there is no need, as Garde demands, to abandon literary criticism as a method for understanding these poems. Garde makes a false distinction between the work of literary criticism and the capabilities of the Anglo-Saxon laity, and underestimates the poems' original audience – forgetting, it seems, that these same readers and auditors participated in a lively and extremely complex tradition of vernacular heroic verse. My goal, therefore, is not to discount the importance of allegorical exegesis in the world of Anglo-Saxon literature, or to argue that the Junius poems could not be read in that light. I would like, however, to expand the sphere of these poems to consider how comparatively less educated Anglo-Saxons, to whom Sigemund might well have been more familiar than Jerome or Augustine, could experience biblical history through poetry. How might an audience steeped in the historical method of *Beowulf* and *Deor* have responded to these retellings of Genesis and Exodus? In addition to making the world of the ancient Middle East more familiar to an English lay audience, how might these poems also have created an affective relationship between that audience and the events described? I am not suggesting that the manuscript or its contents were necessarily designed to provoke such readings; rather, I want to imagine how the poems, as they exist in this form, could have held certain meanings for one kind of audience.

We are brought back, of course, to Bede, and to Augustine's efforts to make Christianity more familiar to his English flock by creating, albeit unintentionally, a hybrid religious culture. Indeed, many critics have emphasized the ways in which Germanic culture assimilated Christianity rather than being colonized by it, especially with respect to biblical verse.[35] As Arthur Skemp puts it, 'scriptural story, motive, and conception were modified ... at the points where the temperament, the ideals, and the structure of society which they expressed or embodied, failed to harmonize

---

34 Judith N. Garde, *Old English Poetry in Medieval Christian Perspective: A Doctrinal Approach* (Cambridge: D.S. Brewer, 1991), 27; emphasis in original. See also Judith N. Garde and Bernard J. Muir, 'Patristic Influence and the Poetic Intention in Old English Religious Verse,' *Journal of Literature and Theology* 2 (1988): 49–68.

35 As in Anne Savage, 'The Old English *Exodus* and the Colonization of the Promised Land,' *New Medieval Literatures* 4 (2001): 39–60.

with those of the Anglo-Saxon.'[36] Critics are now less likely to think of literature in terms of 'temperament,' but Bennett Brockman points out that 'if the Cain and Abel episode of *Genesis A* is any indicator, it is more accurate to surmise that the Old English poet was impressed much more by biblical history, by a new store of legends intelligible within the ancient Germanic social and moral framework, than by exegetical theology or a radically new way of looking at life.'[37] Likewise, Charles Wright finds a poem like *Genesis A* to be more in the tradition of the Universal History than the catechetical *narratio*. In his analysis, the poet is far more interested in the literal events of the biblical narrative than in the possibility of allegorical or typological meditations on them.[38] Thomas Hill states, quite simply, that 'the Old English *Genesis A* is before all else a historical poem.'[39] But it is history with great potential for cultural impact. Nicholas Howe has seen the Old Testament poems as a means by which the Anglo-Saxons worked through their own relationship to a complicated cultural history, reflecting the acknowledgment of a pagan background and traditions in the light of the Christianity to which they were now equally committed. For Howe, a poem like *Exodus* not only offers a way in which the Anglo-Saxons could align their history with that recounted in the Old Testament, in their zeal to become a new chosen people; it actually '*resists* figural interpretation … because its poet was too deeply interested in the idea of migration as a means of understanding his native history.'[40] Howe locates the poem's meaning and importance in its relevance not as a prefiguration of New Testament events, but rather as an analogue for the migration history of the Anglo-Saxons themselves. It is the Exodus as historical event, not as a figure for baptism or salvation, that interests the poet

---

36 Arthur R. Skemp, 'The Transformation of Scriptural Story, Motive, and Conception in Anglo-Saxon Poetry,' *MP* 4 (1907): 423–70 at 436.

37 Bennett A. Brockman, '"Heroic" and "Christian" in *Genesis A*: The Evidence of the Cain and Abel Episode,' *MLQ* 35 (1974): 115–28 at 116. The same could be said of Michael D. Cherniss, 'Heroic Ideals and the Moral Climate of *Genesis B*,' *MLQ* 30 (1969): 479–97.

38 Charles D. Wright, '*Genesis A* ad litteram,' in *Old English Literature and the Old Testament*, ed. Michael Fox and Manish Sharma (Toronto: University of Toronto Press, forthcoming). I am grateful to Professor Wright for sharing his essay with me.

39 Thomas D. Hill, 'The "Variegated Obit" as an Historiographic Motif in Old English Poetry and Anglo-Latin Historical Literature,' *Traditio* 44 (1988): 101–24 at 101.

40 Nicholas Howe, *Migration and Mythmaking in Anglo-Saxon England* (New Haven: Yale University Press, 1989; repr. Notre Dame: University of Notre Dame Press, 2001), 104; emphasis added.

and his readers alike because of the way it resonates with their particular concerns as descendants of a migratory people who also think of themselves as God's chosen *folc*.

Ruth Ames suggested quite some time ago that the Junius poems could very easily be read as thoroughly Christian without being necessarily allegorical; she posits the figure of the Old Testament Christ as a site of confluence for Old Testament, New Testament, and Anglo-Saxon audience, and she points to Christ's presence in the Junius illustrations of Old Testament scenes as evidence that God's presence, in the Second Person of the Trinity, was assumed throughout history by poet and audience alike.[41] This Christological reading efficiently connects the poems of Junius 11, from the *Genesis*, which begins, as Roberta Frank has noted, with wordplay on 'word' that indicates the presence of Christ as *Logos* at the Creation, to the Christ of *Christ and Satan*, who recounts the whole of created history and its salvific significance.[42] Such a heterogeneous perspective on biblical history – that it joins Anglo-Saxon readers to the ancient Hebrews through bonds of commonality, and that it holds immediate interest for a relatively broad audience – has a great deal in common with how the Anglo-Saxons conceived of their relationship to the ancient Germanic past through poems like *Deor*, *The Ruin*, and *Widsith*. And, as Edward Irving, Jr, reminds us (writing about *Exodus*), 'a narrative poem of this kind is aesthetically effective not because it obtrusively keeps drawing our attention to its similarity to another story but because it is first of all a vivid and "true" literary experience in itself.'[43]

But the question of temporality and its relation to the aesthetic has even greater significance in biblical narrative than it did in the stories of mythic and legendary history. The advent of Christ broke history into what came before and what has come since; it is no coincidence that the Western tradition dates its own history in terms of that world-changing event. Christ

---

41 Ruth M. Ames, 'The Old Testament Christ and the Old English *Exodus*,' *Studies in Medieval Culture* 10 (1977): 33–50.

42 Roberta Frank, 'Some Uses of Paranomasia in Old English Scriptural Verse,' *Speculum* 47 (1972): 207–26, especially 211–15. T. Hill has also noted the importance of Christ's presence at the Creation in *Christ and Satan*, where Satan is described explicitly as rebelling against Christ rather than God; see 'The Fall of Satan in the Old English *Christ and Satan*,' *JEGP* 76 (1977): 315–25.

43 Edward B. Irving, Jr, '*Exodus* Retraced,' in *Old English Studies in Honour of John C. Pope*, ed. Robert B. Burlin and Edward B. Irving, Jr, 203–23 (Toronto: University of Toronto Press, 1974), 211.

fulfils what the Anglo-Saxons called the Old Law (*ealde æ*) and replaces it with the New Law (*niwe æ*); the Old Law can henceforth be understood only according to its spiritual meaning in relation to the New Law, rather than in its literality.[44] In theological terms, then, structures of temporality condition the possibility of salvation, and misunderstanding the relationship between past and present can have grave consequences that extend into eternity. How vernacular poetry conceives of that temporality is crucial for understanding the role of Anglo-Saxon biblical verse for its readers, then and now. Ancient patristic writers and modern theologians alike struggle to understand the nature of time in Christian history, and the Christian tradition itself produces various methods for thinking about the significance of past to present and future. How those methods are deployed and their relationship to formal concerns are the subject of this chapter.

In what follows, I want to look first at how Anglo-Saxon poetic form conditions an understanding of divine, as opposed to historical, temporality. The opening lines of *Genesis A* and Cædmon's *Hymn* both deal with the dizzying ramifications of contemplating the beginnings of human history. Drawing liberally on an Augustinian conception of divine and earthly temporalities, both texts formally reaffirm the inherent complexity of time in the Christian tradition. With the binary of divine eternity and earthly temporality firmly established, the Junius poems go on to break it down by subverting the strictures of historical time through aesthetic experience, bringing various historical events together through narrative juxtaposition and placing them all before the reader, who participates both intellectually and affectively in the affirmation of a Christian faith for which past, present, and future all bear equal significance for the story of human salvation. As we shall see, the tendency of the Junius poems to take biblical events and figures out of context for comparative purposes is a powerful tool for generating affective connections between readers and the past. But even contemporary writers feared that those readers might then misunderstand the relative importance of different historical moments, to the eternal detriment of their souls; and we will end with a brief look at Ælfric's anxieties over form, temporality, translation, and salvation – anxieties perhaps prompted by the Junius poems themselves.

---

44   Dorothy Haines has surveyed this tradition in the Anglo-Saxon context; see 'Unlocking *Exodus* ll. 516–532,' *JEGP* 98 (1999): 481–98.

II. In the Beginning: Confronting Origins in Genesis

When the apparition in Cædmon's dream commands him to sing, he begins at the beginning, with the 'principium creaturarum.'[45] In beginning, as Cædmon begins, *in principio*, I want to explore how Cædmon's *Hymn* and the opening lines of *Genesis A* position themselves (and their readers) in relation to the foundations of the created world, and to show how closely that creation is bound up with the idea of narrative.[46] Cædmon's first creative endeavour recounts the very first creative endeavour, the Creation of the world; indeed, Bruce Holsinger has recently suggested a pun on *sceop/ scop* at 5a.[47] Cædmon's *Hymn* paraphrases Genesis 1:1 ('in principio creavit Deus caelum et terram') in a stunning display of verbal artistry:

> Nu sculon herigean   heofonrices weard,
> meotodes meahte   and his modgeþanc,
> weorc wuldorfæder,   swa he wundra gehwæs,
> ece drihten,   or onstealde.
> He ærest sceop   eorðan bearnum
> heofon to hrofe,   halig scyppend;
> þa middangeard   moncynnes weard,
> ece drihten,   æfter teode
> firum foldan,   frea ælmihtig.[48]   (1–9)

---

45 *HE* 4.24. 'beginning of all created things.' D.R. Howlett credits Cædmon with a highly developed theological understanding and finds Trinitarian doctrine in the *Hymn*'s structure and punctuation; see 'The Theology of Cædmon's Hymn,' *Leeds Studies in English* 7 (1974): 1–12.

46 Laurence Michel has examined the parallels between these two texts and the Preface of the Mass in 'Genesis A and the *Praefatio*,' *MLN* 62 (1947): 545–50; see also Gollancz, *Caedmon Manuscript*, lx, and Ferdinand Holthausen, ed., *Die ältere Genesis mit Einleitung, Anmerkungen, Glossar, und der lateinischen Quelle* (Heidelberg: C. Winter, 1914), 91.

47 Bruce Holsinger, 'The Parable of Cædmon's *Hymn*: Liturgical Invention and Literary Tradition,' *JEGP* 106 (2007): 149–75 at 166.

48 Elliott van Kirk Dobbie, ed., *The Anglo-Saxon Minor Poems*, ASPR 6 (New York: Columbia University Press, 1942), 106. 'Now we must praise the guardian of the heavenly kingdom, the might of the creator and his purpose, the work of the father of glory, as he established the beginning of every wonder, the eternal lord. He, the holy Creator, first shaped heaven as a roof for the children of the earth; then the guardian of mankind, the eternal lord, afterwards created the world, the earth for the people, almighty lord.' All translations are my own unless otherwise noted.

The origin of Cædmon's creative activity recounts the origin of the Creation itself, and links the beginning of Old English poetry to the beginning of universal history. In addition to linking Anglo-Saxon traditional culture to the origins of Christian history, Cædmon's *Hymn* is a formal apotheosis of Anglo-Saxon alliterative verse.[49] The poem is a study in contrasts, and the simplicity of its message is underscored by the complexity of its delivery. Its nine lines comprise two sentences, both of which are densely packed with the characteristic stylistic features of the form – alliteration, chiasmus, apposition, repetition, and variation. There are seven variations of the titles for God, not counting pronouns, none of which is simply 'God.' The first sentence has a four-part compound object: God, the *heofonrices weard*, his *meahte* and his *modgeþanc*, and his *weorc*. The nature of that *weorc* is defined in a subordinate clause (3b–4) with the apposite subjects *he* and *ece drihten*. The second sentence further elaborates on the *weorc* from line 3. The subject, God, is reiterated five times by four titles and a pronoun. The action of the sentence falls on two direct objects: *heofon* and *middangeard* (which is also *foldan*). The opposition between heaven and earth is underlined by their structural separation; they are the objects of two separate but parallel verbs, *sceop* and *teode*, in two separate clauses. The coordinating conjunctions *ærest*, *þa*, and *æfter* establish a temporal hierarchy between heaven and earth and emphasize both their separation and their opposition, and the repetition of God as the subject of both clauses shows their unity as created objects. The accumulation of subjects and objects simultaneously in parallel and in opposition to each other enhances the notion of God's creative activity in shaping heaven and earth. Such stylistic accumulation also enhances the creative activity of Anglo-Saxon grammar and syntax in the aesthetic shaping of a biblical paraphrase.

In addition to staging the dialectical relation of form and content, the poem affirms the peculiar temporality of a human being contemplating the Creation, an event outside human history. Its opening words locate us as agents in the present moment (*Nu*) and within a community of active listeners implied by the plural present tense verb 'sculon.' Within three lines, however, the subject of the action has shifted from us to God, and the tense has shifted from present to past, thereby underscoring the historical separation between humanity and the moment of the Creation. With the single past tense verb *onstealde*, the temporal world in both its senses – as

---

49 Holsinger has also argued that the prosody of Cædmon's *Hymn* owes as much to the Latin tradition of accentual-syllabic verse as it does to the Germanic tradition, so that the poem is a formal as well as a cultural hybrid ('Parable,' 167–75).

both worldly and subject to time – is created in a single instant. The *or* that completes the alliterative pattern of line 4 indicates clearly that this is the beginning, a definitive point that marks a boundary between eternity and temporality. Yet the alliteration of line 3 crosses this temporal boundary, joining the object of our present praise, *weorc wuldorfæder*, to the *wundra* that he created in that distant past. Our connection to the created world is expressed at the level of content, too, despite the historical distance. The act of Creation itself is human-directed; God created the heavens for the children of the earth, *eorðan bearnum*; and *firum foldan* in apposition to *middangeard* tells us that earth likewise was created for their benefit. Humanity is separated from the moment of the Creation in time, as the verb tense reminds us, but the way in which humanity is a part of God's creative purpose is literalized in the use of *eorðan bearnum* and *firum* as indirect objects of *sceop* and *teode*. The sentence describing the activity of the Creation (lines 5–9) is bounded by nominatives referencing God (*he* and *frea ælmihtig*), and thus the concept of God as the beginning and the end is literalized (Rev. 22:13) and the limits of human history, past and future, within the eternity of the divine, are marked out. This is where Old English poetry begins, at the beginning of time itself, and the *Hymn* situates its Anglo-Saxon audience at that moment of origin as well.

Like Cædmon's *Hymn*, *Genesis A* begins firmly in the present tense. Also like Cædmon's *Hymn*, it opens with an exhortation to praise God:

> US IS RIHT MICEL   ÐÆT we rodera weard,
> wereda wuldorcining,   wordum herigen,
> modum lufien.[50]   (1–3a)

Our duty, in the present moment – in any present moment – is to praise God. Alliteration in these opening lines links *we* to the *weard* and *wereda wuldorcining* we must praise, as well as to the *wordum* with which we offer that praise. Among those *wordum* are the words of the poem that follow, and the narration of biblical history, of God's hand working among human events, is first and foremost praise of God's work. In addition to the duty to praise, however, the opening lines expound the nature of divine temporality:

---

50 Doane, *Genesis A*. Quotations are cited by line number. 'It is very fitting for us that we should praise with words and love with our hearts the guardian of the skies, the glorious king of hosts.'

                      he is mægna sped,
heafod ealra   heahgesceafta,
frea ælmihtig.   næs him fruma æfre,
or geworden   ne nu ende cymþ
ecean drihtnes   ac he bið a rice
ofer heofenstolas ...[51]

                                                            (5b–8a)

God's existence is outside temporality, and he is both eternal and never-changing. His power and his primacy are always in the present tense, and he is without beginning or end. God is contemporaneous with *us*, just as he was with humans at every other moment in human history.[52] The poetics here work once again to hold contrasting elements in balance. Double alliteration links the elements *fruma æfre* and *frea ælmihtig* in the preceding half-line; alliteration similarly holds together the words for beginning, end, and eternity: *or, ende, ecean,* and *a*. With the establishment of the created world, however, temporality is introduced into the poem, once again with the double sense of 'temporal.' The creation of the angels and the upper heavens introduces the past tense verb 'heold' [held] (9b). With the introduction of the 'sweglbosmas' [heavens] (9b) into the poem, the created world begins to take shape, and Creation is bounded by time. As a result, the rest of the poem's action is narrated in the past tense. Whereas God's nature is expounded as eternal, the nature of the angels even before the Fall is shown to be decidedly temporal by means of the poem's use of verb tense: they 'hæfdon gleam and dream' [had joy and ecstasy] (12b) as well as 'beorhte blisse' [bright bliss] (14a), and both rhyme and alliteration emphasize the joys and happiness that were but are no more. Patristic theology wrestled with various concepts of time and their implications for understanding biblical history. According to Augustine, the angels occupy a temporal space somewhere between the eternity of God and the temporality of humankind; he writes that 'ac per hoc etsi semper fuerunt, creati sunt, nec si semper fuerunt, ideo Creatori coaeterni sunt ... Quamuis nullo tempore sine illa [creatura]; non eam spatio transcurrente, sed manente

---

51 'A beginning, an origin, was never created for him, nor now does the end of the eternal lord come, but he is always powerful over the thrones of heaven.'

52 The eternal present of the divine is what Walter Benjamin seems to have in mind in his use of the term *Jetztzeit* [Now-Time], which is where he locates the moment of historical illumination, the recognition of the constellation, that allows the past to be redeemed. See *Theses on the Philosophy of History*, in *Illuminations*, ed. Hannah Arendt, trans. Harry Zohn (New York: Schocken, 1968), 253–64 at 261.

perpetuitate praecedens.'[53] Gerhart Ladner equates Augustine's formulation with the scholastic notion of *aevum*, a time with a beginning but no end, and finds that 'while transition from eternity to time thus begins with the angels ... time in the strict sense begins with the completion of instantaneous and simultaneous though six-partite creation [the hexameral Creation].'[54] And, as William Labov reminds us, temporal juncture is the foundation of narrative.[55] Narrative thus enters into historical time with the act of Creation (Cædmon's *He ærest sceop*), where that creation is immediately established as fallen: the joys and revelry, bliss and splendour, are things of the past rather than the present.[56]

Both poems are thoroughly Augustinian in their formulation of the Creation, in separating temporality from eternity and understanding the temporal as not only subordinate but always already fallen, subject to change whereas God is unchanging.[57] As Ernst Kantorowicz has written, 'time, *tempus*, was the exponent of transitoriness; it signified the frailty of this present world and all things temporal, and bore the stigma of the perishable. Time, rigorously severed from Eternity, was of inferior rank. For whereas the Eternity of God was conceived of as a Now-and-Ever without Time, the fugitive Time showed all the weakness of the evanescent moment.'[58] The absolute separation between eternity and temporality is reinforced here by the contrast between the eternal present of divine power

---

53 12.16.79–80, 95–7. *Sancti Aurelii Augustini De Civitate Dei libri XI–XXII*, ed. Bernard Dombart and Alphons Kalb, CCSL 48 (Turnhout: Brepols, 1955). 'Even though the angels have always existed, they were created; neither, if they have always existed, are they therefore co-eternal with the Creator ... He was at no time without them, for He preceded them not by the passage of time, but by His abiding eternity.' All translations are taken from Augustine, *The City of God against the Pagans*, ed. and trans. R.W. Dyson (Cambridge: Cambridge University Press, 1998).

54 Gerhart B. Ladner, *The Idea of Reform: Its Impact on Christian Thought and Action in the Age of the Fathers* (Cambridge, MA: Harvard University Press, 1959), 167–85 at 181; see also his 'excursus' entitled 'Some Patristic Distinctions Concerning Eternity, Aevum, and Time,' in *Idea of Reform*, 443–8. See also Ernst H. Kantorowicz, *The King's Two Bodies: A Study in Mediaeval Political Theology* (Princeton: Princeton University Press, 1957), 275–83, especially 280 n14.

55 William Labov, 'Some Further Steps in Narrative Analysis,' *Journal of Narrative and Life History* 7 (1997): 395–415.

56 Constance B. Hieatt traces the repetition of verbal structures that highlight the idea of division throughout the poem; see 'Divisions: Theme and Structure of *Genesis A*,' *NM* 81 (1980): 243–51.

57 *Confessions*, 11–12. See *Sancti Augustini Confessionum libri XIII*, ed. Luc Verheijen, CCSL 27 (Turnhout: Brepols, 1981).

58 Kantorowicz, *King's Two Bodies*, 275.

and glory and the delimited temporality of created beings, signified by the use of the present tense on the one hand and the past tense on the other. The beginning of the poem thus separates the content of its narrative – the history of creation and created beings – from the eternity of God. The separation between temporality and eternity is the foundation of the ineffability of God's plan for the world; it gives rise to typological reading as one way of making sense of events whose meaning is not apparent because the framework of salvation history is not fully comprehensible from a temporal perspective.

As modes of interpretation, typology and constellation share an investment in the connection of disparate events across a historical time line. Like the constellation, typology connects individual events based on their relevance to one another; for example, the sacrifice of Isaac in Genesis is connected to an event thousands of years later, the Crucifixion. Indeed, Erich Auerbach's seminal formulation of figuration insists that *figurae* must be concrete historical events, grounding typology, like the constellation, in the materiality of human experience.[59] Also like the constellation, typology reveals the presence of the eternal divine in the realms of human history. Yet unlike the kinds of historical constellations staged by heroic verse, Christian typology operates within a set teleology; it does not separate events from their historical time line, and events are always related through a third term: salvation. Typology always points toward salvation, and the temporal boundary of Christ's advent in the world defines the relative significance of events before and after that moment. Its configurations are limited and unidirectional; as Jean Daniélou defines it, 'a type is an event which offers likeness to something in the future, but yet does not really fulfil this something ... The type must bear a resemblance to what is typified and at the same time show clearly that it is nothing more than a type and not the reality itself.'[60] This view explicitly privileges the New Testament fulfilment over the Old Testament figure, which, as Richard Emmerson notes, 'can be dismissed (*dismissa figura*) once the fulfillment is accomplished or understood.'[61] In the resulting hierarchy, the sacrifice of Isaac can never be as meaningful as Christ's sacrifice, because, as a type, it

---

59   Erich Auerbach, 'Figura,' in *Scenes from the Drama of European Literature* (New York: Meridian, 1959), 11–76 at 56–7.

60   Jean Daniélou, *From Shadows to Reality: Studies in the Biblical Typology of the Fathers,* trans. Wulstan Hibberd (London: Burns and Oates, 1960), 125.

61   Richard K. Emmerson, '*Figura* and the Medieval Typological Imagination,' in *Typology and English Medieval Literature,* ed. Hugh T. Keenan, 7–42 (New York: AMS, 1992), 12.

is incomplete in itself. The significance of the sacrifice of Isaac is fixed, to use Daniélou's terminology, as a shadow of the reality it prefigures; in the light of the Crucifixion, the significance of Isaac's sacrifice fades away. The redemption of such lost historical moments, however, is precisely the project of the constellation as a mode of historical understanding. In the constellation, meaning proliferates, and the relative significance of events is in constant flux, depending on the point of view of the reader, but they are never dismissed outright.

Typology and constellation also have drastically different relationships with the present. In the constellation, the present is the key element in the production of meaning; redemption comes through the recognition of the constellation in the *Jetztzeit*, not the promise of future illumination. Typology, on the other hand, has the necessary effect of holding the present moment in abeyance in its inexorable drive toward a pre-identified, if yet unknown, future; the present is irrelevant because, as Giuseppe Mazzotta puts it, 'history has come to a closure, but we still wait for the end; the sense of history has been revealed, but we still see through a glass darkly.'[62] The space of time between the Incarnation and the Day of Judgment is a liminal one in which history is at an end, but the future has not yet arrived.[63] As a result, typology is unable to manifest any theory of the present. Instead, all past events point toward a single teleological fulfilment that has yet to be realized. The model of figure and fulfilment links past and future, and it teaches readers to interpret all historical moments as evidence of God's foreordained plan; as Auerbach writes, 'all history … remains open and questionable, points to something still concealed … The event is enacted according to an ideal model which is a prototype situated in the future and thus far only promised.'[64] Auerbach's figuration encodes teleology as the Christian historical method par excellence, whereas Anglo-Saxon alliterative verse is, if not directly opposed to teleology, at least reluctant to renounce the present in the way salvation history demands.

Instead of leading off with typology, then, *Genesis A* articulates a relation of the Anglo-Saxon present to the origins of temporality through the act of narration. Whereas Augustine and even Cædmon situated the beginning

---

62 Giuseppe Mazzotta, *Dante, Poet of the Desert: History and Allegory in the Divine Comedy* (Princeton: Princeton University Press, 1979), 7.
63 See Giorgio Agamben, *The Time That Remains: A Commentary on the Letter to the Romans*, trans. Patricia Dailey (Stanford: Stanford University Press, 2005), especially 69–78.
64 Auerbach, 'Figura,' 58–9.

of time at the Creation, *Genesis A* locates the origins of temporality specifically in the actions and desires of created beings. The extent to which the majority of the poem is a faithful translation of the Latin is evident from a mere glance at Doane's edition of *Genesis A*, which prints the Latin source material alongside the Old English text. Yet the poem, as a hybrid text, also makes liberal use of traditional poetic structures like envelope patterns to reshape the source material, as Colette Stévanovitch has shown, the result being both formal and thematic recursion.[65] Most important, the beginning of its narrative departs significantly from its source: *Genesis A* starts with an extrabiblical preface recounting the Fall of the Angels at some length (12b–91) before it describes the Creation. In this schema, the angels' rebellion and subsequent fall serve as the impetus for God's creation of the world, and of humankind especially. *Genesis A* offers this extrabiblical information, without commentary, in the body of the text itself; it becomes incorporated into the main narrative, as much a part of the story of Genesis as Adam and Eve, Cain and Abel, Noah, and Abraham. In fact, the Fall of the Angels is what establishes temporality in the poem; it is the foundation not only of the narrative, but of time itself in the scheme of the Creation. The ways in which this poem thinks through its relation to the past and to the idea of an origin set it apart, not only from the Latin biblical text on which it is based, but also from a strictly teleological understanding of biblical history.

The move to narrative, and to poetic narrative in particular, shows how Anglo-Saxon biblical verse puts its own stamp on the understanding of biblical history. The dichotomy of eternity and temporality is spatialized, in Augustine, by a dichotomy between the *caelum caeli* and earth. For Augustine, this dichotomy leads to contemplation of the creation of the world, beginning with the ten orders of angels, as coextensive with the creation of time.[66] It is significant, therefore, that *Genesis A* grounds its expression of temporality not simply in the act of the Creation that separates us from God, but rather in the story of the Fall of the rebellious Angels. From its brief contemplation of temporality and eternity, the poem leaps directly to narrative: not the Creation narrative that opens the Bible it purports to re-present, but the apocryphal story that grounds the poem's main theme of obedience. The reasons for this inclusion are not

---

65 Colette Stévanovitch, 'Envelope Patterns in *Genesis A* and *B*,' *Neophilologus* 80 (1996): 465–78.

66 *Confessions*, 12.8–16.

necessarily theological; they are primarily thematic and follow established patristic precedent but are interpretable solely within the context of the poem as well. By moving from the abstractions of praise and eternity to a concrete narrative example of the failure to praise, the poem establishes both the advent of temporality and the relative positions of 'us' (1a) and the 'engla þreatas' [troops of angels] (13b) in history. The mutability of the created world is demonstrated dramatically in the story of the angels, who trade joys and happiness for torment and sadness, the *caelum caeli* for the deepest hell, and who change from God's cohort to his adversaries. Temporality, defined in opposition to the unchanging eternity of the divine, is characterized by the recognition of difference between then and now. Then, the angels had 'gleam and dream' [joy and ecstasy] (12b); now, they suffer punishment for their sins. Then was unity with God in heaven; now is discord and exile from the Edenic homeland. The recognition of those differences is precisely what narrative allows us to achieve by staging change as a process that is both originary and ongoing. Yet the distance of pre- or extrabiblical history is surmountable by the act of narration that brings angels and readers together in the aesthetic experience.

Part of that 'bringing together' consists in bridging, or perhaps effacing, cultural difference as well, and this opening moment of temporal juxtaposition also grounds the poem's hybrid aesthetic. In addition to elaborating on an apocryphal tradition, the *Genesis A* account of the Fall of the Angels provides an opportunity to elaborate on the Germanic tradition of the poetic form by drawing from the poetic lexicon to introduce and characterize the actors in this drama. The angels are cast as noble thegns who honour their lord and sing his praises, and their initial existence shares in the purity and eternity of God:

> synna ne cuþon,
> firena fremman   ac hie on friðe lifdon
> ece mid heora aldor.[67]   (18b–20a)

The unity and happiness of the prelapsarian angels is likened to the idealized life of the Germanic war-band with their lord in the hall. When we recall that the loss of this hall-life is what motivates the lyrical elegies of *Deor* and *The Wanderer*, the angels' exile from heaven becomes both

---

67 'They knew nothing of sins, how to commit crimes, but they lived in peace eternally with their lord.'

meaningful and strikingly affective for the Germanic Christian.[68] The cause of exile is likewise familiar to followers of the heroic tradition: disloyalty to the lord. What shatters this heavenly unity is the *oferhygd* [pride] (22b) and *gedwild* [error] (23a) of the chief of the angels, who no longer wished to honour God and sing his praises. When the angels put their own interests and desires ahead of God's, the result is predictable:

> þa wearð yrre god
> and þam werode wrað   þe he ær wurðode
> wlite and wuldre.   sceop þam werlogan
> wræclicne ham   weorce to leane …[69]
>
> (34b–37)

The angels' crime consists in the actions of supposedly loyal thegns who have turned their backs on their lord, preferring instead to raise themselves up as equals to him. They fail to adhere to their appropriate social positions as created beings; more than that, however, casting them as a Germanic war-band makes their disloyalty an act of personal betrayal against their lord. The social disorder that follows indicates the chaos resulting from disobedience. Just as the content of the narrative is shaded with heroic colouring, so too the poetic form helps to emphasize the contrast between the previous honour of a heroic troop and the painful exile of the traitors. Alliteration once again serves to link contrasting elements: the magnificence and glory God earlier bestowed (*wurðode* / *wlite and wuldre*) on this band of angels (*werod*), and the anger and hostility with which he subsequently repays their treachery by exiling them (*wearð* … *wrað* / *werloga* / *wræclic*).

Like Augustine, the *Genesis A* poet has spatialized the dichotomy between the eternal divine in the *caelum caeli* and created existence; in *Genesis A*, however, that spatialization is conceived as the creation not of earth, but of hell. By launching its narrative not with Gn 1:1 but with a vivid apocryphon, *Genesis A* sets up the poem's ethical framework in specifically Anglo-Saxon terms. The relationship between God and created

---

68   For a useful overview of the theme of exile in Old English literature, see the collected essays in Stanley B. Greenfield, *Hero and Exile: The Art of Old English Poetry*, ed. George Hardin Brown (London: Hambledon, 1989). On the link between exile and Christian belief, see Stephen H. Goldman, 'The Use of Christian Belief in Old English Poems of Exile,' *Res publica litterarum* 2 (1979): 69–80.

69   'Then God became angry and hostile towards the host whom he earlier honoured with brightness and glory. He created for the traitors a wretched home in retribution for their deeds.'

beings is understood by figuring God as a Germanic lord and the angels as his thegns – the bond between them is a personal one. The thegns' rebellion illustrates the need to observe this hierarchy, and their exile to a newly created hell both re-establishes order in heaven and creates a series of empty thrones that God can then resettle.[70] The fallen angels lament the loss of their heavenly home, not unlike the lordless men who wander through the Old English elegies; they, too, have been punished for their sins, both religious and secular, with exile from their homeland. The expulsion of the renegade angels thus paves the way for the creation of the world; but it has also paved the way for a Germanicized understanding of Genesis as a narrative recounting events that took place in discernible historical relation to one another, and within a hybrid cultural framework that enhances and personalizes the moral dimension of the events.

As a result, the reader of *Genesis A* is prepared to understand biblical history as the story of individuals' relationships with God. The theme of obedience, which has rightly been seen by Lucas as the thread that holds the Old English *Genesis*, and perhaps the entire Junius 11, together,[71] is personalized, but it is also removed from the explicit context of salvation history. Obedience and loyalty are understood as virtues in secular as well as religious life, and the opening of *Genesis A* serves to remind readers of their individual obligations toward God. The Fall of the rebellious Angels is an object lesson, and its utility as such becomes all the clearer when the narrative recurs in the interpolation of *Genesis B*, as we shall see shortly.[72] For the moment, it is enough to note that the opening of *Genesis A* has accomplished two things. First, like Cædmon's *Hymn*, it has reiterated a patristic understanding of the created world as irrevocably separated from God and from eternity, but it has also acknowledged the paradox of humanity's distance from, and dependence on, this moment of origin. But *Genesis A* goes one step further in addressing the paradox of historical origin: it launches narrative as a way of understanding the moment of origin in its particularity, but also of drawing that unreachable moment into relation with the present. *Genesis A* does not present the Creation as

---

70 See Haines, 'Vacancies in Heaven: The Doctrine of Replacement and *Genesis A*,' *N&Q* 44 (1997): 150–4.

71 Lucas, 'Loyalty and Obedience in the Old English *Genesis* and the Interpolation of *Genesis B* into *Genesis A*,' *Neophilologus* 76 (1992): 121–35.

72 Lucas suggests that 'when the interpolated *Genesis B* is looked at within the context of the whole poem *Genesis* loyalty is seen to have some point. Loyalty alone may not be sufficient to prevent death, but, accompanied by good intentions, it does prevent damnation' ('Loyalty and Obedience,' 132).

ineffable, as Augustine and Cædmon do; it is bound in causal relation to the rebellion and Fall of the Angels from the 'heaven of heaven.' More important, the event that precipitates Gn 1:1 – sin against God – is infinitely iterable, and both the sin and its punishment, exile, have been staged in terms that resonate strongly with the heroic values of Anglo-Saxon culture.[73] The Creation of the world thus has its origin in narrative causality, and in a series of events that will be restaged, again and again, throughout the Old Testament and, in fact, throughout human history. There is something utterly fascinating, and characteristically Anglo-Saxon, in the idea that our existence stems ultimately from that first, prebiblical Fall, and that decay should give rise to a work of art.

III. Pride, Punishment, and Promise in *Genesis*

The iterability of narratives of sin and their inherent similarity become evident when the Fall of the Angels that opens *Genesis A* is retold in the interpolated section of the poem, *Genesis B*. In its retelling, the narrative of the Fall becomes part of a constellation for the reader; it is no longer just the moment of origin for the created world and human history, but also an exemplum of sin and its punishment that is connected thematically and causally to the first human sin, the Fall of Man. In recounting the rest of the hexameral Creation narrative (lines 92–234), *Genesis A* adapts Genesis with great fidelity. Although the poem suffers the loss of one or more leaves in the middle of the third day's work (Gn 1:10; page 8 in the manuscript), its recounting of the creation of light and dark, the firmament, and the earth closely parallel the Vulgate narrative, and it seems reasonable to assume that the missing leaves were equally faithful to their source.[74] Following the lacuna, the *Genesis A* narrative picks up again with the creation of Eve, condensing the two narratives of the creation of humankind (Gn 1:26–31 and Gn 2:7, 15–25) into one smooth narrative: God first creates

---

73 Larry McKill has argued that the contrasts developed in these opening lines set the agenda for the whole poem, which contrasts those who are obedient to God with those who are not. See 'Patterns of the Fall: Adam and Eve in the Old English *Genesis A*,' *Florilegium* 14 (1995–6): 25–41; and also Hieatt, 'Divisions.'

74 High-quality digital images of Junius 11 are available online; see Oxford Digital Library, 'Bodleian Library MS. Junius 11,' *Early Manuscripts at Oxford University*, http://image.ox.ac.uk/show?collection=bodleian&manuscript=msjunius11. Detailed codicological descriptions of the manuscript can be found in Doane, ed., *Genesis A*, 3–24; and Raw, 'The Construction of Oxford, Bodleian Library, Junius 11,' *ASE* 13 (1984): 187–207.

Eve (Gn 2:18–22) and then blesses the First Couple and gives them dominion over all the earth (Gn 1:28–30).[75] With humanity created and established in Paradise, things really begin to get interesting, both narratively
and codicologically. The Vulgate moves directly from the creation of Eve
to her conversation with the serpent. In the Junius version, however, the
narrative takes a considerably more circuitous route. After naming the
four rivers that flow out of Paradise (Gn 2:10–14), the scribe ends in the
middle of a leaf (page 12) with perhaps 10 cm of writing space left empty.
There is a leaf or leaves missing between this point and the top of page 13,
where the interpolated *Genesis B* begins in the middle of a sentence. It is
impossible to say what material filled the page or pages that are missing; as
the manuscript stands, however, the narrative of *Genesis B* picks up more
or less where *Genesis A* left off, though in a very different style and with
very different aims. And with this interpolation, the verse *Genesis* shifts
from a more or less straightforward adaptation of the Vulgate material to
a considerably more psychologized treatment, not only of the Fall of
Adam and Eve but of the recapitulated Fall of the Angels that is juxtaposed against it. The change in style is due, of course, to the fact that the
source of *Genesis B* is an Old Saxon *Genesis* poem rather than the Bible;
the stylistic differences are so pronounced that Eduard Sievers was able to
postulate the existence of the Old Saxon source nearly two decades before
it was actually discovered.[76] Although the shift is jarring, it produces a
very specific representation of the Fall and pushes the reader toward a
particular mode of interpreting it.

The interpolation of *Genesis B* is disruptive on a number of levels. It
disrupts the established shape of the poem; instead of a straightforward
adaptation of the biblical source, *Genesis B* presents a highly stylized and
imaginative retelling of the Fall. It disrupts the poem's relationship with its
source material, in departing dramatically from the Vulgate narrative so as
to expand the emotional and psychological impact of a crucial moment in
salvation history. But it also disrupts the established narrative temporality
of the poem. God's words to Adam and Eve launch the extant interpolation at more or less the same place that *Genesis A* broke off, but scarcely a

---

75 Owing to the loss of one or more leaves between lines 168 and 169, it is impossible to
say how the poet handled the adaptation of Gn 1:11–2:17, but his rearrangement of Gn
1: 28–30 to follow the creation of Eve shows him altering the verses of the Vulgate to
make better narrative sense in his poem.

76 See Eduard Sievers, *Der Heliand und die angelsächsische Genesis* (Halle: Niemayer, 1875);
and Karl Zangemeister and Wilhelm Braune, 'Bruchstücke der altsächsichen Bibeldichtung aus der Bibliotheca Palatina,' *Neue Heidelberger Jahrbücher* 4 (1894): 205–94.

dozen lines later, the narrative returns to the first day of the Creation with the establishment of the ten orders of angels and Lucifer's rebellion. Instead of moving forward to Gn 3:1, the story jumps backward, resurrecting the Fall of the rebellious Angels from the first day of the Creation and re-presenting it as prefatory to the Fall of Adam and Eve. The theme of the interpolated material is clearly obedience, and the result of juxtaposing the Fall of the Angels with the Fall of Man is to establish a series of contrasts and similarities between the fallen angels and the fallen humans. The angels refuse to bow in obedience to God; Adam and Eve disobey God's injunction against eating from a certain tree. The angels are cast out of heaven as punishment for their sin; Adam and Eve are cast out of Paradise. The angels suffer the torments of hellfire and freezing cold in their new abode; Eve suffers the pains of childbirth, and Adam endures hard physical labour in order to provide sustenance for his family. Both expulsions are permanent: the angels can never return to heaven, and Adam and Eve can never get past the angel with the flaming sword, who guards the gates to Paradise and symbolizes the absolute division between the life of Paradise and this present life.

The contrasts between the two, however, are equally important.[77] The angels sin through pride and wilfulness; Lucifer (unnamed in *Genesis B* until God designates him as Satan after his fall at line 345) deliberately and with clear intent sets himself up as a rival to God's power:

> ... engyl ongan   ofermod wesan.
> ahof hine wið his herran,   sohte hetespræce,
> gylpword ongean,   nolde gode þeowian.
> cwæð þæt his lic wære   leoht and scene,
> hwit and hiowbeorht.   ne meahte he æt his hige findan
> þæt he gode wolde   geongerdome,
> þeodne þeowian.   þuhte him sylfum
> þæt he mægyn and cræft   maran hæfde
> þonne se halga god   habban mihte
> folcgestælna.[78]   (262–71a)

---

77 Michael Cherniss has shown how the heroic diction of the poem serves to heighten the moral elements of those contrasts; see 'Heroic Ideals.'

78 All quotations are taken from Doane, ed., *The Saxon Genesis: An Edition of the West Saxon* Genesis B *and the Old Saxon Vatican* Genesis (Madison: University of Wisconsin Press, 1991), and are cited by line number. 'The angel began to be excessively proud. He raised himself up against his lord, chose hateful speech, boasting words against him, and did not wish to serve God. He said that his body was bright and beautiful, white

Lucifer's internal rebellion immediately expresses itself in a coup; his action is not only contrary to God's will, but meant to supersede it. It is for these sins – pride, disobedience, and treachery – that Lucifer and his own hearth-troop are sent to hell. Adam and Eve, like Lucifer, sin through the desire for self-determination, but the poet takes some pains to sympathize with them.[79] Their disobedience to God is prompted by the lies and deceptions fed to them by Satan's emissary; according to the poet, Eve believes, in fact, that she is obeying God's command in eating from the tree he formerly forbade:

heo dyde hit þeah þurh holdne hyge,   nyste þæt þær hearma swa fela,
fyrenearfeða   fylgean sceolde
monna cynne   þæs heo on mod genam
þæt heo þæs laðan bodan   larum hyrde
Ac wende þæt heo hyldo   heofoncyninges
worhte mid þam wordum   þe heo þam were swelce
tacen oðiewde   and treowe gehet...[80]   (708–14)

---

and radiant. He could not find it in his heart to desire vassalage to God, to serve the prince. He thought to himself that he had more strength and power than holy God could have companions in war.'

79 The poem's apparent sympathy for Eve and Adam is a point of general consensus in the criticism; see, for example, Evans, 'Background,' especially pt II; John F. Vickrey, 'The Vision of Eve in *Genesis B*,' *Speculum* 44 (1969): 86–102, and 'The *Micel Wundor* of *Genesis B*,' *SP* 68 (1971): 245–54; and T. Hill, 'The Fall of Angels and Man in the Old English *Genesis B*,' in *Anglo-Saxon Poetry: Essays in Appreciation for John C. McGalliard*, ed. Lewis E. Nicholson and Dolores Warwick Frese, 279–90 (Notre Dame: University of Notre Dame Press, 1975), and 'Pilate's Visonary Wife and the Innocence of Eve: An Old Saxon Source for the Old English *Genesis B*,' *JEGP* 101 (2002): 170–84. But see also Rosemary Woolf, 'The Fall of Man in *Genesis B* and the *Mystère d'Adam*,' in *Studies in Old English Literature in Honor of Arthur G. Brodeur*, ed. Stanley B. Greenfield, 187–99 (Eugene: University of Oregon Press, 1963); and Doane, *Saxon Genesis*, 139–53. *Genesis B*'s Eve has also been the locus of much recent feminist criticism; see Gillian R. Overing, 'On Reading Eve: *Genesis B* and the Readers' Desire,' in *Speaking Two Languages: Traditional Disciplines and Contemporary Theory in Medieval Studies*, ed. Allen J. Frantzen, 35–63 (Albany: State University of New York Press, 1991); and Susannah B. Mintz, 'Words Devilish and Divine: Eve as Speaker in *Genesis B*,' *Neophilologus* 81 (1997): 609–23.

80 'But she did it with a loyal spirit, she did not know that so many harms, terrible hardships, would follow for humankind because she took to heart the teachings that she heard from the hateful messenger, but she believed that she would gain the grace of the king of heaven through the words which she offered to the man as a sign and promised her good faith.'

Although Adam and Eve choose freely to eat the apple, their sin humanizes them for the audience, and the gentle ease with which they fall into sin is quite different from Lucifer's impassioned desire for sovereignty, in degree if not in kind. Unlike the angels, the first response of the humans on realizing their mistake is to pray for God's mercy and forgiveness, prostrating themselves and asking for a penance, which they will eagerly perform (777b–783a). Their response is the proper one, all the more clearly visible for its proximity to Lucifer's overweening and unrepentant pride. As Janet Ericksen has suggested, the model of penitence in *Genesis B* is a particularly affective one, especially when read in conjunction with the illustrations depicting Adam and Eve's nakedness as a visual sign of their guilt.[81] Prayers of repentance and petitions for forgiveness are the models that the poem's audience should emulate; to do otherwise, as the Fall of the Angels demonstrates, is to invite swift and permanent divine retribution.

Repetition and contrast are key features of Old English poetry in general, and they contribute to the poem's art in *Genesis B* in particular.[82] The structural and poetic constellation of the two Fall narratives, separated in historical time but conjoined in narrative space, serves to emphasize the ways in which they are linked by both their similarities and their differences. Yet the two incidents are related not just in the elements of their plots. They are also bound through causality; the punishment of Lucifer and his cohort inspires him with the desire to ruin God's favoured creation, humanity, as well:

'is þæs ænga styde   ungelic swiðe
þam oðrum þe we ær cuðon
hean on heofonrice …

…

            þæt me is sorga mæst
þæt adam sceal,   þe wæs of eorðan geworht,
minne stronglican   stol behealdan,
wesan him on wynne   and we þis wite þolien,
hearm on þisse helle.'[83]   (356–8a, 364b–8a)

---

81 Janet S. Ericksen, 'Penitential Nakedness and the Junius 11 *Genesis*,' in *Naked before God: Uncovering the Body in Anglo-Saxon England*, ed. Benjamin C. Withers and Jonathan Wilcox, 257–74 (Morgantown: West Virginia University Press, 2003).

82 See G.C. Britton, 'Repetition and Contrast in the Old English *Later Genesis*,' *Neophilologus* 58 (1974): 66–73.

83 'This tight spot is very unlike the other one that we knew before … It is the greatest sorrow to me that Adam, who was made from earth, should have my strong throne, that he should have joys, and we should suffer this torment, pain in this hell.'

The contrast between the heavenly home they once knew and the hellish one they now occupy is compounded by the knowledge that another of God's creatures, Adam, now occupies Satan's former place, both in God's affections and in his Edenic abode. Satan's own fall, therefore, is the impetus for his desire to force history to repeat itself, by tricking Adam and Eve into disobeying God and earning their own banishment. *Genesis B* thus offers a more compelling explanation for the Fall of Man than the biblical text itself provides, and presumably than the parallel text of *Genesis A* provided before it was lost. As Andrew Cole has said of the Old Saxon *Genesis*, *Genesis B*'s source, 'readers of this poem know that the Fall happened ... Those same readers surely want dramatised explanations as to how they, Adam and Eve, fell when things were so right.'[84] The hexameral narrative has no explanatory force for an event like the Fall; the six days of the Creation bear no relation to the causality or the outcome of Adam and Eve's disobedience. *Genesis A* does little to explain the significance of events, preferring the unadorned narrative of its Latin source to the allegorical, typological, or explanatory. *Genesis B*, on the other hand, seeks to explain; it looks for relations of meaning between historically disparate events and brings them together in order to explicate the Fall in the fullness of its meaning. Its constellation makes the most of Anglo-Saxon poetic form to supplement the biblical narrative and draw the reader into the story: what would you do if you were Eve?[85] More than that, its fortuitous position within *Genesis A* allows readers to place the Fall narratives in their relative positions historically while still capitalizing on the associative power of juxtaposing those narratives outside historical temporality. It is impossible to say whether the compiler intended to produce these effects by fusing the two pieces into one text. What is clear, however, is that the opening epic of Junius 11 presents its audience with two distinct yet compatible modes for reading history: by comprehending events and their place in historical temporality, and by apprehending events in relation to

---

84 Andrew Cole, 'Jewish Apocrypha and Christian Epistemologies of the Fall: The *Dialogi* of Gregory the Great and the Old Saxon *Genesis*,' in *Rome and the North: The Early Reception of Gregory the Great in Germanic Europe*, ed. Rolf H. Bremmer, Kees Dekker, and David F. Johnson, 157–88 (Paris: Peeters, 2001), 187–8.

85 Doane identifies this as the 'tropological' function of *Genesis B*: 'The poem works as a moral poem by forcing the audience to exercise correct perception and correct choice ... The target of the action is the audience's moral life, the purpose not the exploration of biblical text or meaning per se, but the relation of the history of the First Times to the inner and outer lives of the audience now living near the Final Time' (*Saxon Genesis*, 113).

one another thematically. Most significantly, it demonstrates that multiple modes of meaning can coexist within a single text.

Unlike the beginning of the interpolation, its end is in no way indicated in the manuscript. A point separates its last line from the next line of *Genesis A*, but in a manuscript where some 95 per cent of the verse half-lines are indicated by scribal pointing,[86] this point is hardly significant. From there, Gn 3:8, *Genesis A* resumes a comparatively frenetic pace, taking the reader sequentially through the next nineteen chapters of Genesis with no further disruptions or dislocations in the narrative. By comparison with the surrounding text of *Genesis A*, *Genesis B* has a clear purpose: to encourage reflection on the possible meanings of the Fall, not exclusively in terms of a salvific telos or a linear narrative causality, but in terms of its relation to previous and subsequent historical events – and to the present situation of its readers, whose behaviour it hopes to guide. The Fall comes about because of events that have already taken place, before the creation of humankind; and its impact is felt in the fallen state of the poem's readers. *Genesis A* teaches its readers to familiarize themselves with the major events of Old Testament history *qua* history, not necessarily as prefigurations of events in the New Testament. *Genesis B*, on the other hand, teaches its readers how to put that knowledge to use, by modelling the constellation of Old Testament events to reveal their fuller meaning through similarity and contrast.

The remainder of *Genesis A* touches on all the highlights of the biblical narrative through Gn 22:14, including the expulsion from Eden, Cain's murder of Abel, the Flood, the Tower of Babel, Abraham's wanderings, and the sacrifice of Isaac. It is worth noting here that these events are also touchstones of Christian typology, foreshadowing key moments of the New Testament and the promise of salvation history. Yet at each of these moments, *Genesis A* looks resolutely to the past, to previous events in its own narrative, and looks forward only to include its audience in the experience of the narrative. Even in its apostrophes to the audience, the poem does not refer to the later events surrounding the coming of Christ that these Old Testament events are supposed to prefigure. Instead, the poem shuttles back and forth between narrative present, narrative past, and the present of its audience, linking these key time frames in its presentation of history. The poem sets its audiences, both Anglo-Saxon and modern, on a

---

86 Hall, 'Epic of Redemption,' 21. See also O'Brien O'Keeffe, *Visible Song: Transitional Literacy in Old English Verse* (Cambridge: Cambridge University Press, 1990), 179–86.

par with Adam and Eve, Cain and Abel, Noah, Abraham, and Isaac. Although the history of the New Testament certainly remains in the background for those readers, the poem itself never references it, despite its occasional tendency to address the audience and direct its interpretation of a particular event. *Genesis A* thus intertwines the history of the Old Testament and of its readers through the theme of sin and punishment, the outward form of which is exile. The link between biblical wanderings and what Howe called the 'migration myth' goes to the heart of the Anglo-Saxon historical consciousness: 'Through the memory of migration, Anglo-Saxon England found its myth of the past and the future. This myth may be thought of as a map of the imagination, as an ordering of experience into an evocative image by which the culture could sustain itself.'[87] For Howe, *Exodus* is the unsurpassed image of migration, around which Anglo-Saxon historical consciousness coalesced into an image of the English as heirs to the Hebrew nation; it is also the key narrative device by which the poems of Junius 11 represent the movement through human history.[88] As Paul Battles has shown, however, *Genesis A* has its own investments in the idea of migration, particularly with respect to Abraham's peripatetic wanderings around a geographically indistinct Middle East.[89] Battles, like Howe, sees the migration myth as foundational to structuring the Anglo-Saxons' understanding of the biblical past by casting it in familiar terms; he finds that '*Genesis A* employs the traditional theme of "Migration" to develop an implicit analogy between the dispersal of Noah's descendants at Babel and the Germanic tribes' coming to England. Biblical and Anglo-Saxon cultural origin myths are superimposed, and their point of contact is migration.'[90] *Genesis A* thus constitutes hybridity in yet another form, in not only importing Germanic imagery and diction into its battle scenes and heroic epithets, but also incorporating a traditional theme so as to bring Anglo-Saxon readers closer to the biblical past.

Battles identifies eight migration passages in *Genesis A*, all of which depart from their source to elaborate on the theme of migration. It is curious, however, that he does not identify any of the scenes of exile before the Flood as migration passages, despite the fact that they specifically involve

---

87 Howe, *Migration and Mythmaking*, 6–7.
88 Howe, 'Falling into Place: Dislocation in the Junius Book,' in *Unlocking the Wordhord: Anglo-Saxon Studies in Memory of Edward B. Irving, Jr*, ed. Mark C. Amodio and Katherine O'Brien O'Keeffe, 14–37 (Toronto: University of Toronto Press, 2003).
89 Paul Battles, '*Genesis A* and the Anglo-Saxon "Migration Myth",' *ASE* 29 (2000): 43–66.
90 Battles, '*Genesis A*,' 66.

the loss of one *eðel* and the search for another. For example, when the *Genesis A* narrative picks up again on page 40 of Junius 11, Adam and Eve face God and receive their punishment; God commands Adam,

'þu scealt oðerne   eðel secean,
wynleasran wic,   and on wræc hweorfan
nacod niedwædla   neorxnawanges ...'[91]   (927–9)

The poem assiduously reminds us that the exile of human existence, instantiated with Adam and Eve's expulsion from Eden, can be traced directly back to that first sin of disobedience; and subsequent sin is likewise described with reference to the original sin. Accordingly, Cain's murder of Abel is immediately linked back to Eve's eating the apple, and his punishment, like hers, is exile from the homeland; like his parents, Cain must 'on wræc hweorfan' [go in exile] to seek 'eðelstowe / fædergeardum feor' [a homeland far from his father's home] (1014b, 1052b–1053a).[92] Like the angels whose fall gave rise to both temporality and narrative, humans who sin against God are punished by being cast out of community with the divine and forced into a new, less hospitable homeland. This theme of exile is carried throughout Junius 11; in *Daniel*, the Hebrews' Babylonian captivity is construed as punishment for falling away from God's teaching (lines 1–78), and Daniel warns Nebuchadnezzar that God 'ðec wineleasne on wræc sendeð' [will send you, friendless, into exile] (line 568).[93] The suffering in Hell in *Christ and Satan* is also characterized as 'wadan wræclastas' [wandering the paths of exile] (120a).[94]

---

91   'You must seek another homeland, a more joyless encampment, and go in exile from Paradise, a poor naked wretch.'

92   Wright has shown, however, that *Genesis A* uses the 'branches of sin' motif to expand on the biblical narrative and cast Cain, rather than Adam and Eve, as the author of evil in the world, thereby marking an important distinction between the two events; see 'The Blood of Abel and the Branches of Sin: *Genesis A, Maxims I*, and Aldhelm's *Carmen de uirginitate*,' *ASE* 25 (1996): 7–19.

93   R.T. Farrell, ed., *Daniel and Azarias* (London: Methuen, 1974). Earl R. Anderson has suggested that *translatio imperii* is one of the poem's main themes; see 'Style and Theme in the Old English *Daniel*,' *ES* 68 (1987): 1–23. Robert E. Bjork connects the Hebrews' disobedience, emblematized by a scene of drunkenness preceding their conquest, to the parallel scene in the Old English *Judith* that precedes Holofernes' demise; see 'Oppressed Hebrews and the Song of Azarias in the Old English *Daniel*,' *SP* 77 (1980): 213–26 at 214–18.

94   George Philip Krapp, ed., *The Junius Manuscript*, ASPR 1 (New York: Columbia University Press, 1931). All quotations of *Christ and Satan* are taken from this edition

At each instance of exile, however, these poems paradoxically create a link between the biblical event and the present community of readers and listeners evoked by the poem itself. *Genesis A* uses apostrophes to the audience at these moments of exile, explicitly drawing its readers into relation with the narrative, implicating them in the drama of human suffering, and reminding them of their connection to the figures and events from the biblical past by virtue of their own exilic condition, both cultural and spiritual. The narration of Adam and Eve's expulsion departs from the Vulgate in order to address the audience directly: 'Hwæt, we nu gehyrað hwær us hearmstafas / wraðe onwocan and woruldyrmðo' (939–40).[95] The 'we' and its present tense verb call attention to the poem's readers and open up a space for critical reflection on the aesthetic experience and the meaning of historical relation. How do we, in the present, respond to the expulsion of Adam and Eve from Eden? How do we process the idea that our current suffering has its roots in an event from the distant biblical past? Similarly, when Cain commits the first murder, we are reminded almost instantly that this, too, is a result of Eve's sin, and that we, as readers, are implicated:

> we þæt spell magon,
> wælgrimme wyrd,   wope cwiðan
> nales holunge   Ac us hearde sceod
> freolecu fæmne   þurh forman gylt
> þe wið metod æfre   men gefremeden,
> eorðbuende   siððan adam wearð
> of godes muðe   gaste eacen.[96]   (995b–1001)

The passage links four separate time frames in the space of seven lines: the present tense of the *we* who *magon … cwiðan*, the literary present of Cain's crime, its precedent in Eve's sin, and the moment of Adam's creation. The poem's audience is implicated in the narrative at all these moments, as sinners like Cain, as those who have suffered the effects of Eve's

---

and are cited by line number. The poem has more recently been edited by Robert Emmett Finnegan, ed., *Christ and Satan: A Critical Edition* (Waterloo, ON: Wilfrid Laurier University Press, 1977).

95 'Listen, we now hear how tribulations and worldly wretchedness began to afflict us harshly.'

96 'We may bewail that story with weeping, that cruel fate, not without cause, but the beautiful woman harmed us grievously through the first sin that men ever committed against God, the dwellers of earth, since Adam was imbued with a soul from God's mouth.'

sin, and as those who, like Adam, are imbued with the gift of a soul from God. Once again, the audience is drawn into self-conscious relation to its biblical predecessors as part of the historical constellation surrounding the idea of sin and punishment. The relations called forth are necessarily unique; readers will respond differently to this confrontation with the past depending on factors such as gender, class, education, occupation, and so on.[97] But each reader will also be able to forge affective connections with these particular examples of a universal human condition: sin.

If exile is the punishment for sin, then the promise of a homeland is the reward for virtue, and *Genesis A* certainly sees this promise in the stories of Abraham and Noah. Both patriarchs, significantly, are charged with reestablishing a homeland in the wake of human sin; God gives Noah an *eðelstol* [homeland] as well as dominion over the land, plants, and animals, just as God initially charged Adam with their care (1514b);[98] and Abraham's quest to establish a final, permanent homeland seems successful by the time the poem ends.[99] The passages detailing Abraham's narrative are, in fact, exemplary of heroic style as well as form: replete with heroic epithets for Abraham and overflowing with set pieces and battle sequences that expand significantly on the biblical sources, the second half of *Genesis* embodies the literary hybridity that reconstitutes Christian meaning by combining it with Germanic form.[100] These migrations are the ones that have captured Howe's and Battles's imaginations as models for the Anglo-Saxons' consciousness of their own historical wanderings, but they take

---

97 Overing, for example, has explored the effects of gender on reading Eve in *Genesis B*, both for Eve and for a feminist critic; see 'On Reading Eve.'

98 The verbal echoes between lines 196–205, where God gives Adam dominion over the animals, and lines 1512–17, where God offers the same to Noah, are quite stunning, with an emphasis on increasing offspring (*tyman*) and filling the earth (*eorðan fyllan*), and on the wild animals (*wilde deor*) and birds (*heofonfuglas*), which are given into the control of humans (*on geweald geseald*); but the same is true of the biblical source (Gn 1:28–9 and 9:1–4).

99 Abraham's sacrifice of the ram, at which he 'sægde leana þanc / and ealra þara þe he him sið and ær, / gifena, drihten forgifen hæfde' [said thanks for the blessings and all those things, the gifts, which God had given him, before and since] (2934b–2936) seems in many ways to fulfil the poem's opening lines, the behest to give thanks and praise to God.

100 Battles, '*Genesis A*,' 47–8; and Orchard, 'Conspicuous Heroism: Abraham, Prudentius, and the Old English Verse *Genesis*,' in Liuzza, *MS Junius 11*, 119–36, repr. from *Heroes and Heroines in Medieval English Literature: A Festschrift Presented to André Crépin on the Occasion of His Sixty-fifth Birthday*, ed. Leo Carruthers, 45–58 (Woodbridge: D.S. Brewer, 1994).

on new shades of meaning when set alongside the specifically punitive exiles of the fallen angels, Adam and Eve, and Cain. As points of historical and ideological contact, the motifs of sin and exile, virtue and migration, play off one another to create a pattern of connections between the audience and divinity, humanity, the Creation, the Fall, punishment, and a nascent sense of redemption. That these categories are mediated through historical narrative, and through the formal structures of juxtaposition and repetition, demonstrates the extent to which the historical consciousness of Old Testament history finds itself adapted, and adaptable, within the stylistic context of Anglo-Saxon verse.

IV. Crossing Seas and Time: *Exodus* and *Christ and Satan*

If we are attentive to the ways in which the *Genesis* poems instruct us to read biblical history, then perhaps the structure of historical narrative in *Genesis B*, especially in the light of those same temporal structures elsewhere in heroic historical poetry, goes some way toward explaining some of the structural cruxes in the other Junius verse, especially *Exodus*. *Exodus* is a notoriously difficult poem, and its abrupt digressions into earlier Old Testament history and didacticism have continually frustrated readers who search for aesthetic unity. It is certainly possible, perhaps even probable, that this poem's repetitions and digressions are the result of bad exemplars or mistakes in copying. Even if that is the case, however, how might reading these aporias like an Anglo-Saxon, proficient in a constellative mode of historical understanding, produce certain effects? Like *Genesis*, *Exodus* opens itself up to a complex and nuanced allegorical interpretation by the knowledgable reader, as scholars from J.E. Cross and S.I. Tucker to James Earl have shown.[101] But, also like *Genesis*, *Exodus* does not demand this kind of interpretation, and the basic elements of the

---

101 Of all the Junius poems, *Exodus* is the one that scholars seem most insistent on identifying as intentionally allegorical in its construction: J.E. Cross and S.I. Tucker, 'Allegorical Tradition and the Old English Exodus,' *Neophilologus* 44 (1960): 122–7, and also their explication of lines 289–90 from an allegorical perspective in 'Appendix on Exodus ll. 289–90,' *Neophilologus* 44 (1960): 38–9; James W. Earl, 'Christian Traditions in the Old English *Exodus*,' *NM* 71 (1970): 541–70; and Lucas, 'Old English Christian Poetry: The Cross in *Exodus*,' in *Famulus Christi: Essays in Commemoration of the Thirteenth Centenary of the Birth of the Venerable Bede*, ed. Gerald Bonner, 193–209 (London: SPCK, 1976). John P. Hermann offers both a strict allegorical reading and a more psycho-social 'counterreading' in *Allegories of War: Language and Violence in Old English Poetry* (Ann Arbor: University of Michigan Press, 1989), 57–89.

narrative coexist comfortably in the kind of historical framework familiar to readers of heroic poetry. Irving summarizes the situation most succinctly:

> *Exodus* then, it seems to me, offers its message of human salvation largely in heroic terms, terms perhaps quite unfamiliar or uncongenial to Latin exegetes ... What we should note in *Exodus* is the way the traditional heroic imagination seizes this idea and expresses it in its own energetic fashion, with its own strong contrasts and dramatic heightening. By such means the narrative of the escape from Egypt becomes almost entirely self-sufficient, just *there*; it does not have to be pushed impatiently aside so that we can get at its true 'meaning.' Those who would too closely imitate the old exegetes in the way they read the poem do it no service, and perhaps neglect the powerful and valid religious experience the poem offers.[102]

Howe has already shown how *Exodus* could have helped Anglo-Saxons work out their relationship to their Germanic and Christian origins.[103] The hybridity of Germanic and biblical elements in *Exodus* is a point of agreement in the scholarship; if anything, the thoroughly Germanic aesthetic of the poem predominates. The fleeing Israelites are described as an army preparing for battle, and their encounter with the Egyptian army is forestalled by the opening of the Red Sea to allow their passage. The preponderance of martial terminology in the description of both the people and the events (including the beasts of battle circling Pharaoh's army at lines 161–9) is a deliberately historicizing motif, which casts the Israelites in the role of heroic warriors almost to the point of absurdity.[104] When the poet describes the appointment of the Israelite army, for example, he is insistent that the leaders of the army did not allow any inexperienced warriors to join their contingent,

ne him bealubenne   gebiden hæfdon
ofer linde lærig,   licwunde spor,
gylpplegan gares.[105]   (238–40a)

---

102   Irving, '*Exodus* Retraced,' 220.
103   Howe, *Migration and Mythmaking*, 72–107.
104   A historicizing motif does not necessarily preclude an allegorical reading; Wright notes that the lion standard of the tribe of Judah serves the purposes of both historical verisimilitude and allegorical referent. See C. Wright, 'The Lion Standard in *Exodus*: Jewish Legend, Germanic Tradition, and Christian Typology,' in Liuzza, *MS Junius 11*, 188–202; rev.; originally pub. *ASNSL* 227 (1990): 138–45.
105   'nor [those who] had experienced a grievous wound over the rim of a shield, a bodily wound, from the combat with spears.' All quotations are taken from Lucas, ed., *Exodus*, and are cited by line number.

One is forced to wonder how any of the Israelites were able to become battle-hardened warriors while living as slaves in Egypt. The drowning of the Egyptian army in the Red Sea is likewise described in terms more generally applied to battlefield carnage (lines 447–515), and the victorious Israelites collect war-booty and sing their *hildespell* [battle-song] in triumph (lines 565–90). That *Exodus* dresses biblical history in Germanic trappings is beyond doubt; what is at stake here, however, is how those trappings produce new kinds of meaning in the narrative. Like *Genesis*, the poem draws on formal connections to the Germanic aesthetic tradition in order to facilitate readers' understanding of their historical relationship to the biblical narrative.

Of crucial importance, therefore, are the so-called interpolated passages: reflections on Noah (lines 362–76) and a somewhat lengthier treatment of Abraham (lines 377–446). Although early scholarship saw these passages as interpolations disruptive of the unity of the poem, there is no reason to believe that they are not original.[106] Lucas unifies the poem's digressions under the theme of 'salvation by faith and obedience'; Daniel Anlezark points to a long tradition of pairing these two episodes in reflections on the importance of faith; and Irving argues that 'the dogmatic content of the story seems to involve two complementary ideas: first, the need for (and difficulty of) obeying God; and second, the reward which comes to those who trust and obey him ... The Abraham and Noah episodes serve to reinforce the central siginificance of that action.'[107] Stanley Hauer argues convincingly that the patriarchal digression is integral to the poem's design, his argument based in part on the presence of two features that will occupy our attention momentarily, thematic parallels and an interest in genealogy.[108] Far from viewing it as tangential, Hauer suggests that 'the

---

106 Lucas points out in his edition of *Exodus* that 'OE poetry is not primarily narrative. The Aristotelian desire for unity of time, place and action is the result of the introduction of these ideas into England in the Renaissance. To criticize the poem on such grounds is to impose upon it the norms of another age' (61). For an overview of the critical history of the poem's textual integrity, see Lucas, *Exodus*, 30–3.

107 Lucas, *Exodus*, 61–9; Daniel Anlezark, 'Connecting the Patriarchs: Noah and Abraham in the Old English *Exodus*,' *JEGP* 104 (2005): 171–88; Irving, ed., *The Old English Exodus* (New Haven: Yale University Press, 1953), 29. See also Robert T. Farrell, 'A Reading of OE. *Exodus*,' *RES*, n.s., 20 (1969): 401–17. Paul F. Ferguson argues for the digression's aesthetic as well as thematic unity with the rest of the poem; see 'Noah, Abraham, and the Crossing of the Red Sea,' *Neophilologus* 65 (1981): 282–7.

108 Stanley R. Hauer, 'The Patriarchal Digression in the Old English *Exodus*, Lines 362–446,' *SP* 78, no. 5 (1981): 77–90. Hauer also argues that the digressions on Noah and Abraham serve as links to the allegorical meaning of the Exodus through Christological typology (86–9).

patriarchal digression is at the heart of *Exodus*,' and Phyllis Portnoy has concretized this suggestion with an analysis of the digression as an example of that emblematic Anglo-Saxon poetic technique, ring composition.[109] That these two allusions also make explicit connections to key episodes in the poem that precedes it in the manuscript only highlights the constellative nature of the manuscript's reception. Indeed, it is possible – desirable, even – to read these seemingly disruptive narrative moments analogously to the interpolation of *Genesis B*: as integrated parts of the text as it was received by its audience, and as indicators of how readers might have understood the historical relations Junius 11 lays out.

Like the Old Testament itself, as well as a great deal of Anglo-Saxon literature, *Exodus* figures those historical relations primarily in the genealogical mode, by charting history in terms of relationships of filiation between human beings. R. Howard Bloch argues that the shift from clan to genealogy as a mode of understanding kinship instantiates a 'representational paradigm characterized by linearity, temporality, verticality, fixity, [and] continuity.'[110] But the genealogical mode of the *Exodus* digressions is characterized by repetition and juxtaposition, features which Bloch himself says slow the progress of narrative and threaten to disrupt its continuity.[111] The twelve cohorts of the Israelite army are divided along tribal lines, a division emphasizing their patriarchal descent from the sons of Jacob (although only the tribes of Judah, Reuben, and Simeon are named). These designations emphasize the differences, and even the hierarchical ranking, among the tribes, but they also recognize an originary unity that underwrites, and perhaps even overrides, those differences. At the moment of salvation and highest drama, as the Israelites parade anxiously through the dry bed of the Red Sea, the poem pauses to reflect on the tribes' relation to their patriarchal origins:

>   Him wæs an fæder,
> leof leodfruma, landriht geþah,
> frod on ferhðe, freomagum leof.[112]   (353b–355)

---

109 Hauer, 'Patriarchal Digression,' 90; Portnoy, 'Ring Composition and the Digressions of *Exodus*: The "Legacy" of the "Remnant",' *ES* 82 (2001): 289–307.

110 R. Howard Bloch, *Etymologies and Genealogies: A Literary Anthropology of the French Middle Ages* (Chicago: University of Chicago Press, 1983), 93.

111 Bloch, *Etymologies*, 103.

112 'They had a single father, beloved founder of the people, who received the land-right, wise in his heart, beloved by his kinsmen.'

The twelve tribes are unified by their common descent from Abraham, and this knowledge of origins is made explicit in its attribution to 'þa þe mægburge mæst gefrunon, / frumcyn feora, fæderæðelo gehwæs' (lines 360–1).[113] The genealogists are the ones who know history as consisting in the relationships among people through time. Yet those relationships are not simply a matter of straightforward descent; genealogy, as a kind of constellation, enacts both unity and differentiation by staging degrees of separation and the division and conjoining of family lines. Genealogy reveals how individuals are connected by blood, but it also creates hierarchies; hence the differentiation of the twelve tribes based on their descent from the different sons of Jacob.[114] Although these differences have been acknowledged in the poem's description of military organization, at this key moment the poem seeks genealogical unity. The significance is that the Israelites currently fleeing Egypt are connected to one another by their historical knowledge of their common patriarch. The commonality stretches back even beyond Abraham, however, to Noah, who kept humanity alive during the Flood. Here, the digression takes its supposedly allegorical turn. Noah is mentioned as an object lesson; he survived the Flood because

Hæfde him on hreðre   halige treowa;
forþon he gelædde   ofer lagustreamas
maðmhorda mæst,   mine gefræge.[115]   (366–8)

Noah's faith is what maintains humanity in the face of almost certain destruction, and the parallels with the Israelites' faith in God during their flight from Egypt is too close to be missed. From the beginning of *Exodus*, God has protected the Israelites; he has punished the Egyptians for enslaving his chosen people (lines 30–53), shielded the fleeing Israelites from the harsh desert elements (71b–124) and from their pursuers (204b–207), and parted the Red Sea (lines 278–98). Noah, as the first human in Genesis to

---

113 'those who inquired the most into genealogy, into the origin of men, the patrilineal descent of each person.'

114 Genealogy performs a similar function in *Genesis A*, in which the poem draws a clear distinction between the descendants of Cain (lines 1049–1103) and those of Seth (1104–1245a). Indeed, the pretext for the Flood is the remixing of the two lines; God loves the sons of Seth until they begin seeking wives from among the kin of Cain (1245b–52).

115 'He held in his heart the holy covenant; because of this, he carried over the waters the greatest treasure-hoard, as I have heard.'

demonstrate faith in God above his own desires, is a fitting appositive to the faithful Israelites, whose salvation has just been secured. But his relation to both Israelites and Anglo-Saxon Christians is not simply or merely allegorical; as forefather of the entire surviving human race, Noah also draws the poem's readers into the genealogy, acknowledging both their connection to and their distance from the Israelites of the poem.[116] The inclusion of Noah forms a constellation with the Israelites and the readers, emphasizing moments of faithful obedience. Just as God connects the two shores of the Red Sea by creating a path out of chaos, *Exodus* connects the Israelites, Noah, and its readers.

In moving from Noah to Abraham, again genealogically, *Exodus* forges a connection between two iconic images of faith and obedience in Genesis, and both Noah and Abraham ultimately refer back to the Israelites, whose story this digression interrupts. Abraham has already been mentioned twice in the poem, once in its opening lines designating the poem's actors as 'Abrahames sunum' [the sons of Abraham] (18b), and once when Moses encourages the desperate Israelites, caught between the Red Sea and the Egyptian army, to pray to 'se ecea Abrahames God' [the eternal God of Abraham] (line 273). These references remind both the Israelites and the poem's audience of the special relationship between God and the chosen people; that relationship is figured genealogically, and *Exodus* uses the genealogical structure to jump from the Red Sea crossing to Noah to Abraham and back again, thereby underscoring the thematic relevance of Noah's faith and Abraham's obedience to the salvation of the Israelites through their covenant with God.[117] Since the readers are also implicated in that genealogy by common descent from Noah, they are drawn into the historical constellation that evokes faith, obedience, covenant, and salvation at distinct but connected moments of biblical history.[118] The poem's

---

116 This is the connection that is reified by the genealogy of Alfred's father Æthelwulf, going back through Noah to Adam, s.a. 855 in the Anglo-Saxon Chronicle; see Janet Bately, ed., *MS A*, The Anglo-Saxon Chronicle: A Collaborative Edition 3 (Cambridge: D.S. Brewer, 1986).

117 The poet of *Daniel* makes a similar move when Azarias prays to God from the fiery furnace and invokes God's promises to Abraham, Isaac, and Jacob (311–14a); the three youths have already been characterized as 'Abrahames bearn' [sons of Abraham] (193b).

118 Steven Kruger has also suggested that the blurring of oppositions in *Exodus* works, like genealogy and heroic diction, to focus the audience's attention on the historical content of the text; similarities between the Israelites and the Egyptians, for example, put life and death and war on an equal, and very human, footing. See 'Oppositions and Their Opposition in the Old English *Exodus*,' *Neophilologus* 78 (1994): 165–70. The West Saxon royal genealogies explicitly traced their origins through a fourth son of Noah,

hybridity, like that in *Genesis A* and *B*, is thus dependent on form as well as content: like the significance of the allusions to Sigemund and Heremod in *Beowulf*, the *Exodus* allusions to Noah and Abraham depend on knowledge of a wider body of narrative, but that knowledge need not be typological or allegorical in order to serve the poem's purpose.[119] The poem envisions biblical history as a series of stories familiar to its readers – from homilies, from liturgical lections, even from the poem that precedes it in Junius 11 – that allow them to forge the same temporal connections encouraged by the tradition of vernacular heroic poetry, but without limiting those connections to the preordained telos of salvation history. Most important, it places the readers themselves within the historical framework of the poem, as sons of Abraham whose faith, like that of the Israelites, is both tested and rewarded.

   The poem's return to its main narrative is as jarring as the beginning of *Genesis B*; following God's promise to Abraham to establish his people in Canaan (lines 443–6), approximately 10 cm of blank space remains on page 163 of Junius 11. Pages 164–5 are blank, presumably left so for illustrations, though it is impossible to tell how much text, if any, may have been intended for these pages. Page 166 (a verso) opens with a initial, indicating the beginning of a new section, but the action plunges us in medias res, with the walls of water crashing down upon the Egyptians and the Israelites safely on the other side of the Red Sea. The remainder of the poem illustrates the reward for faith, in the salvation of the Israelites, as well as the punishment for non-belief, in the drowning of the Egyptians. Like the preparations for battle, the slaughter is described in martial terms, and ramparts and shields, wounds and blood echo through the final passages of the poem. The Israelites end by looting the bodies of the dead Egyptians for 'Iosepes gestreon' [Joseph's wealth] (588b), and the action concludes with a final allusion to the genealogical descent of Moses' people, the confirmation of their role as God's chosen people, and the promise of a return from exile. More unusually, the poem takes a turn here toward the

---

born on the ark; see T. Hill, 'The Myth of the Ark-Born Son of Noe and the West-Saxon Royal Genealogical Tables,' *Harvard Theological Review* 80 (1987): 379–83.

119 Indeed, Germanic elements in the text have even been seen as specific vehicles for allegorized Christian content; Frank notes that 'The passages in *Exodus* that seem most "Germanic" are precisely those in which I would expect to find a mythological dimension, that is, a traditional Christian meaning, being explored.' See Frank, 'What Kind of Poetry Is *Exodus*?' in *Germania: Comparative Studies in the Old Germanic Languages and Literatures*, ed. Daniel G. Calder and T. Craig Christy, 191–205 (Wolfeboro, NH: D.S. Brewer, 1988), 196.

homiletic; in lines 516–48 there is a switch to the present tense to address the audience directly about the significance of these events.[120] We will return to this passage below, but for the moment I want to note that with this direct address to the audience, *Exodus* makes explicit the connections that were implicit in the patriarchal digression: the idea that these events have special significance in the present moment, and that the audience is directly implicated in an experience of that significance.

If *Exodus* implicates its readers in the biblical narrative through both genealogy and direct address, then *Christ and Satan* reinforces that implication through repeated admonitions to its audience to bear in mind (*gemunan* or *gehycgan*) the history of sin and its consequences in the Bible.[121] Using a method not unlike that of *Deor*, *Christ and Satan* selects a series of high points from the epic sweep of biblical history and places them side by side, and not necessarily in chronological order, to allow its readers to contemplate the sources and consequences of sin in the present moment. The poem is non-narrative, and its thematic focus is the contrast between suffering in hell and joy in heaven, as well as the various modes of behaviour that earn a place in each *ham*, or home.[122] In terms of content, *Christ and Satan* repeats itself almost ad nauseam; the Fall of the Angels is retold no fewer than four times in the first four hundred lines, and it is referenced repeatedly as the proximate cause of the devils' current suffering. Satan, in fact, is the poem's primary exemplum; it is his sin of *oferhygd*, mentioned

---

120 Rosemary Huisman has offered a reading of the poem's opening lines, with their oral-derived 'Hwæt, we … gefrigen habbað' [Lo, we have heard/learned by asking] (1), that insists on the universality of the poem's meaning from the beginning; see 'Anglo-Saxon Interpretative Practices and the First Seven Lines of the Old English Poem *Exodus*: The Benefits of Close Reading,' *Parergon*, n.s., 10, no. 2 (1992): 51–7.

121 The placement of *Christ and Satan* at the end of Junius 11 has been the subject of much critical contention. It is clearly separate from the Old Testament poems in being demarcated as *Liber II* in the manuscript, and it is not copied by the same scribe who wrote *Genesis*, *Exodus*, and *Daniel*. Lucas theorized that *Christ and Satan* was incorporated into the manuscript sometime after its original construction, but codicological studies by Raw have shown it to be integral to the manuscript's design; see Lucas, 'On the Incomplete Ending of *Daniel* and the Addition of *Christ and Satan* to MS Junius 11,' *Anglia* 97 (1979): 46–59; and Raw, 'Construction.' The literary integrity of the poem is not so clear; see Hall, 'Epic of Redemption' and 'On the Bibliographic Unity of Bodleian MS Junius 11,' *AN&Q* 24 (1986): 104–7; and Ericksen, 'The Wisdom Poem at the End of MS Junius 11,' in Liuzza, *MS Junius 11*, 302–26.

122 Forms of *ham* occur 26 times in *Christ and Satan*'s 729 lines of text; compared to only 9 occurrences in *Genesis A* and *B* (2936 lines), this fairly high concentration suggests a vested interest in the idea of homeland.

five times,[123] that earns him the torment of hell, which is figured, following the model in *Genesis*, as a place of exile.[124] The poem oscillates among brief narrative passages recounting moments in salvation history; reflections by main characters, mostly Satan and Christ, on the contrasts between heaven and hell; and direct-address admonitions to the reader to *gehycgan* [think about] these contrasts as a guide to earning redemption and a place in the heavenly homeland. The messages of *Genesis* and *Exodus* – that God punishes sin with exile but has promised to help his chosen people to their new homeland – meet the Christological narrative, where God, in the person of Christ, does in fact redeem his people, 'Adames cyn' (406a) and 'Abrahames cynn' (459b), from the depths of hell and lead them to the promised *eðel* of heaven.

Christ and Satan thus fulfils the promise of the Old Testament narratives that precede it in Junius 11, but not just in the typological sense of figure and fulfilment.[125] In no way does the poem refuse either typology or teleology; yet read from the perspective of the historical understanding encoded by *Genesis* and *Exodus*, it uses the hybrid form of Germanic Christian verse to full effect, underscoring its salvific message. The relations among the various speeches in the poem are historical as much as they are thematic. The connections between Old Testament and New Testament juxtapose brief narratives drawn from biblical history, and they are interspersed with connections to both the present moment, in addressing the poem's readers, and the future, in the projection of a Judgment Day and salvation that are yet to come. The poem begins with a brief account of the Creation and the Fall of the Angels, followed by the lament of the fallen angels in hell. For almost two hundred lines, the poem presents dialogue between Satan and the other devils interspersed with descriptions of their torturous environs. In the dialogues, the fallen angels recount the

---

123 *Oferhygd* occurs at 50a, 69a, 113a, 196a, and 369a; in the first four cases, it is Satan's own word for his sin.

124 'Forðon ic sceal hean and earm hweorfan ðy widor, / wadan wræclastas, wuldre benemed, / duguðum bedeled, nænigne dream agan / uppe mid ænglum, þes ðe ic ær gecwæð / þæt ic wære seolfa swægles brytta, / wihta wealdend' [Therefore I, depressed and miserable, must wander all the more widely, tread the paths of exile, deprived of glory, separated from benefits, [and] have none of that joy up above with the angels, since I earlier said that I myself was the giver of joy, the ruler of created beings] (119–24a).

125 Hugh Keenan finds unity in the anomalies of *Christ and Satan* through a typological reading of Satan as a type of the damned at Judgment Day; see '*Christ and Satan*: Some Vagaries of Old English Poetic Composition,' *Studies in Medieval Culture* 5 (1975): 25–32.

miseries they suffer in heat, cold, torment, and bondage, and they appor-
tion blame for the *oferhygd* that earned them this punishment to the leader
who first told them that they could rise up against God and control all of
creation. These repeated (and repetitious) narratives of sin and punishment, set alongside the poem's descriptions of the *ham* in hell itself, serve
as illustrative examples, and the poem's occasional asides to the audience
encourage them directly to take heed from these warnings, choose devotion to God over selfish desires, and earn a place in the *eðel* of heaven
rather than in hell. An account of the Harrowing of Hell, the Fall of Man,
the Resurrection, Pentecost, and the Ascension leads to a fourth admonition to the audience; a description of Judgment Day precedes a fifth; and
the poem concludes, oddly, with a description of Christ's temptation in
the desert and Satan's return to hell.[126]

Christ and Satan reinforces its message through structural devices that
have come to seem familiar at this point: repetition of a familiar short narrative and its juxtaposition against other meaningful, but temporally distant, narratives. The narrative passages, told mostly through the direct
speech of characters like Satan, Eve, and Christ, serve as pretexts for vivid,
if repetitive, descriptions of the torments of hell, which in turn serve as
exempla for the passages of present tense, direct-address admonition to
readers to learn from Satan's example:

> Forþan sceal gehycgan   hæleða æghwylc
> þæt he ne abælige   bearn waldendes.
> Læte him to bysne   hu þa blacan feond
> for oferhygdum   ealle forwurdon.
> Neoman us to wynne   weoroda drihten,
> uppe ecne gefean,   engla waldend.[127]   (193–8)

---

126   On the Harrowing of Hell tradition in Anglo-Saxon England, see Jackson J. Campbell, 'To Hell and Back: Latin Tradition and Literary Use of the "descensus ad inferos"
in Old English,' *Viator* 13 (1982): 107–58. The chronological disjunction from
Judgment Day back to the Temptation of Christ has been a source of discomfort for
many critics and has occasioned numerous attempts to assert unity; see Keenan,
'*Christ and Satan*'; and Stévanovitch, 'Envelope Patterns and the Unity of the Old
English *Christ and Satan*,' *ASNSL* 233 (1996): 260–7. T. Hill suggests that Satan's
peculiar punishment at the end of the poem, to measure out the space of Hell with his
hands, makes Satan the *metod* of Hell; see 'The Measure of Hell: *Christ and Satan*
695–722,' *PQ* 60 (1982 for 1981): 409–14.

127   'Therefore each man must determine that he not offend the son of the ruler. Let it be
an example to them how the glittering enemies all perished because of arrogance. Let
us choose for delight the lord of hosts, eternal joy above, the ruler of angels.'

Through this process, figures in the poem serve as historical exempla for the audience, and the salvific connection between historical events is made clear by removing them from linear temporality and placing them directly side by side. Eve sums up their significance quite succintly: 'Hwæt, þu fram minre dohtor, drihten, onwoce / in middangeard mannum to helpe' (437–8).[128] The words link Eve through genealogy to both Mary and Christ; they remind us, as Eve herself just has (408–19), of the story of the Fall of Man and its consequence of exile from the heavenly home, and they promise a redemption that is immediately delivered to Eve and the rest of *Abrahames cynn* as Christ leads them 'up to eðle' [up to the homeland] (459a). Christ himself elaborates further, recounting Adam and Eve's sin through Satan's temptation, their exile from the *eðel* of Paradise, and his own decision to rescue 'min handgeweorc' [my handiwork] from their suffering in hell by becoming human and suffering himself for their redemption (469b–511a; 487b). Christ's speech isolates the Fall, Crucifixion, and Redemption as the main events of salvation history, made significant by their collocation in the space of his words as well as in the understanding of the Christian subject. Past, present, and future are all linked through narrative: the past history of sin, both biblical and personal; the present moment of Christ's reign in heaven; and the future salvation of readers at their own death and on Judgment Day.

The temporal dilation and telescoping of historical narrative in this poem helps to create a sense of dislocation for the audience, and the frequent direct-address admonitions encourage readers to pause and reflect on the meaning of narratives of sin, punishment, and redemption in their own particular contexts. The contingent temporality of humanity is reinforced, as it was in the opening lines of *Genesis A*, by a contrast between the eternal time of the divine and the proscribed temporality of creation, indicated once again by God's unique perspective on the world:

He selfa mæg   sæ geondwlitan,
grundas in geofene,   godes agen bearn,
and he ariman mæg   rægnas scuran,
dropena gehwelcne.   Daga enderim
seolua he gesette   þurh his soðan miht.[129]   (9–13)

---

128 'Behold, you were born from my daughter, Lord, in middle earth [the temporal world] as a help to the people.'
129 'He alone, God's own son, is able to look over the sea, the foundation of the ocean, and he is able to enumerate the showers of rain, each of the drops. He alone established the number of days through his true power.'

God alone has the ability to fully perceive and completely understand the expanse and detail of his creations, and one of these creations is time itself: the *daga enderim* are, like each drop of rain, fully known only to God. As the poem itself asks, 'Hwa is þæt ðe cunne / orðonc clene nymðe ece god?' (17b–18).[130] The changes in verb tense from present tense *mæg* to past tense *gesette* mirrors the similar move at the beginning of *Genesis A* to introduce temporality alongside both narrative and the Creation. Once again, verb tense illustrates the contrast between God's extratemporal, all-encompassing perspective and the limited, highly contingent perspective of humanity, including the poem's readers. In *Christ and Satan*, however, readers have a more self-consciously realized opportunity to partake of the extratemporal perspective of God, precisely through the medium of narrative poetry that has, throughout Junius 11, surmounted historical distance and brought Old Testament history into the presence/present of its audience. Verb tense once again works to place the audience in a particular relationship with the content of the poem. Five present tense passages direct readers to interpret the poem's dialogues as encouragement to work toward heaven and avoid sin,[131] and the present tense descriptions of the glory of heaven partake of both divine eternity and the interest of the present moment, in contrast to the past tense with which the devils describe heavenly joys. For them, the joy of heaven is always only in the past; for the poem's readers, however, it exists in the present and, they hope, the future.[132]

In the first four hundred lines of the poem, readers encounter a seemingly endless cycle of lament, blame, and admonition; the devils bemoan their suffering, recall its cause, and offer blame to themselves and to Satan, while the narrative voice encourages readers to learn from their example. This cycle of endless repetition even approximates, for the poem's readers, the eternal suffering of hell, and the perpetual lament stretches, without a break, from the moment of the angels' fall to the Harrowing of Hell. Christ's arrival in hell interrupts the endless flow of eternity with a definitive moment of narrative action:

---

130 'Who is it that can fully know such skill but the eternal God?'
131 At 193–223, 282–314, 348–64, 593b–96, and 642–64.
132 At, for example, the description of Christ enthroned at 579–93a and the future judgment at lines 597–641.

Þa him egsa becom,
dyne for deman, þa he duru in helle
bræc and begde ...[133]   (378b–380a)

He bursts in to rescue the trapped souls of the righteous, his agency in
stark contrast to the enforced passivity of the devils, who must remain
bound and suffering, with no hope of any change. The Harrowing links
Old Testament narrative, specifically the Falls of the Angels and of Man,
with the New Testament promise of salvation, and it differentiates the parallel Fall narratives by offering the hope of redemption to humankind
alone. In true typological fashion, the relationship between the Fall of the
Angels and the Fall of Man is clarified and takes on its full Christian significance only in the light of the New Testament event of the Harrowing
of Hell. Christ appears to the humans in hell as a heroic saviour, and *Christ
and Satan* ends, appropriately, with a final showdown between the
eponymous hero and adversary.

In *Christ and Satan*, narrative is explicitly not the point; rather, brief
narrative allusion and recapitulation serve to establish historical relations
between events, including the event of the poem itself, which returns us to
the question of temporality first raised by Cædmon's *Hymn* and the opening of *Genesis A*. Like *Deor*, *Christ and Satan* provides a space for philosophical reflection on the problem of sin and its implications for the individual Christian, as elaborated by the historical examples of *Genesis*,
Exodus, and even (to a lesser extent) *Daniel*. Unlike its Junius predecessors, however, *Christ and Satan* includes the future in its temporal calcu-
lus, and its inclusion of the present is explicit rather than implicit. In this
way, the poem offers its readers a glimpse of biblical history that approximates the divine perspective on human existence; like God, readers exist
outside the time of the narrative and already know the end before they
have begun to read. Just as Cædmon's creative activity mirrored the first
divine Creation, the poet of *Christ and Satan* takes on the role of creator
and imbues his poem with the perspective of the Creator, and the parallel
between poetic narrative and the Creation is striking. Christ himself establishes the frame of reference; the historical significance of these disparate
events, for the reader in the present moment, is made manifest through
Christ's Incarnation and his Ascension, two of the events included in this

---

133 'Then terror came to them, the din preceding the judge, when he burst through and
broke down the doors of hell.'

apotheosis of the constellation. The hybrid Anglo-Christian poem is thus able to reassert the meaning of salvation history; its collocation of disparate events, linked through causality, once again offers exempla, with the poem itself directly implicating readers in that collocation by means of its repeated address to their powers of interpretation and understanding. The aesthetic activity of literary production embodies the historical relations it strives to represent, taking readers outside the present moment to gaze upon the evidence of God's hand among human events.

V. Bare Narrative and Biblical Gloss: Scripture, Orthodoxy, and the Vernacular

The affective power of Anglo-Saxon Christian verse, which constellates biblical history to reinforce Christian identity for its readers, is clear; but the implications of that power and the question of its orthodoxy are less so, and both Junius 11 and other contemporary texts reveal some anxiety over the possibility of misinterpreting biblical events taken out of context. That this mode of reading biblical history was not the only, or the most desirable, one, even within the Junius poems themselves, is evident in the didactic digression in *Exodus* that precedes Moses' speech on the far side of the Red Sea (lines 523–48). This digression instructs readers to search for the spiritual as well as the literal meaning of the text:

> Gif onlucan wile   lifes wealhstod,
> beorht in breostum,   banhuses weard,
> ginfæsten god   Gastes cægon,
> run bið gerecenod,   ræd forð gæð ...[134]   (523–6)

Allegorical reading, the poem explains, links the Israelites' successful passage of the Red Sea to the soul's triumphant passage through the exile of temporal existence to the promised land of heaven (530b–548). Lucas assumes that 'any informed Christian will interpret the scriptures not only for their literal meaning but also for their spiritual meaning, to be perceived by means of typological and allegorical exegesis'; and Dorothy Haines insists that this passage refers to Christ as the key to unlocking the

---

134 'If the mediator of life, bright within the breast, the guardian of the body, wishes to unlock the ample benefits with the keys of the Spirit, secrets will be explained, wisdom will come forth.'

meaning of the Old Testament for post-Incarnation Christians.[135] If the process of allegorical reading outlined in lines 516–48 were as automatic as Lucas and others have assumed, however, the poem would not need to instruct its audience in figural interpretation. In fact, allegorical reading pulls readers in quite a different direction from the one in which the patriarchal digression pulls them. There, examples from biblical history were meant to demonstrate the Israelites' need for faith in order to overcome their tribulations; just as Noah and Abraham were preserved by their faith, so too the Israelites are saved by theirs. These historical connections, mediated through genealogy and the juxtaposition of disparate events, teach about the need for faith throughout history in the temporal world. In all three cases, God saves the faithful from literal, not figurative, hardship – as the angel saves the three youths from the very real threat of the fiery furnace in *Daniel*. Although the allegorical reading encouraged by the didactic digression certainly provides a possible (and popular) interpretation of the events of Exodus, that reading is not the only possible one. Given the demonstrated aptitude of Anglo-Saxon verse for connecting historical events without reference to figuration, the poem itself seems caught between these two historical modes. On the one hand, it validates a historical reading of the Old Testament events it constellates and encourages an understanding of them as salvific, as evidence of God's work among humankind, but with reference specifically to the temporal world. On the other hand, it argues explicitly for an allegorical interpretation of these same events. As the passage demonstrates, there was a perceived need to encourage Anglo-Saxon audiences to understand the biblical past allegorically, as opposed to merely literally or historically. This need is certainly evident in one of the largest surviving corpora of vernacular writing dedicated to the theological formation of the laity: the work of Ælfric. As we shall see, Ælfric's repeated insistence on the typological understanding of the Old Law in the light of the New makes explicit some of the assumptions of the *Exodus* poet, as well as the stakes involved in competing modes of historical understanding.

The translation of scripture into the vernacular was always an enterprise fraught with difficulty at every level. In addition to the labour of rendering Latin writings in a structurally very different language, translators like Ælfric also worried about the ramifications of making scripture, especially the Old Testament, available to foolish people, who might misinterpret it and be led astray. Ælfric in particular was acutely aware of how closely

---

135 Lucas, ed., *Exodus*, 142, n. to ll. 523–6; Haines, 'Unlocking *Exodus*.'

form and content were tied to meaning, and he knew that changing the form of a text – from Latin to English, or from prose to verse – would have significant and unpredictable ramifications for the content as well. Yet the demand for Old Testament stories in the vernacular was sufficient for Ælfric himself to produce extensive versions of the Old Testament in Old English. His translation of Genesis, his homilies *De initio creaturae* and *Hexameron*, and his *Treatise on the Old and New Testament*, also known as the *Letter to Sigeweard*, offer highlights from the narrative of Genesis and place them explicitly and self-consciously in the typological and teleological scheme of salvation history.[136] *De initio creaturae*, for example, presents an overview of salvation history from the Creation to the Last Judgment. It moves efficiently through highlights from the Old Testament (the Creation, Adam and Eve, Noah, the Tower of Babel, and the Exodus) and key moments in the life of Christ (the Annunciation, the calling of the Twelve Apostles, the trial and Crucifixion, the Harrowing of Hell, and the Resurrection). In this homily, the Old Testament is clearly a precursor of the New Testament, although Ælfric does not elaborate on typological connections between the Old and New Testament events; as Katherine O'Brien O'Keeffe writes, 'he is careful to include only those Old Testament events which require little exegesis to make a simple point clear ... Each of these events, though open to higher exegesis, is also accessible at the literal level of God's acting among men.'[137] He also treats extrabiblical material here, including the creation of the ten orders of angels, Lucifer's rebellion, and the punishment of the fallen angels – but he uses these stories to explain that evil came into the world through the free choice of created beings. The emphasis that God 'let hi habban agenne cyre' [allowed them to have their own choice] at their creation reappears at the moment of their punishment and at the expulsion of Adam and Eve from Paradise, and Ælfric uses the same words to describe the eternal soul God gives to

---

136 *De initio creaturae*, in *Ælfric's Catholic Homilies: The First Series*, ed. Peter Clemoes, EETS, s.s., 17 (Oxford: Oxford University Press, 1997), 178–89; hereafter *CH* I; *Exameron Anglice or the Old English Hexameron*, ed. S.J. Crawford (Hamburg: H. Grand, 1921; repr. Darmstadt: Wissenschaftliche Buchgesellschaft, 1968); *The Old English Heptateuch and Ælfric's Libellus de ueteri testamento et nouo*, ed. Richard Marsden, EETS, o.s., 330 (Oxford: Oxford University Press, 2008). On Ælfric's uses of Genesis throughout his work, see O'Brien O'Keeffe, 'The Book of Genesis in Anglo-Saxon England' (PhD diss., University of Pennsylvania, 1975), 104–71, and 'Three English Writers on Genesis: Some Observations on Aelfric's Theological Legacy,' *Ball State University Forum* 19, no. 3 (Summer 1978): 69–78. Ælfric also treated events narrated in *Exodus* and *Daniel* in his work; see Remley, *Biblical Verse*, 88 n174.

137 O'Brien O'Keeffe, 'Three English Writers,' 71.

every person, along with free will.[138] The Fall of the Angels, then, is an opportunity for Ælfric to illuminate a theological concept within this homily.[139] Ælfric appears quite willing to approach extrabiblical material in the context of homiletic exegesis, when he is able to control the text's meaning through his explication. In the translation of the primary source, however, he is on his guard against the possible misapprehensions of the *dysig* [foolish] man or the 'mæssepreost' [mass-priest] who 'cuðe be dæle Lyden understandan' [could only partly understand Latin] (13–15).[140] Without access to the original form of scripture, illiterate or semiliterate Christians might be unable to access the true or correct meaning of the text. Yet access to that message was crucial for salvation; that is precisely the problem that Cædmon and the Junius poets attempted to address in earlier centuries. Unlike his predecessors, however, Ælfric is hesitant to alter the form of the Vulgate. For these readers, and in the absence of an overtly exegetical context, Ælfric holds himself to the strictest limits lest his translations should prove *gedwolsum* [misleading].

Ælfric attempts to mitigate the danger of misreading by keeping his translation as close to the Latin text of the Vulgate as is reasonably possible in a language so different from Latin, what he terms *þa nacod gerecednis* [the bare narrative]. He intends to set the words out in English exactly as they were dictated to Moses by God, except where the modes of expression in English are so different from those in the Latin that he must rearrange the order of the words. Even this, he fears, may lead readers into error. He adheres strictly to his promise 'na mare awritan on Englisc þonne þæt Liden hæfþ' [to write no more in the English than is present in the Latin] (line 98) by translating Genesis line by line wherever possible and recounting nothing that is not present in the Vulgate. As elsewhere in his work, he eschews apocryphal details, preferring instead *þa nacod gerecednis*. As Paul Szarmach puts it, 'Ælfric's narrative impulse means his presentation of the Bible primarily as story, secondarily as text for analysis. As far as audience effect is concerned, the audience hears primarily narrative as narrative is heard, not, say, a sequence of embedded moral principles.'[141] That part comes later. Ælfric's desire for his readers, in this respect, runs

---

138 *CH* I, 179 lines 27–8, 180 line 53, and 184 lines 156, 175–6.
139 On Ælfric's use of sources on the Fall of the Angels, see Michael Fox, 'Ælfric on the Creation and Fall of the Angels,' *ASE* 31 (2002): 175–200.
140 *Prefatio* to Genesis, in Marsden, *Old English Heptateuch*, 3–7. All quotations are taken from this edition and are cited by line number.
141 Paul E. Szarmach, 'Ælfric as Exegete: Approaches and Examples in the Study of the *Sermones Catholici*,' in *Hermeneutics and Medieval Culture*, ed. Patrick J. Gallacher and Helen Damico, 237–47 (Albany: State University of New York Press, 1989), 241.

contrary to literature's capacity for representing the people and events from distant times and places: his translations work not to enliven the Old Testament, but to insist on its morbidity.

In the *Prefatio* to Genesis, which is transmitted with all three copies of his translation of Genesis,[142] Ælfric expresses both his intentions and his concerns: he has begun his translation at the request of Ealdorman Æthelweard, but he worries that it is a very *pleolic* [hazardous] undertaking, because 'ic ondræde gif sum dysig man ðas boc ræt, oððe rædan gehyrþ, þæt he wille wenan þæt he mote lybban nu on þære niwan æ swa swa þa ealdan fæderas leofodon, þa on þære tide' (lines 9–12).[143] Ælfric is acutely aware of the historical separation between his medieval audience and the people whose narratives he is translating, as well as the confusion that might arise for readers who are unable to grasp the idea of historical difference. Yet it is not just a matter of temporal separation that underwrites Ælfric's concern; it is not simply that the ancient Hebrews had different (and perhaps less desirable) customs from those of the Anglo-Saxons. Ælfric's sense of historical separation turns on the central event of Christian history and its irrevocable effects on the relationship between past and present. The Crucifixion produces a definitive rupture in Christian history; with the Incarnation, Passion, and Resurrection, Old Testament law was fulfilled and rendered henceforth inoperable. The coming of Christ meant that Moses' law was no longer sufficient for the new people of God, and Ælfric insists on the theological importance of that separation: 'Gyf hwa wyle nu swa lybban æfter Cristes tocyme swa swa men leofodon ær Moises æ, oþþe under Moises æ, ne byð se man na cristen, ne he furþon wyrðe ne byð þæt him ænig cristen man mid ete' (lines 21–4).[144] One's identification as Christian, and thus one's salvation, depends upon the ability to recognize the difference between the Old Law and the New, and to affirm the New above the Old: after the Advent of Christ, there is no going back, only forward. To remove Old Testament narratives or figures from their historical context and place them alongside New Testament or present-day narratives or figures without acknowledging the crucial element of historical

---

142 In Cambridge, University Library, Ii. 1. 33 (x. xii²); Oxford, Bodleian Library, Laud Misc. 509 (s. xi²); and the lavishly illustrated London, British Library, Cotton Claudius B. iv (s. xi¹), also known as the Old English Illustrated Hexateuch.

143 'I fear that if some foolish man reads this book or hears it read, that he will expect that he can live now under this new law, just as the old fathers lived then in that time.'

144 'If anyone now wishes to live, after the coming of Christ, just as men lived before the law of Moses or under the law of Moses, that man is no Christian, nor is he even worthy that any Christian man might eat with him.'

separation, as the Junius poems do, is tantamount, for Ælfric, to disavowing the significance of the Crucifixion as representing not only a historical paradigm shift, but the single defining moment of Christian history. In Ælfric's insistence on historical separation, the different historical investments of the constellation and Christian teleology become most apparent. In Junius 11, poetry connected readers with biblical history and helped them work out a relationship with the distant past in the hope of future salvation. For Ælfric, however, the present is not the goal of historical narrative; past events are significant only in so far as they point toward the telos of redemption. In this way, says Ælfric in the *Prefatio*, 'man mæg understandan hu deop seo boc ys on gastlicum andgite, þeah þe heo mid leohtlicum wordum awriten sig' (lines 74–5).[145] A thoroughly typological understanding of the Genesis narrative is painstakingly elaborated in the *Libellus de ueteri testamento et nouo*.[146] Here, Ælfric summarizes the high points of the Genesis narrative – the Creation, the Fall, Cain and Abel, the Flood, Abraham, and Isaac – and pauses after each summation to explain its typological connection to New Testament events. 'Adam,' he writes, 'getacnude, þe on ðam sixtan dæge gesceapen wæs þurh God, urne Hælend Crist, þe com to þissere worulde and us geedniwode to his gelicnisse' (14–16).[147] A variety of men from the Old Testament also signify Christ: Abel, Seth, Noah, Isaac, Joshua, David, and Solomon. Eve, in her turn, signifies the Church, and Abraham is a type of God. On the whole, Ælfric explicates the entire Old Testament as a prefiguration of New Testament events: the Old Testament is clearly sacred history, meant to be read not as a means to understanding either past or present, but rather as the illustration of prophecy and fulfilment that leads to salvation. Such an illustration depends on the absolute separation of the Old Law from the New: 'Moyses æ wæs, and witegan soþlice, oð Iohannes wearð acenned þe Crist gefullod' (506–7).[148]

---

145 'one can understand how deep this book is in its spiritual meaning, although it may be written with light words.'

146 In Marsden, *Old English Heptateuch*, 201–30. All quotations are taken from this edition and are cited by line number. The *Libellus* is transmitted, along with the *Prefatio* to Genesis and translation of Genesis, in Laud Misc. 509; a fragmentary version survives in a late twelfth century collection of homilies, many of them by Ælfric, in Oxford, Bodleian Library, Bodley 343.

147 'Adam, who was created by God on the sixth day, signifies our saviour Christ, who came to this world and renewed us in his image.'

148 'The law of Moses and the prophets existed then, until John was born, who baptized Christ.' See Mk 11:13 and Lk 16:16.

Ælfric sees the duality of figural interpretation as a salvific imperative: there are two parts to history, the figure and the fulfilment, or the literal and the spiritual. This duality is pervasive; in the *Prefatio* to Genesis, he argues that God gave humans two eyes, ears, nostrils, lips, hands, and feet to signify the doubleness of the Old and New Testaments (lines 108–11). He also emphasizes the unity of God's plan for history in his explication of the opening verses of Genesis in the *Prefatio*, an explication demonstrating the presence of God in all Three Persons at the moment of Creation; and he repeatedly urges readers to focus on the *gastlice andgyt* [spiritual content] of the biblical narrative rather than its literal meaning. In this, he claims, he is following the example of Christ and his apostles, who 'us tæhton ægþer to healdenne, þa ealdan gastlice and þa niwan soþlice mid weorcum' (106–8).[149] It is thus the perception of Genesis' *gastlice andgyt* that will benefit readers of Ælfric's translation by urging them to good works. Readers must learn to separate the spiritual from the literal, just as they must work to keep the past separate from the present. Yet it is precisely this allegoresis that is most likely to elude an uneducated audience – hence Ælfric's repeated warnings in his letters and prefaces, and his pleas to scribes to copy his work accurately and emend any errors they might find. The fact that the conscientiously instructive *Prefatio* to Genesis was transmitted with all three surviving copies of the translation is compelling evidence of its role in instructing readers how to proceed with the biblical material. Readers of Oxford, Bodleian Library, Laud 509, moreover, would have found instruction in both the *Prefatio* that precedes the translation of Genesis and the treatise *De ueteri testamento et nouo* that follows the Heptateuch.[150]

That Ælfric needs to elaborate – and defend – a theory of typological reading indicates his assumption that his audience would not automatically have read the Old Testament figurally; and that his instructional preface travels so closely with the translation reveals a certain amount of anxiety about that fact. This anxiety extended beyond Ælfric's own composition to the contexts in which biblical exegesis could take place. Benjamin Withers, for example, sees a correspondence between the sense of duality in a typological interpretation and the duality of the manuscript of Ælfric's *Prefatio* in the Old English Illustrated Hexateuch, in which the opening lines of the *Prefatio* and the opening image of the Fall of the Angels combine to 'introduce into [the Hexateuch] a Christian interpretation absent from the literal

---

149 'showed us to observe them both, the old spiritually, and the new in reality, with works.'

150 For the manuscript contents, see Ker, *Catalogue*, no. 344.

Old Testament text.'[151] The passage from *Exodus* quoted above certainly echoes these concerns, despite the fact that modern critics seem to assume the opposite. In his attempts to avoid the possibility of theological error, and to ensure the salvific potential of scripture, Ælfric casts past and present as an incommensurate binary. Biblical history becomes a realm of absolute alterity, a place whose customs and traditions are incomprehensible in Anglo-Saxon terms and have meaning only inasmuch as they prefigure the New Testament narrative of redemption. How different this vision of history is from that of the Germanic war trappings that brought the Israelites of *Exodus* into the space of Anglo-Saxon experience, or from that of the Fall of the Angels that helped Anglo-Saxon readers to see themselves in the Fall of the first humans. It is tempting to speculate that the roughly contemporaneous Junius 11, so carefully planned and executed, complete with lavish illustrations, was precisely the kind of threat that Ælfric meant to counter with his more orthodox and formally precise rendition of Old Testament materials. Where Ælfric's vision of biblical history kept the past at bay and focused instead on the future, the Old English poems of Junius 11 used verse and image to bring the past very much to life for its present readers.

V. Hybridity, Teleology, History

Both Ælfric's translations and the Junius poems seek to fulfil the goal laid out by Bede at the founding moment of Old English vernacular literature: to bring the message of scripture to those unable to read Latin. The hymn that Cædmon sings on the Creation, born as it is out of textual gloss, allegorizes the status of vernacular literature in relation to its Latin counterpart: marginal, secondary, at one remove from the original.[152] Yet, for its audience, the vernacular verse has a primacy that the Latin could never achieve because of its limited accessibility, and Bede himself had such respect for the artistic integrity of the Old English original that he consciously refrained from translating it into Latin verse for fear of marring

---

151 Benjamin C. Withers, 'A "Secret and Fevered Genesis": The Prefaces of the Old English Hexateuch,' *Art Bulletin* 81, no. 1 (March 1999): 53–71 at 53. For a facsimile of Claudius B. iv, see *The Old English Illustrated Hexateuch*, ed. C.R. Dodwell and Peter Clemoes, EEMF 18 (Copenhagen: Rosenkilde and Bagger, 1974).

152 Savage notes that Old English verse seems to have had a cultural status parallel to, rather than below, Latin literature and finds it utterly lacking in the apologetics so frequently found in Middle English versifications of biblical material. See ' Colonization of the Promised Land,' 39–42.

its aesthetic.[153] A notion of the aesthetic is central to this story; Bede repeatedly refers to Cædmon as putting scripture 'optimo carmine' [into excellent verse] and creating 'carmen dulcissimum' [the most melodious verse].[154] It is, in fact, the very beauty of Cædmon's verse that makes it an effective tool of Christian instruction. Bede is not concerned by the fears that plague Ælfric nearly three centuries later; for the eighth century historian, the value of Cædmon's gift lies in its ability to communicate the messages of scripture to an audience who would otherwise lack such illumination. The motivation behind Cædmon's songs, Bede tells us, was that 'homines ab amore scelerum abstrahere, ad dilectionem uero et sollertiam bonae actionis excitare curabat,' and the aesthetic impact of his poetry is precisely what allowed him to do this.[155] Cædmon's *Hymn* and the Junius poems all use the beauty of poetry to transmit a message of Christian faith, all the while taking full advantage of the audience's nostalgia for the aesthetic traditions of their pagan heroic past.

In this way, Anglo-Saxon biblical verse exemplifies the cultural hybridity that results from the meeting of pagan Germanic and Latin Christian cultures. As we have seen, in the meeting of these two cultures, one does not dominate and replace the other; instead, both cultures are altered by the contact. Anglo-Saxon biblical verse is most certainly not the Bible, and it is possible to understand such verse in ways that differ significantly from the ways of Christian orthodoxy. Not only that, but the differences introduced by the hybrid form can call into question the authority of the original: 'Deprived of their full presence, the knowledges of cultural authority may be articulated with forms of "native" knowledges or faced with those discriminated subjects that they must rule but can no longer represent. This may lead ... to questions of authority that the authorities – the Bible included – cannot answer.'[156] 'Questions of authority' are precisely what a translator like Ælfric works to contain, for what is at stake in the translation of scripture in Anglo-Saxon England is not just cultural dominance, but theological truth – the salvation of the Christian subject. Given these stakes, perhaps Ælfric was right to fear less literal adaptations. As his prefaces demonstrate, there is no room for ambivalence in the interpretation of scripture. Salvation depends on recognizing the authority of the

---

153 See n10 above.
154 *HE* 4.24.
155 *HE* 4.24. 'He sought to turn his hearers away from delight in sin and arouse in them the love and practice of good works.'
156 Bhabha, *Location of Culture*, 164.

New Law over the Old, as well as the primacy of the New Testament over the Old. It requires Christian subjects to orient themselves away from both past and present and look toward the future. Yet Anglo-Saxon biblical verse does the opposite. Its form encourages readers to think about past and present, rather than future; or to consider the future as part of a constellation in which past and present are equally important elements. It pulls Old Testament narratives out of the continuum of salvation history, eschewing typology for a different kind of historical consciousness. As a hybrid form, it reflects the dominant ideology of Latin Christianity, but with an ambivalence that troubles the neat temporal distinctions of salvation teleology and interjects the present as a key element of historical consciousness.

The introduction of Christianity changes Anglo-Saxon poetry, and by extension Anglo-Saxon culture; that is Bede's point in recounting the story of Cædmon. But Anglo-Saxon poetry also changes Christianity, and the changes prove, in some ways, incommensurate with the Latin tradition it purports to translate. The success of this poetry is strongly evident in its survival; the production of the *de luxe* Junius 11 in the twilight years of Anglo-Saxon England was a careful and deliberate undertaking. Yet the production of that manuscript may have been just the sort of thing that caused Ælfric to launch his own project of translation, thereby combating what he felt to be *gedwolsum*, or misleading, in the ambivalence of a hybrid form. That hybridity situates Anglo-Saxon England firmly in relation to the biblical origins of a salvation telos, and it recuperates a Christian identity for its Anglo-Saxon audience by rediscovering the present in narratives of the ancient past. Instead of connecting Anglo-Saxon England to its heroic forebears in Germanic tradition, Anglo-Saxon biblical verse claims an equally distant and legendary tradition as part of its own cultural patrimony in its own cultural terms. In Cædmon's *Hymn*, Anglo-Saxon audiences find themselves at the Creation of the world, and in Junius 11, Christian salvation emerges as a very Anglo-Saxon creation indeed.

The form of Anglo-Saxon poetry thus lends its shape to the narrative of biblical history. But historical verse was not limited to the far-distant past of the ancient Hebrews, nor to the pre-Christian Germanic heroes of legend and myth. At the heart of the poetic corpus lie a handful of heroic verses composed in commemoration of contemporary, or roughly contemporary, events: *The Battle of Maldon*, *The Battle of Brunanburh*, *The Capture of the Five Boroughs*, *The Death of Edward*, and several other poems that mark significant events and leaders in the late tenth and the eleventh centuries. The impetus of these verse memorials is not hard to fathom: in honouring kings and fallen heroes by means of heroic verse, the poets impart to their subjects the same grandeur and glory that colours the stories of Beowulf, Sigemund, Welund, Mæðhild, Eormanric, and other giants of Germanic legend. Yet Byrhtnoth, Athelstan, and Edward are not heroes of legend. They are contemporary political leaders, and their immortalization in verse tells us a great deal about the perceived role of historiography in the late Anglo-Saxon period. That the poets and scribes who chronicle the decline and fall of Anglo-Saxon England should choose to represent their own social world in the forms of the ancient heroic world speaks volumes about their investment in a particular vision of the present and its relationship to a particular vision of the past. As a form of historiography, these poems show Anglo-Saxon literary culture responding to the Anglo-Saxons' own present using an aesthetic practice that historicizes contemporary events, thereby offering a cultural space for remembering, repeating, and working through the battles, martyrdoms, and conquests that define the late Anglo-Saxon age.

3 Verse Memorials and the Viking Conflict

Thus founded on the rupture between a past that is its object, and a present that is the place of its practice, history endlessly finds the present in its object and the past in its practice. Inhabited by the uncanniness that it seeks, history imposes its law upon the faraway places that it conquers when it fosters the illusion that it is bringing them back to life.

Michel de Certeau, *The Writing of History*

In a small chapel in the southeast corner of Ely Cathedral, above the tomb of the sixteenth century bishop Nicholas West, there is a row of seven arched niches created to commemorate seven benefactors of Ely from the late Anglo-Saxon period.[1] The niche on the far right holds the remains of Ealdorman Byrhtnoth, who fell fighting the Vikings at the Battle of Maldon in 991 AD and is honoured as a hero in the roughly contemporaneous poem *The Battle of Maldon*. In the niche on the far left rest the bones of Archbishop Wulfstan of York (d. 1023 AD), who composed his most famous work, the *Sermo Lupi ad Anglos*, in response to the same kinds of Viking attacks that took Byrhtnoth's life. These two men are among the most famous from the last decades of Anglo-Saxon England, in large part because of the literary works with which they were associated. Wulfstan's homilies, treatises, law codes, and commonplace books testify to the range and vitality of late Anglo-Saxon literary production, and his work is imbued with a strong desire to ensure the nation's salvation through the piety

---

1 On the history of Bishop West's chapel and the remains buried there, see John Crook, '"Vir optimus Wlfstanus": The Post-Conquest Commemoration of Archbishop Wulfstan of York at Ely Cathedral,' in *Wulfstan, Archbishop of York: The Proceedings of the Second Alcuin Conference*, ed. Matthew Townend, 501–24 (Turnhout: Brepols, 2004).

of its people. Byrhtnoth's encomium in *The Battle of Maldon*, on the other hand, is one of the most frequently cited examples of the heroic code in Anglo-Saxon literature; Byrhtnoth is portrayed as a Germanic warlord leading his faithful *comitatus* to death and glory with brave words and valiant deeds. Both kinds of writing tried, quite self-consciously, to work through the process of historicizing contemporary events within a recognizable historiographical framework, but they approached the question in very different ways. Just as they occupy opposite ends of Bishop West's chapel in Ely Cathedral, Wulfstan and Byrhtnoth represent opposite techniques and forms of history-writing in the late Anglo-Saxon period: one that seeks the meaning of events in their relation to a Christian telos, and one that looks to the heroic tradition to shape its understanding of historical events. These two modes of historiography both illustrate and give rise to very different modes of historical understanding; as we shall see, Wulfstan and the *Maldon* poet construe events and their significance in strikingly dissimilar ways.

The Battle of Maldon, along with *Beowulf* and *The Battle of Brunanburh*, serves to codify the heroic ethos for most Anglo-Saxon scholars.[2] That

---

2 *The Battle of Maldon*, ed. Donald G. Scragg (Manchester: Manchester University Press, 1981). Greenfield and Calder treat *Maldon* in a chapter entitled 'Secular Heroic Poetry'; and the more recent literary history of Fulk and Cain places the poem in the category of 'Germanic Legend and Heroic Lay.' See Stanley B. Greenfield and Daniel G. Calder, *A New Critical History of Old English Literature* (New York: New York University Press, 1986), 149–54; R.D. Fulk and Christopher M. Cain, *A History of Old English Literature* (Malden, MA: Blackwell, 2003), 220–4. Greenfield and Calder write of the heroes of *Maldon* that 'their conduct reflects the heroic code embodied in the old Germanic *comitatus* as described by Tacitus: obedience, loyalty, fortitude, self-sacrifice in repayment for the lord's prior generosity – with the addition of the Christian virtues of trusting in God and submitting to His will' (150), which Fulk and Cain describe as the poem's 'oddly Tacitean attitudes' (222). The *Cambridge Companion to Old English Literature* likewise sees *Maldon* as exemplary of the heroic ethos; see Katherine O'Brien O'Keeffe, 'Heroic Values and Christian Ethics,' in *The Cambridge Companion to Old English Literature*, ed. Malcolm Godden and Michael Lapidge, 107–25 (Cambridge: Cambridge University Press, 1991). For a fuller treatment of *Maldon* specifically, see George Clark, '*The Battle of Maldon*: A Heroic Poem,' *Speculum* 43 (1968): 52–71. Virtually every critic of *Maldon* takes for granted the poem's dependence on a heroic tradition centring on the bonds of loyalty between a lord and his retainers, but see especially Rosemary Woolf, 'The Ideal of Men Dying with Their Lord in the *Germania* and in *The Battle of Maldon*,' *ASE* 5 (1976): 63–81; Roberta Frank, 'The Ideal of Men Dying with Their Lord in *The Battle of Maldon*: Anachronism or *Nouvelle Vague*?' in *People and Places in Northern Europe, 500–1600: Essays in Honour of Peter Hayes Sawyer*, ed. Ian Wood and Niels Lund, 95–106 (Woodbridge: Boydell, 1991); and Joseph Harris, 'Love and Death in the *Männerbund*: An Essay with Special Reference to the *Bjarkamál* and *The Battle of Maldon*,' in *Heroic Poetry in the Anglo-Saxon Period:*

two of the classically heroic poems in the Anglo-Saxon canon deal with the stuff of history, as opposed to legend, cannot but have implications for our examination of Anglo-Saxon historical consciousness. Indeed, popular understanding paints a vivid and romantic picture of Anglo-Saxon poetry as the literary inheritor of a long Germanic tradition descended from the ancient scops, who stored the history of their people in metrical form in their capacious and inventive memories; Widsith, with his catalogue of kings, tribes, and heroes, is a case in point, as is the scop who immediately turns Beowulf's victory over Grendel into song.[3] But the passage from *Beowulf* also depicts the use of heroic verse to commemorate a current event, to turn into history the deeds of a contemporary hero, and it is in this context that we must place the similarly commemorative *Battle of Maldon*.

Maldon, then, can serve as a case study in how the particular ideology of heroic history adapts to events that are local and immediate rather than legendary and distant and emerges as an aesthetic remedy to a moment of crisis in historical discourse.[4] The Viking attacks of the late tenth and early eleventh centuries prompted emotionally and ideologically charged writings both in England and on the Continent, and in a period as well documented and controversial as the reign of Æthelred II, the rhetoric of contemporary prose texts has attracted a great deal of critical attention from scholars demonstrating the ideological power of these texts over contemporary (and, for that matter, modern) readers.[5] Yet the ideological force of

---

Studies in Honor of Jess B. Bessinger, Jr., ed. Helen Damico and John Leyerle, 77–114 (Kalamazoo, MI: Medieval Institute Publications, 1993).

3 *Widsith*, ed. Kemp Malone (London: Methuen, 1936); *Beowulf*, ed. Friedrich Klaeber, 3rd ed. (Boston: D.C. Heath, 1950), 867b–874a. See Introduction and chap. 1 above.

4 The heroic code is a literary creation rather than a lived ideology. Nevertheless, it is a problematic rubric because no one poem or text defines it; rather, these values are a constellation of ideas found throughout the wider corpus of Anglo-Saxon literature, especially in poems such as *Beowulf*, *Widsith*, *The Wanderer*, *The Battle of Brunanburh*, and *The Battle of Maldon*. As these poems demonstrate, the heroic mode is oriented toward the Germanic past, and it is necessarily a historical or historicized form of narration. For definitions of the heroic code and its applicability to *The Battle of Maldon*, see G. Clark, 'Heroic Poem,' 57–60; Thomas D. Hill, 'History and Heroic Ethic in *Maldon*,' *Neophilologus* 54 (1970): 291–6; and O'Brien O'Keeffe, 'Heroic Values,' 107–13.

5 Cecily Clark offers a close reading of how the Chronicle's rhetorical stance shifts over time, in 'The Narrative Mode of *The Anglo-Saxon Chronicle* before the Conquest,' in *England before the Conquest: Studies in Primary Sources Presented to Dorothy Whitelock*, ed. Peter Clemoes and Kathleen Hughes, 215–35 (Cambridge: Cambridge University Press, 1971). Jonathan Wilcox compares the pessimistic rhetoric of the Chronicle during the reign of Æthelred with the idealistic mode of *The Battle of Maldon*, in '*The Battle of Maldon* and the *Anglo-Saxon Chronicle*, 979–1016: A Winning Combination,' *Proceedings of the Medieval Association of the Midwest* 3 (1996): 31–50.

Maldon, while no less powerful than that of the Anglo-Saxon Chronicle or Wulfstan's *Sermo Lupi ad Anglos*, is rarely studied as part of the historiographical tradition, being rather confined to the realm of poetry with its attendant designation of 'fiction.' The Battle of Maldon, however, is not fiction; it took place on 10/11 August 991, and its commemoration in a contemporary heroic poem points to its importance not merely as a historical event, but also as a possible tool for both shaping and revealing the cultural identity of Anglo-Saxon England.[6]

Vernacular historiography has long been seen as a lynchpin of early English identity, and scholars have focused most often on a long tenth century, from Alfred to Æthelred, as the site of its genesis.[7] That identity, as

---

Malcolm Godden explores the implications of Wulfstan's *Sermo Lupi ad Anglos* as a contemplation of the Viking problem, in 'Apocalypse and Invasion in Late Anglo-Saxon England,' in *From Anglo-Saxon to Early Middle English: Studies Presented to E.G. Stanley*, ed. Malcolm Godden, Douglas Gray, and Terry Hoad, 130–62 (Oxford: Clarendon, 1994), especially 152–9. The classic essay on Wulfstan's structure and style is Stephanie Hollis, 'The Thematic Structure of the *Sermo Lupi*,' *ASE* 6 (1977): 175–95.

6 The difficulty of the relationship between *The Battle of Maldon* and history (whatever we mean by that term) is evident in the sheer volume of articles dealing with the question. See O.D. Macrae-Gibson, 'How Historical Is *The Battle of Maldon*?' *Medium Ævum* 39 (1970): 89–107; N.F. Blake, 'The Genesis of *The Battle of Maldon*,' *ASE* 7 (1978): 119–29; A.N. Doane, 'Legend, History and Artifice in "The Battle of Maldon",' *Viator* 9 (1978): 39–66; John Scattergood, '*The Battle of Maldon* and History,' in *Literature and Learning in Medieval and Renaissance England: Essays Presented to Fitzroy Pyle*, ed. John Scattergood, 11–24 (Dublin: Irish Academic Press, 1984); Paul Dean, 'History versus Poetry: The Battle of *Maldon*,' *NM* 93 (1992): 99–108; G. Clark, 'Maldon: History, Poetry, and Truth,' in *De Gustibus: Essays for Alain Renoir*, ed. John Miles Foley, 66–84 (New York: Garland, 1992); and Craig R. Davis, 'Cultural Historicity in *The Battle of Maldon*,' *PQ* 78 (1999): 151–69. In the last few decades, scholars seem to have reached a general consensus that although the broad outline of the poem may be accurate, the details and speeches are certainly fictitious interpolations created by the author from either oral tradition, written sources (some of which are now lost), or his own imagination. It should be noted, however, that Frank Stenton found its representation convincing enough as late as the mid-twentieth century; see his oft-cited passage in *Anglo-Saxon England*, 3rd ed. (Oxford: Oxford University Press, 1971), 376–7.

7 For an important discussion of how we understand the people we call Anglo-Saxons, see Susan Reynolds, 'What Do We Mean by "Anglo-Saxon" and "Anglo-Saxons"?' *Journal of British Studies* 24 (1985): 395–414. Sarah Foot examines Alfred's literary program as an attempt to create political unity by blending various tribal histories into a shared Christian/Germanic inheritance; see 'The Making of *Angelcynn*: English Identity before the Norman Conquest,' *TRHS*, 6th ser., 6 (1996): 25–49. Patrick Wormald compares the early emergence of the English nation, and its lasting success as what he calls an 'ideological artefact,' to the relative lack of unity in other early medieval states, in '*Engla Lond*: The Making of an Allegiance,' *Journal of Historical Sociology* 7 (1994): 1–24.

Nicholas Howe has demonstrated most effectively, depends in large part on an image of the Anglo-Saxons as a new Israel, a chosen people of God whose history of conquest and conversion testifies to their worthiness, and this image appears widely throughout Anglo-Saxon literature.[8] From Eusebius to Bede, the history of a people's salvation and their rise to prominence as a nation are one and the same. For these historians, the shape of history is an ongoing, unidirectional progression from sin to redemption to ultimate salvation, and that progress is measured in the historical events that take place among a particular people. The Viking attacks at the turn of the millennium are a moment of crisis for this version of English history, as military defeat and eventual conquest seem to call English worthiness into question. Both the Battle of Maldon and *The Battle of Maldon* play an important role in this literary history, in large part because the poem eschews the providential narrative of sin, punishment, and redemption as an explanatory model for the English defeat.[9] Certainly the telos-driven historical model was current in the early eleventh century, when Wulfstan wrote his *Sermo Lupi ad Anglos* to admonish the English that their sins were the cause of the Viking invasions, and when the Anglo-Saxon Chronicle lamented the loss of the heroic valour that led earlier generations of the Cerdicings to found a nation.[10] As we saw in the previous chapter, however, the teleology of the salvation narrative often finds itself fragmented and disassembled by the traditional forms of Anglo-Saxon verse. And the *Maldon* poet, faced with the task of commemorating a military defeat and the loss of one of the kingdom's highest-ranking nobles, makes the formally and rhetorically significant choice to render his commemoration in heroic verse. This choice has particular consequences for how the resulting poem encourages its readers to think about the battle, its fallen leader, and its historical consequences, in terms of both

8 Nicholas Howe, *Migration and Mythmaking in Anglo-Saxon England* (New Haven: Yale University Press, 1989; repr. Notre Dame: University of Notre Dame Press, 2001).

9 Salvation history was the dominant model in England as well as elsewhere during the early Middle Ages, from Bede's *Historia ecclesiastica gentis Anglorum* onward; see Introduction above.

10 *Sermo Lupi ad Anglos*, in *The Homilies of Wulfstan*, ed. Dorothy Bethurum (Oxford: Clarendon, 1957), 267–75; hereafter *Sermo Lupi*. Later medieval histories of England, particularly those by twelfth century historians from William of Malmesbury to Geoffrey of Monmouth, would take a similar position to explain and justify the domination of the Normans after 1066. See R. William Leckie, Jr, *The Passage of Dominion: Geoffrey of Monmouth and the Periodization of Insular History in the Twelfth Century* (Toronto: University of Toronto Press, 1981); and Michelle R. Warren, *History on the Edge: Excalibur and the Borders of Britain, 1100–1300* (Minneapolis: University of Minnesota Press, 2000).

the historicity of the event itself and its relation to other historical monuments of the Anglo-Saxon tradition. In offering such encouragement, the poem (and its author) refuses the teleology of a linear historical narrative and opts instead for a more ambiguous mode of historical representation. That is not to say that the poem is not Christian; it is produced in a thoroughly Christian context,[11] the Viking enemy is a definitively pagan Other,[12] and the hero dies with a prayer on his lips.[13] Yet this inherent Christianity alone does not shape the poem's understanding of the event as history; its historical consciousness also draws from the fragments of the heroic tradition and the hybridity to which they can give rise. As John Halbrooks puts it, 'the entire poem conveys ideals both of quasi-pagan heroism and Christian self-sacrifice'; and Peter Clemoes sees the poem as 'a branch of the "mixed" state of verse which developed when … the symbolic system was adapted to human existence redefined by Christ's redeeming incarnation and ascension.'[14] Like other contemporary writings such as those of Wulfstan and the Anglo-Saxon Chronicle, *The Battle of Maldon* sees the Viking attacks as significant, but not necessarily as evidence that the country is sliding toward perdition.

A key distinction between historiography based in a salvation narrative and historiography rooted in the heroic tradition is one of temporality; that is, each mode of history imagines a distinctive relationship between the past and the present. Christian salvation history presents time as a progression toward the Day of Judgment, with well-defined boundaries between past and present and a clearly articulated telos of meaning. Historical events within the salvation narrative have meaning primarily in relation to

---

11 Bernard F. Huppé, *Doctrine and Poetry: Augustine's Influence on Old English Poetry* (New York: State University of New York Press, 1959), 236–8; Blake, 'The Battle of Maldon,' *Neophilologus* 49 (1965): 332–45; and Morton W. Bloomfield, 'Beowulf, Byrhtnoth, and the Judgment of God: Trial by Combat in Anglo-Saxon England,' *Speculum* 44 (1969): 545–59.

12 G.C. Britton, 'The Characterization of the Vikings in "The Battle of Maldon",' *N&Q* 210 (1965): 85–7; and Paul E. Szarmach, 'The (Sub-) Genre of *The Battle of Maldon*,' in *The Battle of Maldon: Fiction and Fact*, ed. Janet Cooper, 43–61 (London: Hambledon, 1993).

13 For differing interpretations of this moment, see Bloomfield, 'Patristics and Old English Literature: Notes on Some Poems,' *Comparative Literature* 14 (1962): 36–43; and J.E. Cross, 'Oswald and Byrhtnoth: A Christian Saint and a Hero Who Is Christian,' *ES* 46 (1965): 93–109. John Niles even reads Byrhtnoth's death as a sacrifice of 'vicarious atonement' in 'On Sacrifice and Atonement,' in *Old English Heroic Poems and the Social Life of Texts* (Turnhout: Brepols, 2007), 243–52.

14 John Halbrooks, 'Byrhtnoth's Great-Hearted Mirth, or Praise and Blame in *The Battle of Maldon*,' *PQ* 82 (2003): 235–55 at 239; and Peter Clemoes, *Interactions of Thought and Language in Old English Poetry* (Cambridge: Cambridge University Press, 1995), 409.

the telos of ultimate salvation, and these histories draw on the past only to move their audience toward the primary goal of future redemption. In contrast, the historical sensibility of heroic poetry maintains a strong focus on the interrelation of present and past by taking events and actors as fragments of a whole that is reconstructed through aesthetic mediation. In place of the homogeneous, empty time of salvation history, heroic history offers time filled with the nostalgic, living memory of a past that continually resurfaces in its enduring relevance, however fictively construed, to contemporary life. Heroic history creates a paradoxical vision of the past as both constitutive of and radically separate from the present; yet, as we have seen in the constellations of *The Ruin, Deor, Widsith,* and the Junius poems, this dialectic can be effectively mediated by classical Anglo-Saxon verse like *Maldon,* whose chiastic structure embraces ambiguity and contradiction. Vernacular verse historiography thus offers an alternative method for finding unity between past and present in the otherwise random context of human history. With nostalgia as its primary aesthetic, Anglo-Saxon historical poetry fosters a cultural identity founded not on a common faith in future salvation, but on a shared belief in a glorious past and its continuing significance for the present. Through the poetic medium, the heroic history of a long-lost Germanic homeland finds new life in the present, and nostalgic longing drives the narrative of what it means to be English. *The Battle of Maldon* serves as a nexus for this constellation of nostalgia, aesthetics, history, and ideology.

Understanding the function of nostalgia as an ideological force in this aesthetic context is a fundamental first step in determining the relationship between Anglo-Saxon historical poetry and the world that we assume it represents. For contemporary readers, heroic history served a certain ideological and even emotional purpose; for modern readers, it helps to construct an idea of what those medieval readers and their world were like. The heroic universe generated in *Maldon* and similar poems is a fictional construct, but it is one that bears a particular relationship to the context of tenth century politics: the world that created this heroic universe was one that not only desired but desperately needed to believe in its existence. Svetlana Boym distinguishes between two types of nostalgia, restorative and reflective. Whereas reflective nostalgia focuses on individual memory and meditates on history and the passage of time, restorative nostalgia seeks to reconstruct that history, to restore the lost origin.[15] It is the restorative form of nostalgia that gives birth to a tradition and provides

---

15 Svetlana Boym, *The Future of Nostalgia* (New York: Basic, 2001), 41–55.

the blueprint for a national identity built around the idea of an originary loss – in the case of the Anglo-Saxons, the continental homeland that was lost when they migrated to the island, as Howe has amply demonstrated. The Anglo-Saxons' loss of their original Germanic homeland does not, paradoxically, leave them adrift in a sea of possible identifications; rather, that originary loss provides the condition of possibility for a unitary group identity, and Howe has shown that the poetic tradition invents an ethnic identity, grounded in the very absence of the common homeland the tradition seeks to reconstruct. If *The Battle of Maldon* is an inauthentic witness to the events of 10/11 August 991, then, it is also an important manifestation of the ways in which those events had meaning for a contemporary audience and in which we, as modern readers, are forced to perceive them today.

In this chapter, I want to look at the genealogical relations between a few key texts from the late Anglo-Saxon period that show how the aesthetic form of alliterative verse and the kind of historical understanding it encodes are brought to bear on the representation of contemporary historical events, as opposed to those of myth or legend. In particular, I want to think about how the historical temporality employed by alliterative verse is transformed into an aesthetics of nostalgia, thereby forging a dialectical relation with the past in response to the needs of a particular historical present. *The Battle of Maldon* draws on the aesthetics of nostalgia to glorify a military defeat that was one among many during the period 980–1014. Whereas other contemporary vernacular accounts of this period – most notably the Anglo-Saxon Chronicle and Wulfstan's *Sermo Lupi ad Anglos* – find little to celebrate in the ongoing Viking conflict, *Maldon* envisions the battle not as an ignominious rout, but as a triumph of the heroic spirit of Anglo-Saxon England. As a representation of the event, *Maldon* borrows its historicity from the heroic tradition, in seeking to restore something that has been lost. As a result, the poem's theory of history, and of the role of historiography, takes it in a very different direction from that taken by the telos-oriented theory of history underwriting Wulfstan's work, which draws instead on a 'fall of Britain' tradition articulated by earlier writers such as Gildas, Bede, and Alcuin. When read against one another, these texts give rise to vastly divergent ways of thinking about the past in relation to the present, and of thinking about the historicity of the present in relation to its representation for both present and future audiences. I am not the first person to place these texts in dialogue with one another or to notice their contrasts, but I want to suggest that the commemoration of a contemporary event in heroic verse could be an argument for a particular way of thinking about English history. Rather than imagining themselves halfway down the road to hell, the audience of *The Battle of Maldon* is charged to remember the bravery and honour of their ancestors and to think about how those values might have meaning for their present.

I. Historical Models for Interpreting Pagan-Christian Conflict

A study of the ideology of history in late Anglo-Saxon England must begin with Howe's *Migration and Mythmaking in Anglo-Saxon England*, which outlines the development of the migration myth as an ideological force throughout the Anglo-Saxon period. The shared belief that they were descended from the Angles, Saxons, and Jutes who had first come to the island as mercenaries in the late fifth century, and the mythic memory of that lost Germanic homeland perpetuated through vernacular poetry and prose, functioned to provide a common identity for the Anglo-Saxons who consumed these texts. Howe traces a long historical arc from Gildas through Bede and Alcuin to Wulfstan that uses narratives of foreign attack and invasion to build and reinforce a sense of manifest destiny for the Anglo-Saxons: they hold the island because God, angered by the sinfulness of the Britons, chose them to cross the Channel as pagans, and then sent Augustine of Canterbury to convert them to Christianity in fulfilment of that destiny. Howe links these two things together – the myth of the Germanic homeland and the crossing of the sea as God's chosen people – by means of the figure of the biblical Exodus. He surveys a wide range of Anglo-Saxon texts, from poetry to homilies to law codes, in order to uncover Anglo-Saxon writers drawing explicit parallels between the Anglo-Saxons and the Israelites, and he demonstrates the power of a cultural myth of migration to unify a people with one another and with their history.

Howe's description of the migration myth is compelling, and it has reshaped the way that Anglo-Saxonists think about historical narrative in Anglo-Saxon England. As a cultural myth, the idea of migration combines both Germanic and biblical traditions in much the same way that the Junius poems do, allowing the Anglo-Saxons to see themselves in both the heroes of Germanic legend and the Old Testament patriarchs. Yet the strain of historiography that Howe traces, from Gildas and Bede through Alcuin to Wulfstan, is invested in a particular form of historical understanding that follows the teleological contours of the salvation narrative. This is hardly surprising; in developing the migration myth, Anglo-Saxon writers such as Bede turned first to the structures of salvation history to set the events of the *adventus Saxonum* in a larger framework of meaning.

The theoretical stakes of this historical mode are overwhelmingly teleological, and are firmly rooted in a vision of the future in which the otherwise random events of human history make sense in terms of a larger (and often incomprehensible) framework.[16] This model asserts the absolute alterity of a past that leads to, but is differentiated from, the present; both find meaning as part of a single, unchanging historical design, and both indicate the direction future events will take.[17] From Eusebius on, Christian historians charted the teleological progression of a people toward salvation, but the model could serve as a powerful explanatory force for current as well as past events. Because history reveals God's hand working on earth, tribulations such as warfare, famine, and plague can quite easily be understood as God's punishment of a people in need of correction if they are to achieve ultimate salvation.

Interpreting historical calamity as divine retribution is hardly new to Christian historiography; Paulus Orosius, whose *Historiarum aduersum paganos libri VII* was an important source for both Gildas and Bede, was prompted by Augustine to write with the explicit intention of countering those who claimed that the barbarian incursions of the early fifth century were a punishment of Rome for abandoning pagan deities in favour of the Christian God.[18] Orosius followed Augustine's dictum that divine providence 'solet corruptos hominum mores bellis emendare atque conterere itemque uitam mortalium iustam atque laudabilem talibus adflictionibus exercere,'[19] seeing universal history as evidence of a specifically Christian

---

16 Hayden White writes, 'Since no given set or sequence of real events is intrinsically tragic, comic, farcical, and so on, but can be constructed as such only by the imposition of the structure of a given story type on the events, it is the choice of the story type and its imposition upon the events that endow them with meaning' (*The Content of the Form: Narrative Discourse and Historical Representation* [Baltimore: Johns Hopkins University Press, 1987], 44).

17 The similarity to typology is not insignificant here; typology is also a formal way of understanding the relationship between past and present, as outlined in chap. 2 above.

18 *Pauli Orosii Historiarum aduersum paganos libri VII*, ed. Karl Zangemeister, CSEL 5 (Vienna, 1882). All subsequent quotations are taken from this edition. For a translation, see *Seven Books of History against the Pagans: The Apology of Paulus Orosius*, trans. Irving Woodworth Raymond (New York: Columbia University Press, 1936). All translations of Orosius are taken from this edition. On Orosius's theology of history, see Hans-Werner Goetz, *Die Geschichtstheologie des Orosius* (Darmstadt: Wissenschaftliche Buchgesellschaft, 1980), especially chaps 1–2. On Augustine's request, see Orosius, 1.Prol.

19 *Sancti Aurelii Augustini De Ciuitate Dei libri I–X*, ed. Bernard Dombart and Alphons Kalb, CCSL 47 (Turnhout: Brepols, 1955), 1.1.25–7. 'often corrects and destroys the corrupt ways of men by wars, and tests the righteous and praiseworthy by such afflictions of this mortal life.' All translations are taken from Augustine, *The City of God against the Pagans*, ed. and trans. R.W. Dyson (Cambridge: Cambridge University Press, 1998).

God's hand working among humanity. Moreover, these hardships are sent by God as a test, 'probatamque uel in meliora transferre uel in his adhuc terris·propter usus alios detinere';[20] Orosius himself writes that 'iure ab initio hominis per bona malaque alternantia, exerceri hunc mundum sentit quisquis per se atque in se humanum genus uidet.'[21] From examples of war, famine, plague, and devastation spanning human history up to the fall of Rome, Orosius demonstrates that life under pagan gods was just as harsh as life under Christ, but with no promise of eventual salvation. Orosius's widespread popularity is evidenced by some 245 manuscripts and fragments still extant,[22] as well as by the influence of his work on centuries of writers who followed him. His influence in England was equally strong throughout the Anglo-Saxon period; and in the late ninth century, Alfred considered Orosius's *Historia aduersum paganos* among the 'books most necessary for all to know' in his great program of vernacular translation.[23]

Orosius's *Historia aduersum paganos* covers world history up to his present time, and it paints a picture of the pagan world as rife with unnatural behaviours, incest, cannibalism, parricide, mariticide, and crossdressing. The world was in a state of constant warfare: 'quae ne sic saltem sese, ut commoti maris fluctus quamuis molibus magnis sequuntur, sed undique diuersis causis uocabulis formis malisque excitata coaceruataque concurrunt.'[24] Orosius contrasts the lives of the pagans in former ages, who never knew a peaceful existence, with those of his fellow Romans,

---

20 Augustine, *Civitate Dei*, 1.1.27–9. 'either conveying them to a better world when they have been proved, or detaining them still on this earth for further service.'
21 Orosius, *Historia*, 1.1.10. 'Everyone who sees mankind reflected through himself and in himself perceives that this world has been disciplined since the creation of man by alternating periods of good and bad times.'
22 Janet M. Bately and D.J.A. Ross, 'A Check List of Manuscripts of Orosius "Historiarum adversum paganos libri septem",' *Scriptorium* 15 (1961): 329–34. Bately and Ross write: 'Conceived as a religious and political tract for the times the History against the Pagans came to enjoy a lasting and widespread popularity because, despite its ephemeral purpose, it contained all the essential facts of universal history in a brief and readable form, which saved the student much hunting in the numerous volumes of Livy or Pompeius Trogus; and at the same time its Christian philosophy of history was in accord with the medieval outlook. It became, therefore, the standard universal history text of the Middle Ages and no school, college or monastic library of any pretensions could afford to lack a copy' (329).
23 For the Old English translation of Orosius, see *The Old English Orosius*, ed. Bately, EETS, s.s., 6 (London: Oxford University Press, 1980).
24 5.24.10. 'Moreover, these wars do not follow one another like the stormy waves of the sea, however great their force may be, but these waves of strife, stirred up by various causes, pretexts, forms, and evils arising on all sides and heaped together into a mass, dash upon one another.'

who had tasted peace and could gain it again: 'atque utinam ipsum depulsorem huius uel modicae inquietudinis precarentur, cuius munere hanc ignoratam aliis temporibus iugitatem pacis habuerunt.'[25] In addition to demonstrating the superiority of the Christian God over pagan gods, then, Orosius offers a corollary to the theory of suffering as God's punishment for sin: prayer and repentance can bring about the relief of suffering, if God wills it. Most important, for Orosius universal history demonstrates that the conditions of human life have been steadily improving, especially since the advent of Christ; this progressive notion of history implies that the future, in which salvation holds out its promise, will be better than the past. Put together, these elements added up to a compelling philosophy of history for early medieval Christians facing pagan incursions.

Orosius's historiographical model, and in particular its power to explain the meaning of catastrophic events and to offer hope by means of the promise of future salvation, was particularly well suited to the political climate of an island under invasion by a conquering force. Robert Hanning traces the development of a 'fall of Britain' tradition that follows a cyclical course of invasion, conquest, and depravity; one group comes to inhabit the island through God's grace, only to lose their right to dominion through sinfulness, when God sends another group of people to supplant them as punishment. These cycles play themselves out through the *adventus Saxonum* and the Norman Conquest, and they are invoked by historians throughout the Middle Ages.[26] The earliest instance of the 'fall of Britain' tradition is recounted in the sixth century *De excidio Britanniae* of Gildas, which would in turn serve Bede as a source for the history of pre-Conversion England.[27]

---

25 1.21.19. 'If only they would pray to Him who can end this period of unrest, trifling though it be, and to Whom they owe this continued peace which was unknown to other ages!'

26 See Robert W. Hanning, *The Vision of History in Early Britain: From Gildas to Geoffrey of Monmouth* (New York: Columbia University Press, 1966); for its particular Anglo-Saxon deployments in times of national crisis, see Howe, *Migration and Mythmaking*, 8–71. This tradition also had important implications for how British history was perceived by later medieval historians; see Leckie, *Passage of Dominion*.

27 *The Ruin of Britain and Other Works*, ed. and trans. Michael Winterbottom (London: Phillimore, 1978); all quotations and translations are taken from this edition. On Gildas's use of Orosius, see Neil Wright, 'Did Gildas Read Orosius?' *Cambridge Medieval Celtic Studies* 9 (1985): 31–42; repr. in *History and Literature in Late Antiquity and the Early Medieval West: Studies in Intertextuality* (Aldershot: Variorum, 1995), chap. 4. On Bede's debt to Gildas, see 'Historical Introduction,' in *Bede's Ecclesiastical History of the English People*, ed. and trans. Bertram Colgrave and R.A.B. Mynors (Oxford: Clarendon, 1969), xxxi (hereafter *HE*; all quotations and translations are taken from this edition); and Molly Miller, 'Bede's Use of Gildas,' *EHR* 90 (1975): 241–61.

Gildas, well trained in Roman rhetoric,[28] would have found a clear parallel for the onslaught of the pagan Anglo-Saxons in the barbarian hordes who sacked Rome and gave Orosius occasion to write his *Historia aduersum paganos*. In fact, his text is less historical than polemical;[29] he attributes the loss of British dominion to a general turning away from Christian orthodoxy. Their depravity indicates their unworthiness to rule; as N.J. Higham comments, 'the superior morality of the Romans, as God's designated rulers of the world, was sufficient to enable them, on occasion, to protect Britain, despite the continuing collapse of the relationship between the Britons and God.'[30] For Gildas, the Britons' lack of faith, rather than their lack of military readiness, explains their inability to fend off the pagan Saxon invaders from overseas, and he spends far more time castigating his fellow Britons than he does describing the activities of the Saxons. In short, 'the actions of virtuous Romans were adequate to drive out the barbarians but the sins of the Britons were such that, whenever the Romans departed, they were incapable, without assistance, of effective resistance.'[31] The bulk of Gildas's treatise points to the specific flaws of church and state that have earned this divine retribution. Significantly, however, a providential model of history offers Gildas an explanation not only of why disasters occur, but also of what people can do to prevent them, and Gildas urges the Britons to repent of their sins in hopes of staving off the Saxon incursions.[32]

Gildas's precedents come from biblical narrative itself. The Old Testament offers him numerous examples of those who break faith with God being punished, and the New Testament leaves him caught between God's mercy and God's judgment; he notes that 'peculiari ex omnibus nationibus populo ... dominus non pepercit, cum a recto tramite deviarint, quid tali huius atramento aetatis facturus est?'[33] Britain's history, he claims,

---

28 See Michael Lapidge, 'Gildas' Education and the Latin Culture of Sub-Roman Britain,' in *Gildas: New Approaches*, ed. Michael Lapidge and David Dumville, 27–50 (Woodbridge: Boydell, 1984).

29 On the problem of historical verisimilitude in Gildas's treatise, see E.A. Thompson, 'Gildas and the History of Britain,' *Britannia* 10 (1979): 203–26, and 'Gildas and the History of Britain: Corrigenda,' *Britannia* 11 (1980): 344; and Patrick Sims-Williams, 'Gildas and the Anglo-Saxons,' *Cambridge Medieval Celtic Studies* 6 (1983): 1–30.

30 N.J. Higham, *The English Conquest: Gildas and Britain in the Fifth Century* (Manchester: Manchester University Press, 1994), 22–3.

31 Higham, *English Conquest*, 23.

32 See, for example, Winterbottom's Preface in *Ruin of Britain*, 5–9.

33 *De Excidio* 1.13. 'When they strayed from the right track the Lord did not spare a people that was peculiarly his own among all nations ... What then will he do with this great black blot on *our* generation?' (emphasis in original).

is saturated with rebellion against proper authority, both temporal and divine, and the island's leaders have turned against both God and Rome. As punishment for this rebelliousness God first sent the Scots and Picts, and then the Saxons.[34] Although the Britons finally defeated the Saxons at Badon Hill, the country has not recovered its former glory: 'Sed ne nunc quidem, ut antea, civitates patriae inhabitantur; sed desertae dirutaeque hactenus squalent, cessantibus licet externis bellis, sed non civilibus.'[35] From the history he has cited, both biblical and insular, Gildas draws the lesson that such decadence will earn further punishment from God and likens himself to the prophets 'qui os quodam modo dei organumque spiritus sancti, mortalibus prohibentes mala, bonis faventes extitere.'[36] His treatise is a complaint and a prophecy, recounting events from the past in the hope that they will serve as a warning to his contemporaries to amend their corruption.

The historical outcome, however, is what Gildas predicts, rather than what he hopes. The Saxons ultimately drive the remaining Britons out of what is now England, taking dominion for themselves. Whereas Gildas sees such developments as God's punishment of the Britons, however, Bede turns the model on its head and interprets them instead as God's sanction of the Anglo-Saxons as replacements for the dissolute Britons. The Anglo-Saxons' memory of their pagan past complicated their identity as Christians, and Howe points out that Bede's use of the migration myth, coupled with Gildas's view of the Anglo-Saxons as a punishment sent by God, allows Bede to reconstrue the *adventus Saxonum* as God's designation of a chosen people.[37] According to Bede, after the Roman legions pulled out, the Britons were unable to defend themselves against the Irish and the Picts from the west and north, so they called on Saxon mercenaries to help them repel the Celtic invaders. These Saxons and their continental neighbors, the Angles and Jutes, subsequently settled in Britain, driving the Britons into Wales and establishing the future Anglo-Saxon England.[38] Like Gildas, Bede attributes this loss of dominion to the depravity of the Britons:

---

34 *De Excidio* 14 and 22–4.
35 *De Excidio* 26.2. 'But the cities of our land are not populated even now as they once were; right to the present they are deserted, in ruins and unkempt. External wars may have stopped, but not civil ones.'
36 *De Excidio* 37.3. 'who were in a sense the mouth of God and the instrument of the holy spirit, favouring the good and forbidding men the bad' (translation adapted from Winterbottom).
37 Howe, *Migration and Mythmaking*, 48–71.
38 *HE* 1.12–16.

Cessante autem uastatione hostili, tantis frugum copiis insula quantas nulla retro aetas meminit, affluere coepit, cum quibus et luxuria crescere et hanc continuo omnium lues scelerum comitari adcelerauit, crudelitas praecipue et odium ueritatis amorque mendacii, ita ut, si quis eorum mitior et ueritati aliquatenus propior uideretur, in hunc quasi Brittaniae subuersorem omnium odia telaque sine respectu contorquerentur. Et non solum haec saeculares uiri sed etiam ipse grex Domini eiusque pastores egerunt, ebrietati animositati litigio contentioni inuidiae ceterisque huiusmodi facinoribus sua colla, abiecto leui iugo Christi, subdentes. Interea subito corruptae mentis homines acerua pestis corripuit, quae in breui tantam eius multitudinem strauit, ut ne sepeliendis quidem mortuis uiui sufficerent; sed ne morte quidem suorum nec timore mortis hi, qui supererant, a morte animae, qua peccando sternebantur, reuocari poterant. Vnde non multo post acrior gentem peccatricem ultio diri sceleris secuta est ... Quod Domini nutu dispositum esse constat, ut ueniret contra inprobos malum, sicut euidentius rerum exitus probauit.[39]

The connection between the Britons' dissipation and the subsequent plague and conquest is explicit: for Bede, 'events clearly showed' that their suffering was 'ordained by God' as a punishment for their sins. If drunkenness, strife, cruelty, mendacity, and heresy were not quite enough to justify the Saxon conquest, an even worse crime of the Britons is their failure to convert the pagan Anglo-Saxons: 'Qui inter alia inenarrabilium scelerum facta, quae historicus eorum Gildas flebili sermone describit, et hoc addebant, ut numquam genti Saxonum siue Anglorum, secum Brittaniam incolenti, uerbum fidei praedicando committerent. Sed non tamen diuina

---

39 *HE* 1.14. 'After the enemy's depredations had ceased, there was so great an abundance of corn in the island as had never before been known. With this affluence came an increase of luxury, followed by every kind of foul crime; in particular, cruelty and hatred of the truth and love of lying increased so that if anyone appeared to be milder than the rest and somewhat more inclined to the truth, the rest, without consideration, rained execrations and missiles upon him as if he had been an enemy of Britain. Not only were laymen guilty of these offences but even the Lord's own flock and their pastors. They cast off Christ's easy yoke and thrust their necks under the burden of drunkenness, hatred, quarrelling, strife, and envy and other similar crimes. In the meantime a virulent plague suddenly fell upon these corrupt people which quickly laid low so large a number that there were not enough people left alive to bury the dead. Yet those who survived could not be awakened from the spiritual death which their sins had brought upon them either by the death of their kinsmen or by fear of their own death. For this reason a still more terrible retribution soon afterwards overtook this sinful people for their fearful crimes ... As events plainly showed, this was ordained by the will of God so that evil might fall upon those miscreants.'

pietas plebem suam, quam praesciuit, deseruit; quin multo digniores genti memoratae praecones ueritatis, per quos crederet, destinauit.'[40] In his analysis, Bede deftly converts the pagan invaders into 'the people whom [God] foreknew,' and he introduces Augustine of Canterbury, chief among the 'much worthier heralds of the truth,' in the very next paragraph. The Angles and Saxons whose rapacious conquest Gildas lamented have now become a new chosen people of God and the rightful inheritors of the island's considerable bounty.

If the ideology of dominion transmitted from Orosius and Gildas through Bede justified the victory of the pagan Anglo-Saxons, it is not surprising to see those same Anglo-Saxons, now Christian, turn once again to salvation history in the face of a similar pagan threat from across the waves. When a group of Norse raiders sacked Lindisfarne in 793, initiating a century of raiding in England, Alcuin responded from Charlemagne's court with letters and a poem reflecting this historiographic inheritance. In a letter to Æthelred of Northumbria, Alcuin warns:

Atentius considerate, fratres, et diligentissime perspicite ne forte hoc inconsuetum et inauditum malum aliqua inauditi mali consuetudine promereretur. Non dico quod fornicationis peccata prius non essent in populo, sed a diebus Ælfwaldi regis fornicationes, adulteria, et incestus inundauerunt super terram, ita ut absque omni uerecundia etiam et in ancillis Deo dicatis hec peccata perpetrabantur. Quid dicam de auaritia, rapinis, et uiolentis iudiciis, dum luce clarius constat quantum ubique hec crimina succreuerunt et populus testatur spoliatus?[41]

---

40 *HE* 1.22. 'To other unspeakable crimes, which Gildas their own historian describes in doleful words, was added this crime, that they never preached the faith to the Saxons or Angles who inhabited Britain with them. Nevertheless God in His goodness did not reject the people whom He foreknew, but He had appointed much worthier heralds of the truth to bring this people to the faith.'

41 *Two Alcuin Letter-Books*, ed. Colin Chase (Toronto: PIMS, 1975), 53–6 at 54. 'Consider carefully, brothers, and examine diligently, lest perchance this unaccustomed and unheard-of evil were merited by some unheard-of evil practice. I do not say that formerly there were no sins of fornication among the people. But from the days of King Ælfwold fornications, adulteries and incest have poured over the land, so that these sins have been committed without any shame and even against the handmaids dedicated to God. What may I say about avarice, robbery, violent judgments? – when it is clearer than day how much these crimes have increased everywhere, and a despoiled people testifies to it' (*English Historical Documents, c. 500–1042*, ed. and trans. Dorothy Whitelock, EHD 1, 2nd ed. [London: Eyre Methuen, 1979], 843).

Like both Gildas and Bede, Alcuin reads the devastation of Lindisfarne as a punishment for sin, and admonishes the brothers to be on their guard against further cause for punishment. Like Gildas, Alcuin explicitly acknowledges history as a source for this explanation: 'Qui sanctas legit scripturas et ueteres reuoluit historias et seculi considerat euentum, inueniet pro huiusmodi peccatis reges regna et populos patriam perdidisse.'[42] For sins like these, the Britons lost dominion of the island, and their fate presages a similar one for unrepentant Anglo-Saxons as well. Alcuin's letters to Æthelheard, archbishop of Canterbury, to the monks of Wearmouth and Jarrow, and to the bishop and monks of Lindisfarne repeat and reinforce this concern; Colin Chase notes that 'it recurs constantly, not only in the letters discussed above, but also in those which do not refer to the destruction of Lindisfarne.'[43] Alcuin's historical model, adopted from Gildas, provides solutions as well as explanations; like his sixth century precursor, he urges his readers to offer prayers for their sins to prevent God's wrath from striking again in Viking form.

In addition to these letters, however, Alcuin historicizes the event, and its impact on Anglo-Saxon historical consciousness, in verse. His poem on the sack of Lindisfarne both commemorates the event and places it in the context of universal history. In so treating it, Alcuin emphasizes the historical relation between the suffering caused by the Vikings at Lindisfarne and the suffering caused by other enemies at other times and places throughout history; the sack of Lindisfarne is a particular example of a universal principle that illustrates the causality of sin and suffering. After surveying the collapse of great peoples and kingdoms through ancient and biblical history, much as Orosius does, Alcuin ends with an admonition:

Si quid displicuit Christo iam cuncta videnti,
    Moribus in vestris corrigite hoc citius,
Ut pius egregium conservet pastor ovile,
    Ne rapidis capiat hoc lupus insidiis.
Non est quippe deus poenis culpandus in istis,
    Sed nostra in melius vita ferenda cito,

---

42 Chase, *Alcuin Letter-Books*, 54. 'Whoever reads the Holy Scriptures and ponders ancient histories and considers the fortune of the world will find that for sins of this kind kings lost kingdoms and peoples their country' (Whitelock, *EHD*, 843).
43 Chase, *Alcuin Letter-Books*, 6; for the letters to Æthelheard, to the monks of Wearmouth and Jarrow, and to the bishop and monks of Lindisfarne, see 71–6, 44–50, and 50–2.

Et pia flectenda est precibus clementia nostris,
Quatenus a nobis transferat ipse plagas:
Atque suis clemens praestet solacia servis,
    Tempora concedens prospera cuncta quibus,
Hymnidicas laeta laudes ut mente canamus
Celsithroni cuncti semper ubique simul …[44]

Once again, human suffering is linked causally to human sin; tribulations are sent to test the faithful, and if the faithful prove worthy by amending their behaviour, then they will be rewarded with peace and prosperity in this life or, failing that, with salvation in heaven. In the poem, as well as in the letters, Alcuin reads the Viking attack as a judgment on the Christian faithful (or faithless), and his writings historicize the event by locating it within the teleology of salvation history. The cyclical nature of this teleology means that by writing about historical tragedy, an author like Orosius, Gildas, Bede, or Alcuin can urge his readers to mend their ways of life and conform to religious orthodoxy. Witness Bede: 'Siue enim historia de bonis bona referat, ad imitandum bonum auditor sollicitus instigatur; seu mala commemoret de prauis, nihilominus religiosus ac pius auditor siue lector deuitando quod noxium est ac peruersum, ipse sollertius ad exsequenda ea quae bona ac Deo digna esse cognouerit, accenditur.'[45] Knowing about the past can help to predict the future because of the patterns that recur; sin always leads to suffering that can be remedied only through repentance, which leads to ultimate salvation. Coupled with the generally progressive notion of Christian history, these recurring patterns move humanity steadily toward

---

44 Ernst Dümmler, ed., *Poetae Latini aevi Carolini*, vol. 1, MGH, Poetarum Latinorum medii aevi, 1 (Berlin, 1881), 229–35 at 235. 'If anything in your behaviour displeased Christ / who sees all things, correct it swiftly, / so that the pious shepherd may save the excellent fold / and the wolf not capture it by his swift snares. / For God is not to be blamed for these our punishments, / but our lives should swiftly be improved / and our prayers should appeal to His kindly mercy, / so that He take tribulation away from us, / and grant solace in His clemency to His slaves, / bestowing prosperity at all times upon them, / that with joyous minds we may all sing hymns in praise / of Him who is enthroned on high everywhere at once' (from Peter Godman, ed. and trans., *Poetry of the Carolingian Renaissance* [Norman: University of Oklahoma Press, 1985], 127–39 at 137–9).

45 *HE*, Preface. 'Should history tell of good men and their good estate, the thoughtful listener is spurred on to imitate the good; should it record the evil ends of wicked men, no less effectually the devout and earnest listener or reader is kindled to eschew what is harmful and perverse, and himself with greater care pursue those things which he has learned to be good and pleasing in the sight of God.'

salvation, by offering examples from the past as moments that are similar to, but crucially distinct from, the present. Alcuin's letters and poem thus condense and explicate the tradition inherited from Bede, Orosius, and especially Gildas, and they do so explicitly to help his readers cope with an external threat to the integrity of the devastated monastic communities.

When faced with military threats from the outside, then, English writers frequently turned to Orosius's historical model, written initially to respond to the fall of Rome, to offer both explanations and remedies. As a discourse of history that emerges both at moments of crisis (in Orosius, Gildas, and Alcuin) and in times of more deliberate reflection (in Bede), it embodies what Howe calls a 'curious blend of eschatology and history' that would prove eminently useful for capturing the anxious, fearful days of the late Viking Age in England.[46] This mode of historical understanding is not without its own nostalgia, either; it embodies Boym's reflective nostalgia, meditating on the differences, in a qualitative sense, between then and now. More important, however, it links human action, and the adherence to certain standards of behaviour, with the outcome of historical events. As these writers clearly believed, Christian virtue could help to protect a people from temporal affliction. This belief was shared by Archbishop Wulfstan in the late tenth and early eleventh centuries, when England faced not the seasonal Viking raids of Alcuin's day, but a full-fledged invasion that once again threatened to overturn the dominion of the island. In Gildas's Britons, Wulfstan would have recognized kindred spirits to his own flock, and he would have shuddered at the fate that awaited them. From Gildas to Wulfstan, 'history repeats itself – or threatens to repeat itself – because God works through the same pattern: the island must be cleansed of its sinful inhabitants by heathen outsiders.'[47] The presence of foreign invaders indicates that the English have strayed from their path to salvation, and they must return to it in order for history to resume its progress.

II. The 'Fall of Britain' and the Viking Challenge in England

When Viking attacks on England resumed in 980, after a hiatus of nearly a century, they were of a very different sort from the earlier incursions, and they lasted for more than three decades with little successful response from the English leadership. Æthelred's reign is therefore often portrayed

---

46 Howe, *Migration and Mythmaking*, 17.
47 Howe, *Migration and Mythmaking*, 12.

as Anglo-Saxon England's darkest hour,[48] and this was the situation that prompted Archbishop Wulfstan of York to compose, among other things, the famous *Sermo Lupi ad Anglos*.[49] Patrick Wormald comments that Wulfstan's life's work was to bring the English people back to the law of God through the law of the king, an ideology that radically shifted the relationship between law and religion: 'Wulfstan becomes more than a preacher of genius who drafted laws too. He was the new English kingdom's main exponent of the Biblical ideal that God's People be ruled in accordance with His will: the pre-eminent ideal of Charlemagne's kingship.'[50] This fusion of faith and statecraft has long been recognized as fundamental to all Wulfstan's work.[51] As an archbishop and trusted royal adviser to both Æthelred and Cnut, Wulfstan had ample opportunity to link the affairs of state to an ecclesiastical worldview, and he took an active role in promoting religious values through political administration. His prolific composition of both homilies and law codes offered multiple venues for forwarding this agenda, and his pastoral leadership was effective enough to sustain him as a prominent figure of national importance on both sides of the Danish conquest.[52] In all his writings, Wulfstan is clear about the

---

48 This view has been challenged by both Simon Keynes, 'The Declining Reputation of King Æthelred the Unready,' in *Ethelred the Unready: Papers from the Millenary Conference*, ed. David Hill, 227–53 (Oxford: British Archaeological Reports, 1978), and *The Diplomas of King Æthelred 'The Unready', 978–1016: A Study in Their Use as Historical Evidence* (Cambridge: Cambridge University Press, 1980); and Pauline Stafford, 'The Reign of Æthelred II: A Study in the Limitations on Royal Policy and Action,' in Hill, *Ethelred the Unready*, 15–46, and *Unification and Conquest: A Political and Social History of England in the Tenth and Eleventh Centuries* (London: Edward Arnold, 1989).

49 The dating of the *Sermo Lupi* has been the subject of much debate; the date of 1014 comes from the rubric introducing the sermon in London, British Library, Cotton Nero A. i: 'SERMO LUPI AD ANGLOS QUANDO DANI MAXIME PERSECUTI SUNT EOS, QUOD FUIT ANNO MILLESIMO .XIIII. AB INCARNATIONE DOMINI NOSTRI IESU CRISTI.' See Wilcox, 'Wulfstan's *Sermo Lupi ad Anglos* as Political Performance: 16 February 1014 and Beyond,' in Townend, *Wulfstan*, 375–96. Godden argues for an earlier date for the sermon in 'Apocalypse and Invasion.' Despite disagreements about the specific date, there is scholarly consensus that the sermon is very much a response to the contemporary situation of Viking attacks and invasion.

50 Wormald, *The Making of English Law: King Alfred to the Twelfth Century*, vol. 1, *Legislation and Its Limits* (Oxford: Blackwell, 1999), 27. On Wulfstan's works in the context of his role as lawmaker, see pp. 449–65.

51 For the definitive treatment, see Whitelock, 'Archbishop Wulfstan, Homilist and Statesman,' *TRHS*, 4th ser., 24 (1942): 25–45.

52 On Wulfstan's influence in late Anglo-Saxon England, see Milton McC. Gatch, *Preaching and Theology in Anglo-Saxon England: Ælfric and Wulfstan* (Toronto:

relationship between Christian virtue and national prosperity: a nation where the people are virtuous, from king to common man, prospers, and a nation that admits of depravity founders.

It is no surprise, then, to see Wulfstan making liberal use of the historical model that so appealed to Gildas and Alcuin as he turns his pen to the task of understanding the continuing devastation wrought by the Vikings on England. He combines a keen awareness of the suffering caused by current events with a traditional concern for the souls of his flock, and the two are linked in the belief that the Viking attacks are God's punishment for the sins of the English. Hence, if the English repent, the attacks will cease; bodies and souls alike will be saved. Wulfstan looks to writers like Alcuin and Abbo of Saint-Germain-des-Prés as precedents for how to think about Viking attacks in literary terms.[53] Abbo's poem on the Siege of Paris, the *Bella Parisiacae urbis*, was written to commemorate the victory of the Parisians over the Vikings, who sailed up the Seine in 885 and were eventually warded off through prayers to St Germain and other saints who came to the city's defence.[54] Abbo writes explicitly for the sake of 'mansuri aliarum tutoribus urbium exempli,'[55] and like Alcuin, he attributes the attacks to vice among the Parisians, namely arrogance, lust, and a taste for fine clothes. Wulfstan knew Alcuin's work, and it is possible that he knew Abbo's popular poem as well.[56] Certainly these writings on Viking attack show a unity of purpose

University of Toronto Press, 1977); and Joyce Hill, 'The Benedictine Reform and Beyond,' in *A Companion to Anglo-Saxon Literature*, ed. Phillip Pulsiano and Elaine Treharne, 151–69 (Oxford: Blackwell, 2001).

53 On Wulfstan's familiarity with Alcuin, see Bethurum, *Homilies of Wulfstan*, 98–101; and Neil Ker, 'The Handwriting of Archbishop Wulfstan,' in Clemoes and Hughes, *England before the Conquest*, 315–31 at 326–7. London, British Library, Cotton Vespasian A. xiv, believed to have been prepared at Wulfstan's request, contains a number of Alcuin's letters on the sack of Lindisfarne; see Chase, *Alcuin Letter-Books*, 39–43, 44–50, 50–2, 53–6, and 71–6; see also Gareth Mann, 'The Development of Wulfstan's Alcuin Manuscript,' in Townend, *Wulfstan*, 235–78.

54 On Abbo's influence, see J.E. Cross and Alan Brown, 'The Literary Impetus for Wulfstan's *Sermo Lupi*,' *Leeds Studies in English*, n.s., 20 (1989): 271–91. The *Bella Parisiacae urbis* was certainly known in tenth century England, but whether Wulfstan actually read it is unclear. See Patrizia Lendinara, 'The Third Book of the *Bella Parisiacae urbis* by Abbo of Saint-Germain-des-Prés and Its Old English Gloss,' *ASE* 15 (1986): 73–89 at 73 n3.

55 'Dilecto fratri Gozlino,' in *Abbon: Le Siège de Paris par les Normands*, ed. and trans. Henri Waquet (Paris: Société d'édition 'Les Belles Lettres,' 1942), §2. 'a lasting example to those who needed to defend other cities' (translation adapted from Waquet).

56 Wulfstan's knowledge of Gildas, whom he references at the end of the *Sermo Lupi*, likely comes via Alcuin's letters; see, for example, Dorothy Whitelock, 'Two Notes on

in explaining foreign incursions as the wages of sin – Paul Szarmach has even called them a (sub)-genre[57] – and their example shapes Wulfstan's explanation of the current Viking conflict. The *Sermo Lupi* drives its message home with a galloping rhythm and mnemonic alliteration in Wulfstan's distinctive style.[58] His reliance on rhythm and alliteration has frequently prompted comparisons with the poetic tradition; Andy Orchard has shown how his compositional style parallels oral traditional composition, and a large part of Wulfstan's rhetorical effectiveness is already embedded in these stylistic choices.[59] For an oral audience, the rhythm and the alliteration cue emphasis on important words and concepts, and it is abundantly clear, both stylistically and thematically, which words are the important ones in the *Sermo Lupi*: 'Ne dohte hit nu lange inne ne ute, ac wæs here 7 hunger, bryne 7 blodgyte, on gewelhwylcan ende oft 7 gelome. And us stalu 7 cwalu, stric 7 steorfa, orfcwealm 7 uncoþu, hol 7 hete 7 rypera reaflac derede swyþe þearle.'[60] Alliteration, and even rhyme with 'stalu 7 cwalu,' connect and emphasize a lengthy list of sins that function almost as appositives to one another, thereby reinforcing the didactic tone of the sermon; the aesthetic effect is one of being overwhelmed by the sheer quantity and variety of sins practised by the English. Wulfstan returns again and again to this technique, each time adding to the burden of sinfulness borne by both the Anglo-Saxons and his listening (or reading) audience:

> Wearð þes þeodscipe, swa hit þincan mæg, swyþe forsyngod þurh mænig-
> fealde synna 7 þurh fela misdæda: þurh morðdæda 7 þurh mandæda, þurh
> gitsunga 7 þurh gifernessa, þurh stala 7 þurh strudunga, þurh mannsylena 7

Ælfric and Wulfstan,' *MLR* 38 (1943): 122–6 at 125–6. Howe credits Wulfstan with a fuller knowledge of Gildas, although it can't be proved; see *Migration and Myth-making*, 20–4.

57 Szarmach, '(Sub-)Genre,' 44. The attacking Vikings provide a pagan 'other' to support the self-identification of Christians both in individual polities and as part of a larger Christendom.

58 On Wulfstan's unique style, see Karl Jost, 'Einige Wulfstantexte und ihre Quellen,' *Anglia* 56 (1932), 265–315; Angus McIntosh, 'Wulfstan's Prose,' Sir Israel Gollancz Memorial Lecture 1948, *PBA* 35 (1949): 109–42; and Bethurum, *Homilies*, 24–49 and 87–98.

59 A.P.McD. Orchard, 'Crying Wolf: Oral Style and the *Sermones Lupi*,' *ASE* 21 (1992): 239–64.

60 *Sermo Lupi*, lines 55–9. 'For a long time now nothing has prospered either here or elsewhere, but there has been war and hunger, burning and bloodshed in every region again and again. And stealing and slaughter, plague and pestilence, murrain and disease, calumny and malice and rapine plunder have injured us very gravely.' All quotations are taken from Bethurum, *Homilies*, and all translations are my own.

þurh hæþene unsida, þurh swicdomas 7 þurh searacræftas, þurh lahbrycas 7 þurh æwswicas, þurh mægræsas 7 þurh manslyhtas, þurh hadbrycas 7 þurh æwbrycas, þurh siblegeru 7 þurh mistlice forligru. And eac syndan wide, swa we ær cwædan, þurh aðbricas 7 þurh wedbrycas 7 þurh mistlice leasunga forloren 7 forlogen ma þonne scolde.[61]

Following models in Gildas and Alcuin, Wulfstan explicates the relationship between these sins and the Viking incursions as directly causal. Because of these numerous and varied crimes, God has not only sent the Vikings to harry England, but also granted them victory, much to Wulfstan's dismay:

Ful earhlice laga 7 scandlice nydgyld þurh Godes yrre us syn gemæne, understande se þe cunne, 7 fela ungelimpa gelimpð þysse þeode oft 7 gelome. Ne dohte hit nu lange inne ne ute, ac wæs here 7 hete on gewelhwilcan ende oft 7 gelome, 7 Engle nu lange eal sigelease 7 to swyþe geyrgde þurh Godes yrre, 7 flotmen swa strange þurh Godes þafunge þæt oft on gefeohte an feseð tyne 7 hwilum læs, hwilum ma, eal for urum synnum.[62]

Gildas and Bede both attributed the success of the *adventus Saxonum* to the sinfulness of the Britons, which made them unworthy in God's eyes to hold the island. Likewise, in Wulfstan's view, the inability of the English to meet the Viking challenge casts doubt on their worthiness as God's chosen people. In previous centuries, God used the Vikings to test his

---

61 *Sermo Lupi*, lines 131–40. 'This nation, so it seems, has for a long time been made sinful through manifold sins and through many misdeeds: through murder and through evil deeds, through avarice and through gluttony, through theft and through pillaging, through traffic in people and through heathen vices, through betrayals and through deceptions, through lawbreaking and through lawlessness, through attacks on relatives and through manslaughter, through injuries to those in holy orders and through adultery, through incest and through various adulteries. And also many more than should be are lost and ravaged widely, as we said before, through oathbreaking and pledgebreaking and various lies.'

62 *Sermo Lupi*, lines 106–13. 'Very cowardly laws and shameful tributes are common to us, through the wrath of God, understand it who can; and many misfortunes befall this people again and again. For a long time now nothing has prospered, within or without, but there has been raiding and persecution on every side, again and again. And for a long time now the English have been entirely without victory and too much disheartened through God's anger, and the seamen so strong through God's consent, that in battle often one will put to flight ten, and sometimes fewer, sometimes more, all because of our sins.'

people, and ultimately found them worthy (in commemorative texts such as the *Bella Parisiacae urbis*, if not in historical reality). England's experience of Viking attacks in the early eleventh century differs greatly from its experience of these former raids. They are not the temporary and seasonal harassments of the earlier Viking age, but protracted engagements with an enemy bent on invasion and conquest. As a result, Wulfstan's tone is more akin to Gildas's tone of despair than to Alcuin's of remonstrance and, ultimately, hope. Wulfstan accordingly turns directly to Gildas's example to propose prayer and penance as a remedy, and to forecast the doom of the English if they fail to adopt it:

> Ac la, on Godes naman utan don swa us neod is, beorgan us sylfum swa we geornost magan þe læs we ætgædere ealle forweorðan. An þeodwita wæs on Brytta tidum Gildas hatte. Se awrat be heora misdædum hu hy mid heora synnum swa oferlice swyþe God gegræmedan þæt he let æt nyhstan Engla here heora eard gewinnan 7 Brytta dugeþe fordon mid ealle. And þæt wæs geworden þæs þe he sæde, þurh ricra reaflac 7 þurh gitsunge wohgestreona, ðurh leode unlaga 7 þurh wohdomas, ðurh biscopa asolcennesse 7 þurh lyðre yrhðe Godes bydela þe soþes geswugedan ealles to gelome 7 clumedan mid ceaflum þær hy scoldan clypian. Þurh fulne eac folces gælsan 7 þurh oferfylla 7 mænigfealde synna heora eard hy forworhtan 7 selfe hy forwurdan. Ac utan don swa us þearf is, warnian us be swilcan; 7 soþ is þæt ic secge, wyrsan dæda we witan mid Englum þonne we mid Bryttan ahwar gehyrdan. And þy us is þearf micel þæt we us beþencan 7 wið God sylfne þingian georne.[63]

The move toward Gildas is very telling; as Alcuin did more than two centuries earlier, Wulfstan finds a clear parallel between the Britons of the

---

63 *Sermo Lupi*, lines 174–90. 'And so, in the name of God let us do as need be, protect ourselves as we most eagerly might, lest we all perish together. There was a wise man among the Britons called Gildas. He wrote about their misdeeds, how by their sins they grieved God so greatly that he finally let the English invaders conquer their land and destroy the British nobility altogether. And that happened, as he said, because of the robbery of the rich and because of the coveting of ill-gotten property, because of the lawlessness of the people and because of unjust judgments, because of the laziness of bishops and because of the vile cowardice of God's messengers who all too often kept silent about the truth and mumbled in their cheeks when they should have cried out. Because of the foul luxury of each of the people and because of gluttony and because of manifold sins they destroyed their realm and they themselves perished. But let us now do as is needful, take heed ourselves from such things; and it is true what I say, that we know of worse deeds among the English than we ever heard of among the Britons. And therefore it is needful for us that we think about ourselves and plead eagerly with God himself.'

fifth century and the Anglo-Saxons of his own time, and the recurring pattern of sin and punishment gives him grounds to predict the Anglo-Saxons' future course. Yet the turn to history also allows him to differentiate the English from the Britons, in both good and bad ways. The English, he reminds his audience, were the ones who ultimately gained control of the island through God's will, not the ones who lost his favour. He also notes, however, that the sins of the English today are far worse than those of the fifth century Britons; he thus makes their case historically specific at the same time that it resonates with earlier examples. Also like Alcuin, he takes Gildas's warning – along with his historical knowledge of the Britons' ultimate defeat – so as to build a case for repentance as a remedy for current tribulation. Wulfstan takes the same view of history that motivated Bede, and trusts that on learning of the calamities suffered by bad people, readers or listeners will seek to change their own lives to follow God's law and avoid sin. For Wulfstan, this historical paradigm provides contemporary events with meaning while simultaneously bringing them under some semblance of human control; as the Chronicle entries demonstrate, the Viking situation was clearly out of English control by the time Wulfstan began drafting the *Sermo Lupi*, even if it was as early as 1009.[64] Along with providing meaning, however, his chosen historical paradigm realigns English history with Christian history and its cyclical progression toward salvation. Just when it seems that the world is coming to an end, Wulfstan offers a path to salvation in place of the expected apocalypse – especially in the light of the coming millennium.[65] His rhetorical stance reinscribes England, on the verge of conquest, into the larger identity of Christendom, and thus preserves a sense of England's integrity at a moment of crisis. Perhaps most important, Wulfstan offers a practicable course of action whereby all those considered English can contribute to the salvation of

---

64 Hollis argues for an early dating of the longest version of the *Sermo Lupi*, and suggests that the shorter versions are later abridgments of the original, although she offers no dates; see 'Thematic Structure,' especially 176–8. Godden, in 'Apocalypse and Invasion,' proposes that all three versions were written within two years, but reverses Hollis's ordering; the longest version is also the last, written in late 1014; see especially 150–2.

65 Godden writes that 'the Old Testament parallels suggest the cyclic repetition of divine punishment and repentance rather than the once-only end of all things; they imply divine anger with the chosen people rather than the destruction of the whole world' ('Apocalypse and Invasion,' 155). But see Hollis, who argues in 'Thematic Structure' that the careful stylistic construction of the sermon, the representation of the Vikings as Antichrist, and the idea that the people's sins will occasion the Last Days point toward an apocalyptic understanding of the Viking attacks.

their nation through the salvation of their own souls. The Viking attacks serve as a call for renewed piety among the English, and the intensity of the destruction and devastation is directly proportional to the intensity of the repentance required to bring it to an end.

Religious rhetoric, prayers, and penance were not the sum total of England's plan to stave off the Viking threat; Æthelred also pursued diplomatic avenues with fellow Christian rulers in Normandy and Scandinavia.[66] In 994 he stood sponsor at Olaf Tryggvason's baptism, hoping that the Christianity of a Danish king and English support of his bid to conquer and convert Norway would keep England safe from attack. His marriage to Emma of Normandy in 1002 was a similar attempt to secure the allegiance of a foreign, Christian ruler against the Vikings. These diplomatic efforts, like Wulfstan's homily, were attempts to link England with the larger world of Christendom. Even at home, Æthelred's policy was influenced by England's identity as a Christian nation with a role to play in salvation history, as well as by the belief that human beings were not only responsible for the evils that afflict our world, but also capable of gaining God's grace so as to heal them. In 1009, he issued an edict – drafted by Wulfstan, no less – decreeing as follows:

[Prol.] Ealle we beþurfan, þæt we geornlice earnian, þæt we Godes miltse 7 his mildheortnesse habban moton 7 þæt we þurh his fultum magon feondum wiðstandan.

[1] Nu wille we, þæt eal folc to gemænelicre dædbote þrig dagas be hlafe 7 wirtum 7 wætere, þæt is on Monandæg 7 on Tiwesdæg 7 on Wodensdæg ær Michaeles mæssan.

[2] 7 cume manna gehwilc bærefot to circan buton golde 7 glæncgum, 7 ga man to scrifte.

[2.1] 7 gan ealle ut mid halidome 7 clipian inweardre heortan georne to Criste.

[2.2] 7 sceote man æghwilce hide pænig oððe pæniges weorð.

...

---

66 Theodore M. Andersson delineates the diplomatic effort (ultimately unsuccessful) to divide enemies and secure a peaceful neighborhood, in 'The Viking Policy of Ethelred the Unready,' in *Anglo-Scandinavian England: Norse-English Relations in the Period before the Conquest*, ed. John D. Niles and Mark Amodio, 1–11 (Lanham, MD: University Press of America, 1989). This theme was suggested earlier by James Campbell, 'England, France and Germany: Some Comparisons and Connections,' in Hill, *Ethelred the Unready*, 255–70.

[3] 7 gif hwa þis ne gelæste, ðonne gebete he þæt, swa swa hit gelagod is: bunda mid XXX p[ænigum], þræl mid his hide, þegn mid XXX scill[ingum].[67]

Wulfstan's influence is evident in both Æthelred's and Cnut's law codes, but an edict like this demonstrates the power of this historical ideology at all levels and in all corners of the Anglo-Saxon social world. Moreover, the public nature of these texts – meant to be read aloud as homilies, or proclaimed as law – suggests that people may well have seen repentance, prayer, and the eradication of sinful behaviour as means by which to alter the current course of English history and realign it on the path to salvation, which the writings of Bede had indicated to be England's destiny. From these documents, readers construct an image of England as a Christian nation, first and foremost, whose teleological destiny lies in its survival through prayer and piety. In this discursive climate of Christian historiography and its extensive influence, a poem like *The Battle of Maldon* appears all the more incongruous, with its glorification of a military rather than a spiritual response to pagan attack. It is thus essential to ask why, amid a strong environment of Christian moralizing, a commemorative poem opts for the archaic glory of the Germanic warrior rather than that of the *miles Christi* in the context of Christian-Viking conflict.

III. A Call to Arms: Poetry, Heroism, and Historical Response

The dismal narrative of the Anglo-Saxon Chronicle, written well after the Danish conquest of England, paints a picture of millennial England as a kingdom in perpetual decline, without hope of fighting off the Danish invaders, and ruled by an incompetent king who duly earned the sobriquet 'Unready.' This standard account of the decline and fall of Anglo-Saxon

---

67   VII Æthelred, in Felix Liebermann, *Die Gesetze der Angelsachsen*, 3 vols (Halle: Max Niemeyer, 1903–16; repr. Aalen: Scientia, 1960), 1:262. 'We all need to work eagerly so that we might have God's mercy and his compassion and so that we may through his help withstand our enemies. Now we desire that all the nation fast as a common penance for three days on bread and herbs and water, that is on Monday, on Tuesday, and on Wednesday before Michaelmas. And every man should come barefoot to church without gold and ornaments, and everyone should go to confession. And all should go out with the relics and call from their inmost hearts eagerly on Christ. And each hide should pay one penny or the value of one penny … And if anyone does not fulfil this, then he will pay for it as it is ordained by law: the freeman with 30 pennies, the slave with his skin, the thegn with 30 shillings.'

England leaves readers with the distinct impression that Æthelred's kingship was weak, unsteady, and doomed to failure. For the chronicler, the
eventual outcome of Æthelred's Viking policies overshadowed the other
events of his reign; as a retrospective narrative, the account is unavoidably
coloured by the knowledge of England's eventual conquest by the Danes.[68]
In recent years, scholars such as Simon Keynes and Pauline Stafford have
mounted increasingly convincing arguments that Æthelred's reign was far
from the unqualified disaster it has seemed.[69] That being said, however, the
unmitigated dolour with which the Chronicle recounts more than three
decades of attempts to defend England against the Vikings leaves a powerful impression. These annals strike readers immediately as considerably
fuller and more detailed than the annals for the earlier parts of the tenth
century; Cecily Clark has even argued that 'from about 991, the annalist,
enlarging the borders of his garments, begins to offer explanations of the
events he records, and also comments on them.'[70] Yet these explanations
do not centre on a lack of Christian virtue among the English; as Fred
Robinson has remarked, 'the entries in the *Anglo-Saxon Chronicle* from
the time of the battle of Maldon to the end of the twelfth century make
surprisingly few references to God working through history.'[71] Instead,
they opt for a distinctly heroic ethos of historical causality. Alice Sheppard
sees these annals as particularly invested in a heroic notion of lordship and
warrior valour; the Chronicle in general, she argues, overtly posits kingship as a form of Germanic lordship, and Æthelred's failure to protect his
people and secure the bonds of loyalty from his nobles forecasts the failure
of the kingdom.[72] The Chronicle, Sheppard suggests, paints Æthelred as a
leader undeserving of his people's loyalty, so that the witan's acceptance of
their conqueror, Cnut, is not a betrayal of the Anglo-Saxon people, but a
heroic step taken on their behalf.[73] The question of proper lordship, along

---

68 Stafford points out that Æthelred's reputation for incompetence allows the monarchy
    to remain a stable institution once the individual and incompetent monarch is replaced
    by a more apt leader, such as Cnut. See 'Reign of Æthelred II,' 15.
69 Keynes, 'Declining Reputation' and *Diplomas*; Stafford, 'Reign of Æthelred II' and
    Unification and Conquest.
70 C. Clark, 'Narrative Mode,' 225.
71 Fred C. Robinson, 'God, Death, and Loyalty in *The Battle of Maldon*,' in *J.R.R.
    Tolkien, Scholar and Storyteller: Essays* in Memoriam, ed. Mary Salu and Robert T.
    Farrell, 76–98 (Ithaca: Cornell University Press, 1979), 87.
72 Alice Sheppard, *Families of the King: Writing Identity in the* Anglo-Saxon Chronicle
    (Toronto: University of Toronto Press, 2004), especially 71–93.
73 Sheppard, *Families*, 94–120.

with the sense of havoc wreaked on a nation whose leaders do not live up to the heroic standard, underscores the Chronicle's narrative of 983–1016, which yearns for a military salvation delivered not by God, but by a hero. The Viking attacks on England resumed in 980, when 'wæs Suðhamtun forhergod fram scipherige 7 seo burhwaru mæst ofslegen 7 gehæft; 7 þy ilcan geare wæs Tenetland gehergod; 7 þy ilcan geare wæs Legeceasterscir gehergod fram norðscipherige.'[74] The following years saw a regular repetition of these coastal attacks, and after a decade or so, the Chronicle begins to offer tacit explanations for their continuation in accounts of bad leadership, often consigning to infamy the names of the ealdormen responsible for the failed defence. For example, s.a. 992, manuscript C records that

Þa gerædde se cyning 7 ealle his witan þæt man gegadrede ealle ða scipu þe ahtes wæron to Lundenbyrig, 7 se cyning þa betæhte þa fyrde to lædenne Ælfrice ealdormenn 7 Þorede eorlle 7 Ælfstane bisceope 7 Æscwige bisceope, 7 sceoldon cunnian meahton hy þone here ahwær utan betreppan. Þa sende se ealdorman Ælfric 7 het warnian ðone here, 7 þa on ðære nihte þe hy on ðone dæig togædere fon sceoldon, þa sceoc he on niht fram þære fyrde him sylfum to myclum bysmore, 7 se here ða ætbærst, butan an scyp þær man ofsloh; 7 þa gemette se here ða scypu on Eastenglum 7 of Lundene, 7 hi ðær ofgeslogan micel wæl.[75]

The plan is a good one by both historical and heroic standards: the king, who should not in any case lead the battle himself, turns the management of his forces over to his trusted noblemen; manuscript F notes that Ælfric in

---

74   Katherine O'Brien O'Keeffe, ed., *MS C*, The Anglo-Saxon Chronicle: A Collaborative Edition 5 (Cambridge: D.S. Brewer, 2001). 'Southampton was ravaged by a naval force and most of the inhabitants slain or taken captive; and in the same year Thanet was harried; and in the same year Cheshire was harried by a northern naval force.' All quotations of the Anglo-Saxon Chronicle are taken from the relevant volume of the Collaborative Edition, and all translations are my own.

75   'The king and all his councillors declared that all the ships that were of use should be gathered at London, and the king then entrusted the force to the leadership of Ealdorman Ælfric and Earl Thored and Bishop Ælfstan and Bishop Æscwig, and they were to try, if they could, to trap the Danish army anywhere at sea. Then Ealdorman Ælfric sent to warn the Danish army, and then in the night before the day on which they were to engage in battle, he fled by night from the army, to his own great shame, and then the Danish army escaped, except one ship that was destroyed; and then the Danish army met the ships from East Anglia and from London; and they slew a great many there.'

particular was 'an of þan þa se cing hæfde mæst truwe to.'[76] But Ælfric's treachery and the slaughter that results reveal a breakdown in the chain of command, to say nothing of the heroic ideal of the warlord and his *comitatus*. This episode is an early indication of the disorganization that would plague the English forces in the decades to come, and Ælfric is not the only leader to fail in his duty. S.a. 993, we learn that 'þa gegaderede man swiðe micle fyrde, 7 þa hi togædere gan sceoldon, þa onstealdan þa heretogan ærest þone fleam: þæt wæs Fræna 7 Godwine 7 Fryþegyst.'[77] Again the English nobility flees from battle, and this picture of cowardice becomes more and more vivid as the annals continue. In 1003, Ælfric once again led the army, 'ac he teah ða forð his ealdan wrencas'[78] and feigned illness as an excuse not to fight. At this point, the chronicler lays out in no uncertain terms that 'þonne se heretoga wacað þonne bið eall se here swiðe gehindrad,'[79] thereby making concrete the hitherto implied link between the behaviour of the ealdormen and the losses of the English army.[80] By 1009, the chronicler's disgust with the English leadership is clear:

> Her on þissum geare wurdan þa scypu gearwe ... 7 hiora wæs swa feala swa næfre ær þæs, ðe us bec secgað, on Angelcynne ne gewurdon on nanes cyninges dæge, 7 hi man ða ealle togædere ferode to Sandwic 7 ðær sceoldon licgan 7 þisne eard healdan wið ælcne uthere. Ac we ða gyt næfdon þa gesælða ne þone wyrðscype þæt seo scypfyrd nyt wære þissum earde þe ma ðe heo oftor ær wæs.[81]

The chronicler goes on to tell of more treachery, this time by Ealdorman Eadric and his brother, Brihtric. By 1010, there seems to be little hope for an English victory; 'þeah mon þonne hwæt rædde þæt ne stod furðon

76   Peter S. Baker, ed., *MS F*, The Anglo-Saxon Chronicle: A Collaborative Edition 8 (Cambridge: D.S. Brewer, 2000). 'One of those in whom the king trusted most.'

77   MS C. 'A great army was gathered, and when they should have engaged in battle, the leaders first started the flight: they were Fræna, Godwine, and Frythegyst.'

78   MS C. 'But he was up to his old tricks.'

79   MS C. 'When the leader weakens, the whole army is much hindered.'

80   See T. Hill, '"When the Leader Is Brave ...": An Old English Proverb and Its Vernacular Context,' *Anglia* 119 (2001): 232–6.

81   MS C. 'In this year the ships [commissioned by Æthelred in 1008] were ready ... and there were so many of them as never before had been in England in the day of any king, from what books tell us, and they were all brought together at Sandwich and were to lie there and protect this country from every foreign army. But we still had not the good fortune or the honour that the naval force might be of use to this country, any more than it often had been before.'

ænne monað; æt nextan næs nan heafodman þæt fyrde gaderian wolde, ac ælc fleah swa he mæst mihte, ne furðon nan scir nolde oþre gelæstan æt nextan.'[82] In 1011, the chronicler proclaims that 'ealle þas ungesælða us gelumpon þuruh unrædas,'[83] laying the literary groundwork for Æthelred's reputation as the 'Unready.'[84]

That the chronicler blames specific individuals and 'unrædas' for England's military woes represents a crucial departure from the sin-and-punishment causality promulgated by Latin Christian historians. At the same time that Wulfstan was blaming English sinfulness for Danish aggression, the chronicler seems to ascribe the situation to the lack of support shown by Æthelred's nobles, as evidenced by the passages quoted above. Nowhere does the Chronicle invoke generalized sin and depravity among the people, and the absence of such a judgment marks a significant difference from Wulfstan's response to the same events. In lieu of the miraculous intervention of God and his saints that Abbo offered as exempla, the ideology expressed in the Chronicle seeks heroism and lordship. Several instances of bravery and successful leadership among the English are noted in contemporary sources like the *Vita Oswaldi*, which records inspirational leadership after the heroic fashion in a battle that took place months before Maldon:

> Factum est durissimum bellum in occidente, in quo fortiter resistentes nostrates (qui dicuntur Deuinsyce) uictoriam sancti triumphi perceperunt, adquisita gloria. Ceciderunt plurimi ex nostris, pluriores ex illis. Nam occisus est ex nostris miles fortissimus nomine Stremwold, cum aliis nonnullis – qui bellica morte magis elegerunt uitam finire quam ignobiliter uiuere.[85]

---

82 MS C. 'Although something might be decided, it did not stand even a month; at last there was no leader who would gather an army, but each fled as best he could, and finally no shire would help the next.'
83 MS C. 'All these disasters happened to us because of bad policy.'
84 As Simon Keynes notes, however, the byname does not actually appear in the textual record until the thirteenth century; see 'Declining Reputation,' 240–1.
85 Michael Lapidge, 'The *Life of St Oswald*,' in *The Battle of Maldon, A.D. 991*, ed. Donald G. Scragg, 51–8 (Oxford: Basil Blackwell, 1991), 52. 'A savage battle took place in the west, in which our men (who are called Devonshiremen), opposing them bravely, achieved the triumph of a victory and its accompanying glory. Many of our men fell, but far more of theirs. In fact one of our men, a valiant soldier called Stremwold, was killed along with several others who chose to end their lives by death in battle rather than to live on in shame' (translation from Lapidge, 'Life of Oswald,' 54).

Even the generally pessimistic Chronicle commemorates some of England's fallen heroes; s.a. 988, we read 'wæs … Goda se defenisca þegen ofslagen 7 mycel wæl mid him,'[86] and Byrhtnoth's death is mentioned s.a. 991.[87] S.a. 998, 999, and 1001,[88] the chronicler records attempts at English defence in which the warriors showed courage but lacked leadership and inevitably fled the field or were slaughtered. Manuscript A s.a. 1001 records that 'þa com þær togeanes Hamtunscir 7 him wið gefuhton; 7 ðær wearð Æþelweard cinges heahgerefa ofslegen 7 Leofric æt Hwitciricean 7 Leofwine cinges heahgerefa 7 Wulfhere bisceopes ðegn 7 Godwine æt Worðige, Ælfsiges bisceopes sunu, 7 ealra manna an 7 hund eahtatig; 7 þær wearð þara Denescra micle ma ofslegenra, þeah ðe hie wælstowe geweald ahtan';[89] and MSS CDE add the narrative of the brave but futile defence mounted by the men of Devon and Somerset at Pinhoe. Finally, s.a. 1004, Ealdorman Ulfcetel leads his troops to block the Danes from returning to their ships; his forces are described as fighting 'fæstlice' [steadfastly] and kill many Danes, but in the end, 'ðær wearð Eastengla folces seo yld ofslagen,'[90] and the Danes, though reduced in number, are eventually able to reach their ships. These commemorations of named individual leaders, their courage, and their ability to keep an army together and on the field indicate that the English view of the Viking battles wasn't completely dismal; there were moments of faith in the country's leaders even in the face of defeat. It is important, however, that these moments are patterned on the heroic values that stem from the vernacular poetic tradition.

The questions of treachery and loyalty that permeate the Chronicle accounts reflect certain ideals of the conduct becoming an English nobleman. The fact that the *comitatus* was a literary rather than a lived ideal has been firmly established; tenth century Anglo-Saxons did not live in a mead-hall with their lord and did not pledge their lives and services to him

---

86 MS C. 'Goda the Devonshire thegn was killed and many died with him.'
87 In MSS ACDE.
88 In MSS CDE; the entry s.a. 1001 is also found in MS A.
89 Janet M. Bately, ed., *MS A*, The Anglo-Saxon Chronicle: A Collaborative Edition 3 (Cambridge: D.S. Brewer, 1986). 'The people of Hampshire came together and fought against [the Danes] there, and there Æthelweard the king's high-reeve was slain and Leofric from Whitchurch and Leofwine the king's high-reeve and Wulfhere the bishop's thegn and Godwine from Worthy, Bishop Ælfsige's son, and eighty-one men in all; and there many more of the Danes were killed, although they had control of the place of slaughter.'
90 MS C. 'The flower of the East Anglian people was slain.'

in return for gifts of armour and gold rings.[91] The relationships between lord and thegns in late Anglo-Saxon England had more to do with politics and personality than with honour and tradition.[92] That does not mean, however, that the heroic ideal of loyalty between lords and thegns had no cultural significance; on the contrary, texts such as *Beowulf*, *Maldon*, and the Chronicle poems demonstrate the level of currency it enjoyed throughout the late Anglo-Saxon period. The heroic ethos valorizes the twin virtues of loyalty and bravery, dictating that a man's primary responsibility is to fight well in the service of his lord. Despite its impracticability as a political system, the prevalence of the heroic code in Anglo-Saxon literature gives it an ideological force that has the power to shape beliefs, interpretations, and even actions. I would not argue that Byrhtnoth's men really died with brave speeches on their lips, as the poem maintains; but I would suggest that offering these literary examples in the face of a chronically ineffectual military defence might represent an attempt to defend the integrity of English identity and recall the success and the unity of English troops under Athelstan and Edmund decades before by using the same poetic form that memorialized their earlier victories – indeed, the same form that immortalized the heroes of legend.[93]

If a heroic English identity finds expression in some of the Chronicle passages, it is positively codified by the 325-line fragmentary poem on the Battle of Maldon. The question of loyalty, a touchstone of the heroic code and the central theme of the poem, takes on new ideological force in what is clearly a moment of crisis for England. *The Battle of Maldon* makes use of a form – alliterative verse – that resonates with the notions of glory, history, and unity, which are missing from current events, and that also eschews causality, linearity, and teleology as historical methods. The method of invocation in alliterative verse is allusive and vertical; it assembles a constellation of fragments that requires activity on the part of its readers to fill in the gaps out of their own knowledge. Epic poetry has meaning because an audience knows what to expect; the characters, the storylines, and the rhetorical conventions that dictate the actions of heroes and villains alike are all familiar, and invoke levels of meaning beyond and outside the story

---

91 See Woolf, 'The Ideal of Men Dying'; and Frank, 'Anachronism or *Nouvelle Vague?*'
92 Stafford outlines the formation of relationships between kings and ealdormen in late Anglo-Saxon England in *Unification and Conquest*, especially 150–61. See also Sheppard, *Families*, 26–50.
93 See chap. 4 below.

at hand.[94] Historical events like the Battle of Maldon, however, have the disadvantage of failing to provide the clear-cut villains and dramatic speeches that would allow Anglo-Saxons to assimilate them into a familiar pattern, and history-writing thus faces a formal challenge. As Hayden White puts it,

> in order to effect this transformation, the events, agents, and agencies represented in the chronicle must be encoded as story elements; that is, they must be characterized as the kind of events, agents, agencies, and so on, that can be apprehended as elements of specific story types ... When the reader recognizes the story being told in a historical narrative as a specific kind of story – for example, as an epic, romance, tragedy, comedy, or farce, – he can be said to have comprehended the meaning produced by the discourse.[95]

Once encoded as story elements, events, agents, and agencies can fit into the generic structure that invokes them. As a poem in the heroic tradition, *Maldon* gives its readers all the information they need to make sense of the historical fragments that it invokes – the location of the battle, its major actors, the fact of defeat, and the mechanisms of bravery and loyalty on the one hand, and cowardice and treachery on the other – and that can be construed as explanations for the outcome. Although, as Craig Davis notes, *Maldon* does not invoke the heroic tradition directly by alluding to characters and events from myth and legend, the poem's deployment of the familiar forms of heroic verse cue the audience's response and condition their understanding of the event as a part of the historical tradition.[96] And, as Elizabeth Tyler has commented, the traditionality of that form is itself revealing: 'To compose classical Old English verse in the tenth and eleventh centuries, when other, less strict, forms of verse were emerging in English was a conscious choice, and the conventionality of Old English poetics would not have been perpetuated unless it had a value.'[97]

---

94 On the metonymic invocations of traditional poetic structures, see particularly John Miles Foley, 'Oral Traditional Aesthetics and Old English Poetry,' in *Medialität und mittelalterliche insulare Literatur*, ed. Hildegard L.C. Tristram, 80–103 (Tübingen: Narr, 1992), especially 82–93; 'Signs, Texts, and Oral Tradition,' *Journal of Folklore Research* 33 (1996): 21–9; and *Immanent Art: From Structure to Meaning in Traditional Oral Epic* (Bloomington: Indiana University Press, 1991).
95 White, *Content of the Form*, 43.
96 Davis, 'Cultural Historicity,' 155.
97 Elizabeth M. Tyler, 'Poetics and the Past: Making History with Old English Poetry,' in *Narrative and History in the Early Medieval West*, ed. Elizabeth M. Tyler and Ross Balzaretti, 225–50 (Turnhout: Brepols, 2006), 237.

Just as providential history offered Wulfstan a model for integrating the chaos of Viking attack, heroic poetry provides a framework within which to make sense of a major defeat in the defence both of Maldon and of 'eþel þysne, / Æþelredes eard' [this homeland, Æthelred's realm] (52b–53a).[98] Edward B. Irving comments that '[the poet] has created a heroic poem out of brute fact. He has been obliged to forego the great resources of the epic poets – the romantic glamour of antiquity and strange beings, or the plot and characters already long cherished by the audience ... Instinctively he has known how to use style to suggest this epic world and to make it function as a part of his own poem.'[99] Irving hits on the poet's chief challenge: that of creating a traditional work of art from historical fact rather than from stock characters and plot elements. Because of the conventions of heroic poetry, readers of *Maldon* know what kinds of behaviour to expect from the various players in the drama; the meaning or significance of the event is dictated to a large degree by generic expectations based on a familiar form. Byrhtnoth becomes a latter-day Beowulf; the men who flee the battle are branded traitors; the Vikings are simply the enemy. The nuances and complexities of the tumultuous political scene that was Æthelred's reign become blurred by the need for a unified English identity in the face of a common threat; in this case, that identity is forged upon a shared heroic past rather than a vision of future salvation. In *Maldon*, the Vikings' paganism serves to underscore their difference from the Anglo-Saxon heroes rather than their role as agents of God's wrath, as they were in the *Bella Parisiacae urbis* and the *Sermo Lupi*,[100] and the Christianity of the English army is a given historical fact, not a typological rhetorical theme. The poem makes clear that Byrhtnoth's men fight not for their faith, but for lord and land.[101] And notwithstanding Byrhtnoth's final speech, in

---

98 All quotations are from Scragg, *Maldon*, and all translations are my own.

99 Edward B. Irving, Jr, 'The Heroic Style in *The Battle of Maldon*,' *SP* 58 (1961), 457–67 at 467.

100 Britton demonstrates that the main role of the Vikings in *Maldon* is to point up the heroism of their English adversaries ('Characterization'). More recently, Niels Lund has attempted to elucidate 'The Danish Perspective' in Scragg, *Maldon, A.D. 991*, 114–42. Niles and Amodio's *Anglo-Scandinavian England* brings to light many of the more subtle and nuanced perceptions of the Vikings at this time.

101 C. Clark makes this clear by contrasting Byrhtnoth with the more overtly Christian hero of the *Chanson de Roland*; see 'Byrhtnoth and Roland: A Contrast,' *Neophilologus* 51 (1967): 288–93. But see Christopher M. Cain, who argues that the *Maldon* poet writes with an eye to the coming apocalypse, namely, the millennium and the end of Anglo-Saxon England, in 'The "Fearful Symmetry" of *Maldon*: The Apocalypse, the Poet, and the Millennium,' *Comitatus* 28 (1997): 1–16.

which he prays to God to show him mercy and take his soul to heaven just before he is cut down by 'hæðene scealcas' [heathen soldiers] (181a), the hero is presented not as a defender of the faith, but as 'þæs folces ealdor, / Æþelredes eorl' [the leader of the people, Æthelred's nobleman] (202b–203a). His brave leadership in battle and his loyalty to his lord and king, not his faith, define his character.[102]

The scene is set when Byrhtnoth

Het þa hyssa hwæne   hors forlætan,
feor afysan   and forð gangan,
hicgan to handum   and to hige godum.[103]   (2–4)

He takes charge even before the start of the battle, by offering guidance to his men in both word and deed. The warriors respond precisely as warriors should; each one marches forward full of resolve and determination:

Offan mæg …
…
             to þære hilde stop.
Be þam man mihte oncnawan   þæt se cniht nolde
wacian æt þam wige,   þa he to wæpnum feng.
Eac him wolde Eadric   his ealdre gelæstan,
frean to gefeohte;   ongan þa forð beran
gar to guþe.   He hæfde god geþanc

---

102 This presents an interesting contrast with another Germanic poem on Christian-Viking conflict, the late ninth century *Ludwigslied*; see *Althochdeutsche Literatur*, ed. Horst Dieter Schlosser (Frankfurt/Main: Fischer, 1989), 274–7 at 277. For the political context of the *Ludwigslied*, see Holger Homann, 'Das Ludwigslied – Dichtung im Dienste der Politik?' in *Traditions and Transitions: Studies in Honor of Harold Jantz*, ed. Lieselotte E. Kurth, William H. McClain, and Holger Homann, 17–28 (Munich: Delp, 1972). Hincmar himself authors a distinctly different account of the battle at Saucourt in the *Annales Bertiniani*, ed. Georg Waitz, MGH, Scriptores rerum Germanicarum in usum scholarum, 5 (Hannover, 1883). Trude Ehlert explores the implications of Christian typology in the *Ludwigslied* in 'Literatur und Wirklichkeit – Exegese und Politik: Zur Deutung des Ludwigsliedes,' *Saeculum* 32 (1981): 31–42, especially 31–5.
103 'Commanded each of the warriors to release his horse, to drive it far away and to go forward on foot, to think on brave deeds and bold thoughts.'

þa hwile þe he mid handum   healdan mihte
bord and brad swurd ...[104]   (5a; 8b–15a)

Even at the level of form, the poem emphasizes its heroic context. In each line, the alliteration calls attention to the trappings of heroic warfare that decorate the poem: appositives for war, battle, weapons, and lord cluster around named figures like Offa's kinsman and Eadric in addition to Byrhtnoth, offering proof of these characters' fitness and propriety as warriors. The aesthetic method is not dissimilar to Wulfstan's in the *Sermo Lupi*, but whereas Wulfstan offers an endless catalogue of negative examples, *Maldon* compiles instances of honour and glory as moral desiderata.[105] The actions of individuals are the ground upon which the battle will be won or lost, and the men of Kent declare their support for Byrhtnoth by stepping forward with weapons and refusing to 'wacian æt þam wige.'[106] Byrhtnoth exhorts the troops not to be afraid, and he himself fights among them, significantly placing himself 'þær he his heorðwerod holdost wiste' [where he knew that his hearth-companions were most loyal] (line 24). The leader's chosen place to fight is not where the soldiers are biggest, bravest, or strongest, but where they are most loyal, a detail explicitly reinforcing what was implicit in the behaviour of Offa's kinsman and Eadric: loyalty is the paramount virtue of the heroic warrior. In the poem, however, these men are not simply loyal men, but the 'hearth-companions' of the ancient Germanic *comitatus*. The invocation of the heroic tradition both thematically and lexically indicates immediately the generic conventions that will govern this narrative; readers know that they can expect bravery, loyalty, and honour from the heroes of *Maldon*.

---

104 'Offa's kinsman stepped up to the battle. By that, all might know that the young man would not weaken at the fight, when he seized his weapons. Also Eadric wished to support his lord, his leader in the battle; he began then to bear forth his spear to the battle. He had a strong purpose so long as he might hold with his hands the shield and the broad sword.'

105 Helen Phillips offers a brilliant close reading of these poetic forms, commenting that 'constant references to hands and holding are elements in two of the poem's most important effects in creating the illusion that an English defeat is an English victory: the motif of firmness and the tendency to focus on small-scale bodily action and on action by an individual' ('The Order of Words and Patterns of Opposition in the *Battle of Maldon*,' *Neophilologus* 81 [1997]: 117–28 at 121).

106 Ralph W.V. Elliott notes the significance of the warriors' unquestioning obedience to Byrhtnoth's call to arms, concluding that 'in the irresistible challenge of heroic obedience Byrhtnoth and his men find their fulfillment' ('Byrhtnoth and Hildebrand: A Study in Heroic Technique,' *Comparative Literature* 14 [1962]: 53–70 at 70).

In the first twenty-five lines of the poem, the roles and responsibilities of the English army are categorically laid out: the soldiers must simply stand fast in battle, and the general must encourage and exhort the soldiers, leading by example. The distinction between loyal and disloyal soldiers will thus be based on who scatters and who doesn't, and the moral weight of that distinction is made clear from the very beginning of the poem.[107] Eadric and Offa's kinsman declare their intention not to weaken in the fight; Wulfstan, Ælfhere, and Maccus similarly

> noldon æt þam forda   fleam gewyrcan,
> ac hi fæstlice   wið ða fynd weredon
> þa hwile þe hi wæpna   wealdan moston.[108]   (81–3)

The problem of a dispersing army, which proves recurrent in the Chronicle entries and finally disastrous to the Maldon campaign itself, is never an option for the heroic warrior. Byrhtnoth, furthermore, states explicitly that he fights

> ... gealgean   eþel þysne,
> Æþelredes eard,   ealdres mines
> folc and foldan.[109]   (52–4a)

He offers a reason for fighting, beyond the glory and fame promised by heroic poetry: the defence of the lord, homeland, and people, which are further emphasized and glorified by the alliteration (*eþel* / *Æþelredes* / *eard* /*ealdres* and *folc* / *foldan*). In this moment, the defence of Maldon transcends its regional focus to symbolize the defence of all England, and *Maldon* becomes a vehicle for Wormald's notion of England as an 'ideological artefact' promoted through a literary-historical medium.[110] It even offers, as Bradley Ryner has recently argued, a particular kind of subjectivity for the fallen warriors, who assert agency through their choice to continue the struggle rather than opt for surrender or tribute – the fact that their agency ends in death only makes their subjective victory stronger.[111]

---

107 The legal weight of this distinction becomes clear upon examination of some of the later law codes; see below.
108 'would not take flight from the ford, but they held out steadfastly against the enemy as long as they were able to wield weapons.'
109 'To defend this homeland, Æthelred's realm, my lord's people and his country.'
110 See n7 above.
111 Bradley D. Ryner, 'Exchanging Battle: Subjective and Objective Conflicts in *The Battle of Maldon*,' *ES* 87 (2006): 266–76.

As the poem, along with the battle, progresses, the values of courage and loyalty are reiterated time and time again. The poet uses various poetic locutions to indicate that the company held out against the enemy – 'nolde wacian' [would not weaken] (9b–10a), 'standan and þone stede healdan' [stand and hold the place] (line 19), 'noldan ... fleam gewyrcan' [would not take flight] (line 81), 'gearowe stodon' [stood ready] (100b), 'healdan fæste' [held firmly] (102b–103a), 'stodon stædefæste' [stood steadfast] (127a), and 'gangan forð' [went forth] (170a) – before Byrhtnoth, struck down by a Danish spear, 'ne mihte þa on fotum leng fæste gestandan' [could no longer stand fast on his feet] (line 171). Byrhtnoth embodies the ideal of the warrior who stands fast and fights until he can stand no more; he dies, fairly early in the poem, fulfilling the duty to offer an example to his men. This point is driven home by the assertion that two of his warriors, Ælfnoth and Wulfmær, fall beside him, thus demonstrating to the other soldiers their willingness to follow their lord's example. The *Vita Oswaldi* similarly presents Byrhtnoth in the role of a brave war-leader:

Quam gloriose quamque uiriliter, quam audacter suos incitauit princeps belli ad aciem, quis urbanitate fretus potest edicere? Stabat ipse statura procerus, eminens super ceteros ... Percutiebat quoque a dextris, non reminiscens cigneam caniciem sui capitis, quoniam elemosine et sacre misse eum confortabant. Protegebat se a sinistris, debilitationem oblitus sui corporis, quem orationes et bone actiones eleuabant. Cumque pretiosus campi ductor cerneret inimicos ruere et suos uiriliter pugnare eosque multipliciter cadere, tota uirtute cepit pro patria pugnare. Ceciderunt enim ex illis et nostris infinitus numerus; et Byrihtnoðus cecidit, et reliqui fugerunt.[112]

He battles bravely for his men, his country, and his God. In contrast to *Maldon*, however, the *Vita Oswaldi* records the dispersal of the army after Byrhtnoth's death without offering a word of censure against the men

---

112 Lapidge, 'Life of Oswald,' 53–4. 'Who, sustained with eloquence, could say how gloriously, how bravely, how boldly the battle-leader exhorted his men in the battle-array? He himself was tall of stature, standing above the rest ... He struck blows from his right side, not paying heed to the swan-white hair of his head, since alms and holy masses gave him consolation. He protected himself on the left-hand side, forgetful of the weakness of his body, for prayers and good deeds uplifted him. When the estimable champion saw his enemies rush forward, and saw his own men fighting bravely and falling in droves, he began to fight for his country with all his might. For an infinite number of them and us fell; and Byrhtnoth fell, and those remaining fled' (Lapidge, 'Life of Oswald,' 54–5).

who fled and focusing instead on the fact that 'Dani quoque mirabiliter sunt uulnerati, qui uix suas constituere naues poterant hominibus.'[113] The poem offers a very different portrayal of the flight:

Hi bugon þa fram beaduwe   þe þær beon noldon:
þær wurdon Oddan bearn   ærest on fleame,
Godric fram guþe,   and þone godan forlet
þe him mænigne oft   mear gesealde;
he gehleop þone eoh   þe ahte his hlaford,
on þam gerædum   þe hit riht ne wæs,
and his broðru mid him   begen ærndon,
Godwine and Godwig,   guþe ne gymdon,
ac wendon fram þam wige   and þone wudu sohton,
flugon on þæt fæsten   and hyra feore burgon,
and manna ma   þonne hit ænig mæð wære,
gif hi þa geearnunga   ealle gemundon
þe he him to duguþe   gedon hæfde.
Swa him Offa on dæg   ær asæde
on þam meþelstede,   þa he gemot hæfde,
þæt þær modelice   manega spræcon
þe eft æt þærfe   þolian noldon.[114]   (185–201)

The leaders of the flight are named, and their flight is characterized in terms of their desires: they *þær beon noldon*, and they *guþe ne gymdon*. Perhaps most important, they were motivated to save their own lives, thus placing their personal interests above those of the land, people, and king they were fighting to protect. Those who fled *forlet* this exemplary leader in defiance not only of vows they had made earlier, but also of the implicit heroic contract between a lord and his thegns. The poem evaluates their

---

113 Lapidge, 'Life of Oswald,' 54. 'The Danes too were severely wounded: they were scarcely able to man their ships' (Lapidge, 'Life of Oswald,' 55).

114 'Those who didn't want to be there then fled from the battle: there Odda's sons were the first in flight, Godric [fled] from the battle, and abandoned the good man who had often given him many horses; he leapt upon the horse that had been his lord's, up on the trappings, which was not right, and both his brothers fled with him, Godwine and Godwig, they did not heed the battle, but turned from the fight and sought the woods, fled to safety and saved their lives, and many more than was at all honourable, if they had all remembered the favours that he had often done for them. Thus Offa had said to him earlier in the day at the assembly, when he held the meeting, that many spoke bravely there who would not hold fast in time of need.'

flight in terms of this contract; Godric abandons *þe him mænigne oft mear gesealde*, and none of the three men is guided by a sense of the proper behaviour mandated by the memory of *ealle … þe he him to duguþe gedon hæfde*. In this context, there is no doubt in the mind of poet or reader that *hit ne riht wæs*, and that the defence of Maldon fails because the warriors' actions were not *mæð*.

While this contract bore little resemblance to actual lordship relations in tenth century England, the legal provisions for dealing with deserters in V and VI Æthelred and again in II Cnut point up the very real significance of loyalty and the disastrous effects of these kinds of breaches, especially in battle, as the Chronicle entries above illustrate. V Æthelred decrees that '[28] 7 gif hwa buton leafe of fyrde gewende, þe se cyning sylf on sy, plihte him sylfum oðða wergylde, [28.1] 7 se þe elles ham of fyrde gewende, beo se CXX scill[inga] scyldig,'[115] and VI Æthelred [35] repeats the decree almost verbatim. II Cnut specifies that '[77] And se man, þe ætfleo fram his hlaforde oðða fram his gefearam for his yrhðe, sy hit on scypfyrde, sy hit on landferde, þolige ealles þæs þe he age 7 his agenes feores; 7 fo se hlaford to þam ehtan 7 to his lande, þe he him ær sealde. [77.1] 7 gif he bocland hæbbe, ga þæt þam cyninge to hande.'[116] Like VII Æthelred cited above, these law codes demonstrate that the ideals represented in literary texts were, to varying degrees, lived out by (or at least legislated for) many contemporary Anglo-Saxons, whether the ideals came from the Christian tradition, as in VII Æthelred, or from heroic poetry, as in the codes cited here. They also indicate that flight in battle was widespread enough to require legislation against it. These particular codes, however, highlight the continued relevance of heroic ideals for tenth and eleventh century England, when the welfare of the nation was at stake and treachery and betrayal threatened to harm much more than one's honour or reputation.[117]

---

115 Liebermann, *Gesetze*, 1:244. 'And if anyone should depart without leave from the army where the king himself is, he risks himself or wergild, and he who otherwise departs home from the army shall owe 120 shillings.'

116 Liebermann, *Gesetze*, 1:364. 'And the man who flees from his lord or from his companions because of his cowardice, whether on a naval expedition or a land expedition, shall lose all that he has and his own life; and his lord shall receive the property and his land, which he had earlier given to him. And if he should have *bocland*, that shall come into the king's possession.'

117 Hugh Magennis has pointed out the pervasiveness of treachery and betrayal as themes of the Anglo-Saxon literature copied during this period, and suggested that they resonated strongly with late Anglo-Saxon readers. See *Images of Community in Old English Poetry* (Cambridge: Cambridge University Press, 1996), especially 15–31.

Unlike the *Vita Oswaldi, Maldon* refrains from taking a neutral stance on the scattering army; rather, it paints the leaders of the flight as traitors to Byrhtnoth and further censures the rout through the heroic portrayal of those who stayed to continue the fight and who died *ðegenlice* – as thegns should, in the service of their lord.

The remaining men make their courage known through brave speeches; these speeches are certainly a poetic invention, but they also demonstrate the generic conventions involved in writing a poem of praise for contemporary historical figures. The speeches most clearly reveal the heroic ideology underlying the poetic representation, and they arise from the audience's expectations rather than from any historical reality. Ælfwine, son of Ælfric, voices the traditional duties of a warrior according to the poetic ideal, which has already been betrayed by his fleeing comrades:

'Gemunaþ þa mæla   þe we oft æt meodo spræcon,
þonne we on bence   beot ahofon,
hæleð on healle,   ymbe heard gewinn:
nu mæg cunnian   hwa cene sy.
Ic wylle mine æþelo   eallum gecyþan,
þæt ic wæs on Myrcon   miccles cynnes;
wæs min ealda fæder   Ealhelm haten,
wis ealdorman   woruldgesælig.
Ne sceolon me on þære þeode   þegenas ætwitan
þæt ic of ðisse fyrde   feran wille,
eard gesecan,   nu min ealdor ligeð
forheawen æt hilde.   Me is þæt hearma mæst:
he was ægðer min mæg   and min hlaford.'[118]   (212–24)

Once again, alliteration emphasizes the heroic diction of Ælfwine's speech; he invokes boasts on the benches, heroes in the hall, and the nobility of the lineage (*æþelo* / *eallum* /*ealda* / *Ealhelm* / *ealdorman*) that upholds the connection between *eard* and *ealdor*. Ælfwine already speaks of himself in the past tense ('ic *wæs* on Myrcon miccles cynnes'), perhaps forecasting his

---

118 'Remember now the times when we often spoke over mead, when we raised boasts on the benches, heroes in the hall, about hard struggles: now we can test who is brave. I want to make my noble heritage known to all, that I was from a great kin among the Mercians; my grandfather was called Ealhelm, a wise ealdorman and prosperous. Nor shall thegns among that people taunt me that I wished to leave this army, to seek my home, now that my leader lies cut down in battle. To me that is the greatest pain: he was both my kinsman and my lord.'

intention to die fighting, if necessary. But more important is the link he establishes between nobility and honouring the promises made in the mead-hall; they are the very promises that Offa warned Byrhtnoth would be broken when he needed them most. Ælfwine intends to set an example in contrast to that of the men who fled, and both defines his duties in words for the benefit of his audience and then lives up to them in his actions. As Offa says in return, 'Hwæt, þu, Ælfwine, hafast ealle gemanode, / þegenas to þearfe' (231–2a).[119] He expresses the need for each man to encourage his fellows in the fight, declaring that 'Us Godric hæfð, / earh Oddan bearn, ealle beswicene' (237b–238),[120] and finally condemning him roundly: 'Abreoðe his angin, / þæt he her swa manigne man aflymde' (242b–243).[121] The other supporters of Byrhtnoth follow suit: Leofsunu, the yeoman Dunnere, the Northumbrian hostage Æscferth, Edward the Tall, Æthelric, Wistan, Oswold, Eadwold, Byrhtwold, and another Godric abandon class and regional distinctions to assert their unity through their fallen lord. These men are all individually named, a technique ensuring that their reputations will live on after their deaths; many of them even deliver bold, hortative speeches meant to inspire others to similar feats of loyalty. Their position is perhaps most succinctly expressed by Dunnere:

> unorne ceorl,   ofer eall clypode,
> bæd þæt beorna gehwylc   Byrhtnoð wrece:
> 'Ne mæg na wandian   se þe wrecan þenceð
> frean on folce,   ne for feore murnan.'[122]   (256–9)

Like the scop's song immortalizing Beowulf's fight with Grendel directly following the battle itself, The Battle of Maldon turns current events into history through the medium of heroic poetry, thereby investing them with both meaning and historical significance. The poetic form, as Helen Phillips has argued, is a mimetic re-enactment of the action of the poem itself, one that brings the poem's audience even closer to the event, at the same time that the invocation of the heroic mode sets the actors and actions apart from the everyday by aligning them with larger-than-life heroes in spirit,

---

119 'So you, Ælfwine, have encouraged everyone, thegns in the fight.'
120 'Godric, the craven son of Odda, has betrayed us all.'
121 'Damn his action, that he should put so many men to flight here.'
122 'The simple peasant called out over them all, bid that each of the warriors should avenge Byrhtnoth: "He must never flinch who thinks to avenge his lord among the people, nor care for his life."'

if not in direct allusion.[123] The poem seems, paradoxically, to suggest that the Anglo-Saxon inheritance of Germanic glory both is and is not a part of contemporary English identity.

The routing of the English army thus becomes a moral as well as a military defeat for the deserters, who have failed to fulfil the promise of their heroic ancestors.[124] The poem offers a framework for interpreting the battle at Maldon, and the morality it champions runs parallel to the morality of salvation history. It is certainly possible that the end of the poem, now lost, originally made a turn toward Wulfstan's model and advocated prayer and repentance. It could likewise have ended with a general call for all Englishmen to take up arms and defend their homeland against the invading Danes, but that too is pure speculation. Some scholars, such as Keynes and John Niles, have even seen the poem as a contribution to the debate over Æthelred's policy of paying tribute to the Vikings.[125] As it stands, however, *The Battle of Maldon* does not offer a solution to the Viking problem, and it does not champion a particular course of action for Æthelred and his nobles.[126] Rather, like Wulfstan's writings, it locates the general evils that have contributed to the decay of English society. The constellation of ideas that make up the heroic warrior ethos stands in stark contrast to the behaviour of late tenth and early eleventh century leaders like Ealdormann Ælfric, and *Maldon* uses this contrast to delineate the problems facing the Anglo-Saxon army. These problems, moreover, are situated along a specifically historical axis. The military prowess that carried the day at Brunanburh and was glorified in that poem is no longer standard among the English, and contemporary English warriors are by and large unequal to the Viking challenge. The heroic code was no more real to the soldiers of 937 than it was to those of 991; the only difference is that in 937 the English won, and in 991 they lost. In the face of that defeat, however, *The Battle of Maldon* bears witness to the heroic spirit of the Anglo-Saxon poetic tradition by representing key figures as the embodiment of the heroic ideal in their words and deeds. That spirit is immortalized in literary form, resurrected from the past by the same text that mourns its passing. Like the dialectical image of the ruin, it signifies both

---

123 Phillips, 'Order of Words.'

124 Scragg also points out the poet's moralistic tendencies in his Introduction in *Maldon*, 37–40.

125 Keynes, 'The Historical Context of the Battle of Maldon,' in Scragg, *Maldon, A.D. 991*, 81–113; and Niles, 'Maldon and Mythopoesis,' *Mediaevalia* 17 (1994): 89–121.

126 But see Niles, who argues in 'Maldon and Mythopoesis' that *Maldon* was written to explain Æthelred's policy of paying tribute to the Vikings.

nostalgia and hope; the very act of acknowledging what is lost brings it once more to consciousness, thereby conferring new life on values that seem to have died. This is nostalgia in the restorative, rather than the reflective, mode. Locating a warrior ethos in the men who died at Maldon paradoxically suggests that the heroic spirit lives on, and that the England serving as the setting of *Maldon* is a land of heroes, though perhaps not as many as it needs.

The paucity of heroes, of course, is precisely what the annalist of the Anglo-Saxon Chronicle seems to lament: that England lacks the heroic spirit that would allow it to fend off the Vikings and achieve the glory of its forebears. As Jonathan Wilcox puts it, 'the chronicler forcefully portrays the collapse of a society which fails to live up to the ideals expressed by those characters in the poem who stay to fight to the end.'[127] *The Battle of Maldon* does not write the Danish conquest into the larger patterns of salvation history, but opts instead for the larger patterns of heroic history. The defeat at Maldon is not God's punishment of a sinful people; rather, it is the outcome of a failure on the part of the nation's leaders to live up to the heroic standard. For both Wulfstan and the *Maldon* poet, the Viking attacks are the result of England's failure to live properly; what constitutes proper living, however, is dictated on the one hand by Christian orthodoxy, and on the other by the tradition of heroic poetry. In both cases, the writers turn to the past in search of explanatory models for contemporary events. But whereas Wulfstan's models in Gildas and Alcuin urge audiences to repent and look forward to future salvation, the *Maldon* poet remains oriented toward the past, oscillating between nostalgia for heroic glory and the faint glimpses of that glory in Byrhtnoth and his *heorðwerod*. What emerges from this reading of *Maldon* is both an appreciation of how the poem speaks to the specific concerns of its historical context and new evidence for the unique role of poetry in structuring historical understanding. Heroic history, as an alternative to Wulfstan's providential model, shows Anglo-Saxon England an image of itself as a nation rooted in a glorious past, and nostalgia thus becomes a key element in our understanding of Anglo-Saxon attitudes to both their history and their present.

IV. Nostalgia and Redemption

Perhaps the most powerful ideological effect of *Maldon*, then, is its redemption, in the Benjaminian sense, of an early eleventh century present

---

127 Wilcox, 'Winning Combination,' 45.

through the fragments of the past that resonate with it. For Benjamin, history is melancholic; like Boym's restorative nostalgia, its foundations rest on the loss of originary meaning, and its drive comes from the desire to restore the fullness of that meaning. In representing the fragments of the past – heroic ideals, loyalty, bravery, and war-gear – *Maldon* rescues them from oblivion and redeems them by understanding them in terms of the present.[128] Certainly the present moment of *Maldon's* composition is one in need of the promise of redemption; recording a moment of cultural crisis, the poem rescues meaning from defeat by employing a nostalgic view of history to paint over the degradation of contemporary events through the invocation of a glorious history in which both poet and readers want to believe. Unlike Wulfstan and the chroniclers, who condemn the present moment as hopeless, the *Maldon* poet finds in the chaos of the Viking crisis an opportunity for the redemption of Englishness. The historicity, in Jameson's sense of the term, of *The Battle of Maldon* 'defamiliarizes' the event and 'allows us that distance from immediacy which is at length characterized as a historical perspective.'[129] By separating readers from their own present by means of the aesthetic mechanism of alliterative verse, nostalgia creates a space in which the emotional responses to history – mourning loss, celebrating glory, honouring heroes, condemning cowards – can take place at a safe distance. Yet readers remain connected to the event, and the poem's invocation of a fragmentary past – for modern readers, both the incomplete poem and the tradition to which it metonymically refers – makes these remnants a powerful ideological force.

In the case of *The Battle of Maldon*, the poet faces a need to cast a staggering military defeat in a positive light for the tribute poem he has been commissioned to write. Heroic history, with its aesthetic of nostalgia, removes the battle from its contemporary context and provides historical distance through narrative. At the same time, the elements of tradition intrinsic to the heroic mode provide a framework for understanding the event not as a tragic loss, but as an opportunity for glory, or *dom*, for the brave warriors who fought to honour their lord. The poem redeems the past, in the Benjaminian sense, by rescuing those fragments of the tradition.

---

128 See Walter Benjamin, *Theses on the Philosophy of History*, in *Illuminations*, ed. Hannah Arendt, trans. Harry Zohn (New York: Schocken, 1968), 253–64; and Max Pensky, *Melancholy Dialectics: Walter Benjamin and the Play of Mourning* (Amherst: University of Massachusetts Press, 1993), especially 20–45.

129 Fredric Jameson, 'Nostalgia for the Present,' in *Postmodernism, or, The Cultural Logic of Late Capitalism*, 279–96 (Durham: Duke University Press, 1991), 284.

Even as it lends authority to *Maldon*'s shaping of history, the tradition it-self is reinforced by its own invocation; as an ideological construct, the heroic mode is an amorphous paradigm, constantly being revised with each invocation and unlocatable in any single rendering. Because it exists everywhere and nowhere at once, the heroic tradition has the power to shape historical discourse without being confined to a single meaning or context; it transcends historical time, bridging the distances between past, present, and future, to shield the tragedy of the Maldon defeat behind a veneer of historical continuity. Heroic history thus becomes an equally suitable vehicle for nationalism. Unlike the salvation teleology that Bede envisioned for the Anglo-Saxons, however, the heroic model constructs England as a nation for whom history charts not the rise to greatness, but greatness as a continuous ontological state: as it is, was, and always will be.

Wulfstan's turn to the past is a reflective one; he sees in the Britons a cautionary tale for his contemporaries, but he emphasizes the historical separation between then and now as a disjunction between the Anglo-Saxons' salvific destiny and their present course. The passage of time is crucial for Wulfstan, because his Anglo-Saxon audience is that much closer to Judgment Day than Gildas's Britons were. The *Maldon* poet, on the other hand, makes no distinction between a heroic ethos derived from myths and legends of the fifth century and the brave speeches he puts in the mouths of the late tenth century men who fought and died for their lord, Byrhtnoth. The poem's nostalgia is of the restorative type; for *Maldon*, the fragments of a heroic past can be reassembled to create a pic-ture of valour and glory in the present day. Like the speaker of *The Ruin*, the *Maldon* poet laments the loss of a great civilization, but both poems also show how the ruins of that greatness persist in the present and can be reconstructed through an aesthetic experience. In response to the apoca-lyptic rhetoric of a homily like the *Sermo Lupi*, *The Battle of Maldon* counters with a vision of history that rejects notions of progress altogether in favour of recuperating the present in terms of the past.

As readers far removed from the historical context of the period we study, our perceptions of the Anglo-Saxons are coloured in large part by the literature that survives, and the fact that so much of this literature deals with heroic themes and legendary history leads us to think of its creators in some of the same terms. Despite the obvious historical disjunction be-tween the Germanic war-band and the late Anglo-Saxon state, the values encoded in heroic literary texts continued to influence and motivate the people who read them; and the resulting ideology – in which living well consists in being willing to die for lord and country – could be a powerful antidote to the sense of despair produced by the ever-degenerating situation with respect to the Vikings. *The Battle of Maldon* demonstrates that not only were heroic ideals alive and well, if not widely practised, in millennial England, but they also played a considerable role in how contemporary writers chose to represent their own historical moment. That this same historical moment is often credited with the genesis of the earliest English nationalism indicates the magnitude of the question of historical representation and how it shapes our understanding of Anglo-Saxon England.

The tradition of heroic history employed by the *Maldon* poet has the same goal as the providential model favoured by Wulfstan: to unify and integrate a group in terms of their identity in the face of devastation by an outside force. To a degree, it also works to bring a seemingly uncontrollable course of events under English control; if the defeat at Maldon is due to the cowardice of the men who fled the field, then encouraging English bravery in battle, like encouraging English prayer and repentance, could help the English protect themselves and their realm against future incursions. But its more immediate effect is to offer a site for grounding an English identity that is badly shaken by the prospect of defeat. The heroic stance taken by *The Battle of Maldon* does not address the concerns of a contemporary audience by direct relevance to contemporary culture; rather, it removes the disaster of the Maldon campaign from the murky political waters of Æthelred's England and places it instead in a context in which loyalty and treachery, fighting and fleeing, are free of moral ambiguity. *Maldon* gazes nostalgically backward toward a time when things were simpler and the English were victorious, but that backward gaze provides a foundation on which to build an understanding of the present. The political intricacies that made the determination of a Viking policy so difficult for Æthelred and his advisers have no bearing on the heroic world of the poem, and its current fragmentary state prevents us from ever knowing whether the poet eventually endorses a particular approach to the Viking problem. The text as it survives reinforces a link between English identity and military heroism that pervades the literary tradition and conditions the historical understanding of its readers.

For modern readers, whose desire is directed to discerning the world of the Anglo-Saxons through their poetry rather than coping with the cultural trauma of military and political annihilation, *The Battle of Maldon* demonstrates one of the many ways in which the Anglo-Saxons envisioned their cultural identity and their relationship to history. Heroic history imagines Englishness as the inheritor of the grand Germanic tradition, a forceful identity that appears again and again throughout Anglo-Saxon literature, but most especially in the vernacular historical texts. The early Chronicle poems, as we shall see in the next chapter, employ the same aesthetic of nostalgia to link the tenth century West Saxon kings with their ancient and mythical forebears; here, as in *Maldon*, the poetry works as propaganda to engender a national identity that recognizes the authority of a strong, centralized ruler and outlines a powerful but ambiguous national destiny. But the nation whose course was charted by Bede, Alcuin, and Wulfstan in their salvation histories has not died, and as we shall see, the national identity generated by heroic history gradually merges with a more universal sense of England as a Christian nation, which ultimately allows the idea of Englishness to survive the Norman Conquest. Because of its lack of specificity and its origin as a discursive construct, heroic Englishness is flexible enough to accommodate a wide range of historical changes and remain intact, beginning with the defeat at Maldon in 991. In the social, political, and literary context of millennial England, amid more pressing concerns, the nostalgic and antiquarian note sounded by *The Battle of Maldon* could easily ring hollow. Instead, it captures and distils the elements of a unique cultural identity and asserts the persistent dignity of a people who may have lost the battle, but have not given up on the war.

In witnessing the transformation of current events into historical discourse, we can see how poetic form conditions the ideological content of historical representation, and fighting the ideological war is, it would seem, the main task of historical poetry. We have already noted in passing some crucial similarities between *The Battle of Maldon* and the traditional verse of the Anglo-Saxon Chronicle; poems such as *The Battle of Brunanburh*, *The Capture of the Five Boroughs*, and *The Death of Edward* also work to historicize and defamiliarize contemporary events through aesthetic distancing. Yet the Chronicle verse has a different story to tell about the role of poetry in the historical consciousness of late Anglo-Saxon England. The same profound nostalgia for a heroic past underscores these verse memorials, but the chronological and geographical range of their production – to say nothing of the range of verse forms the Chronicle incorporates, far beyond the basic alliterative long line – allows for a much broader analysis of the role of poetic form in historiography. The canonical Chronicle verse forms a literary counterpart to *The Battle of Maldon*, in connecting the ruling Wessex dynasty to a long tradition of heroism and victory. If the traditional forms of Old English verse prompt a historical consciousness steeped in nostalgia and heroic glory, however, then the gradual transformation of those forms into another kind of poetry, incorporating poetic techniques apart from alliterative metre, signals the transformation of historical consciousness as well. This transformation is precisely what the verse of the Anglo-Saxon Chronicle will allow us to witness, as the heroic Anglo-Saxon England of the tenth century gradually gives way to the Anglo-Norman England of the post-Conquest era.

4 Poetic Memory: The Canonical Verse of the Anglo-Saxon Chronicle

In the traditional songs which form their only record of the past the Germans celebrate an earth-born god called Tuisto. His son Mannus is supposed to be the fountain-head of their race and himself to have begotten three sons who gave their names to three groups of tribes – the Ingaevones, nearest the sea; the Herminones, in the interior; and the Istaevones, who comprise all the rest.

Tacitus, Germania

When Tacitus describes the Germans and their interest in their own history, two key features are immediately apparent: their investment in tracing their ancestry to euhemerized gods, and the record of the past in 'traditional songs.'[1] The Anglo-Saxon Chronicle demonstrates a similar investment in tracing origins and in traditional songs, though its deployment of these factors differs significantly from that of the Germans Tacitus describes. When the author of the Chronicle's A-text begins the narration of Anglo-Saxon history with a genealogy built on the traditional heroic model, he invokes that nostalgic past in the service of interpreting and authorizing the present:

ÞY GEARE ÞE WÆS AGAN FRAM CRISTES ACENnesse .cccc. wintra 7 .xciiii. uuintra, þa Cerdic 7 Cynric his sunu cuom up æt Cerdicesoran mid .v. scipum; 7 se Cerdic wæs Elesing, Elesa Esling, Esla Gewising, Giwis Wiging, Wig Freawining, Freawine Friþugaring, Friþugar Bronding, Brond Bęldæging, Bęldæg Wodening ... Se Eþelwulf wæs Ecgbryhting, Ecgbryht Ealhmunding,

---

1 Tacitus, *The Agricola and the Germania*, trans. Harold Mattingly, rev. trans. S.A. Handford (Harmondsworth: Penguin, 1970), 102. See also *Cornelii Taciti opera minora*, ed. M. Winterbottom and R.M. Ogilvie (Oxford: Clarendon, 1975).

Ealhmund Eafing, Eafa Eopping, Eoppa Ingilding, Ingild Cenreding, 7 Ine
Cenreding 7 Cuþburg Cenreding 7 Cuenburg Cenreding, Cenred Ceolwalding,
Ceolwald Cuþwulfing, Cuþwulf Cuþwining, Cuþwine Celming, Celm
Cynricing, Cynric Cerdicing.[2]

The chronicler looks back to the period of the *adventus Saxonum*, the first
arrival of the Anglo-Saxons on the island, and he links the patron of his enterprise, Alfred, through direct paternal lineage to those first conquerors,
Cerdic and Cynric. But his invocation of that specific fiction of history also
directs a reader's interpretation of the following information; that is, since
the A-text begins by invoking a heroic mode, we are to read the deeds of the
Cerdicing dynasty as those of heroes – more important, as those of people
who are authorized, by tradition and by antiquity, to rule the Anglo-Saxons.
At the ninth century moment of its creation, the Chronicle looks back nostalgically to the fifth century, but it is nostalgic in the Jamesonian sense of a
'nostalgia for the present.'[3] The manuscript's opening regnal list asserts two
kinds of origins: the first, a chronological origin from the birth of Christ,
and the second, an ethnic origin from the arrival of Cerdic, who traces his
own lineage to Woden. The A-text thus instantiates the very tradition on
which it will base its claims to authority and those of the Anglo-Saxon kings
it chronicles. The chief purpose of this prefatory matter is to link the
Chronicle's patron, King Alfred, with the ideological power of Anglo-Saxon
England's hybrid origins, both Christian and Germanic, both human and
divine. Most important, it ends with the record of Alfred's accession following his father and his brothers: 'Þa feng Ęlfred hiera broþur to rice, 7 þa was
agan his ielde .xxiii. wintra 7 .ccc. 7 .xcvi. wintra þæs þe his cyn ærest

---

2 Janet M. Bately, ed., *MS A*, The Anglo-Saxon Chronicle: A Collaborative Edition 3
   (Cambridge: D.S. Brewer, 1986), 1. 'In the year when 494 years had passed since the
   birth of Christ, Cerdic and his son Cynric landed at Cerdic's Shore with five ships; and
   Cerdic was the son of Elesa, Elesa the son of Esla, Esla the son of Gewis, Giwis the son
   of Wig, Wig the son of Freawine, Freawine the son of Frithugar, Frithugar the son of
   Brond, Brond the son of Beldæg, Beldæg the son of Woden ... Æthelwulf was the son of
   Ecgbryht, Ecgbryht the son of Ealhmund, Ealhmund the son of Eafa, Eafa the son of
   Eoppa, Eoppa the son of Ingild, Ingild the son of Cenred, and Ine the son of Cenred
   and Cuthburg the son of Cenred and Cuenburg the son of Cenred, Cenred the son of
   Ceolwald, Ceolwald the son of Cuthwulf, Cuthwulf the son of Cuthwine, Cuthwine
   the son of Celm, Celm the son of Cynric, Cynric the son of Cerdic.' All translations are
   my own.
3 See pp. 4–6 above.

Westseaxna lond on Wealum geeodon.'[4] Alfred's rule is sanctioned by the long-standing dominion of his ancestors, going back nearly four centuries, and if there is a telos governing the narrative of the Chronicle, it is West Saxon kingship. The genealogy s.a. 855, where Æthelwulf's death is recorded, re-emphasizes the teleology, this time extending the Wessex lineage beyond Woden through Noah to Adam. The A-text author's use of nostalgia thus provides an ideological framework for interpreting the history of the island, and that framework is aimed at validating the authority of the West Saxon dynasty who rule England not at the beginning, where the Cerdicings' mythic origins are located by this nostalgic narrative, but in the moment of the creation of the text.

Numerous scholars have commented on the role of these genealogies in asserting West Saxon hegemony.[5] Their relationship to Tacitus's 'traditional songs' is remarkable; not only do they trace the lineage of the Anglo-Saxons to divine origins, but they also take the form of alliterative metre. Thomas Bredehoft has analysed the genealogy that prefaces the A-text of the Chronicle, as well as other genealogies that occur in the Common Stock, and has found that not only do they alliterate (as elite genealogies often do; think of Hrothgar and his sons Hrethric and Hrothmund in *Beowulf*, for example), but they also form regular metrical half-lines.[6] The genealogies, then, are heroic verse; although they offer no narrative, they evoke a series of moments in time and show how those moments are connected, by means of both the formal device of alliteration and invocation of the continuity of history. Furthermore, as Jennifer Neville has recently pointed out, the structure of these genealogies 'radically disrupts the uni-directional flow of time which fundamentally makes a chronicle what it is' by simultaneously tracing relationships both forward and backward through time.[7] Such temporal dislocation, and the

---

4 Bately, *MS A*, 2. 'Then Alfred their brother succeeded to the kingdom, and he was then twenty-three years old and it was 396 years since his ancestors had first conquered the land of the West Saxons from the Britons.'

5 See, for example, Kenneth Sisam, 'Anglo-Saxon Royal Genealogies,' *PBA* 39 (1953): 287–348; David N. Dumville, 'The West Saxon Genealogical Regnal List and the Chronology of Early Wessex,' *Peritia* 4 (1985): 21–66, and 'The West Saxon Genealogical Regnal List: Manuscripts and Texts,' *Anglia* 104 (1986): 1–32; and Sarah Foot, 'The Making of *Angelcynn*: English Identity before the Norman Conquest,' *TRHS*, 6th ser., 6 (1996): 25–49.

6 Thomas A. Bredehoft, *Textual Histories: Readings in the* Anglo-Saxon Chronicle (Toronto: University of Toronto Press, 2001), 14–38.

7 Jennifer Neville, 'Making Their Own Sweet Time: The Scribes of *Anglo-Saxon Chronicle A*,' in *The Medieval Chronicle II: Proceedings of the 2nd International Conference on*

possibilities it raises for historical consciousness, bear no small similarity to the kind of history encoded by heroic verse, and the relationship of this nostalgic framing device of the 'myth of origins' to the heroic poetry that also commemorates certain actors and events in the Anglo-Saxon Chronicle merits further investigation.

The greatest difficulty facing scholars who study the Anglo-Saxon Chronicle is, of course, the fact that it does not exist as a single text, but as a series of compilations and redactions occupying eight extant manuscripts and perhaps dozens of hypothetical ones.[8] This complicated transmission history makes it impossible to speak of any one version as 'the' Chronicle, and the range of variations forecloses any attempt at a unifying or totalizing reading. Yet this often frustrating text allows us to witness the production of Anglo-Saxon history in multiple locations and at different times during the Anglo-Saxon period, including the years following the Norman Conquest. In the Chronicle, we can see the development of a vernacular historiographic tradition that covers a wider geographic and temporal range than any other medieval history does; instead of being limited to a single author's or locale's perspective, we can see what constituted Anglo-Saxon historical

---

the Medieval Chronicle Driebergen (Utrecht 16–21 July 1999), ed. Erik Kooper, 166–77 (Amsterdam: Rodopi, 2002), 172.

8 I include in this count manuscript G (London, British Library, Cotton Otho B. xi, fols 39–47 + Additional 34652, fol. 2 [Winchester, s. x med + s. xi¹]), mostly destroyed in the Cotton Fire but reconstructed from fragments, transcripts, and collation with other manuscripts by Angelika Lutz (Die Version G der angelsächsichen Chronik [Munich: Wilhelm Fink, 1981]). The fragmentary manuscript H (London, British Library, Cotton Domitian ix, fol. 9 [s. xii¹]) contains only two annals, neither of which includes a poem. The other Chronicle manuscripts are Cambridge, Corpus Christi College 173, fols 1v–32v (Winchester, s. ix/x–xi²; MS A); London, British Library, Cotton Tiberius A. vi, fols 1–34 + A. iii, fol. 178 (Abingdon, s. x²; MS B); London, British Library, Cotton Tiberius B. i, fols 115v–164 (Abingdon or Canterbury, s. xi¹–xi²; MS C); London, British Library, Cotton Tiberius B. iv, fols 3–86 (Worcester or York, s. xi med. –xi²; MS D); Oxford, Bodleian Library, Laud Misc. 636 (Peterborough, s. xii¹, xii med.; MS E); and London, British Library, Cotton Domitian viii, fols 30–70 (Christ Church, Canterbury, s. xi/xii; MS F). On the transmission history of the Anglo-Saxon Chronicle, see Charles Plummer, Two of the Saxon Chronicles Parallel, 2 vols (Oxford: Clarendon, 1892–9), 2:xxiii–cii; Dorothy Whitelock, ed., with David C. Douglas and Susie I. Tucker, The Anglo-Saxon Chronicle: A Revised Translation (New Brunswick: Rutgers University Press, 1961); Antonia Gransden, Historical Writing in England, c. 550 to c. 1307 (Ithaca: Cornell University Press, 1974), 32–41; and Janet Bately, The Anglo-Saxon Chronicle: Texts and Textual Relationships, Reading Medieval Studies Monographs 3 (Reading: University of Reading, 1991). For more detailed examinations of specific manuscripts, see the individual volumes of The Anglo-Saxon Chronicle: A Collaborative Edition, ed. David Dumville and Simon Keynes, 9 vols (Cambridge: D.S. Brewer, 1983–).

discourse at different times and places in the nation's history. We can also witness the production of that historical discourse in a variety of forms, from the standard prose annal to the highly formalized genealogies and, finally, to the verse passages incorporated into the annals beginning s.a. 937 (MSS ABCD). With the exception of the bilingual manuscript F and the two annals that comprise manuscript H, every manuscript uses poetry in multiple instances to portray certain events.[9] These poems cover a wide range of styles and genres; they include epideictic verse, encomia, apostrophes, and commentary; they chronicle military victories, marriages, the deaths of kings and princes, and the abuse of power; they range in tone from heroic to hagiographic; and they focus on the interests of both secular and ecclesiastical authorities. In short, they run the gamut in terms of both style and content, and they display a wide range of form as well.

The nature and role of these verse passages have remained unclear and comparatively unexamined through the history of Chronicle scholarship, and in what follows I want to consider the Anglo-Saxon Chronicle as a species of *prosimetrum*, a genre that mixes prose and verse for varying rhetorical purposes. Specifically, I want to examine how the use of heroic poetry as a form of history sets certain events apart from others recounted in the Chronicle, and how the historical consciousness encoded by that form operates as an ideological force in tandem with other aspects of the Chronicle's production, such as the genealogies. The canonical Chronicle poems memorialize the scions of the Alfredian House of Wessex in much the same way that *The Battle of Maldon* commemorated the fallen heroes of Byrhtnoth's *heorðwerod*, by deploying the aesthetics of nostalgia to historicize contemporary (or near-contemporary) events as the stuff of legend.[10] Like *Maldon*, the Chronicle verse encourages its audience to

---

9 And even F contains abridged versions of the poems found in other manuscripts s.a. 958 (for 959), 979, and 1011; see Peter S. Baker, ed., *MS F*, The Anglo-Saxon Chronicle: A Collaborative Edition 8 (Cambridge: D.S. Brewer, 2000).

10 Five poetic passages in the Chronicle follow the regular metrical patterns of classical Old English verse and were canonized in *The Anglo-Saxon Minor Poems*, ed. Elliott van Kirk Dobbie, ASPR 6 (New York: Columbia University Press, 1942), 16–26 and 146–51. ASPR also includes a sixth poem, *The Death of Alfred*, which Dobbie describes as 'partly in prose, partly in verse' due to the irregularity of its metre (xlii). These poems go under the familiar titles of *The Battle of Brunanburh* (937), *The Capture of the Five Boroughs* (942), *The Coronation of Edgar* (973), *The Death of Edgar* (975), *The Death of Alfred* (1036), and *The Death of Edward* (1065). In addition to these six, there are twelve passages that distinguish themselves from standard prose and have been treated at various times as verse. These so-called irregular verse passages are the subject of chap. 5 below.

imagine its subjects as the embodiment of a heroic past that is reconstituted in late Anglo-Saxon England; here, however, the heroism resides in the nation's rulers and helps to connect them to the people. In addition, like the Junius poems, these texts stand as products of a cultural hybridity that turns Old Testament patriarchs into Germanic *hlafordas* and Anglo-Saxon war leaders into *milites Christi*. In the context of the Anglo-Saxon Chronicle, itself a composite text, hybridity takes many and varied forms. The Chronicle poems are, as Martin Irvine has suggested, 'an act of poetic nostalgia,' but they are also a deployment of that nostalgia for particular political and ideological ends.[11]

I. Thinking about Form: The Chronicle as *prosimetrum*

The mixture of prose and verse in the Anglo-Saxon Chronicle is not unique; the Latin genre known as *prosimetrum* enjoyed something of a golden age during the medieval period, although a version in vernacular historiography is rather unusual for so early a date.[12] A form carried over from late Antiquity, *prosimetrum* identified a work in which both verse and prose were used to convey the meaning of the text. Classical examples include allegorical-philosophical works such as Martianus Capella's *De nuptiis Philologiae et Mercurii* and Boethius's *De consolatione Philosophiae*, both of which enjoyed widespread popularity throughout the Middle Ages. As a genre, *prosimetrum* has attracted comparatively little critical attention, perhaps because of the linguistic, geographical, and chronological breadth of the form.[13] Its study is also complicated by the inherent

11 Martin Irvine, 'Medieval Textuality and the Archaeology of Textual Culture,' in *Speaking Two Languages: Traditional Disciplines and Contemporary Theory in Medieval Studies*, ed. Allen J. Frantzen, 181–210 (Albany: State University of New York Press, 1991), 202.

12 For an overview of the Latin *prosimetrum* tradition, see Peter Dronke, *Verse with Prose from Petronius to Dante: The Art and Scope of the Mixed Form* (Cambridge, MA: Harvard University Press, 1994); and Bernhard Pabst, *Prosimetrum: Tradition und Wandel einer Literaturform zwischen Spätantike und Spätmittelalter*, 2 vols (Cologne: Böhlau, 1994).

13 Until recently, the study of *prosimetrum* has remained limited to its use in specific texts; since 1994, however, three full-length studies have appeared. See Dronke, *Verse with Prose*; Pabst, *Prosimetrum*; and Joseph Harris and Karl Reichl, eds, *Prosimetrum: Cross-Cultural Perspectives on Narrative in Prose and Verse* (Cambridge: D.S. Brewer, 1997). Studies of individual texts useful to the student of Old English literature include Kurt Otten, *König Alfreds Boethius* (Tübingen: Niemeyer, 1964); Allan A. Metcalf, *Poetic Diction in the Old English Meters of Boethius* (The Hague: Mouton, 1973); and

difficulties in defining the genre. Some scholars confine the definition to only those texts conceived, as a whole, by a single author, and in which the verse and prose sections contribute equally and differently to the explication of meaning.[14] Indeed, the texts that served as models for medieval writers followed this form, and the earliest *prosimetra* of the Middle Ages were conceived as coherent texts.[15] Classical models were primarily allegorical-philosophical works like those of Martianus and Boethius; in the Middle Ages, however, the genre found specific resonances with historical narrative as well, and surfaced in both hagiographical and historical texts from the mid-ninth century onward.[16] Many well-known historical texts incorporated both verse and prose, including Bede's *Historia ecclesiastica*, the *Historia Langobardum* of Paul the Deacon, the *Annales Fuldenses*, Dudo of Saint-Quentin's *Gesta Normannorum*, and the *Chronicon* of Thietmar of Merseburg. The use of poetry works both formally and rhetorically in these texts to underscore moments of high emotional investment in praise songs and death laments, as well as providing the author with an alternative voice or voices in which to express apostrophes and commentary on events; it allows authors to capitalize on a 'genre that exploits the tension between prose and poetry and at the same time also makes use of the different possibilities of these types of discourse.'[17]

Preben Meulengracht Sørensen, 'The Prosimetrum Form 1: Verses as the Voice of the Past,' in *Skaldsagas: Text, Vocation, and Desire in the Icelandic Sagas of Poets*, ed. Russell Poole, 172–90 (Berlin: Walter de Gruyter, 2001). In omitting vernacular texts from consideration, the surveys by Dronke and Pabst make an overwhelmingly large topic somewhat more manageable, but they also exclude a significant portion of relevant literature. The collections edited by Poole and by Harris and Reichl provide an important corrective to this tendency to divorce Latin and vernacular literature.

14 Pabst argues for such a definition at some length (*Prosimetrum*, 12–15).

15 The genre of *geminus stilus* or *opus geminatum*, also descended from classical exemplars, seems to offer an equally important locus for the comparative study of the use of prose and verse. For an overview, see Peter Godman, 'The Anglo-Latin *opus geminatum*: From Aldhelm to Alcuin,' *Medium Ævum* 50 (1981): 215–29; and Gernot Wieland, '*Geminus stilus*: Studies in Anglo-Latin Hagiography,' in *Insular Latin Studies*, ed. Michael Herren, 113–33 (Toronto: PIMS, 1981). This category of mixed form involves writing two parallel texts, one in prose and one in verse, that both explore the same ideas and includes the schoolroom practice of paraphrasing prose in verse, and vice versa. *Geminus stilus* or *opus geminatum* enjoyed considerable popularity in Anglo-Saxon England.

16 Pabst, *Prosimetrum*, 601.

17 Edith Marold, 'The Relation between Verses and Prose in *Bjarnar saga Hítœlakappa*,' in Poole, *Skaldsagas*, 75–124 at 75.

In Anglo-Saxon England, *prosimetrum* was found primarily in hagiography and spiritual writings; the *De virginitate* of Aldhelm and Bede's *Vitae S. Cuthberti* are well-known examples of the Latin *opus geminatum* tradition as it continued in England, but the later *Translatio et miracula S. Swithuni* by Lantfred of Winchester is the earliest true example of the mixed form within a single text.[18] The form spans the centuries of Anglo-Saxon cultural production, from Bede's *Historia ecclesiastica* to the late eleventh century *Vita Aedwardi Regis*.[19] But the use of mixed form in the Anglo-Saxon Chronicle forces us to consider the translation of that tradition from a Latin to a vernacular setting. Indeed, the bulk of scholarship on *prosimetrum* has tended to focus, for obvious reasons, on the Latin tradition and its continuation into the Middle Ages; the genre is more rarely examined in regard to vernacular texts, and the examinations that have been undertaken are found within studies of individual texts rather than in broad surveys of the genre.[20]

Critical interest in *prosimetrum*, both in the Middle Ages and in recent scholarship, focuses on the genre as offering a rare opportunity to observe the differences in how prose and verse function in the same environment, where the formal contrast between verse and prose is highlighted by their

---

18 Pabst, *Prosimetrum*, 661–5. Later sermons by Ælfric have also caused debate among scholars as to their status; Ælfric's diction contains much that mirrors the poetic tradition, and the classification of 'rhythmical prose' does not always seem to account for his style. See chap. 5 below, and Bredehoft, 'Ælfric and Late Old English Verse,' *ASE* 33 (2004): 77–107. Aldhelm, *Carmen de virginitate*, in *Aldhelmi opera*, ed. Rudolf Ehwald, MGH, Auctores antiquissimi, 15 (Berlin: Weidmann, 1919), 327–471, and *Prosa de virginitate*, ed. Scott Gwara, CCSL 124 and 124A (Turnhout: Brepols, 2001). Bede, *Two Lives of Saint Cuthbert: A Life by an Anonymous Monk of Lindisfarne and Bede's Prose Life*, ed. and trans. Bertram Colgrave (Cambridge: Cambridge University Press, 1940; repr. 1985), and *Bedas metrische 'Vita Sancti Cuthberti,'* ed. Werner Jaager (Leipzig: Mayer and Müller, 1935). Lantfred of Winchester, *Translatio et miracula S. Swithuni*, in *The Cult of St Swithun*, ed. and trans. Michael Lapidge, Winchester Studies 4.ii (Oxford: Clarendon, 2003), 252–333.

19 *Bede's Ecclesiastical History of the English People*, ed. and trans. Bertram Colgrave and R.A.B. Mynors (Oxford: Clarendon, 1969); *Vita Ædwardi Regis qui apud Westmonasterium requiescit*, ed. and trans. Frank Barlow, 2nd ed. (Oxford: Clarendon, 1992).

20 Such studies include Otten, *König Alfreds Boethius*; Metcalf, *Poetic Diction*; Francis R. Swietek, 'Gunther of Pairis and the *Historia Constantinopolitana*,' *Speculum* 53 (1978): 49–79; and Renate Blumenfeld-Kosinski, 'Moralization and History: Verse and Prose in the *Histoire ancienne jusqu'à César* (in B.N. f.fr. 20125),' *Zeitschrift für romanische Philologie* 97 (1981): 41–6.

juxtaposition.[21] The actual functions of the two forms are difficult to define and vary considerably from one text to another. Specific formal differences between verse and prose are equally difficult to identify. Given the extremely wide range of poetic markers available to the modern reader, extending far beyond rhyme, metre, alliteration, and figurative language, it is perhaps easiest to say simply, 'We know it when we see it.' Medieval readers and writers presumably also knew verse when they saw it, since treatises on rhetoric frequently make distinctions between prose and verse.[22] Caroline D. Eckhardt, following Isidore of Seville, finds that prose is 'discourse that is intellectually free: discourse not controlled by expectations of meter and therefore free to follow the shape of ideas rather than linguistic patterns,' whereas poetry is limited in its forms of expression and more suited to emotion than reason.[23] Eckhardt's unambiguous dichotomy between reason and emotion may be over-simple, but in practice verse passages seem to offer an opportunity for authors to interpret, moralize, apostrophize, and generally comment in ways that stand at one remove from the narrative of the prose text.[24] They frequently offer formulaic

---

21 Unfortunately, the evidence does not point to a single conclusion. Some scholars, such as Godman, follow Roman rhetorical theory to argue that writing the same thing in both verse and prose demonstrates the interchangeability of the two forms ('Anglo-Latin *opus geminatum*,' 217). Wieland, in contrast, insists that this kind of duplication, the revision that inevitably accompanied it, and the different audiences for which it was intended all point to the inherent difference between verse and prose ('*Geminus stilus*,' 114–17).

22 Caroline D. Eckhardt, 'The Medieval *Prosimetrum* Genre (From Boethius to *Boece*),' *Genre* 16 (1983): 21–38 at 22. See also Bredehoft on scribal indications of the boundaries between verse and prose, in 'The Boundaries between Verse and Prose in Old English Literature,' in *Old English Literature in Its Manuscript Context*, ed. Joyce Tally Lionarons, 139–72 (Morgantown: West Virginia University Press, 2004). Kristin Hanson and Paul Kiparsky postulate verse and prose as two subsets of literary language; they are distinguished by prose's being a marked form of literary language, and verse's being unmarked. Hanson and Kiparsky argue that prose is marked by its suppression of the qualities that identify stylized language, whereas verse is the stylization of natural features of a language, such as metre. See Hanson and Kiparsky, 'The Nature of Verse and Its Consequences for the Mixed Form,' in Harris and Reichl, *Prosimetrum*, 17–44.

23 Eckhardt, 'Medieval *Prosimetrum*,' 22; see also Harris and Reichl, *Prosimetrum*, 4; and Isidore, *Etymologiae* I.38.1, ed. W.M. Lindsay, *Isidori Hispalensis episcopi Etymologiarum sive Originum libri xx*, 2 vols (Oxford: Clarendon, 1957).

24 See, for example, Pabst, *Prosimetrum*, 1029–48; and Emily Albu, *The Normans in Their Histories: Propaganda, Myth, and Subversion* (Woodbridge: Boydell, 2001), 36.

phrases and conventional interpretations of the events recounted by the annals; that is certainly the case in a poem like *The Death of Edgar*, in which the poet offers moral platitudes in response to historical events. In other cases, however, the bulk of the narrative is told in verse, and commentary, transitions, and summaries are offered in prose.[25] *The Battle of Brunanburh*, for example, offers a full narrative account of a single battle, whereas the prose annals that surround it provide far less detail about the events they record.

However the textual work is divided between prose and verse, the divisions are made clear by the variation of form, and formal juxtaposition contributes to the overall meaning of the text as a whole. In her study of verse quotations in medieval French romance, Maureen Boulton observes that the tension created by this formal juxtaposition not only drives the narrative, but makes it dialogic; that is, the prose and the verse speak to each other in a variety of ways.[26] Verse segments can reinforce the underlying ideology of the prose narrative, or they can make an ironic statement using what Boulton calls the 'poetics of contrast.'[27] In the case of the Chronicle, the poetic form itself, heroic verse, signals the moral and historical valence of the episode by invoking a particular cultural tradition. The mixed form, then, creates an opportunity for a clearly delineated, multi-voiced narrative within a single text, a possibility that plainly appealed to writers of *prosimetrum* such as Boethius and that complicates the unitary vision of history more familiar from the epic. In the Chronicle, formal variation draws attention to particular events, and alliterative metre indicates the context of values in which those events are to be understood.

The Anglo-Saxon Chronicle presents certain challenges to standard definitions of *prosimetrum*. Unlike most of the texts mentioned above as examples of the genre, the Chronicle is not a single text written by a single author; its form, therefore, is not the result of intentional composition, but grows out of the texts' continued development as they were copied, circulated, emended, and edited by a multitude of writers over several centuries. Many scholars, such as Jan Ziolkowski, argue that 'annals and chronicles which happen to include now and then a verse epitaph, other sorts of

---

25 Harris and Reichl, *Prosimetrum*, 7–8.
26 Maureen Barry McCann Boulton, *The Song in the Story: Lyric Insertions in French Narrative Fiction, 1200–1400* (Philadelphia: University of Pennsylvania Press, 1993). Boulton's concept of dialogism draws on M.M. Bakhtin, *The Dialogic Imagination: Four Essays*, ed. Michael Holquist, trans. Caryl Emerson and Michael Holquist (Austin: University of Texas Press, 1981), especially 3–40 and 259–88.
27 Boulton, *Lyric Insertions*, 1–23.

memorial verses, or short occasional verses cited as sources are not to be accorded full status as *prosimetra*.'[28] Yet others insist that we need not abandon the formal knowledge gained from the study of *prosimetrum* in attempting to fathom the role of poetry in less formal or coherent texts, especially those in the vernacular. Extending the definition to include any text that contains both prose and verse, whether written by a single author or not, offers a valuable perspective on the formal aspects of the various Chronicle texts.[29] The writers of these texts chose to use poems alongside prose, and their inclusion of verse among the tenth century annals set a precedent that later continuators seemed happy, even eager, to follow. Moreover, the transition from poems that stood alone as complete annals to verse passages incorporated into longer prose entries indicates that later readers recognized the prosimetric form the Chronicle had adopted, and even fostered its continuation. As Bredehoft has demonstrated, the juxtaposition of verse with prose in a single text offers the opportunity to examine if, and how, readers might recognize the difference, and manuscript evidence indicates that even the irregular Chronicle verse was in fact marked as such by many scribes.[30] If contemporary readers recognized the mixing of forms in the Chronicle as fundamental to reading them properly, then surely modern readers can do no less.

Thinking of the Chronicle as a kind of *prosimetrum*, therefore, can help us understand how the varying formal characteristics of the different Chronicle texts indicate shifting relations between English identity and the documentation of an English past. The heroic memorialization of events that dominates the tenth century Anglo-Saxon Chronicle verse entries capitalizes on cultural nostalgia to uphold the homogeneity of identity between Anglo-Saxon England and the House of Wessex.[31] Their

---

28 Jan Ziolkowski, 'The Prosimetrum in the Classical Tradition,' in Harris and Reichl, *Prosimetrum*, 45–65 at 56; similarly, Pabst, *Prosimetrum*, 606.

29 This wider definition of *prosimetrum* informs the essays collected in Poole, which consider the inclusion of skaldic poetry in later sagas as offering an example of *prosimetrum* that differs, but is not wholly distinct, from Latin forms precisely because they originate with different authors (Poole, *Skaldsagas*, 10–11 and 75).

30 Bredehoft, 'Boundaries between Verse and Prose,' 156–67.

31 As numerous scholars have aptly noted; see, for example, Irvine, 'Medieval Textuality,' 202. On the nostalgia of Anglo-Saxon literature more generally, see Nicholas Howe, *Migration and Mythmaking in Anglo-Saxon England* (New Haven: Yale University Press, 1989; repr. Notre Dame: University of Notre Dame Press, 2001); and Roy M. Liuzza, '*Beowulf*: Monuments, Memory, History,' in *Readings in Medieval Texts: Interpreting Old and Middle English Literature*, ed. David F. Johnson and Elaine Treharne, 91–108 (Oxford: Oxford University Press, 2005).

invocation of the epic tradition lays the foundations of an epic national past; as Mikhail Bakhtin writes in a different context, 'these songs transfer to contemporary events and contemporaries the ready-made epic form; that is, they transfer to these events the time-and-value contour of the past, thus attaching them to the world of fathers, of beginnings and peak times – canonizing these events, as it were, while they are still current.'[32] For Bakhtin, the epic creates history as a monolithic totality in which the nation speaks with a single voice. In the case of Anglo-Saxon England, the early Chronicle speaks with the voice of the West Saxon royal court. The canonical Chronicle verse is invested in forging an ideological link between the nation's leaders and its heroic past; it is another instance of Boym's restorative nostalgia, bridging chronological distance to bring the heroic past into the present of the events it chronicles and of its readers.[33] This nostalgia encounters history as a dialectic; the same form that forges an ideological link also creates a space for ambiguity by disrupting the Chronicle's narrative teleology. As a result, the introduction of verse into a text as unstable as the Chronicle also opens the way for future chroniclers to exploit the formal tension between verse and prose; and as the Anglo-Saxon Chronicle moves out of the West Saxon sphere of influence, the verse entries – particularly the so-called irregular ones – begin to represent alternative voices within the hegemonic historical narrative. Over the next two chapters, I want to explore the development and deployment of verse forms within the Anglo-Saxon Chronicle, first as they work to reconstitute the heroic age for contemporary audiences, and then as they move away from Wessex hegemony and become increasingly diglossic. This diglossia is the focus of the next chapter; first, we must consider how poetry begins to be incorporated into the Chronicle, and what purpose or purposes it serves for the chroniclers and their patrons in the earlier manuscripts (ABC) created and propagated within the court circles of the West Saxon kings.

II. The Study of the Anglo-Saxon Chronicle and the Chronicle Verse

The exact origins of the Chronicle remain hidden,[34] but the text is most often associated with the court of King Alfred and assumed to have been

---

32   Bakhtin, *Dialogic Imagination*, 14–15.
33   See pp. 131–2 above.
34   The composition and transmission of the Chronicle have been studied in great detail by Bately and Audrey L. Meaney. See Bately, *Texts and Textual Relationships*; 'The Compilation of the Anglo-Saxon Chronicle 60 BC to AD 890: Vocabulary as Evidence,'

commissioned during the later years of his reign; the Common Stock runs up to 891, offering a convenient terminus a quo for the primary instalment. The extant manuscripts represent continuations of the original Common Stock written up at various times and in various places, but all trace their origins to the massive program of vernacular textual production of the Alfredian court that produced other literary monuments to history such as the Old English translation of Orosius's *Historiarum aduersum paganos libri VII* and possibly the Old English version of Bede's *Historia ecclesiastica* as well.[35] Unlike the works of Bede and Orosius (and their Old English translations), however, the Anglo-Saxon Chronicle was never a completed text; as a chronicle, it was not meant to represent the coherent view of a single author for a particular audience. Rather, it encompassed a range of viewpoints and ideas and found itself less constrained by the requirements of a unified framework. Scholars have argued that the chronicle form itself originated as marginal annotations in Easter tables,[36] and that their purpose was 'to remind readers of important events so that the full stories and related facts would come to mind,'[37] rather like the fragments of narrative employed by Deor to evoke fuller stories from the poetic tradition. In this respect, a chronicle distinguishes itself from a

PBA 64 (1980 for 1978): 93–129; 'The Compilation of the *Anglo-Saxon Chronicle* Once More,' *Leeds Studies in English*, n.s., 16 (1985): 7–26; and 'Manuscript Layout and the Anglo-Saxon Chronicle,' *Bulletin of the John Rylands University Library of Manchester* 70 (1988): 21–43. See Meaney, 'D: An Undervalued Manuscript of the Anglo-Saxon Chronicle,' *Parergon*, n.s., 1 (1983): 13–38, and 'St. Neots, Æthelweard, and the Compilation of the *Anglo-Saxon Chronicle*: A Survey,' in *Studies in Earlier English Prose*, ed. Paul E. Szarmach, 123–39 (Albany: State University of New York Press, 1986).

35 *The Old English Orosius*, ed. Janet Bately, EETS, s.s., 6 (London: Oxford University Press, 1980); *The Old English Version of Bede's Ecclesiastical History of the English People*, ed. and trans. Thomas Miller, 2 vols, EETS, o.s., 95, 96, 110, and 111 (London: EETS, 1890–8). The Alfredian origin of the Chronicle has long been assumed or at least accepted by scholars. Plummer gives an analysis of the Chronicle's origins and subsequent development (*Saxon Chronicles*, 2:cii–cxxii). More recent scholarship tends to focus on the production of individual manuscripts; see, for example, Bately, *Texts and Textual Relationships*; Cyril Hart, 'The B Text of the *Anglo-Saxon Chronicle*,' *JMH* 8 (1982): 241–99; and Meaney, 'D: An Undervalued Manuscript.' For a thorough overview of recent Chronicle scholarship, see Jacqueline Stodnick, 'Second-rate Stories? Changing Approaches to the *Anglo-Saxon Chronicle*,' *Literature Compass* 3 (2006): 1253–65, http://www.blackwellsynergy.com/doi/full/10.1111/j.1741-4113.2006.00380.x.

36 These arguments date at least to the early twentieth century; see Reginald Lane Poole, *Chronicles and Annals: A Brief Outline of Their Origin and Growth* (Oxford: Clarendon, 1926).

37 Gransden, *Historical Writing*, 30.

history by lacking a specific narrative framework and presenting only fragments of information rather than a coherent argument about the past; like Benjamin's fragments of history, these fragments can be recognized when they flash up at a moment of danger, or they can be lost forever.[38] Antonia Gransden even goes so far as to contrast the form of chronicle with that of history, in asserting that 'chronicles could be written when disturbed political conditions made the pursuit of scholarship and the composition of literary histories difficult.'[39] Whereas histories seek to interpret events and explain their significance, Gransden suggests, chronicles simply record. It is clear that from the historian's perspective, the chronicle format involves less manipulation of the material than more carefully constructed histories, so that chronicles are at once less good in terms of artistry and composition but more valuable in providing the historian with raw material.

But Janet Bately takes issue with this common scholarly assumption and argues that Easter tables are not in fact the model for the Chronicle; she attributes the annal layout to examples found in the epitome appended to Bede's *Historia ecclesiastica*, Isidore's *Etymologies*, and the *Jerome-Eusebius Chronicle*.[40] This line of argument allows us to think of the Chronicle less as a primitive form of historiography and more as a meticulously planned set of records. And although some would argue that the supposed lack of deliberate manipulation makes a chronicle more objective,[41] it is also possible to see chronological ordering itself as a kind of narrative frame, and a chronicle as potentially as invested in interpretation, authority, and justification as any history more broadly conceived.[42] Hayden White argues for three levels of narrativity in history-writing: the annal, the chronicle, and the history. In the annal, the narrative element that provides meaning in historiography is missing; the chronicle, on the other hand, 'often seems to wish to tell a story, aspires to narrativity, but typically

---

38 See chap. 1 above, and Walter Benjamin, *Theses on the Philosophy of History*, in *Illuminations*, ed. Hannah Arendt, trans. Harry Zohn (New York: Schocken, 1968), 253–64 at 255.

39 Gransden, *Historical Writing*, 31.

40 Bately, 'Manuscript Layout,' especially 35–43.

41 Such as Gransden: 'The very second-rateness of chronicles gives them a value to the historian today. The author of a literary history arranged and selected his facts, working them into his theme … But the chronicler was less selective and although a chronicle is jerky to read it is a mine of information' (*Historical Writing*, 31).

42 See Hayden White, *The Content of the Form: Narrative Discourse and Historical Representation* (Baltimore: Johns Hopkins University Press, 1987), 1–25.

fails to achieve it ... It starts out to tell a story but breaks off *in medias res*, in the chronicler's own present; it leaves things unresolved.'[43] Full-blown history, of course, does not suffer from a lack of knowledge about how the story ends; the entire framework, from beginning through middle to end, provides not only a meaningful structure to support the narrated events, but also a guide by which the author can select which events fit into the story and which should be left out. That is precisely what we have already observed in the structure of salvation history; the narrative telos governs the inclusion and interpretation of events within Christian history. For the Chronicle, however, salvation does not serve as its governing telos. If anything, the rule of Alfred and his descendants becomes the end point of Anglo-Saxon history, and past events become meaningful as the road that leads to the dominion of the House of Wessex – the telos of a nationalist historiography.[44] Accordingly, the brief entries in the Chronicle already function, like Easter table marginalia or historical epitomes, to evoke a grander narrative of Anglo-Saxon history, one that, in its form of presentation as well as in its meaning, parallels the heroic tradition.

White's definition of the intermediate form, the chronicle, serves as a reasonable description of the Anglo-Saxon Chronicle, with some important exceptions. The Chronicle begins with brief entries that recapitulate the events comprising the Common Stock, but as successive continuations are added, entries become longer, more detailed, and more narrative: the Chronicle becomes aware of its status as a history in the making. Cecily Clark has shown that, beginning with the first continuation in manuscript A, the Chronicle entries begin to move more toward the form White would define as 'history,' showing greater use of subordination, clauses, connectives, and rhetorical patterning.[45] By the late tenth century, chroniclers are providing considerable detail about, and often commenting on the significance of, the events they describe. As the Chronicle progresses, entries show heightened emotion and more rhetorical flourishes, including the alliteration, metre, and rhyme of the verse passages. But even simple parataxis can imply relations between events, and the Chronicle does

---

43 White, *Content of the Form*, 5.
44 On the Anglo-Saxon Chronicle as a document of English identity, see Patrick Wormald, '*Engla Lond*: The Making of an Allegiance,' *Journal of Historical Sociology* 7 (1994): 1–24; and Foot, 'Making of *Angelcynn*.'
45 Cecily Clark, 'The Narrative Mode of *The Anglo-Saxon Chronicle* before the Conquest,' in *England before the Conquest: Studies in Primary Sources Presented to Dorothy Whitelock*, ed. Peter Clemoes and Kathleen Hughes, 215–35 (Cambridge: Cambridge University Press, 1971), 225.

indeed aspire to, and achieve, narrativity in its use of temporality as a governing structure. Jacqueline Stodnick argues that the physical presentation of the annal numbers, for example, enlists temporality as a structure for the meaning of events, and that even the sparser Chronicle entries realize a narrativity that does not depend on linear discursive forms. Her analysis suggests that we need not be bound by an Aristotelian understanding of narrative in order to explore how historical discourse shapes stories about the past and to open up new paths of inquiry into medieval notions of history and temporality.[46] And these notions can take very simple forms indeed. Peter Clemoes has noted that the Chronicle, in its very layout, is a document of continuity; the dating from the birth of Christ rather than in regnal years, and in particular the fact that the scribes copy out annal numbers even when they have no material to record in those annals, indicates that Anglo-Saxon history continued to progress even when there were no events to record.[47] 'This single form of reckoning running right through was an important feature of the *Chronicle*,' Clemoes writes, 'and evidently it was not enough to cite the reckoning just whenever there was an entry. The series of year numbers starting from Christ's birth must have been significant in its own right and its significance must have lain in its continuity.'[48] The dating used by the Chronicle and its rigidly formal layout thus reinforce the view of Anglo-Saxon history prompted by the genealogies, as one recording the unchanging march to dominion of the Cerdicings. As Clemoes puts it, 'this was not the history of cause and effect; it was a declaration of continuity. The compilers of the 890 *Chronicle* and the genealogist thought alike.'[49] While acknowledging the passage of time, the Chronicle does not insist that historical distance really matters; each annal exists in the present and points irrevocably to a moment in the past, and the spatial relation between those moments is determined by sheer chronology. Their meaning, on the other hand, emerges through contiguity in the connections made by the reader, who is interpreting them in the light of the other events and actors with which a given moment may be compared. Reading the Anglo-Saxon Chronicle, then, involves the flow

---

46 I am grateful to Dr Stodnick for sharing with me her unpublished paper 'The *Anglo-Saxon Chronicle* as Narrative.'

47 On the consistency of layout and use of annal numbers for barren annals, see Bately, 'Manuscript Layout,' 24–31.

48 Peter Clemoes, 'Language in Context: *Her* in the 890 *Anglo-Saxon Chronicle*,' *Leeds Studes in English* 16 (1985): 27–36 at 31.

49 Clemoes, 'Language in Context,' 31.

of thoughts through the successive annal numbers and their arrest as well, at the fruitful annals, where poems and genealogies point simultaneously forward and backward in time: in short, what Benjamin called 'dialectics at a standstill.'[50]

The annalistic structures that differentiate a chronicle from a history, then, also open up the possibility of dialogism within the text, rather than maintaining a unitary monolithic treatment of past events. Although the Anglo-Saxon Chronicle exceeds their definitions in many ways, White and Gransden both make the important point that the chronicle form is not bound by the same ideological limitations and exclusions that govern the production of full histories. The Anglo-Saxon Chronicle's patchwork composition might be understood by some to show a lack of coherent historical sense, but it also frees the texts from the limitations of a more structured and unified historical narrative conceived by a single author. Because the Chronicle was not produced, and does not exist, as a coherent whole, the format was open to alteration by continuators and scribes alike. As the Chronicle grew, it could adapt to meet the changing needs of its various writers and audiences. Part of this adaptation included the incorporation of verse, both as individual annals and as supplements to longer prose entries. And the verse passages draw on a range of traditions as well, depicting the West Saxon kings both as scions of the Woden-descended Cerdic and as defenders of the faith. It is crucial to remember, however, that whereas narrative accounts may contain certain facts, they also contain the rhetorical devices that signal particular interpretations – or, as White puts it, the 'modes of emplotment' that 'represent the facts as displaying the form and meaning of different kinds of stories.'[51] For this reason, the verse passages of the Anglo-Saxon Chronicle become vital witnesses not only to literary experimentation, but also to the shifting roles of historical writing itself and changing ideas about the mission and task of the historian.

On the whole, the Chronicle poems, however they have been defined and with the notable exception of *Brunanburh*, have met with derision from Old English scholars. Alistair Campbell had little time for 'the doggerel of the popular poems of the *Chronicle*.'[52] Stanley Greenfield and

---

50 See chap. 1 above, and Benjamin, *Theses*, 262–3.

51 White, 'Historical Emplotment and the Problem of Truth,' in *Probing the Limits of Representation: Nazism and the 'Final Solution,'* ed. Saul Friedländer, 37–53 (Cambridge, MA: Harvard University Press, 1992), 39.

52 *The Battle of Brunanburh*, ed. Alistair Campbell (London: William Heinemann, 1938), 38.

Daniel Calder find that of the five canonical poems besides *Brunanburh*, 'none of them compares with it in poetic quality,' and they describe a sixth, *William the Conqueror*, as 'doggerel verse.'[53] Donald Scragg finds simply that they 'lack inspiration';[54] and R.D. Fulk and Christopher Cain agree that these 'poems of nationalist aims ... are formally not of high quality.'[55] Yet these evaluations are based on readings that first extract the poems from their Chronicle context and then measure them against the literary standards distilled from *Beowulf*. In so extracting them, scholars fail to see the importance of the poems in their original historical context; that is, the poems are not ancient verse passed down and finally preserved in tenth century manuscripts, but contemporary creations that speak directly to the values and interests of their own historical moment. That they sometimes do so in a form that mimics or imitates classical Old English verse only indicates the ideological power of the verse form and its association with traditions passed on from one generation to the next. Indeed, the metrical regularity of the poems is indisputable, as Julie Townsend has shown;[56] and Katherine O'Brien O'Keeffe has found that regular metre and formulaic language can contribute to accurate copying through manuscript transmission. Perhaps most important, as O'Brien O'Keeffe has discovered, when scribes do alter the text of the Chronicle poems, they tend to employ variants that are drawn from formulaic language and are metrically and contextually appropriate, and that practice helps to ensure that the annal's message will survive more or less intact as it is passed along.[57] Memorializing contemporary events in alliterative metre, then, not only invokes a heroic past; it also encourages accurate transmission of the events being recorded through successive copyings, thereby ensuring the legacy of the West Saxon kings for posterity.

---

53 Stanley B. Greenfield and Daniel G. Calder, *A New Critical History of Old English Literature* (New York: New York University Press, 1986), 247–8. The poems referred to are 942 ABCD, 973 ABC, 975 ABC, 1036 CD, 1065 CD, and 1086 E, and *Brunanburh* is treated separately at 148–9.

54 Donald G. Scragg, 'The Nature of Old English Verse,' in *The Cambridge Companion to Old English Literature*, ed. Malcolm Godden and Michael Lapidge, 55–70 (Cambridge: Cambridge University Press, 1991), 58.

55 R.D. Fulk and Christopher M. Cain, *A History of Old English Literature* (Malden, MA: Blackwell, 2003), 68.

56 Julie Townsend, 'The Metre of the *Chronicle*-verse,' *Studia Neophilologica* 68 (1996): 143–76.

57 Katherine O'Brien O'Keeffe, *Visible Song: Transitional Literacy in Old English Verse* (Cambridge: Cambridge University Press, 1990), 108–37; see also Bredehoft, *Textual Histories*, 42–59.

Working from this perspective, many scholars have found the Chronicle poems an extremely valuable site for the excavation of Anglo-Saxon literary history. Both Neville and Janet Thormann have argued that these poems play a crucial role in the dissemination of an Anglo-Saxon national identity, for which the Anglo-Saxon Chronicle is a primary vehicle.[58] Both see the Chronicle as creating what Benedict Anderson calls an 'imagined community,' a group constituted politically across time and distance by the shared experience of a text;[59] and Neville compares the literary program of Alfred with the educational reforms of Charlemagne, and sees that both had the potential to create a sense of national unity through exposure to literacy. In addition, both Thormann and Irvine have shown how heroic poetry can be a vehicle for nationalism through the repetition of heroic values drawn from a shared cultural heritage;[60] and Nicholas Howe reminds us that the Chronicle, like Bede's *Historia ecclesiastica*, is as strongly invested in England's ties to Rome as in those to the Germanic past.[61] Matthew Townend even sees the most traditional Chronicle verses as examples of Old English praise-poetry and, consequently, as evidence of a latter-day Heroic Age, established in the tenth century.[62] By means of the Chronicle poems, heroic tradition is reconstituted as contemporary ideology, and the Chronicle itself, as *prosimetrum*, makes use of its double structure to combine the teleological narrative thrust of salvation history with the strong pull of nostalgia for the heroic age. Whereas the overall flow of the Chronicle recounts the history of Anglo-Saxon England as a preface to the present age of Alfred and his descendants, the poems set events apart both formally and affectively. The effect of these poetic interludes is to confer historicity on the present. They arrest the flow of events and abstract individual moments from sheer temporality, much as the genealogies do, in order to demonstrate the dialectical relation of past and

---

58 See Janet Thormann, 'The *Anglo-Saxon Chronicle* Poems and the Making of the English Nation,' in *Anglo-Saxonism and the Construction of Social Identity*, ed. Allen J. Frantzen and John D. Niles, 60–85 (Gainesville: University of Florida Press, 1997); and Neville, 'History, Poetry, and "National" Identity in Anglo-Saxon England and the Carolingian Empire,' in *Germanic Texts and Latin Models: Medieval Reconstructions*, ed. K.E. Olsen, A. Harbus, and T. Hofstra, 107–26 (Leuven: Peeters, 2001).

59 Benedict Anderson, *Imagined Communities: Reflections on the Origin and Spread of Nationalism*, rev. ed. (London: Verso, 1991).

60 Irvine, 'Medieval Textuality,' 202–8.

61 Howe, 'Rome: Capital of Anglo-Saxon England,' *JMEMS* 34 (2004): 147–72.

62 Matthew Townend, 'Pre-Cnut Praise-Poetry in Viking Age England,' *RES*, n.s., 51 (2000): 349–70.

present. With poetic form, the Chronicle establishes a clear distinction between a mere record of events as teleology and the significance of particular moments as History.

III. Longing for the Past: Nationalist Nostalgia in the Canonical Chronicle Verse

The poems copied in the Anglo-Saxon Chronicle, and subsequently printed in ASPR, mark a phenomenological shift in the discourse of historiography in late Anglo-Saxon England. Although Germanic poetry has a long tradition of memorializing the past, Anglo-Saxon secular verse, of the kind typified by *Beowulf*, concerns itself primarily with a past far removed from the experience of any Anglo-Saxon poet, reader, or listener; moreover, that long-ago past quickly assumes a legendary quality, and the predominant tone of Anglo-Saxon heroic verse is one of nostalgia for a distant world. As we saw in *The Battle of Maldon*, the adaptation of heroic verse forms to chronicle contemporary, verifiable, real-life events amounts to nothing less than a literary revolution in the writing of English vernacular history, and a poem like *Maldon* makes use of such a poetics in a propagandistic moment charged with nationalist ideology. In the context of the Chronicle, this revolution takes place over a broader span of time, but in order to serve a very similar function as part of the historiographic project: in their form, these verses echo the traditional ancient poetry of the Germanic peoples, filling a role as nationalist propaganda through the century of the nation's consolidation and then, as a melancholy irony, mourning the loss of that national identity with the death of the last West Saxon king. The Germanic and Christian elements of the Anglo-Saxon poetic tradition combine in these poems to form an image of Christian kingship perfected by the descendants of Cerdic at the same time that their power extends to encompass the greatest extent yet of the island and puts them on a par with continental European leaders.

The classical Chronicle verse begins with a direct and undeniable evocation of the heroic style s.a. 937 (MSS ABCD):

Her Æþelstan cyning,   eorla dryhten,
beorna beahgifa,   7 his broþor eac,
Eadmund æþeling,   ealdorlangne tir
geslogon æt sæcce   sweorda ecgum
ymbe Brunnanburh.   Bordweal clufan,
heowan heaþolinde   hamora lafan,

afaran Eadweardes,   swa him geæþele wæs
from cneomægum,   þæt hi æt campe oft
wiþ laþra gehwæne   land ealgodon,
hord 7 hamas.   Hettend crungun,
Sceotta leoda   7 scipflotan
fæge feollan   – feld dænede –
secgas hwate,   siðþan sunne up
on morgentid,   mære tungol,
glad ofer grundas,   Godes condel beorht,
eces Drihtnes,   oð sio æþele gesceaft
sah to setle.   Þær læg secg mænig
garum ageted,   guma norþerna
ofer scild scoten,   swilce Scittisc eac,
werig, wiges sæd.⁶³   (1–20a)

The opening lines of the passage commonly known as *The Battle of Brunanburh* waste no time in establishing the poem's generic stakes; within the first two lines, Athelstan is both *eorla dryhten* and *beorna beahgifa* as well as the simple *cyning*. Like the warriors of *Beowulf*, Athelstan and Edmund fight with *sweorda ecgum* and *hamora lafan*, and they do so in order to defend their land and the people who depend on them, *hord 7 hamas*.⁶⁴ Alliteration ties the names of our heroes firmly to their noble

63 'In this year, King Athelstan, the leader of warriors, ring-giver of men, and his brother also, the atheling Edmund, gained lifelong glory by striking at battle with the edges of swords at Brunanburh. The sons of Edward split the shield-wall, cut down the battle-shields with the leavings of hammers, as befit the nobility inherited from their ancestors, that they should often defend the land, the treasures, and homes, against every enemy through battle. The enemies fell, the people of the Scots and the pirates fell, fated to die – the field darkened – brave men, after the sun, the glorious star, bright candle of God, the eternal lord, came up in the morningtime, shining over the ground, until the noble creature sank to its seat. There many a warrior of the men from the North lay destroyed by spears, shot over the shield, likewise also the Scottish were tired, weary of war.' For the sake of both convenience and coherence, poems common to MSS ABC are quoted from MS A, which served as the base text for Campbell's edition of *Brunanburh* and which is also generally accepted as the oldest of the surviving manuscripts. In an effort to emphasize the importance of these passages' original manuscript context, I have chosen to cite the available Chronicle texts, MSS ABCDEF, from the most recent authoritative edition, Dumville and Keynes, *Collaborative Edition*, rather than from editions taken out of that context, such as Campbell's *Brunanburh* or Dobbie's ASPR editions.

64 A perusal of *A Concordance to the Anglo-Saxon Poetic Records*, ed. Jess B. Bessinger, Jr (Ithaca: Cornell University Press, 1978), shows that phrases like these occur frequently

qualities (*Aþelstan ... eorla dryhten / ealdorlangne tir / afaran Eadweardes / geæþele*), as well as emphasizing the nouns and verbs of battle: *geslogon / sæcce / sweordum; heowan / heaþolinde / hamora; hord / hamas / hettend; fæge / feollan / feld*; and so on. Indeed, Campbell noted that 'the diction [of *Brunanburh*] is almost entirely composed of elements to be found in earlier poems,' and that the poem's metrical structure is equally conservative.[65] *Brunanburh*, then, does not represent poetic innovation, but certainly an innovation in historiography; it historicizes the battle, in Jameson's sense of the term,[66] by creating aesthetic distance for its readers. As a result, the distinction between past and present becomes blurred, so heroic values lose any sense of being anachronistic at the same time that Athelstan and Edmund become larger than life. The tropes of the heroic epic are thus firmly established: the king is a victorious warrior and protector of his people, and the contemporary battle is described in the same terms of glory and heroism that adorn the traditional legends of ancient Germanic heroes. In Thormann's words, 'the traditional heroic language in itself ... enacts a political claim by representing the contemporary event as the reenactment of the values and achievements of the past,' and thereby making the Battle of Brunanburh 'a symbolic locus.'[67] Like the image of the ruin or the heroic diction of *Maldon*, *Brunanburh* resurrects a lost past and gives it new life in the present; at the same time, however, its symbolic function defamiliarizes both the actors and the event. Athelstan and Edmund lose their commonality with their contemporaries and enter the realm of Beowulf and Sigemund as grandsons of Alfred, imbued with the aura of historicity. In terms of its relationship to historical time, *Brunanburh* both recognizes the passage of time and asserts the unchangeability of human experience; it allows for the flow of events, but arrests them at the moment when they resonate significantly with ideas about the past. The Chronicle's other accounts of battles with Vikings, Picts, and Scots, although offering a similar level of detail about the events, do not make the West Saxons into heroes. For example, when Edward the Elder, the father

---

in *Beowulf* and *The Battle of Maldon*, as well as in heroic religious pieces such as *Judith, Juliana, Elene, Andreas, Exodus*, and *Daniel*. The use of these heroic tropes in Anglo-Saxon vernacular adaptations of biblical and early Christian narrative provides an interesting ground for comparison with original Anglo-Saxon material such as the Chronicle verse; see chap. 2 above.

65   Campbell, *Brunanburh*, 38.
66   See pp. 170–1 above.
67   Thormann, '*The Battle of Brunanburh* and the Matter of History,' *Mediaevalia* 17 (1994): 5–13 at 8 and 9.

of Athelstan and Edmund and the son of Alfred himself, defeats both Danes and Scots and secures their submission, the Chronicle records s.a. 920 (MS A)[68] that he went north, built several strongholds, and secured the submission of various named Scots, Danes, English, Norwegians, and Britons. Edward's earlier victories are recorded in similar detail, with many particulars of places and individuals, but nowhere before 937 does the Chronicle invoke the idea of Germanic heroism by means of poetic diction.[69]

The poem also portrays the Mercians and West Saxons as united under Athelstan and Edmund's leadership, fighting together against the combined forces of their enemies, the Scots and Northmen. The Christian-pagan dichotomy is once again brought into play, and the political stakes of such a poem are by no means obscure: echoing the genealogies of the regnal list and the 855 annal,[70] the poem places Athelstan and Edmund firmly within a heroic lineage, their *cneomagum*, which links back not only to Alfred, but through him to both Woden and Adam. This lineage, and the linear flow of continuous time that it represents, is countered when the poem directly invokes the Germanic heroes of the pre-Migration period in its closing lines:

> Ne wearð wæl mare
> on þis eiglande   æfer gieta
> folces gefylled   beforan þissum
> sweordes ecgum,   þæs þe us secgað bec,
> ealde uðwitan,   siþþan eastan hider
> Engle 7 Seaxe   up becoman,
> ofer brad brimu   Brytene sohtan,
> wlance wigsmiþas,   Weealles ofercoman,
> eorlas arhwate   eard begeatan.[71]   (65b–73)

---

68 For 924; see Bately, *MS A*, s.a. 920 n1.

69 The 755 entry in all MSS on the story of Cynewulf and Cyneheard is often cited as a historical example of the heroic code, when Cynewulf's men refuse Cyneheard's offer of amnesty after their lord's death: 'þa cuędon hie þæt him nænig mæg leofra nære þonne hiera hlaford 7 hie næfre his banan folgian noldon.' (MS A; 'then they said that no kinsman was dearer to them than their lord and they would never follow his murderer'). Yet this annal makes no use of either poetic form or poetic diction; the annal itself, though heroic in tone, is utterly prosaic in its execution and reads very differently from the 937 annal.

70 In MSS AD; in MSS BC, the genealogy appears s.a. 856.

71 'Never, before or since, was there a greater slaughter in this island, of people felled by the edges of swords, of which books tell us, the old sages, since the Angles and Saxons came hither from the east, sought Britain over the wide sea, proud warriors, overcame the British, men eager for glory seized the land.'

The Anglo-Saxons' migratory past is thus conjured to evoke both historical distance and Germanic heritage, and the poem is able to assert the ex-
ceptionality of the event by declaring that there was no greater slaughter
in the island from that time to this.[72] Even in this assertion, temporality is
disrupted; the poem jumps from the here and now (*on þis eiglande, þissum*)
through the written authority of *bec* – perhaps the Chronicle itself – to the
Anglo-Saxons who came from the east *ofer brad brimu*, not unlike the
Vikings whom Athelstan and Edmund have just conquered. The passage
simultaneously asserts the similarity of the West Saxons to their conquering forebears and distinguishes between those forebears and the
Vikings, who also *up becoman, / ofer brad brimu Brytene sohtan*, but who
do not at this point achieve an *adventus Danorum*. The alliteration once
again emphasizes the nobility of Edmund and Athelstan, who are *eorlas
arhwate*, and their connection to the *eard* of England itself. The classical
Chronicle poems thus start off with a strong sense of rhetorical purpose,
in serving as historical propaganda for the descendants of Alfred as well as
in drawing attention to a key political moment in an otherwise sparse
stretch of annals. What the poem does not do, and this is crucial, is invoke
the Anglo-Saxons as God's chosen people. The invocation of *Godes condel
beorht* may well signal God's approbation of the Cerdicings, but the battle
is not understood to evince God's hand at work among humans (although
neither does it preclude such an interpretation).

Brunanburh picks up themes already present in earlier Chronicle entries; the annals documenting the reign of Edward the Elder build a repeated image of the king travelling around the island, conquering lands,
and accepting the submission of the various peoples, including Welsh,
Scots, Britons, and Danes, who, significantly, choose him as their leader
and protector.[73] Yet, as we noted in the entry s.a 920, these victories do not
inspire verse memorials akin to *Brunanburh*, although they do celebrate
Edward's military prowess. Casting the annal on Athelstan's victory in
verse, however, raises the historical stakes by elevating his deeds from
those of an idealized Germanic warrior king to those of a true hero in the
epic literary style.[74] And the work the entry accomplishes in glorifying the

---

72 On 'the greatest events in memory,' see Bredehoft, 'History and Memory in the
   Anglo-Saxon Chronicle,' in Johnson and Treharne, *Readings in Medieval Texts*, 109–21
   at 113–19.
73 See, for example, Bately, *MS A*, s.a. 913–25.
74 That the text was recognized as verse by its readers is without question; Bately's edition
   of MS A notes the regular appearance of metrical pointing after half-lines in this annal,
   and O'Brien O'Keeffe identifies these points as the work of a later reader interpreting

leadership of Athelstan – of placing him, in effect, on an equal footing with heroes like Beowulf – is inestimable in terms of its ideological power.[75] Athelstan's merit stems not simply from his being a grandson of Alfred the Great, but from his personal abilities to lead the people, defend the nation, and extend its borders. The poem simultaneously creates and reifies the image of the classical warrior king, and that image quickly becomes more important than the mere reality of the battle itself. Scragg points out that two other grandsons of Alfred fell in the battle; the absence of their names from the poem not only reinforces the suggestion that military victory is a fundamental element of heroic kingship, but also shows how carefully *Brunanburh* guards its ideological investments.[76] The poem does not simply memorialize a king's victory; it removes the battle from the public domain of current events and translates it to the more rarefied sphere of History. The Battle of Brunanburh is no longer merely a military victory, or fodder for political propaganda; both the event and its meaning have become legend through the aesthetic workings of a nostlagic historicity.

Because of *Brunanburh*, Athelstan's image rises above his father's, and that image, now preserved for posterity in epic verse, serves as his legacy to future generations – and as a point of reference for establishing the heroic image of subsequent West Saxon kings, such as his brother, Edmund, honoured in a similarly heroic poem for his reconquest of Mercia in 942 (MSS ABCD). Although it lacks the narrative scope of *Brunanburh*, *The Capture of the Five Boroughs* invests its subject with the same qualities that distinguish the Germanic hero: one who is able to achieve the protection of people and land, and victory in battle. It replicates many of *Brunanburh*'s formal qualities as well; Scragg has proposed that the two texts were composed by the same poet.[77] Like his brother, Edmund takes on the aura of legend by virtue of heroic deeds performed on behalf of his people:

---

the passage as verse and directing future readers to do the same. See Bately, *MS A*, lxiv; and O'Brien O'Keeffe, *Visible Song*, 131–3.

75 Thormann investigates the 'peculiar force' of *Brunanburh* as a product of ideology; that is, 'as an excess the language produces and reflectively invests, precisely as interpretation' ('Matter of History,' 6). She contends that this drive toward interpretation sets the poem apart from mere chronicle as list and forms the basis for a concept of national identity; she discounts the possibility that chronology constitutes a narrative or ideological framework in and of itself.

76 Scragg, 'A Reading of *Brunanburh*,' in *Unlocking the Wordhord: Anglo-Saxon Studies in Memory of Edward B. Irving, Jr*, ed. Mark C. Amodio and Katherine O'Brien O'Keeffe, 109–22 (Toronto: University of Toronto Press, 2003), 116 and n35.

77 Scragg, 'Reading of *Brunanburh*,' 113.

> Her Eadmund cyning,   Engla þeoden,
> maga mundbora,   Myrce geeode,
> dyre dædfruma,   swa Dor scadeþ,
> Hwitanwylles geat   7 Humbra ea,
> brada brimstream.   Burga fife,
> Ligoraceaster   7 Lindcylene
> 7 Snotingaham,   swylce Stanford,
> eac Deoraby.   Dæne wæran ær
> under Norðmannum   nyde gebegde
> on hæþenra   hæfteclommum
> lange þraga,   oþ hie alysde eft
> for his weorþscipe   wiggendra hleo,
> afera Eadweardes,   Eadmund cyning.[78]

Like Athelstan, Edmund receives a range of heroic epithets. His descent from the Cerdicings is emphasized by *afera Eadweardes*, and the poem emphasizes the unity of southern England under a single ruler who is not only *Engla þeoden*, but also *maga mundbora, dyre dædfruma*, and *wiggendra hleo*. The focus on geography is striking; alliteration places emphasis on the place names *Dor* and *Myrce*, as well as connecting those places backward across the caesura to Edmund's heroic epithets (lines 2–3); and the Humber is a *brimstream*, a word found only in *Beowulf* and *Andreas*. It is of more than passing significance for both poet and readers that the people whom Edmund rescues from the Northmen are *Dæne* [Danes] who have been living in England and are crucially distinguished from the *Norðmannum* whom Edmund fights and defeats.[79] Referents can also be ambiguous; is *burga fife* the object of *geeode*, or does it parallel *Dæne*? The fragment works to link the two, making the Danes the object of Edmund's activity. By means of alliteration and apposition, then, *Five Boroughs* joins heroic identity to the land and the people subject to the West Saxon king.

---

78 'In this year king Edmund, leader of the English, protector of men, won Mercia, noble doer of deeds, as it was bounded by the Dore, Whitwell gate, and the Humber River, the wide current. [There were] five boroughs: Leicester and Lincoln and Nottingham, likewise Stamford, also Derby. The Danes were previously oppressed by force under the Northmen, in the fetters of the heathens for a long time, until the protector of warriors freed them, son of Edward, king Edmund, to his honour.'

79 The distinction between Danes, who may be considered fellow countrymen, and Northmen, who are raiders, also appears in the annal for 920 (MS A), in which Edward the Elder secures the submission of 'ge Denisce ge Norþmen' [both Danes and Northmen]. See Allen Mawer, 'The Redemption of the Five Boroughs,' *EHR* 38 (1923): 551–7.

In both *Brunanburh* and *Five Boroughs*, the poems' role as annals is indicated by the extrametrical *Her* that opens each one, but this same *Her* also complicates the relationship to temporality. Clemoes has noted that the formulaic use of *Her* in the Chronicle annals is distinctively English; it also directs attention to what he calls 'the latent paradox in the coincident corporeality and incorporeality of written language.'[80] Specifically, *Her* directs the reader to note both the annal's material existence in the manuscript and the connection of that material object to an event in the past. *Her* thus functions to bridge the distance between a number on a manuscript page and its referent in a past event: 'With its meaning beamed to the present and its grammar to the past, it welded the two together in a regular, formulaic way.'[81] Past and present are thus linked together through a formal structure that is repeated throughout the Chronicle, and the poems *Brunanburh* and *Five Boroughs* fill in the outlines of historical relation with heroic content. Together, these two poems, entered into manuscript A at the same time by Bately's Scribe 3,[82] establish an image of West Saxon kingship that correlates with both the teleological rise to power of Alfred's dynasty and the backward gaze of a heroic nostalgia seen first in the genealogies, reinforced temporally by the Chronicle's dating system and use of *Her*, and now reified in the celebration of Athelstan and Edmund in alliterative verse. Both *Brunanburh* and *Five Boroughs* remove their heroes from the realm of the quotidian and invest them with legendary status using the aesthetics of nostalgia. Athelstan and Edmund can thus serve to ground a heroic notion of the Anglo-Saxon people, but the aesthetic turn also unmoors them from sheer chronology even while asserting incipient historicity.

The heroic presentation of the House of Wessex continues in the prose entries that follow these poems, by continuing the theme of the West Saxon kings as powerful military leaders and noble conquerors, like their ancestors:

[944] AN. .dccccxliiii. Her Edmund cyning geeode eal Norþhymbra land him to gewealdan 7 aflymde ut twegen cyningas, Anlaf Syhtrices sunu 7 Rægenald Guðferþes sunu.

[945] AN. .dccccxlv. Her Eadmund cyning oferhergode eal Cumbra land 7 hit let to eal Malculme Scotta cyninge on þæt gerad þæt he wære his midwyrhta ægþer ge on sæ ge on lande.

---

80 Clemoes, 'Language in Context,' 30.
81 Clemoes, 'Language in Context,' 28.
82 Bately, *MS A*, xxxiv–xxxv.

[946] AN. .dccccxlvi. Her Eadmund cyning forðferde on Sanctes Agustinus mæssedæge, 7 he hæfde rice seofoþe healf gear. 7 þa feng Eadred æþeling his broþor to rice 7 gerad eal Norþhymbra land him to gewealde, 7 Scottas him aþas sealdan, þæt hie woldan eal þæt he wolde.[83]

Alfred's grandsons expand the dominion of the Anglo-Saxons, securing an ever-wider range of land and people for West Saxon control. In prose as well as verse, Edmund proves to be a conquering hero, and when the good king finally departs this life (significantly, the annal points out, on the feast day of the saint who first brought Christianity to the island), his successor and brother, Eadred, continues that tradition with the extension of his dominion throughout Northumbria, even securing the *aþas* [oaths] of the northern Gaels. At the same time, their military conquests spread Christianity to territory earlier held *on hæþenra hæfteclommum* [in heathen fetters], and the Chronicle informs us that Edmund saw both Olaf and Rægnald baptized, thus securing their submission to the rule of king and church together.[84] Yet Christianity is not the governing structure of the Chronicle's history here; Edward the Elder and his sons do not win military victory thanks to God's favour, and the events of the Chronicle do not reveal God's hand at work through them. Rather, the prose entries supplement and reinforce the message of the poetry, in upholding the ideal of heroic kingship as a historical standard. Within a ten-year span of annals, the Chronicle paints an impressive historiographical portrait of the House of Wessex: they are noble kings like the heroic rulers of ancient legend; they exercise their dominion over an ever-increasing range of peoples and places; and they derive their mandate to rule explicitly from their devotion to the people they fight to protect and only implicitly from their devotion to the Christian God.[85]

---

83 *MS A.* '944. In this year King Edmund won all of Northumbria to his control and put to flight two kings, Olaf Sihtricson and Rægnald Guthfrithson. 945. In this year King Edmund overran all of Cumbria and gave it to Malcolm king of the Scots on the conditon that he would be his ally both on sea and on land. 946. In this year King Edmund departed on the feast day of St Augustine, and he held the kingdom for six and a half years. And then Prince Eadred his brother succeeded to the kingdom and brought all of Northumbria into his control, and the Scots gave him oaths that they would do all that he wished.'

84 See MS A, s.a. 942, directly following *Five Boroughs*.

85 The annals for *924–55, which establish this interpretation of Cerdicing history, were entered at one go by Bately's Hand 3 in the mid-tenth century (Bately, *MS A*, xxxiv–xxxvi), a fact suggesting the possibility that their shaping of historical emplotment is both conscious and intentional.

The discursive effects of presenting the West Saxon kings in such a light are politically powerful ones. As contemporary heroic verse, the poems on *Brunanburh* and the *Five Boroughs* exploit a sense of nostalgia, both cultural and historical, to generate an identity for the House of Wessex that evokes the lost past of the Anglo-Saxons' Germanic heritage. At the same time, the prose entries expound the kings' role as defenders of their faith as well as their *hord ⁊ hamas*. By inscribing these royal virtues into a document that purports to serve the interests of the Anglo-Saxon people as their official national history and casting them in a form with such powerful cultural and historical overtones, the early Chronicle verse underwrites certain claims to authority by establishing an equivalency between the actions of the rulers and the cultural memory of the Anglo-Saxons. Athelstan, Edmund, and Eadred all represent the values that typify this ancient heritage, and the House of Wessex comes to symbolize Anglo-Saxon society as a whole; in the discourse of the Anglo-Saxon Chronicle, the leaders embody the spirit of the nation. As the basis for a communal identity, the Chronicle offers tenth century Anglo-Saxon England a picture of its kings, and by extension of itself, as noble, heroic, and worthy to hold and defend the island.

IV. Heroic History and the *miles Christi*: The Chronicle Verse on Edgar and Edward the Confessor

The epic style of heroic verse is not limited to the recounting of military events, however, and the later classical verse in the Chronicle adapts the epic form as a vehicle for memorializing the West Saxon kings more explicitly as heroes of the faith. In poems commemorating Edgar's coronation and death s.a. 973 and 975 respectively (MSS ABC), the subject of these entries is equal parts heroic Germanic king and *miles Christi*; and like the Junius poems, these verses employ heroic diction to describe spiritual, rather than military, glory. As patron of the Benedictine Reform, which established and restored many of the houses and scriptoria responsible for the continuation of the Chronicle manuscripts, Edgar was naturally eulogized by the ecclesiastics who had benefited from his patronage and generosity; and 973 ABC places great emphasis on his role as a servant of the faith. He is still a heroic king, described as 'Engla waldend' [ruler of the English] (1b) and 'niðweorca heard' [hardened by battles] (18b), but instead of placing him in the tradition of ancient Germanic warriors, the poem takes considerable pains to locate him in a chronology dating from the birth of Christ:

7 ða agangen wæs
tyn hund wintra   geteled rimes
fram gebyrdtide   bremes cyninges,
leohta hyrdes,   buton ðær to lafe þa gen
wæs wintergeteles,   þæs ðe gewritu secgað,
seofon 7 twentig;   swa neah wæs sigora frean
ðusend aurnen,   ða þa ðis gelamp.
7 him Eadmundes   eafora hæfde
nigon 7 .xx.,   niðweorca heard,
wintra on worulde,   þa þis geworden wæs,
7 þa on ðam .xxx. wæs   ðeoden gehalgod.[86]   (10b–20)

Neil Isaacs cites these lines as evidence of a 'pedestrian versifier' at work
– 'what else can one call the man who devotes his longest sentence ... to
naming the death-day?'[87] – but given the importance of chronology in the
Chronicle, the poet's care in identifying Edgar's location, and therefore his
significance, within a specifically Christian temporality far outweighs his
apparent lack of skill. The poem establishes Edgar's place in history in
three ways: first, it counts from *gebyrdtide bremes cyninges*, dating according to the years of Christ; second, it identifies Edgar as *Eadmundes
eafora*, locating him within a family history of national leadership; and
finally, it counts the years of Edgar's own life, giving his age as twenty-
nine at his accession but dating his coronation to the year he was thirty. By
emphasizing that he waited until the same year that Christ began his min-
istry to take the crown, although he already held the kingdom, the poem
shows both Edgar's political ability and his recognition of the need for
divine sanction of his reign. Like the opening entries of the Chronicle,
which record both the advent of Christ and the *adventus Saxonum* as moments of origin for Anglo-Saxon England, Edgar becomes the embodiment
of cultural hybridity, a blending of the Christian and the Germanic that is
complementary and generative rather than contradictory and agonistic.

In this poem, the House of Wessex continues to elicit the epithets of heroic tradition, but the focus has shifted from descriptions of battles and warrior

---

86 'And then ten hundred winters had passed, reckoned by numbers, from the birth of
the glorious king, the guardian of lights, except that there were yet seven-and-twenty
winters remaining, as the writings say; so nearly a thousand years had run by for the
lord of victories, when this took place. And the son of Edmund was nine-and-twenty
winters in the world, hardened by battles, when this happened. And in the thirtieth he
was consecrated king.'

87 Neil D. Isaacs, '"The Death of Edgar" (and Others),' *AN&Q* 4 (1965): 52–5 at 52.

values to infusions of Christian teachings. Instead of being surrounded by a troop of warriors, Edgar finds himself amid 'preosta heap, / micel muneca ðreat' [a multitude of priests, a great throng of monks] (8b–9a). The image of the *comitatus*, the Germanic war-band, is recast as a throng of rejoicing priests surrounding the king, and the Germanic leader's responsibility to his people subtly shifts to highlight his obligation specifically to the Church. Edgar is significantly 'to cyninge gehalgod' [consecrated as king] (2b; *gehalgod* is repeated at 20b), a detail indicating not only that he is worthy of kingship, but that the validity of his reign comes from God. Throughout the Old English corpus, *halgian* [to consecrate] is a word that occurs almost exclusively in a religious context; homilies, saints' lives, and religious poems make frequent use of the term, and churches, cities, saints, and bishops are often *gehalgod*, as are the names of God and Christ. As a rule, however, kings are not consecrated in the early Anglo-Saxon period; before Edgar, only Ecgferth is said to have been *gehalgod*,[88] whereas after him, all the Anglo-Saxon kings except for Edward the Martyr are specifically described as *to kinge gehalgod*, a development suggesting that divine sanction became a regular part of confirming succession only after Edgar's coronation.[89] That the poem commemorating his coronation replaces the image of the Germanic warlord with that of the *miles Christi* is consistent with the new emphasis on the duty that kings owe to God, but the language in which it is expressed also mimics the heroic tone of the earlier Chronicle poems.

The subsequent death of the Christian hero, recorded in verse s.a. 975 (MSS ABC),[90] provides another opportunity to present nationalist history using a Christian framework. The verse blends Christian and heroic diction in its opening lines:

---

88 S.a. 785 in all manuscripts. Michael Swanton notes in his translation that this is the first reference to an English king being consecrated; Swanton, trans. and ed., *The Anglo-Saxon Chronicle* (New York: Routledge, 1998), 52 n11. On the significance of royal anointing, see Janet L. Nelson, 'National Synods, Kingship as Office, and Royal Anointing: An Early Medieval Syndrome,' *Studies in Church History* 7 (1971): 41–59, and 'Inauguration Rituals,' in *Early Medieval Kingship*, ed. Peter H. Sawyer and Ian N. Wood, 50–71 (Leeds: University of Leeds School of History, 1977); see also Michael J. Enright, *Iona, Tara, and Soissons: The Origin of the Royal Anointing Ritual* (Berlin: Walter de Gruyter, 1985).

89 Æthelred (MSS CDEF, s.a. 978/979), Edward the Confessor (MSS ACDEF, s.a. 1042/1043), Harold (MSS CD s.a. 1065), William (MSS DE s.a. 1066), and Henry I (MS E s.a. 1100). Several queens in the eleventh and twelfth centuries are also 'gehalgod': Edith (MS E s.a. 1048), Matilda (MS D s.a 1067), and Maud (MS E s.a. 1100).

90 MSS DE preserve a different passage, written in irregular verse, in this annal; see pp. 236–7 below.

Her geendode   eorðan dreamas
Eadgar, Engla cyning,   ceas him oðer leoht,
wlitig 7 wynsum,   7 þis wace forlet,
lif þis læne.[91]   (1–4a)

The poem once again employs the annalistic format with the opening *Her*, and it continues the work of ideological consolidation by invoking both the Christian and the heroic tradition. The phrase *eorðan dreamas*, for example, is found primarily in homiletic texts and also in *Daniel*, but not in heroic verse; and the alliteration with *geendode* emphasizes the transitory nature of human existence that is further expressed in *lif þis læne*.[92] Edgar's death exemplifies the narrative arc of salvation history, in which the concerns of a worldly existence – which are also, coincidentally, the primary concerns of the Chronicle – are put aside in favour of *oðer leoht*. At the same time, however, the poem clings to a heroic depiction of the Cerdicings; Edgar is 'Engla cyning' [king of the English] (2a) and 'beorna beahgyfa' [ring-giver of men] (10a), and his son Edward receives the epithet of 'eorla ealdor' [ruler of men] (12a) despite his also being 'cild unweaxen' [ungrown child] (11b). As heroic leaders, their connection to the people is of a piece with their kingship, and the people 'in ðisse eðeltyrf' [in this homeland] (6a) are invoked as 'leoda bearn, / men on moldan' [the children of the people, men in the country] (4b–5a); but when they are also called 'þa þe ær wæran / on rimcræfte rihte getogene' [those who were properly educated in computation] (5b–6), it becomes clear that these *leoda bearn* are in fact churchmen. It is this context of Edgar's patronage of the Church that informs the remainder of the poem: it records the death, or perhaps just departure, of Bishop Cyneweard, himself a 'tirfæst hæleð' [glorious hero] (13a), and a backlash against the Benedictine Reform in

---

91 'Here Edgar, king of the English, reached the end of the joys of earth, chose for himself another light, beautiful and fair, and abandoned this weak and transitory life.'

92 *Eorðan dreamas* appears in *Daniel*, 30a and 115a, as well as in a homily by Wulfstan for the Tuesday during Rogationtide, a Vercelli homily for the same day, and an anonymous homily for the fifth Sunday after Epiphany (in London, British Library, Cotton Faustina A .ix, fols 27v–31v, cited by Dictionary of Old English transcript in *Old English Corpus*, ed. Antoinette di Paolo Healey [Ann Arbor: University of Michigan Press, 1998]), item [0060(161)], http://quod.lib.umich.edu/o/oec/). See Robert T. Farrell, ed., *Daniel and Azarias* (London: Methuen, 1974); Arthur Napier, ed., *Wulfstan* (Berlin: Weidmann, 1883), 250–65; and Scragg, ed., *The Vercelli Homilies and Related Texts*, EETS, o.s., vol. 300 (Oxford: Oxford University Press, 1992), 196–213.

Mercia.[93] In broadening the scope of its commemoration to include events beyond the royal household, the poem links the death of the West Saxon king to the fate of his land and people, thus reifying the connection between royal identity and national identity and forging a causal connection between human faith in God and historical events. When God's law was overturned following Edgar's death, the people were punished – first with the loss of the hero Oslac, whose departure is narrated with a profusion of heroic phrases,[94] and then with a famine and the appearance of a comet. 'Wæs geond werðeode,' the annal explains helpfully, 'Waldendes wracu wide gefrege' [The vengeance of the Lord was widely known among the people] (33b–34). Perhaps most important, it is God, not a West Saxon king, who eventually rescues the people from their distress:

> þæt eft heofena Weard
> gebette, Brego engla,   geaf eft blisse gehwæm
> egbuendra   þurh eorðan westm.[95]   (35b–37)

The form of heroic poetry here takes the link between king and people, established in *Brunanburh* and *Five Boroughs*, and invests it with the explanatory power of the salvation narrative: the comet and the famine are signs of God's anger at how the English turned on the Church after Edgar's death, and the *eorðan westm* are signs that he has forgiven them once more. In comparison to the prose annals of the A-text, the 975 poem offers interpretation and significance in addition to recording the event; the prose annals, on the other hand, continue to be sparse, and the years of Æthelred's reign and the Danish conquest show only the most cursory attempts at record-keeping. Manuscript C, in contrast, seems to carry the salvation model

---

93 'Ða wæs on Myrceon, mine gefræge, / wide ⁊ welhwær Waldendes lof / afylled on foldan. Fela wearð todræfed / gleawra Godes ðeowa' (16–19a). [Then, as I have heard, praise of the Lord was subverted widely and everywhere in Mercia. Many of the good servants of God were scattered.] On the backlash against the reform following Edgar's death, see Pauline Stafford, 'The Reign of Aethelred II: A Study in the Limitations on Royal Policy and Action,' in *Ethelred the Unready: Papers from the Millennary Conference*, ed. David Hill, 15–46 (Oxford: British Archaeological Reports, 1978).

94 Oslac is 'deormod hæleð' [courageous hero] (24b), 'gamolfeax hæleð' [grey-haired hero] (26b), and 'hama bereafod' [deprived of his home] (28b); and his journey takes him across 'yða gewealc' [the rolling of the waves] (25b), 'ganotes bæð' [the gannet's bath] (26a), 'wætera geðring' [the commotion of the waters] (27b), and 'hwæles eðel' [the whale's homeland] (28a).

95 'Then the Keeper of the Heavens, the Lord of Angels, restored it, gave joy back to each of the island-dwellers through the fruits of the earth.'

over into its prose annals, which present fuller accounts and commentary on events. For example, manuscript C notes 'se miccla hungor' [the great famine] among the English s.a. 976, the prose annal for the year following Edgar's death. Although it makes no direct link between Edgar's death and the famine, the juxtaposition of the two events could suggest causality to a providentially inclined reader. In a similar vein, C also records that Edward was not just killed, but 'gemartyrad' [martyred] s.a. 978; and the account of Æthelred's coronation s.a. 979 is capped by a description of a 'blodig wolcen' [bloody cloud] that was seen for many days and nights. This ominous portent could quite easily be read as connected to the new king's coronation and the mysterious nature of his brother's death. And as events become more dire through the 980s and 990s and into the early part of the new millennium, the C-chronicler, as we have seen, does not hold back in recording his disdain for the English leadership along with the year's events.[96] The dismal narrative of Æthelred's reign could readily be understood as offering evidence of God's judgment on a king who murdered his own brother, and the Chronicle verse accordingly begins to adopt a hybridity akin to that of the Junius poems, in which heroic and salvation histories blend to comprise a uniquely Anglo-Saxon product.

If the classical Chronicle verse increasingly becomes a hybrid product of Christian and Germanic tradition, then the 1065 verse on the death of Edward the Confessor (MSS CD) is a culminating tour de force of the historical poet's art. Unlike the earlier poems, the eulogy for Edward does not stand alone as a separate annal. Instead, it is part of a lengthy annal chronicling the various political and military events of the year, including the dedication of Westminster, founded through Edward's own patronage and his last great act as king. Yet, as O'Brien O'Keeffe has noted, this is really Edward's only act as recounted in the prose annal; the text is far more concerned with Harold's activities in Wales and Northumbria, and Harold's coronation is the final event mentioned s.a. 1065 in both manuscripts.[97] Where Edward does appear, the prose text emphasizes the extent of his piety in founding Westminster, as well as the fact that Edward oversees the dedication of his church just in time to be buried in it – he died eight days later:

And Eadward kingc com to Westmynstre to þam Middanwintre 7 þæt mynster þar let halgian þe he sylf getimbrode Gode to lofe 7 Sancte Petre 7 eallum

---

96 See pp. 153–6 above.
97 O'Brien O'Keeffe, 'Deaths and Transformations: Thinking through the "End" of Old English Verse,' in *New Directions in Oral Theory*, ed. Mark C. Amodio, 149–78 (Tempe: Arizona Center for Medieval and Renaissance Studies, 2005), 167.

Godes halgum, 7 seo circhalgung wæs on Cilda mæssedæig. 7 he forðferde on Twelftan Æfen, 7 hyne man bebyrigde on Twelftan Dæig on þam ylcan mynstre swa hyt her æfter seigð.'[98]

Like the church at Westminster, the verse s.a. 1065 is meant to stand as a monument to the king who will later be known as 'the Confessor.' Introduced by the phrase *swa hyt her æfter seigð* and set off from the preceding text by an initial capital,[99] the encomium memorializes Edward as both Christian king and scion of the great House of Wessex. The self-conscious archaizing of poetic form in the twilight of Anglo-Saxon England is itself enough to provoke a sense of nostalgia, especially in modern readers. O'Brien O'Keeffe offers a detailed comparison of each half-line with formulae from elsewhere in the poetic corpus, and the sheer density of formulaic language connects the poem more solidly to the verse of two centuries earlier than to its literary contemporaries, such as the *Death of Alfred*.[100] Like *Brunanburh*, the *Death of Edward* is a formally conservative, traditional evocation of the heroic tradition, built from fragments of the literary tradition it echoes; like the Anglo-Saxon churches that used Roman stones in their foundations, the *Death of Edward* grounds itself in old material rather than creating something new. Formally, the poem directs its gaze on the past, but the significance of these events has everything to do with the chronicle's present.

The poem once again announces its place in the annals with the opening *Her* and immediately declares investments in both heroic and salvation history:

---

98 O'Brien O'Keeffe, ed., *MS C*, The Anglo-Saxon Chronicle: A Collaborative Edition 5 (Cambridge: D.S. Brewer, 2001). 'And King Edward came to Westminster at midwinter and there he ordered the minster to be consecrated which he himself had built for the praise of God and St Peter and all of God's saints, and the church dedication was on Holy Innocents' Day. And he went forth on Twelfth Night, and he was buried on Twelfth Day in that same minster as it says hereafter.'

99 O'Brien O'Keeffe, *MS C*, s.a. 1065 n14; see also 'Deaths and Transformations,' 165. The presentation of this text in MS D is very similar, with the text seemingly set off by both textual and scribal cues. Like MS C, MS D introduces the poem with the words 'swa hit her æfter sægð'; see G.P. Cubbin, ed., *MS D*, The Anglo-Saxon Chronicle: A Collaborative Edition 6 (Cambridge: D.S. Brewer, 1996). Cubbin notes that 'the *H* [beginning the poem] is large and extends into the margin' (s.a. 1065 n12) and that 'the 7 [following the poem] is as large as the first letter of an annal' but insists that 'there are no indications of verse in the MS' (s.a. 1065 n20). O'Brien O'Keeffe treats the text as verse in her edition but has also asserted that 'the scribe of D did not intend metrical pointing or did not recognize verse' in this annal (*Visible Song*, 135). Bredehoft remarks that 'scribes also frequently marked out poetic passages within prose contexts by the use of capital (or simply large) letters' (*Textual Histories*, 82).

100 O'Brien O'Keeffe, 'Deaths and Transformations,' 168 and 173–8.

Her Eadward kingc,   Engla hlaford,
sende soþfæste   sawle to Criste
on Godes wæra,   gast haligne.[101]   (1–3)

Edward's identity as a proper Germanic lord is firmly established; he is
'hæleða wealdend' [ruler of heroes] (8b) and 'Eadward se æðela' [the noble
Edward] (24a), and he 'weolan brytnode' [distributed treasures] (7b),
phrases calling up images of the lord dealing out gold rings to his loyal
companions in the hall. Family heritage also receives its due emphasis;
Edward's lineage is firmly established as 'byre Æðelredes' [descendant of
Æthelred] (10b), and he is also, perhaps in direct contrast to his father,
'cræftig ræda' [skilled in counsel] (5b). Perhaps most important, his control over all England, including 'Walum 7 Scottum / 7 Bryttum eac' [the
Welsh and the Scots and the Britons as well] (9b–10a), is emphasized as
one of the defining characteristics of his reign. In this portrait, Edward is
a generous and wise leader, one inspiring the loyalty of the warriors who
owe him allegiance from all parts of the island. Edward also embodies his
Anglo-Saxon heritage by replaying the migration history of his ancestors
and overcoming the adversity of exile and displacement in Normandy
during the years of Cnut's rule. Like the biblical heroes in whom the
Anglo-Saxons saw literary models for their own identity, Edward 'wunode
wræclastum' [dwelled in the paths of exile] (17a) after being deprived of
his eðel [homeland], yet another nostalgic gesture toward the ancient
Anglo-Saxon past. As we saw in the Junius poems, being deprived of eðel
and forced to wander on wræclastum marks the breaking of faith with
God; it is the fate suffered by Adam and Eve, by Cain, and by the Israelites
in the desert, and it also informed the myth of migration that was so important to Anglo-Saxon cultural identity.[102] But the king's heroic virtue
leads him to reclaim his throne; more important, he 'eðel bewerode, /
land 7 leode' [defended the homeland, the land and the people] (24b–25a), unlike his father, Æthelred, whose failure to do just that resulted in twenty-
eight years of Danish rule. Edward here is the archetype of the good
Germanic lord, the þeodcyning or people's king, fulfilling his duties to the
people and earning their love and loyalty in return. But in this poet's mind,
the virtues of the good king also clearly destine him for the glories of
heaven, and 'Englas feredon / soþfæste sawle innan swegles leoht' [angels

---

101 MS C. 'Here king Edward, lord of the English, sent his righteous soul to Christ, his
      holy spirit into God's protection.'
102 See chap. 2 above, and also Howe, *Migration and Mythmaking*.

carried his righteous soul into the light of heaven] (27b–28) after he 'sende soþfæste sawle to Criste / on Godes wæra' [sent his righteous soul to Christ, into God's protection] (2–3a).[103] Together, the prose and verse portions s.a. 1065 reinforce the idealized image of Christian kingship embodied in the last scion of the Anglo-Saxon royal house to sit on the English throne.

At the same time, the poem once again helps to historicize contemporary events, by defamiliarizing them in order to clarify the relationship of present to past. O'Brien O'Keeffe discusses at some length 'the poem's complex relationship with time and history' as it is figured both in the archaizing formalism and in the various invocations of chronology within the poem itself.[104] The rigid traditionalism of the verse archaically commemorating Edward marks its own passing, for the *Death of Edward* is the last example of alliterative metre in Old English.[105] Here, the form itself is a ruin, and its reconstruction from fragments of older poems enacts the historical dialectic. Here, instead of resurrecting events, ideals, or actors from the past, the verse breathes life into a dying form, and its passing also mourns the passing of the cultural history it embodies. In the C-text, the narrative of Anglo-Saxon history breaks off in the next annal, which recounts Harold's victory at Stamford Bridge but ends without any mention of Hastings. It is almost as if the chronicler, so focused on the nostalgic image of heroic Anglo-Saxon kingship, cannot bear to include the defeat at Hastings in his backward gaze.[106]

V. Heroic History and Cultural Identity

Like the *Maldon* poet, the various writers of the Anglo-Saxon Chronicle adapted traditional heroic verse forms to a new use, that of describing contemporary events. In the Chronicle verse, the aesthetics of nostalgia activate the same heroic sensibilities that underlie poems like *Beowulf* and

---

103   Other notable figures who place themselves 'on Godes wæra' include Guthlac, Gregory the Great, and Andreas, according to the *Old English Corpus*. Scyld's soul similarly ends up 'on Frean wæra' in the opening lines of *Beowulf*.

104   O'Brien O'Keeffe, 'Deaths and Transformations,' 165.

105   Thomas Cable has argued that the much later poem *Durham* (c. 1100) departs significantly from classical Old English metre; see Cable, 'Metrical Style as Evidence for the Date of *Beowulf*,' in *The Dating of* Beowulf, ed. Colin Chase, 77–82 (Toronto: University of Toronto Press, 1981), and *The English Alliterative Tradition* (Philadelphia: University of Pennsylvania Press, 1991), 52–6.

106   MS D continues to 1080, however, and makes further use of verse as a facet of mourning; see chap. 5 below.

Deor. These poems paint contemporary events with an ancient brush, in locating modern kings and princes among the Germanic heroes of *Widsith*'s catalogue or the *Wanderer*'s elegiac musings, but without the sense of loss that so profoundly defines the speaker of *The Ruin.* The cultural force of these classical Chronicle verses works on a number of levels to present a vision of history that is both radical, in the sense that vernacular historiography is still a relatively innovative form, and highly conservative, both textually and politically. As we have seen, the inclusion of verse passages in historical texts is not a new phenomenon; nor is it unusual to find vernacular examples of the mixed form, although there are few parallels this early. In these poems, the epic form reinforces the monolithic voice of West Saxon hegemony; verse and prose work toward the same end of underwriting the dominance of West Saxon ideology in the formation of an English cultural identity that, as in the Junius poems, explicitly acknowledges and adopts Anglo-Saxon England's hybrid cultural heritages. The continuity that Clemoes sees asserted by the simple adverb *Her* that opens each annal, and the way in which, as Neville has written, the Chronicle 'make[s] all the events from 60 BC to 855 AD themselves into a prologue for Alfred and his immediate predecessors' (and hence for Alfred's descendants as well)[107] reveals a sense of history as a fundamentally unchanging state of human existence. From this perspective, the Chronicle's historical consciousness makes no real distinction between Cerdic in the fifth century and Athelstan in the tenth. They are both part of the same tradition of heroic West Saxon kingship, and the history of their people is not the march to progress or the path to salvation so much as it is the continuity of the ever-same. In these poems, the glorious past, present, and future of Anglo-Saxon England is immediately present to the reader and, simultaneously, held at an aesthetic distance.

Reading these Chronicle poems exposes a process of discursive promotion of political and cultural hegemony that then becomes more clearly visible in the prose portions of the southern Chronicle texts as well; the transparency of propaganda in the poetry cues readers to look for it in other, less obviously structured annals, in which the subtleties of parataxis might let it pass unnoticed. These effects are difficult to witness when the poems are taken from their original context and edited separately; leaving them alongside their prose counterparts allows readers to see how, in the true spirit of *prosimetrum*, the early Chronicle texts make use of contrasting literary forms to highlight a specific interpretation of the events they

---

107 Neville, 'Making Their Own Sweet Time,' 171.

narrate. Perhaps most important, that interpretation combines the legacy of the Germanic heroic age with the image of Christian kingship and of Anglo-Saxon England as God's chosen people. In the Anglo-Saxon Chronicle, history is teleological; but the telos is the present, not future salvation. The celebration of West Saxon kingship asserts unity with the past instead of differentiating past from present, and these Chronicle poems demonstrate that history is continually relevant to the present for its commonalities rather than its differences. They view the present from the perspective of the past, rather than vice versa; the significance of contemporary events lies in their reactivation – their redemption, to use Benjamin's term – of moments of past glory.

Unlike most of the Anglo-Saxon poetic canon, the Chronicle poems are datable, within a reasonable span, simply by virtue of both their content and their manuscript context, a feature allowing scholars to locate their creation in a particular historical moment. This context is also highly specified: they appear only within the manuscripts of the Anglo-Saxon Chronicle, and are not copied into miscellaneous verse collections or other manuscript compilations. This fact alone should be evidence enough that they are best read within that context. Accordingly, they survive as nothing less than monuments carved in verse historiography; rather than being popular songs or traditional epics, these metrical creations are case-specific instruments of West Saxon ideology, inscribed into the official collective memory of Anglo-Saxon England. The Chronicle co-opts the cultural power of the alliterative long line to underwrite the larger text's claims to national identity; the relative stability of poetic form and its mnemonic features consequently transfer some of their permanence to the people and events memorialized in these verses. They are not mere entertainment or embellishment. The classical verse of the Anglo-Saxon Chronicle is to be understood as history of the most enduring kind, history persisting long after the demise of both authors and subjects and working to shape readers' understandings of who and what the Anglo-Saxons were. Just how closely this form of memorialization was tied to the West Saxon royal family will become even more evident as we survey the alternative uses of verse in the manuscripts of the northern recension.

5 Transitional Verse in the Anglo-Saxon Chronicle: Changing the Shape of History

> Philosophically considered, this ancient record is the *second* great phenomenon in the history of mankind. For, if we except the sacred annals of the Jews, contained in the several books of the Old Testament, there is no other work extant, ancient or modern, which exhibits at one view a regular and chronological panorama of a PEOPLE, described in rapid succession by different writers, through so many ages, in their own vernacular LANGUAGE.
>
> James Ingram, *The Saxon Chronicle*, 1823

The close connection between the Anglo-Saxon Chronicle and the people whose history it purports to represent is perhaps one reason why the Chronicle holds such fascination for readers; because it tells us how the Anglo-Saxons thought about their relation to the past, it can also tell us how they pictured themselves as a part of the history they were writing. As we saw in the previous chapter, the picture of Anglo-Saxon England that emerges from the earlier, southern manuscripts of the Chronicle is heavily (though not exclusively) informed by the ideology of West Saxon kingship and by a notion of history as the uninterrupted flow of undifferentiated events that all demonstrate the heroic qualities of the Cerdicings and their people. The shape of this history conforms to the generic expectations of heroic legend, and the poetic forms extant in these Chronicle texts cue audiences to understand events in those terms. When the Chronicle leaves the control of court production, however, it begins to find new uses for historical verse that build on Latin and homiletic models to further a mode of historical representation and interpretation more akin to the providential history favoured by Orosius, Alcuin, and Wulfstan.[1] Though still making use of techniques such as formulaic language and

---

1 See chap. 3 above.

rhythmical patterns to encourage accurate copying, these verses do not evoke the heroic conventions so closely bound to Old English alliterative metre. Instead, they recall distinctive homiletic forms, thus urging readers to contemplate the Christian meaning of historical events and looking toward the future, rather than the past, in order to give the Church a voice in historical discourse. In place of the grand memorials of the classical verse, the rhythmical Chronicle verse provides a literary space for commentary and reflection on the events of the temporal world as evidence of God's plan for the Anglo-Saxons. In place of historical poetry reminiscent of *Beowulf*, the later Chronicle suggests the homiletic discourse of Wulfstan and Ælfric. And in place of a constellation of historical fragments, it offers a distinctly providential narrative.

The chief difficulty in beginning to approach the later Chronicle verse is a categorical one: scholars cannot even agree on how many of these passages actually count as poetry. Certainly the scribes who recorded the verse offer little or no guidance in distinguishing one from the other; in spite of their frequent practice of writing Latin verse in lines, they write all vernacular literature continuously across the page, only irregularly indicating poetic lines by the use of pointing or other markings.[2] Angus McIntosh identifies five stylistic genres of writing for late Old English texts, ranging from classical verse through the debased verse of the Chronicle poems and rhythmical alliteration to ordinary prose.[3] Homilies by both Ælfric and Wulfstan have been printed in lines of verse,[4] and studies of both stylists

---

2 Late Anglo-Saxon scribes do, however, make use of pointing and spacing to mark metrical units in some verse manuscripts; Katherine O'Brien O'Keeffe sees the development of this practice as an index of a cultural shift from orality to literacy in *Visible Song: Transitional Literacy in Old English Verse* (Cambridge: Cambridge University Press, 1990). Thomas A. Bredehoft examines manuscript layout, spacing, and pointing in a range of manuscripts that juxtapose prose and verse, and finds that scribes very often do indicate boundaries between genres, even if metrical units are not specifically marked; see 'The Boundaries between Verse and Prose in Old English Literature,' in *Old English Literature in Its Manuscript Context*, ed. Joyce Tally Lionarons, 139–72 (Morgantown: West Virginia University Press, 2004). Since scribal practice was by no means consistent or regulated, however, it is of limited use in categorically defining a canon of verse or prose, but such pointing does offer some indication of the range of possible verse forms recognized in late Anglo-Saxon England.

3 Angus McIntosh, 'Wulfstan's Prose,' Sir Israel Gollancz Memorial Lecture 1948, *PBA* 35 (1949): 109–42.

4 For example, Eugen Einenkel prints Wulfstan's *Sermo Lupi ad Anglos* as a poem in 'Der Sermo Lupi ad Anglos ein Gedicht,' *Anglia* 7 (1884): 200–3; and Bruno Assmann takes a similar approach to Ælfric's homily on Judith in *Angelsächsiche Homilien und Heiligenleben*, Bibliothek der Angelsächsichen Prosa 3 (Kassel: Georg H. Wigand, 1889), 102–16. J.C. Pope's 1967 edition of Ælfric's homilies, which served until recently as the scholarly

comment on their frequent use of poetic rhythms and tropes.[5] In the past decade, however, scholarship has begun to revisit the issue. Recent work by scholars such as Clare Lees and Seth Lerer questions the utility of such strict definitions of poetry and prose.[6] Most notably, Thomas Bredehoft has championed the cause of the so-called irregular Chronicle verse from a formal standpoint in what amounts to no less than a complete reconsideration of our definitions of poetry in the Anglo-Saxon period. Bredehoft has demonstrated that late Anglo-Saxon verse made liberal use of loose metrical patterns and rhyme that differentiate it from both classical Germanic metre and straightforward prose. His work reveals a wider range of poetic techniques than has previously been acknowledged by Anglo-Saxonists and probes new frontiers in Old English poetics.[7]

In what follows, I would like to venture further into this territory by exploring how the different forms of verse used in different Chronicle manuscripts point toward changing ideas about both the nature and the purpose of historical poetry. Like Bredehoft, I conceive of verse more broadly than as consisting in the classical metre and diction of poems like *Beowulf*, and I posit a temporal shift in the role of vernacular historiographic verse throughout the late Anglo-Saxon period. But I would also

---

standard, also prints the texts in metrical lines; Pope, ed., *The Homilies of Ælfric: A Supplementary Collection*, 2 vols, EETS, o.s., 259 and 260 (London: Oxford University Press, 1967).

5 McIntosh, in 'Wulfstan's Prose,' details the use of metrical half-lines combined with both alliteration and rhyme in Wulfstan's writing. Many Ælfric scholars have similarly noted his favouring of alliterating pairs and poetic diction in specific texts; see, for example, Paul E. Szarmach, 'Ælfric Revises: The Lives of Martin and the Idea of the Author,' in *Unlocking the Wordhord: Anglo-Saxon Studies in Memory of Edward B. Irving, Jr*, ed Mark C. Amodio and Katherine O'Brien O'Keeffe, 38–61 (Toronto: University of Toronto Press, 2003), 44–51 and 55. See also Pope, 'Introduction,' in *Homilies of Ælfric*, 1:105–36; and Malcolm Godden, *Ælfric's Catholic Homilies: Introduction, Commentary, and Glossary*, EETS, s.s., 18 (Oxford: Oxford University Press, 2000), xxxvi–xxxvii.

6 According to Lees, the disciplinary distinction between poetry and prose results in split methodologies that hinder rather than help the study of literary history; see *Tradition and Belief: Religious Writing in Late Anglo-Saxon England* (Minneapolis: University of Minnesota Press, 1999), 22–7. Lerer subtly questions these distinctions on palaeographic grounds, in 'Old English and Its Afterlife,' in *The Cambridge History of Medieval English Literature*, ed. David Wallace, 7–34 (Cambridge: Cambridge University Press, 1999).

7 Bredehoft, *Textual Histories: Readings in the* Anglo-Saxon Chronicle (Toronto: University of Toronto Press, 2001), and *Early English Metre* (Toronto: University of Toronto Press, 2005), 70–98.

argue that shifting poetic styles indicate different political and ideological investments in historical poetry. Whereas the verse of the earlier, predominantly southern Chronicle manuscripts (ABC) generally is formally traditional, metrical, alliterative, and concerned with the commemoration of West Saxon kingship, the verse of the later manuscripts descended from the northern recension (DE) is generally rhythmical rather than metrical, rhyming rather than alliterative, and critical rather than commemorative. The coincidence of form, geography, and ideology in these poems has profound consequences for our understanding of both poetry and historiography. In the first place, the prosodic developments witnessed by the two main recensions of the Chronicle indicate that ideas about what verse forms were appropriate to historical narrative were changing; in the second, they suggest that different parts of the country had different investments in historiography. While the earliest uses of verse in historical narrative drew on nostalgia for the heroic past to memorialize a contemporary historical event, later verse forms entered a transitional phase with a strong relationship to both the style and the sentiments of the turn-of-the-millennium homilists.

In this chapter, I argue not only that the various poetic passages of the Chronicle deserve consideration as part of the poetic canon, but also that such literary consideration reveals some of the ideological investments of the Chronicle as documents of contemporary identity as well as historical record. By broadening the definition of verse to include rhythmical passages replete with poetic imagery, alliteration, rhyme, and other ornaments, it will be possible finally to assess the role and impact of the Chronicle's verse passages as a group, thereby enabling some observations about the changing uses of verse in historical texts from the perspective of literary criticism. This reconsideration of generic literary classifications reveals a diachronic shift from the ideological monolith of epic history in the more traditional Chronicle verse of the earlier manuscripts toward a more dialogic, heteroglossic notion of historical discourse in the later recensions. The changing form of poetry in the Anglo-Saxon Chronicle thus reveals the existence of varying models of historical consciousness throughout the island from the tenth to the twelfth centuries. Although I would not argue that the annalists and poets who compiled these manuscripts were necessarily aware of such ideological investments, it is clear, from a literary standpoint, that the texts themselves bear witness to very different modes of historiography, and that these differences have important implications for our understanding of the Chronicle and the society that created it. The canonical Chronicle verse enters the document as a vehicle for a nostalgic ideology of heroic history, but once it is there, the formal innovation of verse historiography opens up the possibility of other voices entering the text. As we noted in the previous chapter, the variable form of the Chronicle can exploit the tension between verse and prose to heighten the affective power of a certain event, but it also introduces the possibility of a truly heteroglossic treatments of events. In the northern recension, the ambiguity and polyvalence that characterize Old English poetics (and are so celebrated by Benjamin as essential tools for the critical historian) find expression through formal variation. Instead of the monumental identity fostered by the canonical Chronicle verse, the 'irregular' verse passages show later, northern chroniclers utilizing this formal variation to offer commentaries and interpretation that vary considerably from the more or less unified poetic voice of manuscripts ABC. The manuscripts of the northern recension also reflect a variety of political investments, and different sets of annals clearly reveal the political affiliations and sympathies of their authors and compilers.[8] Alternative voices break down the monolithic identity of epic history, and in the Chronicle, the language of history likewise shifts from dogmatic monoglossia to critical polyglossia, fracturing the assertion of national identity as a totality. The alternative voices of the Chronicle verses are the voices of those who have gradually assumed the task of recording history, the monastic houses whose interests extend beyond the West Saxon dynasty. Instead of documenting the triumphs of the West Saxon kings, the later Chronicles represent the wider perspective of a Christian kingdom.

I. The Chronicle Verse: From Heroic History to Rhythm and Rhyme

Addressing the question of form may help us think about the many different uses and contexts of the Anglo-Saxon Chronicle during its development and transmission. Although six of the Chronicle poems are printed in volume 6 of the *Anglo-Saxon Poetic Records* and conform to the metrical rules of 'classical' Old English poetry,[9] various scholars have identified a range of additional verse passages scattered throughout the eleventh

---

8   Stephen Baxter, for example, has shown how differences among C, D, and E align with the pro- or anti-Godwinist sentiments of the regions where the annals where composed; see 'MS C of the Anglo-Saxon Chronicle and the Politics of Mid-Eleventh-Century England,' *EHR* 122 (2007): 1189–1227.
9   These go under the familiar titles of *The Battle of Brunanburh* (937), *The Capture of the Five Boroughs* (942), *The Coronation of Edgar* (973), *The Death of Edgar* (975), *The Death of Alfred* (1036), and *The Death of Edward* (1065). See chap. 4 above.

and twelfth centuries that adopt looser metrical patterns and incorporate rhyme as well as alliteration.[10] Scholarly study of these poems focuses for the most part on their value as poetry, that is, on the extent to which they conform to Old English metrical rules.[11] The problem with this definition of poetry is that it bases aesthetic judgment for an entire culture spanning nearly five hundred years on the metrical form of a single text taken to represent the pinnacle literary achievement of that culture, namely *Beowulf*. In so doing, literary criticism discounts the possibility that other forms of poetic diction may have been popular in Anglo-Saxon England, thus preventing us from fully appreciating the aesthetic contribution – or the literary-historical context – of works like the undervalued Chronicle poems.

The irregular Chronicle poems are not simply throwaway additions or random citations; because they are found almost exclusively in manuscripts descended from the northern recension, they offer an opportunity to examine alternative uses of verse in a historiographic context parallel to that of the southern manuscripts. They also provide significant chronological overlap with the classical Chronicle verse; the earliest of these pieces is found s.a. 959, and they extend into the twelfth century with a

---

10 Eleven passages are codified as verse in Charles Plummer's 1892 edition: 959 DE, 975 DE, 975 D, 979 E, 1011 E, 1057 D, 1067 D, two at 1075 DE, 1086 E, and 1104 E; see 'Introduction,' in *The Anglo-Saxon Minor Poems*, ed. Elliott van Kirk Dobbie, ASPR 6 (New York: Columbia University Press, 1942), xxxii–xliii. All are printed as verse in Plummer, *Two of the Saxon Chronicles Parallel*, 2 vols (Oxford: Clarendon, 1892–9). Since Plummer's edition was the authoritative standard for most of the last century, his presentation of the text and choices about which passages to print as verse have defined the parameters for scholarly discussion of the Chronicle poems. See, for example, Dobbie, who writes that 'it is not always easy to draw the line between irregular meter and rhythmical prose,' and offers 'a list of the passages which are arranged as verse by Plummer' as the official count (*Minor Poems*, xxxiii n1). James Ingram sees two additional verse lines at the opening of 1086 E and a single verse phrase at 1130 E (*The Saxon Chronicle* [London, 1823]). Bredehoft has recently argued that the closing lines of 1003 E are really twelve lines of alliterative verse and that the 1067 D verse on Malcolm and Margaret is really a 35–line poem. See Bredehoft, 'OE *yðhengest* and an Unrecognized Passage of Old English Verse,' *N&Q*, n.s., 54 (2007): 120–2. I am grateful to Dr Bredehoft for sharing with me a copy of his forthcoming article 'Malcolm and Margaret: The Poem in Annal 1067D.'

11 On Old English metrics generally, see Eduard Sievers, *Altgermanische Metrik* (Halle: M. Niemeyer, 1893), which establishes the now standard five-type system of scansion for Old English alliterative verse. Sievers's method is developed further by J.C. Pope, *The Rhythm of Beowulf: An Interpretation of the Normal and Hypermetric Verse-Forms in Old English Poetry* (New Haven: Yale University Press, 1942); and A.J. Bliss, *The Metre of Beowulf* (Oxford: Blackwell, 1958), and *An Introduction to Old English Metre* (Oxford: B. Blackwell, 1962). But see also Bredehoft, *Early English Metre*, especially 21–34.

rhymed couplet s.a. 1104. While none of these verses is found in manuscripts A or B, C contains two of them, and D and E abound with them
and contain progressively fewer classical poems; D has 937, 942, and 1065,
but E preserves none at all. The irregular verse serves a very different purpose from that of the predominant nationalist and royalist themes of the
classical Chronicle verse. In the northern recension, verse passages offer
commentary rather than commemoration; their tone is frequently homiletic, rarely heroic; and they give voice to opinions and concerns that are
often critical of secular powers and have more in common with the historical interpretations of salvation history than with the nostalgia and honour
of a heroic past. In both form and content, they differ greatly from the
classical verse of the southern Chronicle manuscripts, and offer compelling evidence of the link between aesthetic form and historical consciousness that has been so apparent in the heroic verse of the previous chapters.
As a different kind of historical poetry, then, they provoke a different kind
of historical response.

That many of these passages are indeed verse, after a fashion, is a fact
assumed from the beginning of modern Chronicle scholarship and more
concretely demonstrated by recent work in the field. Edmund Gibson's
1692 edition was the first to print passages in a verse layout.[12] In 1823,
James Ingram offered the first edition with an English translation; he
claimed that 'in this edition, also, will be found numerous specimens of
Saxon poetry, never before printed, which might form the ground-work of
an introductory volume to Warton's elaborate annals of English poetry.'[13]
Representing himself as a ground-breaker, Ingram printed fourteen passages as verse, including two phrases that only he considers to be verse.[14]
As the epigraph to this chapter illustrates, Ingram's edition is the product
of a devoted scholarly nationalism in which Old English poetry plays the
part of a national heritage; Ingram cites the Chronicle's importance as the
'original and authentic testimony of contemporary writers to the most
important transactions of our forefathers, both by sea and land, from their
first arrival in this country to the year 1154.'[15] This nationalist-historical

---

12   Edmund Gibson, *Chronicon Saxonicum* (Oxford, 1692).
13   Ingram, *Saxon Chronicle*, iii.
14   The passages are 937 ABCD, 942 ABCD, 959 DE, 973 ABC, 975 ABC (975 DE in a
     footnote), 979 DE (in the Appendix), 1011 CDE, 1036 CD, 1065 CD, both portions of
     1075 DE (the second in a footnote), 1086 E (in the Appendix, adding the preceding lines
     'Witodlice on his timan / hæfdon men mycel geswinc 7 swiðe manige teonan'), and a
     phrase s.a. 1130 E: 'hæge sitteð / ða aceres dæleth.'
15   Ingram, *Saxon Chronicle*, ii.

bent certainly echoes the original ideological purposes of the Chronicle verse, and it had a great influence on how the Chronicle poems were subsequently read, as Daniel Abegg's 1894 study shows.[16] Abegg was the first to study the poems categorically, analysing metre, diction, rhythm, and rhyme as poetic markers. He considered a total of twelve passages as poetic in order to argue that poetry was the backbone of early Anglo-Saxon historiography, and that many of the more detailed annals of the Chronicle were actually prose versions of original poems.[17] The desire for the recovery of a pan-national Germanic historiographic form that predated and rivalled Christian Latin historiography betrays the Romantic sensibilities of Abegg's project; he seems almost as eager as the tenth century classical poets to portray the Anglo-Saxons as heirs to a grand cultural legacy. In spite of these motives, however, his critical methodology is well ordered. Abegg imposes a poetic hierarchy; he collects the passages into two groups, of which he terms one 'gelehrte Annalistendichtungen' [poems by learned annalists] and the other 'Gedichte volkstümlicher Art' [poetry in the popular style].[18] According to Abegg, these popular poems represent a transitional phase in English poetry between classical Old English verse and the freer, more eclectic form of the early Middle English period, such as that found in Laȝamon's *Brut*, and they do not measure up artistically to the classical forms of the first group.[19]

Abegg's approach also illustrates the influence of Benjamin Thorpe's 1861 edition, which was the first to print all the Chronicle manuscripts synoptically. Thorpe is the first editor to comment at any length on the verse passages themselves and their place in the texts:

> I regret my inability to supply any information relative to the authors of the poetic effusions in the Saxon Chronicle. Are they by the writers of the prose narrative, or are they only insertions? The latter seems to me the more probable opinion. Of these, the first, not only in the order of time, but in excellence, is the ode on the Battle of Brunanburh (A.D. 937); and a matter it is of regret

---

16 Daniel Abegg, *Zur Entwicklung der historischen Dichtung bei den Angelsachsen*, Quellen und Forschungen zur Sprach- und Culturgeschichte der germanischen Völker 73 (Strassburg: Karl J. Trübner, 1894).

17 Abegg, *Entwicklung*, 79–102.

18 The two groups correspond largely to Dobbie's division in ASPR: the first contains 937 ABCD, 942 ABCD, 973 A / 974 BC, 975 ABC, and 1065 CD; the second contains 959 DE, 975 DE, 975 D, 1011 CDE, 1036 CD (which Dobbie prints with reservations), 1067 D, and 1076 DE.

19 Abegg, *Entwicklung*, 58.

that the name of its author has irrecoverably perished. Of the other pieces, little can be said in praise; they are rather rhythmical and alliterative prose than poetry; while, on the other hand, the effusion on the assassination of king Eadward, and the account of the murder of the young prince Ælfred, son of the Confessor, may be regarded as unmetrical poetry.[20]

Thorpe's description of these passages as 'poetic effusions' clearly indicates how he felt readers were meant to understand them, and his analysis raises a set of questions that have proved unanswerable by modern scholarship. The questions of who wrote the poems, and whether they were conceived as part of the Chronicle itself or were separate compositions later inserted into the text, approach the crux of their problematic nature. Thorpe prints only eleven passages as verse and is generally unimpressed by their worth as poetry (*Brunanburh* notwithstanding).[21]

The set of passages described today as the Chronicle verse (in ASPR, for example) was established by Charles Plummer's 1892 edition, which was the standard edition for nearly a century.[22] Plummer prints seventeen passages as verse, the highest number of any editor and the standard by which the Chronicle poems have been investigated since. Plummer recognizes a variety of prosodic features as poetic techniques, and although he does not comment specifically on their form, he takes for granted the existence of these poems *qua* poetry. On *The Death of Edgar*, for example, he comments that 'all the chroniclers burst out into panegyrics';[23] he defines the spurious verse at 1011 as a dirge;[24] he finds the D version of 1036 inferior because its omission of Godwine's name 'has destroyed the rhythm ... and has also destroyed the rhyme of the first couplet "gelette, sette"';[25] and he accepts the authority of ballads as sources of history.[26] Plummer seems

---

20   Benjamin Thorpe, ed. and trans., *The Anglo-Saxon Chronicle According to the Several Original Authorities*, 2 vols (London, 1861), 1:xiii.

21   The passages are 937 ABCD, 942 ABCD, 959 DEF, 973 ABC, 975 ABC, 975 DE, 975 D, 1011 CDE, 1065 CD, 1067 D, and 1075 DE (only the first portion).

22   Now superseded by David Dumville and Simon Keynes, eds, *The Anglo-Saxon Chronicle: A Collaborative Edition*, 9 vols (Cambridge: D.S. Brewer, 1983–), of which the six main Chronicle texts have appeared to date (MSS ABCDEF).

23   Plummer, *Saxon Chronicles*, 2:162.

24   Plummer, *Saxon Chronicles*, 2:189.

25   Plummer, *Saxon Chronicles*, 2:212.

26   'Finally, a word of protest must be said against Mr. Freeman's apparent wish to discredit the account of the Chronicle [at 1036], because it "takes the form of a ballad." ... This is what Mr. Freeman says elsewhere on the value of contemporary ballads as authorities

untroubled by the non-classical forms of most of his verse passages, and similarly unruffled by the presence of verse in a predominantly prose historical text. As a part of the Chronicle, then, these verses caused comparatively little consternation;[27] when it comes to the poetic canon, however, an entirely different set of criteria comes into play.

The six-volume *Anglo-Saxon Poetic Records* set out to clearly define the canon of Old English poetry, and that definition was predicated on the exclusion of certain kinds of texts.[28] Elliott van Kirk Dobbie determines that 'in the various manuscripts of the Anglo-Saxon Chronicle, from the year 937 to the end, there are six annals, or parts of annals, which are in sufficiently regular meter to be included in a collective edition of Anglo-Saxon poetry'; in other words, classical Old English verse.[29] His criteria are clearly stated as the metrical rules of classical Old English verse, as defined by Sievers in 1893; in spite of this, he chooses to include 1036 CD, which 'is not regularly alliterative, like the other five poems, but is partly prose and partly irregular rimed verse.'[30] He does not, however, discount the other verse passages as poetry per se; he justifies his inclusion of 1036 CD by 'following the practice of earlier editors,' and he submits that 'a number of other passages in irregular meter, in the later years of the Chronicle, have been omitted from this edition. Since these texts are all to be found in Plummer's edition of the Chronicle, their omission here will be no hardship to scholars.'[31] If their omission is no hardship to scholars, however, it has proved a considerable disadvantage to the texts themselves, and Dobbie's circumlocution on the issue of verse criteria has a profound impact on how we think about Old

---

for history: "The story of Eadric pretending that Eadmund was dead ... no doubt comes from a ballad, but I do not see that that makes it at all untrustworthy. A contemporary ballad such as that of Maldon, or the lost ballad on which [Henry of Huntingdon] must have founded his account of Stamford Bridge, is surely very good authority"' (Plummer, *Saxon Chronicles*, 2:215).

27 But see the various editors of Dumville and Keynes, *Collaborative Edition*, for their own individual, and often conflicting, commentary on whether specific passages should be treated as verse or prose; the matter is far from settled as an editorial and palaeographic concern.

28 George Philip Krapp and Elliott van Kirk Dobbie, eds, *The Anglo-Saxon Poetic Records*, 6 vols (New York: Columbia University Press, 1931–53). The Chronicle poems are found in Dobbie, *Minor Poems*, 16–26 and 146–51, with important comments in the Introduction at xxxii–xliii.

29 Dobbie, *Minor Poems*, xxxii.

30 Dobbie, *Minor Poems*, xxxii.

31 Dobbie, *Minor Poems*, xxxii and xxxii–xxxiii.

English poetry today. The verse passages excluded from ASPR are rarely, if ever, considered in scholarship dealing with either the Chronicle verse or Old English poetry more generally, and overviews of literary history take Dobbie's text as the basis of their discussion, often ignoring the other poems altogether and perpetuating their exclusion. The reason for Dobbie's choice is understandable from a categorical point of view; although he acknowledges them as verse, he cannot confer canonicity on them without disrupting his metrical criteria for Old English poetry, with the result that the standard definition of Old English poetry excludes a wide range of poetical texts written during the Anglo-Saxon period.

The scholars who have found the most value in the non-canonical verse of the Chronicle are those who study the English alliterative tradition; they find important connections between the debased verse forms of the later Chronicle poems and the broader alliterative tradition of the early Middle English period.[32] The styles that lie somewhere in the middle of the continuum between verse and prose may complicate definitions, but they stand as evidence of a rich and diverse literary tradition that existed before the Norman Conquest and survived beyond it in works such as *The Grave*, the *Worcester Fragments*, and Laȝamon's *Brut*.[33] For scholars of the early Middle English period, the more flexible poetics of non-classical verse and rhythmical alliteration, which remain unremarked or derided by Old English scholars, provide the seeds for later poetic inventions and represent a connection between the two traditions over the historical rupture of the

---

32 Many scholars, such as Abegg, McIntosh, and J.P. Oakden, *Alliterative Poetry in Middle English*, 2 vols (Manchester: Manchester University Press, 1930–5), want to see the connection as a form of literary continuity. But see also Thomas Cable, *The English Alliterative Tradition* (Philadelphia: University of Pennsylvania Press, 1991), and the three-essay exchange between Geoffrey Russom and R.D. Fulk ('The Evolution of Middle English Alliterative Meter'; 'Old English Poetry and the Alliterative Revival: On Geoffrey Russom's "The Evolution of Middle English Alliterative Meter"'; 'A Brief Response') chronicled in *Studies in the History of the English Language II: Unfolding Conversations*, ed. Anne Curzan and Kimberly Emmons, 279–314 (Berlin: Mouton de Gruyter, 2004).

33 *The Grave*, in *Die Fragmente der Reden der Seele an den Leichnam in zwei Handschriften zu Worcester und Oxford*, ed. Richard Buchholz, Erlanger Beiträge zur englischen Philologie 6 (Erlangen and Leipzig, 1890), 11. *The Soul's Address to the Body: The Worcester Fragments*, ed. Douglas Moffat (East Lansing, MI: Colleagues Press, 1987). *Laȝamon: Brut*, ed. G.L. Brooke and R.F. Leslie, EETS, o.s., 250 and 277 (London: Oxford University Press, 1963–78).

Conquest.[34] Thus the non-classical poetry of the late Anglo-Saxon period is often valued more highly by scholars outside the field than within it. This problem has been acknowledged, and to some extent addressed, over the past two decades. In a 1989 dissertation, Ellen L. Wert increased the number of poetic passages to sixteen and offered detailed analyses of the poetic devices and metrical schemes at work in each of them.[35] Although some of these passages ultimately fail to conform to her own definitions of poetry,[36] Wert broadens previous definitions considerably, thereby expanding the rubric of Old English poetry to include alternate types of prosody. Her work begins a reformulation of how we define Old English poetry, and that reformulation is continued most fully by Bredehoft, who addresses the question of non-classical form by examining the manuscript context of these poems to determine whether the scribes copying them recognized them as poetry.[37] In approximating Anglo-Saxon determinations of aesthetic value, he finds not only that scribes did recognize and copy many of these annals as poetry, but that 'the *Chronicle*'s evidence for a late-Anglo-Saxon tradition of rhyming verse ... challenges the critical viewpoint that sees the presence of alliteration as the defining characteristic of all Old English verse.'[38] Bredehoft also proposes an overhaul of traditional metrics to better account for a wider variety of prosody in late Old English writings, and offers the most thorough analysis to date of Old

---

34 Numerous scholars have commented on the affinities between Middle English alliterative verse and the Old English homiletic styles of Ælfric and Wulfstan, and recent studies of the tradition reinforce this link. Cable finds a clear break in the alliterative tradition at 1066, arguing that the alliterative verse of the early Middle English period harks back not to Old English metrical verse, but to Old English rhythmical alliteration; see *Alliterative Tradition*, 41–65. McIntosh similarly draws parallels between early Middle English alliterative verse and the rhythmical alliteration of Wulfstan in 'Early Middle English Alliterative Verse,' in *Middle English Alliterative Poetry and Its Literary Background: Seven Essays*, ed. David Lawton, 20–33 (Woodbridge: D.S. Brewer, 1982).

35 Ellen L. Wert, 'The Poems of the Anglo-Saxon Chronicles: Poetry of Convergence' (PhD diss., Temple University, 1989).

36 She finds 979 E, 'The Death of Edward,' for example, to be prose rather than verse (Wert, 'Poetry of Convergence,' 111–12).

37 Bredehoft uses manuscript evidence such as pointing and 'meaningful space,' as well as the margin of error in copying poetic phrases versus prose phrases, to argue that scribes not only recognized verse, but felt less free to alter it than they did prose annals; in addition, they often marked received passages as verse for the benefit of future readers (Bredehoft, *Textual Histories*, 42–59 and 72–118). But see also O'Brien O'Keeffe, who demonstrates that poems are also subject to scribal interpolation (*Visible Song*, 108–37).

38 Bredehoft, *Textual Histories*, 153.

English verse in its most inclusive form.[39] Re-evaluating the Chronicle poems, then, impacts not only our understanding of form and historiography in Anglo-Saxon England, but also our very definitions of what counts as Anglo-Saxon poetry.

Written over several centuries in various places and by many different people, the Chronicle bears witness to a wider range of ideas about what counts as history, and what history-writing should look like, than any individual text possibly could. Cecily Clark's study documents the stylistic and narrative shifts that took place in the compilation of manuscript A;[40] the prosimetric form adopted by the later Chronicle entries similarly indicates an expansion in the range of historiographic possibilities by the early twelfth century. But it also indicates a waning in the classical Old English verse form that originally served to highlight heroic vignettes in the tenth century Chronicle in favour of a movement toward both more detailed and expansive prose entries and the incorporation, rather than the separate use, of verse. The four poems of manuscript A, for example, all make use of classical Old English verse forms. They are all printed in ASPR, and the earliest, *The Battle of Brunanburh*, is the only Chronicle poem to merit substantial scholarly treatment, including an independent edition. In contrast, the much later manuscript E contains twice as many verse passages, but none uses classical alliterative metre, and none is printed in ASPR. Whereas the early Chronicle poems are free-standing poetic texts consisting of all or most of the annals they record, later poems are more likely to be fragments that erupt from an otherwise straightforward prose entry, thus pointing to both a different form and a different purpose behind their composition.

The changes in the verse of the Chronicle should be seen as a general trend rather than as a linear development, however. Rhyme makes an appearance in the tenth century as well as in the later verses,[41] and the 1065 verse on the death of Edward the Confessor employs the classical Old English style with a formality surprising in such a late composition.[42] The general direction of the trend is evident, however, in table 5.1, a graphic

---

39 Bredehoft, *Early English Metre*.
40 Cecily Clark, 'The Narrative Mode of *The Anglo-Saxon Chronicle* before the Conquest,' in *England before the Conquest: Studies in Primary Sources Presented to Dorothy Whitelock*, ed. Peter Clemoes and Kathleen Hughes, 215–35 (Cambridge: Cambridge University Press, 1971).
41 In 975 DE.
42 See pp. 208–11 above.

representation of the occurrence and distribution of verse in five of the surviving manuscripts.[43] Table 5.1 indicates a gradual movement, from top left to bottom right, away from the strictly classical compositions of the earlier manuscripts AB toward the wider range of verse typified by the examples in the later manuscripts DE. These dates seem to suggest that not only did poetry as a medium in the Anglo-Saxon Chronicle survive the death of classical Old English verse forms, but it actually increased in popularity in the later manuscripts, and survived the Norman Conquest to chronicle some of the trials and tribulations faced by the Anglo-Saxons under their new overlords. In the process, however, the form of historical poetry underwent some profound changes, in being transformed from the heroic model of *Brunanburh* and the like to the looser form and commentary-oriented verses of the later Chronicles. Regarding the chronological distribution of the Chronicle poems, it is possible to form a hypothesis not only about the role of poetry in commemorating historical events, but also about the relationship between the older and newer poetic styles.

The distribution is not only chronological, however; it also has a geographical component. The use of alliterative and rhyming verse occurs almost exclusively in the manuscripts that descend from the Chronicle's northern recension, a compilation based on the Common Stock but revised and augmented with Northumbrian annals and information from Bede.[44]

---

43 The bilingual MS F preserves some of these poems in shortened form (959, 979, 1011), but they duplicate the text of E without demonstrating the passages' poetic characteristics, so I have omitted F from my discussion. The remnants of MS G, although recently reconstructed in Lutz's edition, indicate that it is mostly a copy of MS A and contains no new information about the poems; for this reason, I have omitted it as well. MS H has no verse in either of its two annals.

44 Simon Keynes, 'Anglo-Saxon Chronicle,' in *The Blackwell Encyclopaedia of Anglo-Saxon England*, ed. Michael Lapidge, John Blair, Simon Keynes, and Donald Scragg, 35–6 (Oxford: Blackwell, 1999), 36. Whitelock locates the origin of the northern recension at York, in *The Anglo-Saxon Chronicle: A Revised Translation*, ed. Dorothy Whitelock, with David C. Douglas and Susie I. Tucker (New Brunswick: Rutgers University Press, 1961), xiv, and *The Peterborough Chronicle*, EEMF 4 (Copenhagen: Rosenkilde and Bagger, 1954), 28–30. Audrey L. Meaney supports Whitelock's assertion but resists locating its archetype anywhere more specific than 'Northumbria,' in 'D: An Undervalued Manuscript of the Anglo-Saxon Chronicle,' *Parergon*, n.s., 1 (1983): 13–38 at 20–5. Frank Stenton surveys the northern annalistic tradition of York and Chester-le-Street in *Anglo-Saxon England*, 3rd ed. (Oxford: Oxford University Press, 1971), 693–4.

Table 5.1
Distribution of Verse in Five of the Anglo-Saxon Chronicle Manuscripts

	A	B	C	D	E
937	M	M	M	M	
942	M	M	M	M	
959				A	A
973	M	M	M		
975	M	M	M		
975				A	A
975				A	
979				A	A
1003					A
1011			A	A	A
1036			R	R	
1057				?*	
1065			M	M	
1067				R	
1076				R	R**
1076				R	R**
1086					R
1104					R
1130					?*

M = metrical; A = alliterative; R = rhyming
* Though printed as verse by some editors, the status of these passages is questionable; they are not particularly rhythmical and do not rhyme or alliterate.
** These verses are found s.a. 1075 in MS E.

Bredehoft has suggested reading the northern recension as an attempt to broaden the scope of the Chronicle to include material of interest beyond West Saxon 'nationalism,'[45] and the distribution of verse seems to support this assertion. In addition to celebrating the West Saxon royal line,[46] the verse of the northern recension commemorates events of geographically broader significance.[47] Moreover, at least two and possibly three of the verses have been described as being written in the alliterative homiletic

---

45 *Textual Histories*, 67–71.
46 In addition to the standard verses at 937, 942, 1036, and 1065 in MS D, the northern recension includes several rhythmical verses on the Wessex dynasty, at 959 DE, 975 DE, 979 DE, and 1057 D.
47 Such as the marriage of St Margaret to Malcolm of Scotland (1067D), the treachery at the marriage celebration of Earl Ralph (1076/75 DE), and the sufferings of the people under William (1086 E) and Henry I (1104 E).

style of Wulfstan, bishop of Worcester (1002–16) and archbishop of York (1002–23).[48] The effect is to extend the borders imagined by the Chronicle beyond the initial range of West Saxon influence.

It is in the descendants of the northern recension that we first see the influence of French poetic traditions on English verse, with the construction of regular rhymed couplets in 1076/75 DE, 1086 E, and 1104 E; in these descendants we find the verses that make up the transitional style that bridges Old and Middle English poetry.[49] The poems of the DE manuscripts stand apart because they are chronologically later than most of the classical verse of manuscripts ABC, but also because they stem from a recension that departed from the southern tradition shortly after the Chronicle's inception and developed along different lines for the next two centuries. In these circumstances, removed in both time and space from the ideological discourse of West Saxon hegemony, verse historiography developed independent of court patronage and incorporated poetic elements either unavailable or unacceptable to the writers of the texts behind manuscripts ABC. The light cast by this interpretation reveals classical Old English verse as one of the many tools deployed in the service of West Saxon hegemonic ideology, a tool working both to glorify its proclaimed heroes and to solidify an English sense of identity. The scarcity of this kind of verse in later Chronicle manuscripts descended from the northern recension, especially as compared with the density of other poetic passages in the same manuscripts, demonstrates the eventual failure of both the discourse and the form of heroic history. At the same time, however, the Chronicle bears witness to the endurance of verse as a historiographic medium.

If we keep in mind the correlation between geographic and prosodic difference in the two main recensions of the Anglo-Saxon Chronicle, viewing the Chronicle as a kind of *prosimetrum* brings a whole host of new issues to light. It is no coincidence that the poetry that is freer in both its form and its content from the ideology of heroic poetry that eulogized the Cerdicing dynasty would begin to appear in texts the genesis of which is far removed from the Common Stock in both time and place. The extent to which the classical verse form of the poems in manuscripts ABC

---

48 959 DE, 975 D, and possibly 1011 CDE. For the assignment of these passages to Wulfstan, see McIntosh, 'Wulfstan's Prose,' 115; Dorothy Bethurum, ed., *The Homilies of Wulfstan* (Oxford: Clarendon, 1957), 47–8; and Bredehoft, *Textual Histories*, 106–10.

49 I use the term 'transitional' to describe the gradually loosening forms of alliterative verse that many scholars view as the link between Old English and early Middle English alliterative poetry. See, for example, McIntosh, 'Early Middle English Alliterative Verse,' 20–33; and Cable, *Alliterative Tradition*, 41–65.

supports the nationalist project behind Wessex-sponsored historiography becomes clear; in these manuscripts, verse and prose passages augment each other ideologically to produce a unified notion of the Anglo-Saxon people. As long as West Saxon kingship remains strong, it functions as a locus for this unitary identity supported by an epic view of national history. The decline of the epic form, however, coincides with the decline of West Saxon, and eventually Anglo-Saxon, power, and we see a shift in the style and content of the prose annals as well as the verse. The later, northern-derived Chronicle takes on a range of historiographical perspectives, sometimes supporting royal hegemony, sometimes criticizing it, but always offering commentary in both verse and prose that presents a more rounded and heterogenic expression of historical identity. The Chronicle exemplifies the use of *prosimetrum* in both its monoglossic and heteroglossic forms, thereby documenting a shift from historiography as royal propaganda to historiography as evidence of God's hand moving human events – from historiography as remembering and repeating to historiography as working through.[50]

II. Transitional Verse as Alternative Historiography

The irregular Chronicle verse falls roughly into two categories, rhyming verse and rhythmically alliterative verse. Both remain somewhat mysterious and amorphous categories for Anglo-Saxon scholars; their genesis and origins are uncertain, and the extent of their popularity or acceptability among Anglo-Saxon literati is unknown. Michael McKie's study of the origins of rhyme in English verse stresses multiple sources in Church Latin and the works of the Provençal troubadours.[51] E.G. Stanley identifies an early tradition of rhyming that, though often unrecognizable to modern readers accustomed to pure rhyme, is nevertheless in evidence, and he also suggests Church Latin and Old French rhyming verse, as well as Old Norse, as probable influences on later English poets.[52] Much of

---

50 In the Freudian sense of processing an event; see Sigmund Freud, 'Remembering, Repeating, and Working-Through,' in vol. 12 (1962) of *The Standard Edition of the Complete Psychological Works of Sigmund Freud*, trans. and ed. James Strachey, 24 vols (London: Hogarth, 1953–74), 145–56.

51 Michael McKie, 'The Origins and Early Development of Rhyme in English Verse,' *MLR* 92 (1997): 817–31.

52 E.G. Stanley, 'Rhymes in English Medieval Verse: From Old English to Middle English,' in *Medieval English Studies Presented to George Kane*, ed. Edward Donald Kennedy, Ronald Waldron, and Joseph S. Wittig, 19–54 (Wolfeboro, NH: D.S. Brewer,

Stanley's evidence is drawn from the rhyming Chronicle poems as datable examples of an important poetic trend in the transitional period.[53] Rhythmical alliteration, on the other hand, has a rich and well-documented existence outside the examples in the Anglo-Saxon Chronicle and has been studied thoroughly in relation to the works of Ælfric and Wulfstan. The designation of this kind of writing has always been somewhat hazy; whereas some scholars feel that the structural complexity of rhythmical writing distinguishes it from ordinary prose, others are hesitant to call it verse because of its lack of poetic diction and adherence to standard metrical principles. J.C. Pope states definitively that 'the term "rhythmical prose" as applied to Ælfric's compositions must be understood to refer to a loosely metrical form resembling in basic structural principles the alliterative verse of the Old English poets, but differing markedly in the character and range of its rhythms as in strictness of alliterative practice, and altogether distinct in diction, rhetoric, and tone. It is better regarded as a mildly ornamental, rhythmically ordered prose than as a debased, pedestrian poetry.'[54] Yet Pope still prints the homilies in metrical lines rather than as prose, not only underlining the importance of rhythmical structure to the working of the text, but also highlighting the ways in which such texts trouble a strict verse/prose distinction.[55] And Bredehoft has recently argued, from a metrical standpoint, that Ælfric's signature style is more accurately described

---

1988). James W. Earl similarly points to Latin models, particularly those in the hisperic style of Irish Latinists, for the Old English 'rhyming poem,' in 'Hisperic Style in the Old English "Rhyming Poem",' *PMLA* 102 (1987): 187–96. Anne L. Klinck notes the mixed use of rhyme, half-rhyme and assonance in Latin continental verse of the early medieval period, in '"The Riming Poem": Design and Interpretation,' *NM* 89 (1988): 266–79 at 269.

53 Stanley, 'Rhymes,' 28–30. McKie does not consider the Chronicle poems in his analysis.
54 *Homilies of Ælfric*, 1:105.
55 But see also Peter Clemoes's explicit contrast between Ælfric's rhythmical style and poetry: 'Ælfric's sentences have momentum. They have shape. They have a firm and well-articulated grammatical structure ... They are, in fact, sentences which say neither more nor less than their author intended. And their virtues seem all the more remarkable when we remember that traditional vernacular poetry aimed at "stirring the imagination by broad impressions and suggestions" (to use some words of Dr Sisam) and encouraged "spread" and repetition. It is astonishing that Ælfric should have been master of such exact and economical intellectual statement from the start' ('Ælfric,' in *Continuations and Beginnings: Studies in Old English Literature*, ed. E.G. Stanley, 176–209 [London, 1966], 201–2). Anne Middleton likewise states firmly that 'despite its formal resemblance to poetry, [Aelfric's rhythmic style] is defined as prose by Aelfric's own clear terms of classification' ('Aelfric's Answerable Style: The Rhetoric of the Alliterative Prose,' *Studies in Medieval Culture* 4 [1973]: 83–91 at 83).

as verse than as rhythmical prose.[56] The affinity between the irregular Chronicle verse and homiletic discourse therefore has a formal as well as thematic component; when Chronicle poems take on the quality of rhythmical alliteration, they also take on a philosophy of history that accords with salvation rather than epic doctrine.

In an attempt to avoid a problematic dichotomy, McIntosh proposes that 'there is not just verse on the one hand ... and prose on the other ... There are in the late Old English period at least five clearly separable stylistic genres, between which there are important and significant rhythmical distinctions. How many of these five are "verse" and how many are "prose" is a terminological problem which I should prefer to avoid.'[57] McIntosh's delineation of five generic categories addresses the problem of evaluating late Old English literature in the terms of a prose/poetry dyad, and he offers a new possibility by asserting that while '[Ælfric's] *Life of Oswald* may be verse, it is hardly poetry.'[58] With the introduction of a third term, McIntosh seems to suggest that the texts of Anglo-Saxon England are not necessarily well served by traditional (and need we add, modern) definitions of literary form.

N.F. Blake offers a taxonomic compromise in the intermediary term 'rhythmical alliteration.' Blake takes issue with 'rhythmical prose' because the term 'has the unfortunate effect of turning the works written in it into prose works; their close relationship to verse is thus obscured. And although I am aware that works composed in rhythmical alliteration contain many rhetorical features, including rhyme, other than alliteration ... the name emphasizes that the boundary between verse and prose was so blurred that a clear division is impossible.'[59] Blake's approach, which averts false dichotomies and appreciates the fluid nature of the surviving corpus, allows us to appreciate the interplay between aesthetic traditions in the late Anglo-Saxon period while also placing those traditions within a literary practice that eventually leads to the texts of the early Middle English period, thereby providing some continuity (though not necessarily a direct progression) over the all-too-convenient break of 1066. Stanley similarly approaches the style as hailing 'from the borderland of verse and prose,' where a text can move back and forth in its metrical shape and the

---

56 Bredehoft, 'Ælfric and Late Old English Verse,' 78, and *Early English Metre*, 81–90.
57 McIntosh, 'Wulfstan's Prose,' 110.
58 McIntosh, 'Wulfstan's Prose,' 111.
59 N.F. Blake, 'Rhythmical Alliteration,' *MP* 67 (1969): 118–24 at 120.

use of poetic diction is an important factor in its definition.[60] Stanley thus establishes two key criteria for the definition of poetry, metre and diction, both of which play a prominent role in the irregular Chronicle verse. Designating these texts as rhythmically alliterative, and thus emphasizing the important influence of the verse tradition on this equivocal form, can expand our definition of poetry enough to include the irregular Chronicle verse as well as other late compositions and overcome the problems of taxonomy that impede many investigations. Perhaps most important, it recognizes the fluidity of late Anglo-Saxon prosody.

The loose forms that Bredehoft, Stanley, and others identify as characteristic of late Old English metrics are clearly at odds with the strict formalism of classical Old English verse; the question, then, is how the loosening of form, and its affinity with homiletic discourse, affects the historical understanding that is encoded by the later, non-traditional Chronicle verse. The classical verse of manuscripts ABC served a very specific function, namely, the nostalgic memorialization of West Saxon leaders as ideal Christian Germanic kings, but the verse of the northern recension extends beyond memorialization to voice an evaluative, often critical perspective. Removed from the circles of court patronage, the northern exemplar seeks to answer the concerns and interests more relevant to its own audience and patrons, and historical verse functions otherwise than promoting the ideology of West Saxon kingship. These poems do not interpret events through the single heroic lens of past glory; rather, they opt for a range of interpretive possibilities. Many of the rhythmical passages take on the character of the homilies they so closely resemble, by introducing the framework of salvation history alongside the heroic history of the classical verse. Rhymed couplets, on the other hand, tend to emerge at moments of heightened emotion in the historical narrative and emphasize the affective impact of the event. The irregular Chronicle verse, in both its rhythmical and its rhymed forms, thus marks a transitional phase not only in English poetics, but also in the uses and meaning of historiography. With the introduction of this kind of verse, the Anglo-Saxon Chronicle takes on increasing narrativity, and the relationship between prose and verse becomes more

---

60 Stanley thus defines and prints portions of a homily in the style of Wulfstan as verse, on the basis of both their metrical structure and their use of poetic diction; see 'The Judgement of the Damned (from Cambridge, Corpus Christi College 201 and other manuscripts) and the Definition of Old English Verse,' in Learning and Literature in Anglo-Saxon England: Studies Presented to Peter Clemoes on the Occasion of His Sixty-fifth Birthday, ed. Michael Lapidge and Helmut Gneuss, 363–91 (Cambridge: Cambridge University Press, 1985), 390.

complex as verse passages perform the function of commenting and apostrophizing rather than simply memorializing.

The entry for 959 in all the Chronicle manuscripts marks the accession of Edgar, patron of the Benedictine Reform, on the death of his brother Eadwig. In keeping with their general focus on the deeds of the West Saxon kings, the southern manuscripts duly record the accession as an important event. In manuscript A, this event is the only one recorded s.a. 958: 'Her forðferde Eadwig cyng on kalendas Octobris, 7 Eadgar his broðor feng to rice.'[61] Manuscripts B and C add that Edgar 'feng to rice ægðer ge on Westseaxum ge on Myrcum ge on Norðhymbrum, 7 he wæs þa .xvi. wintre,'[62] emphasizing Edgar's control over regions outside Wessex as well as over Wessex itself. In the northern manuscripts, however, the significance of Edgar's accession rests on something other than his West Saxon pedigree; instead, we find a poetic encomium on his good deeds as a benefactor of the Church and supporter of the reform. Introducing the annal with the news that 'Her Eadwig cyning forðferde, 7 feng Eadgar his broþor to rice,' manuscripts D and E go on to record the following:

> On his dagum hit godode georne,   7 God him geuðe
> þet he wunode on sibbe   þa hwile þe he leofode,
> 7 he dyde swa him þearf wes,   earnode þes georne.
> He arerde Godes lof wide   7 Godes lage lufode
> 7 folces frið bette   swiðost þara cyninga
> þe ær him gewurde   be manna gemynde.
> 7 God him eac fylste   þet cyningas 7 eorlas
> georne him to bugon   7 wurden underþeodde
> to þam þe he wolde,   7 butan gefeohte
> eall he gewilde   þet he sylf wolde.
> He wearð wide geond þeodland   swiðe geweorðad,
> forþam þe he weorðode   Godes naman georne

---

61 Janet M. Bately, ed., *MS A*, The Anglo-Saxon Chronicle: A Collaborative Edition 3 (Cambridge: D.S. Brewer, 1986). 'Here Eadwig the king died on the kalends of October, and Edgar his brother succeeded to the kingdom.' All citations of the Chronicle are taken from the relevant volume of Dumville and Keynes, *Collaborative Edition*, and all translations are my own.

62 Simon Taylor, ed., *MS B*, The Anglo-Saxon Chronicle: A Collaborative Edition 4 (Cambridge: D.S. Brewer, 1983). 'Succeeded to the kingdom both in Wessex and in Mercia and in Northumbria, and he was then sixteen years old.' MS C replicates this wording; see O'Brien O'Keeffe, ed., *MS C*, The Anglo-Saxon Chronicle: A Collaborative Edition 5 (Cambridge: D.S. Brewer, 2001).

7 Godes lage smeade   oft 7 gelome
7 Godes lof rærde   wide 7 side
7 wislice rædde   oftost a simle
for Gode 7 for worulde   eall his þeode.[63]   (1–16)

In its form, the passage scarcely resembles classical Old English verse; yet its carefully structured rhythmical patterning sets it apart from ordinary prose, and its distinctive style, with such characteristic phrases as *oft 7 gelome, for Gode 7 for worulde*, and *wide 7 side*, so closely matches that of Wulfstan that many scholars attribute its authorship to him.[64] In addition to a variant aesthetic form, however, this passage introduces a variant notion of the purpose of verse historiography: it sets out, like the classical verses, to praise King Edgar, but its narration of history is shaped by the teleology of Christian salvation rather than by heroic legend. Edgar's kingship has a direct causal relationship with the well-being of his people. While there are hints of such a relationship in the classical poem on Edgar's

---

63 Susan Irvine, ed., *MS E*, The Anglo-Saxon Chronicle: A Collaborative Edition 7 (Cambridge: D.S. Brewer, 2004). 'In his day things quickly got much better, and God granted him that he might remain in peace as long as he lived, and he did, as was needful to him – he earned that deservedly. He spread the praise of God widely, and loved God's law, and restored the peace of the people, more so than any of those kings who came before him in human memory. And God also supported him, so that kings and earls eagerly bowed to him, and became subject to that which he wished, and without fighting he controlled that which he himself wished [to control]. He was greatly celebrated throughout the land of the people because he earnestly honoured the name of God, and reflected on God's law, often and frequently, and spread the praise of God, far and wide, and ruled wisely, often and continuously, for God and for the world, all his people.' S. Irvine prints the poetic passages at 959, 975, 979, two at 1075, 1086, and 1104 as lines of verse and notes that the passage on Ælfheah at 1011 has been identified as 'poetic prose' by Bredehoft (*MS E*, s.a. 1011 n1). G.P. Cubbin does not print any passages as verse in his edition of MS D (Cubbin, ed., *MS D*, The Anglo-Saxon Chronicle: A Collaborative Edition 6 [Cambridge: D.S. Brewer, 1996]). Cubbin insists that 'there is nothing in the MS to indicate verse in this annal' (s.a. 959 n2), but Bredehoft offers a metrical analysis that contradicts this view (*Textual Histories*, 97–8 and 107–8).

64 Karl Jost, 'Wulfstan und die Angelsächsiche Chronik,' *Anglia* 47 (1923): 105–23; affirmed by McIntosh, 'Wulfstan's Prose,' 112; Bethurum, 'Wulfstan,' in Stanley, *Continuations and Beginnings*, 210–46 at 212; and *English Historical Documents, c. 500–1042*, ed. and trans. Dorothy Whitelock, EHD 1, 2nd ed. (London: Eyre Methuen, 1979), 225 n4 and 229 n2. The attribution is accepted by a majority of scholars, and I follow their lead; whether the verses were actually written by Wulfstan himself is not as important to the present discussion as the fact that they make conscious use of a style noted for its affinity with the vernacular verse tradition. On this connection, see A.P.McD. Orchard, 'Crying Wolf: Oral Style and the *Sermones Lupi*,' *ASE* 21 (1992): 239–64.

death,[65] the DE poem makes it a central facet of his reign from the moment of his accession and offers the peace and prosperity of his reign as evidence of his own piety and dedication to God's law. Immediately upon his accession, *On his dagum hit godode georne*, and unlike the kings in the classical poems, Edgar has no need to be a warrior, because *God him eac fylste þet cyningas 7 eorlas / georne him to bugon* without violence. The annal for 959 DE instantiates a new kind of historical poetry, one that serves not merely to commemorate, but to comment on events and offer an interpretive framework distinct from the nationalist doctrine of the earlier, southern Chronicle verse. Instead of praising Edgar as a noble warrior and heroic leader, the poem emphasizes his piety and his devotion to God as the cornerstones of his kingship. The contrast here to the verses on Athelstan and Edmund is striking, especially in the light of the Viking attacks that followed Edgar's reign. The verse looks to the future, rather than the past, in order to elucidate the meaning of Edgar's kingship in a providential context. From this perspective, the time of Edgar takes on the character of a golden age, and the political repercussions surrounding his death in 975 emerge as foreshadowing the Viking conflicts of the late tenth and early eleventh centuries. The nostalgia of the heroic epic, which gazes longingly at the heroic past, no longer serves as a point of reference for understanding Anglo-Saxon history. Rather, these verses look to salvation history as a model for interpretation.

This shift in historical ideology accompanies, or perhaps necessitates, the shift in poetic form, as looser verse forms replace the classical epic form. Instead of the classical verse which eulogizes Edgar s.a. 975 in manuscripts ABC, the DE annal begins with a different poem, rhythmical but not classically metrical, about the West Saxon king, of which more below. Following this alternative eulogy, the passage in manuscript D adds an important caveat about the chaos that befalls Anglo-Saxon England on the death of the monarch whose piety ensured peace among his people:

> On his dagum,   for his iugoðe,
> Godes wiþærsacan   Godes lage bræcon
> Ælfere ealdorman,   7 oþre manega,
> 7 munucregol myrdon,   7 mynstra tostæncton,
> 7 munecas todræfdon,   7 Godes þeowas fesedon,
> þe Eadgar kyning het ær   þone halgan biscop
> Aþælwold gestalian,   7 wydewan bestryptan

---

65 See pp. 205–8 above.

oft 7 gelome,   7 fela unrihta
7 yfelra unlaga   arysan up siððan,
7 aa æfter þam   hit yfelode swiðe.[66]

Alliteration on 'm' carries through lines 3b–6a, highlighting the monks, minsters, and monastic rule that fell victim to Ælfhere and his fellows. The repetition of the conjunction *ond*, meanwhile, piles appositive examples of their evil deeds before the reader. The technique is strikingly similar to Wulfstan's in the *Sermo Lupi* – which is among the reasons that scholars have attributed authorship of the verse to him. Like that homily, the 975 D passage encourages its readers to think of history in terms of the punishment of sins, rather than of the deeds of heroes.[67] With the death of their good Christian king, the Anglo-Saxons find themselves once again plunged into chaos, and the backlash against the churches that had benefited, at the expense of the nobility, during Edgar's reign emerges as the inevitable outcome of evil among the leaders, whom the verse casts as *Godes wiþærsacan*. In deliberately setting up this dichotomy between secular leaders and the servants of God, the passage underscores a teleological interpretation of historical events: because the pious king is dead, and because his successor is so young, there is no secular leader capable of enforcing God's law among ealdormen like Ælfhere, with the inevitable result that the people suffer *fela unrihta / 7 yfelra unlaga*. The wider, providential consequences of Edgar's death, toward which the poem s.a. 975 in manuscripts ABC only gestures, come forth here as the centrepiece of the passage. In contrast to the heroic history expounded by the classical Chronicle poems and *The Battle of Maldon*, these homiletic verses shift the focus of historical narrative from the epic-style commemoration of the West Saxon dynasty to humankind's failure to follow God's plan and the resulting chaos. There is no going back in this model, no redemption of a lost past; there is only movement forward through time in the direction dictated by the Anglo-Saxons' piety, or lack thereof.

---

66 'In his day, because of his youth, God's enemies broke God's law, Ealdorman Ælfhere and many others, and disrupted the monastic rule, and destroyed churches, and drove out monks, and drove away the servants of God, whom Edgar had previously commanded the holy bishop Æthelwold to establish, and often and frequently robbed widows, and afterward many wrongs and evil crimes rose up, and always after that it became much worse.' My lineation. Here, Cubbin notes that 'there are more capitals than normal in this annal, but no explicit marks of verse' (*MS D*, s.a. 975 n3).

67 See pp. 143–51 above.

This rhythmical style sets a new standard for the use of verse in the Anglo-Saxon Chronicle, and when bad things happen, the continuators of the northern versions often follow its example in explaining the cause of events. Such is the case for the murder (or martyrdom) of Edward in 978. Manuscript A records s.a. 978 simply that 'Her wearð Eadweard cyning ofslegen' [In this year King Edward was killed], and manuscript C already adds that he was 'gemartyrad' [martyred]. The northern versions take up the idea of Edward's martyrdom and explicate it, once again, by means of rhythmical alliteration tinged with the overtones of homiletic musings about historical cause and effect. The opening lines, 'Ne wearð Angelcynne nan wærsa dæd gedon / þonne þeos wæs syððon hi ærest Brytonland gesohton' (1–2), recall the closing lines of Brunanburh, in linking the deeds of contemporary Anglo-Saxons with their migratory – and pagan – ancestors.[68] In this case, however, their deeds are not those of heroic warriors defending and consolidating the nation; instead, they consist of the treacherous and craven act of regicide. Using the techniques of repetition and contrast familiar from homiletic discourse, the passage highlights the traitors' opposition to God in the making of history:

Men hine ofmyrðrodon,   ac God hine mærsode.
He wæs on life   eorðlic cing;
he is nu æfter deaðe   heofonlic sanct.
Hine nolden his eorðlican   magas wrecan,
ac hine hafað his heofonlica fæder   swiðe gewrecen.
Þa eorðlican banan woldon his gemynd   on erðan adilgian,
ac se uplica wrecend hafað his gemynd   on heofenum 7 on eorðan
    tobræd.
Þa þe nolden ær to his libbendum   lichaman onbugan,
þa nu eadmodlice on cneowum   abugað to his dædum banum.[69]   (3–11)

The passage builds to an aesthetic crescendo, beginning with brief, pithy statements of contrasting states and adding detail and commentary in each

---

68 MS E, s.a. 979 (for 978). 'There was no worse deed done among the English people since they first sought the land of the Britons.'
69 MS E. 'Men murdered him, but God exalted him. He was in life an earthly king; he is now after his death a heavenly saint. His earthly kinsmen did not wish to avenge him, but his heavenly father has greatly avenged him. The earthly slayers wished to blot out his memory on earth, but the divine avenger has spread out his memory in heaven and on earth. Those who did not wish to submit to his earthly body, they now meekly bow on their knees to his dead bones.'

subsequent line. The rhythmical structuring of narrative assertion and reversal contrasts the earthly with the divine and shows God repeatedly thwarting human attempts to determine historical events, serving as protector and saviour of his loyal subject, Edward. In this sense, God has taken on the role of the Germanic lord who defends the interests and well-being of his subjects and becomes the central actor in the historical narrative. The poem does not eulogize Edward so much as it celebrates God's role in determining human events. Lest we miss this important lesson, the passage closes by stating it explicitly:

> Nu we magon ongytan   þet manna wisdom
> 7 smeagunga   7 heore rædas
> syndon nahtlice   ongean Godes geþeaht.[70]   (12–14)

With this powerful interpretive framework firmly established by the verse passages of the northern recension, readers can produce an explanation for the chaotic events leading to the eventual loss of English sovereignty not once, but twice, in the eleventh century – particularly for those events that have marked Æthelred's reign. Although the Chronicle is notoriously pessimistic in its portrayal of these years, blaming the country's distress on weak leadership and bad counsel, these verse passages trace the source of that distress to the death of Edgar, the last ruler to ensure peace, and the murder of Edward, whose byname of Martyr becomes a powerful propaganda tool for Æthelred's detractors. The southern Chronicle, equally pessimistic in its record of the Æthelred years, does not explicitly take up the notion of salvation history as an explanatory model, in spite of its perpetual popularity. This particular ideology of history finds expression in the rhythmical alliteration that fails to appear in any of the southern manuscripts.[71] The northern version of the Chronicle is thus able to draw a

---

70 MS E. 'Now we may perceive that the wisdom of men and their thoughts and their counsels are nothing compared to God's intentions.'

71 The single exception to this rule is MS C's use of the rhythmical passage on the martyrdom of Archbishop Ælfheah at the hands of the Danes, a passage also found in MSS DE. O'Brien O'Keeffe finds that 'both Rositzke and Plummer (for E) print this passage as verse, but there is no basis, metrical or otherwise, for such treatment' (*MS C*, s.a. 1011 n7). The treatment of the material, however, is too ornamental to be considered mere annalistic prose. Following the rhythmical style of Wulfstan's annals, a series of thematic contrasts depicts a ruler brought low, joy replaced by sorrow, and a devastating attack on Christianity in the very city that first welcomed St Augustine as the apostle of the English more than four centuries earlier. MS C, s.a. 1011, blames the

higher meaning from a chaotic series of events otherwise attributable only to bad leadership. If the Anglo-Saxons have a bad leader, they have little recourse; if, however, their misfortune has come about through neglect of their duties to God, they can always fast and pray.

In emphasizing salvation teleology in the Chronicle texts, and in doing so by employing literary forms most often associated with the homilies of Wulfstan and Ælfric, these passages of rhythmical alliteration subtly detach the burden (and the benefits) of written history from the orbit of the royal court and reorient historiography around the Church. Not only the production but also the interpretation and meaning of history fall under ecclesiastical auspices, a trend that will continue through the remainder of English vernacular historiography in the Chronicle entries of the late eleventh and twelfth centuries. Although the Anglo-Saxon Chronicle's interest in recounting secular events never wanes, the meaning of those events is no longer filtered through the lens of heroic history. Rather, ecclesiastical interests, often at odds with those of secular government, offer their own interpretations of events. Those interpretations are often highly critical of the actors in the drama, even when the actors are kings. As the remaining irregular verse passages show, even when the content of a verse is not homiletic, the critical function remains, and the standard metrical praise of kings and princes is, quite literally, a thing of the past.

The final form the Chronicle verse takes is that of rhymed poetry. Like the homiletic rhythmical alliteration, the rhymed passages speak from a position outside the narrative, commenting on and offering interpretations of the historical events they relate. Although they do not always serve the

---

devastation of Canterbury on the indecision of secular leaders: 'Ealle þas ungesælða us gelumpon þuruh unrædas þæt man nolde him a timan gafol beodon oþþe wið gefeohtan. Ac þonne hi mæst to yfele gedon hæfdon, þonne nam mon frið 7 grið wið hi, 7 naþelæs for eallum þissum griðe 7 gafole hi ferdon æghweder flocmælum 7 heregodon ure earme folc, 7 hi rypton 7 slogon' [All these misfortunes befell us because of bad counsel, because they would not offer them tribute in time or fight against them. But when they had done the most evil, then they were offered peace and tribute; nevertheless, in spite of all that peace and tribute, they went about everywhere in bands and harried our poor people, and they captured and slew]. Anglo-Saxon England thus loses the symbolic and actual head of its Church – an event whose significance within the scope of salvation teleology seems to augur the eventual conquest of England by the Danes in 1013. Keynes assumes the existence of a cult of Ælfheah in London within a few years of his death and explains the translation of his relics in 1023: 'It may be that in the manner of his death Ælfheah had become a symbol of English resistance to the Danes, and that Cnut was concerned to move the focal point of his cult from London to Canterbury, where it might not be so highly charged' (Keynes, 'Ælfheah,' in Lapidge et al., Blackwell Encyclopedia, 7).

same explanatory function as the rhythmical passages or the commemorative role of the classical verse, these poems serve to highlight moments of emotional or narrative intensity within the historical narrative, thus shaping the way a reader might interpret events. The death of King Edgar; the maiming and death of Alfred; the dramatic and politically significant marriage of Princess (later St) Margaret to Malcolm of Scotland, despite her professed devotion to God; and the death of William the Conqueror, among other events, all inspire moments of rhyming verse, to varying degrees of strictness, from the chroniclers. The more substantial of these verse passages chart a development of rhyme in Old English and show its gradual replacement of alliteration as a primary poetic device.

The poem s.a. 975 DE is in many ways more rhythmical than rhyming, but it shows a fascinating blend of traditional form, with alliterating half–lines and heroic diction, and rhyme introduced as a linking device. Replacing the classical poem found in manuscripts ABC,[72] the DE verse likewise honours Edgar as a traditional Germanic king with the epithets 'Angla reccent' [ruler of the English] (1b), 'Westseaxena wine' [friend of the West Saxons] (2a), and 'Myrcene mundbora' [protector of the Mercians] (2b) in quick succession; the alliterative titles also emphasize the extent of Edgar's rule over a variety of English peoples and territories. The verse goes on to impress upon the reader Edgar's influence over international affairs:

Cuð wæs þet wide   geond feola þeoda
þet aferan Eadmundes   ofer ganetes bað
cyningas hine wide   wurðodon side,
bugon to cyninge   swa wæs him gecynde.
Næs se flota swa rang   ne se here swa strang
þet on Angelcynne   æs him gefetede
þa hwile þe se æþela cyning   cynestol gerehte.[73]   (3–9)

Phrases like *aferan Eadmundes* and *ganetes bað* recall classical poetic diction from the parallel annal in ABC and emphasize the verse's links to that literary tradition, replete with its focus on ancestry and use of kennings.

---

72 Cubbin argues that the compiler of D used precursors of C and E as two of his exemplars up to 1016 (*MS D*, xxvii–liii); if this is the case, then the compiler likely had the option to copy the classical verse s.a. 975 C, but chose to insert this one instead.

73 MS E. 'It was widely known throughout many peoples that kings far and wide over the gannet's bath honoured him, the son of Edmund, very much, widely submitted to the king, as was fitting for him. No fleet was so proud, nor army so strong, that it could fetch for itself carrion among the English people as long as the noble king ruled the throne.'

But the half-lines themselves are linked by rhyme. The use of rhyme in this passage might be seen as a bit spurious; but if we bear in mind Stanley's caveat against accepting only the pure rhyme of modern literary definitions,[74] we can find rhymes such as *feola / þeoda, wide / side, cyninge / gecynde, rang / strang, Angelcynne / æþela cyning,* and *gefætte / gerehte,* or six rhymes in nine lines of verse. The passage opens with the traditional technique of alliteration (*Eadgar / Angla, Westseaxena / wine, Myrcna mundbora,* and *aferan Eadmundes*) but closes with rhyme, thus blending the two poetic modes into a single work unified by its heroic theme and diction. As the northern chronicles tell it, the death of Edgar was a tremendous blow not only to his subjects, who went on to suffer decades of bad rule and foreign invasion, but also to the Church, which subsequently suffered retribution for churchmen's earlier preferment in royal grants and charters. As a complement to the rhythmical, Wulfstanian passages on the same event, this poem reminds readers that from a late tenth / early eleventh century point of view, Edgar's death marks the end of peace and prosperity for England.

The poem on the death of Alfred s.a. 1036 CD similarly combines the poetic techniques of alliteration and rhyme to highlight an event of great political and emotional impact.[75] Alfred was an heir to Æthelred II and therefore a potential threat to the Danish kingship; as such, he was summarily dealt with by the ruling forces on his return to England from Normandy. The Chronicle does not hesitate to take sides, by characterizing him in the annal's prose portion as 'se unsceððiga æþeling' [the guiltless prince] who simply wanted to visit his mother. In addition, the prose text recounts the concern of Earl Godwine and the other powerful men who 'hit him ne geþafode' [would not allow him to do it], thus indicating a potential succession struggle that ended in favour of Harold, the son of Cnut, 'þeh hit unriht wære' [although it was not right]. The partisan nature

---

74 'Can we assume that [Old English] poets strove to achieve true rhymes for such occasional ornaments? If, as I think, they did not, hearers (or readers) would not expect true rhymes. Having been accustomed to rhymes less than true for occasional ornament Old English poets might not have striven to provide consistently true rhymes when rhyme recurs regularly, and hearers (or readers) would not have expected true rhyming only' (Stanley, 'Rhymes,' 20).

75 O'Brien O'Keeffe places this poem in the context of legal history and bodily signification in the time of Æthelred and Cnut, whereas the Christian emphasis of the poem works to place the guilt inscribed by Alfred's maiming and death firmly on Godwine; see her 'Body and Law in Late Anglo-Saxon England,' *ASE* 27 (1998): 209–32, especially 212–15 and 230.

of this event is underscored by emotional invocations of the violent and gruesome attacks on Alfred and his companions:

Ac Godwine hine þa gelette   7 hine on hæft sette
7 his geferan he todraf   7 sume he mislice ofsloh.
Sume hi man wið feo sealde,   sume hreowlice acwealde,
sume hi man bende,   sume hi man blende,
sume hamelode,   sume hættode.
Ne wearð dreorlicre dæd   gedon on þison earde
syþþan Dene comon   7 her frið namon.[76]   (1–7)

Leonine rhyme not only links half-lines across the caesura, but also accentuates Godwine's appalling deeds: *gelette / gesette, sealde / acwealde, bende / blende*, and *hamelode / hættode*. The repetition of *sume* presents these atrocities in a catalogue, recalling Wulfstan's technique in the *Sermo Lupi ad Anglos* by piling atrocity upon atrocity.[77] The poem continues to underline the horror of this act by invoking the now familiar locution *Ne wearð dreorlicre dæd gedon on þison earde syþþan ...*, echoing both *Brunanburh* and the verse on Edward's martyrdom s.a. 979 DE.[78] In this poem, rhyme works to provide narrative emphasis, and the occasional alliteration, not conforming to any metrical pattern, supplies ornament but does not structure meaning.

The atrocity of the attacks does find meaning, however, in the interpretive framework offered by salvation history, and the poet urges readers

---

76 MS C. 'But Godwine then oppressed him and cast him into fetters and drove away his companions and killed some of them in various ways. Some of them were sold for money, some cruelly killed, some of them were fettered, some of them were blinded, some hamstrung, some scalped. Such a bloody deed was not done in this country since the Danes came and made peace here.' MS D significantly omits to mention, both in the prose lead-in and in the verse passage itself, that Godwine was the author of these acts; instead, D blames only those 'þe micel weoldon on þisan lande' [who had great power in this land] and begins the poetic passage with the actor 'he' [he].

77 See pp. 146–7 above.

78 Bredehoft has recently noted that the use of phrases like 'the worst in memory' or 'the worst in history' reveal different modes of representing the significance of current events, either in terms of human memory or in terms of recorded history: the latter is explicitly political, whereas the former is more likely to refer to natural or environmental events. See 'History and Memory in the *Anglo-Saxon Chronicle*,' in *Readings in Medieval Texts: Interpreting Old and Middle English Literature*, ed. David F. Johnson and Elaine Treharne, 109–21 (Oxford: Oxford University Press, 2005).

... to gelyfenne   to ðan leofan Gode
þæt hi blission   bliðe mid Criste
þe wæron butan scylde   swa earmlice acwealde.[79]   (8–10)

Once again stressing the blamelessness of Alfred and his comrades, the poem urges belief in the Christian faith to make sense of an incomprehensible historical event; instead of pointing to a cause-and-effect relation between faith and events, the verse offers faith as a solution rather than a reason. Katherine O'Brien O'Keeffe has shown how the verse on Alfred, 'the ambitions of which exceed those of epitaph and look rather to the promotion of a cult of the dead prince,' draws liberally from hagiographic convention in both its content and its aesthetic form.[80] The parallels between *The Death of Alfred* and the commemoration of martyrs in the Anglo-Saxon homiletic tradition also recall, within the context of the Chronicle itself, the death of Alfred's uncle, Edward the Martyr, and play deftly into the politics of dynastic succession.[81] The role of the Church is likewise emphasized as the story of Alfred continues, honouring the monks at Ely who cared for him in his infirmity and buried him 'swa him wel gebyrede, / ful wurðlice, swa he wyrðe wæs' [as properly befitted him, with great honour, as he was worthy] (17b–18) with the assurance that 'seo saul is mid Criste' [the soul is with Christ] (20b). Rhyme once again connects half-lines across the caesura and highlights the actions of Godwine's men ('Sona swa he *lende* on scype man hine *blende*'), Alfred himself ('7 he þar *wunode* ða hwile þe he *lyfode*'), and the monks ('Syððan hine man *byrigde* swa him wel *gebyrede* ... / æt þam *westende* þam styple ful *gehende*')[82] as well as providing links for narrative transition:

Se æþeling lyfode þa *gyt*;   ælc yfel man him *gehet*,
    oð þæt man *gerædde*   þæt man hine *lædde*
to Eligbyrig   swa gebundenne.[83]   (11–13)

---

79 MS C. 'To have faith in dear God that they rejoice blissfully with Christ who were without guilt so wretchedly killed.'

80 O'Brien O'Keeffe, 'Deaths and Transformations: Thinking through the "End" of Old English Verse,' in *New Directions in Oral Theory*, ed. Mark C. Amodio, 149–78 (Tempe: Arizona Center for Medieval and Renaissance Studies, 2005), 158.

81 O'Brien O'Keeffe, 'Deaths and Transformations,' 150–64.

82 MS C; my emphasis. 'As soon as he arrived on the ship he was blinded' (line 14); 'and he lived there as long as he lived' (line 16); 'he was buried as properly befitted him ... at the west end, very near to the steeple' (lines 17 and 19).

83 MS C; my emphasis. 'The atheling yet lived; every evil was ordered for him, until it was advised that he should be taken to Ely thus bound up.'

The death of Alfred marks a moment in which the stakes are high not only in the narrative of Anglo-Saxon history, which relishes the treachery and atrocity of Godwine's acts for the drama they provide, but also in the partisan politics of succession and kingship in England after the Danish conquest. It is no coincidence that in the annal for 1037 directly following this account, 'man geceas Harald ofer eall to cinge' [Harald was chosen everywhere as king], thereby settling the question of succession once the West Saxon heir whose very name conjures an image of historical eminence is no longer a threat.[84] Political instability leads to an atrocity of which the meaning is reconciled through verse and prayer and the outcome once again promotes stability. To commemorate the event in classical metre would be to work a theme at odds with the heroic themes of the earlier poems, but the flexibility of the rhythmical form creates a space in which to express outrage, horror, and sadness within the context of national history. The disjunction between the Anglo-Saxon nationalism underlying the extensive emotional treatment of Alfred's death and the dry, brief notice of the throne's passing to the son of Cnut is underscored by the prose-verse distinction as well. Instead of epic verses celebrating the heroic ideology of the West Saxon dynasty, this portion of the Chronicle evokes the tragedy of a nation drifting irrevocably both from God's law and from its own heroic vision of itself.

With the exception of the classical verse on Edward's death in 1065, which could even be read as antiquarian by virtue of its late date, rhyme is the predominant poetic technique for the remainder of the Chronicle. Given the close connection between traditional alliterative metre and the West Saxon royal family, clearly established by the tenth century verse of the southern Chronicle manuscripts, it seems neither surprising nor out of place to find that form invoked on the death of the last West Saxon king. Nor is it shocking to note that the Chronicle neglects to offer eulogies on the deaths of Swein, Cnut, Harald, and Harthacnut. In contrast, when William dies in 1087, his death is also commemorated in verse, but his eulogy is offered in the form of rhyming poetry. This change both demonstrates the growing dominance of rhyme as a poetic technique in English and underscores the notion that the alliterative long line is a specifically Anglo-Saxon form, unsuitable for the memorial to a Norman king. The

---

84 Edward (later the Confessor) was still alive, but in exile in Normandy, having launched an ultimately unsuccessful invasion attempt at Southampton on Cnut's death in 1035, according to the later Norman sources William of Jumièges and William of Poitiers; see *Vita Ædwardi Regis qui apud Westmonasterium requiescit*, ed. and trans. Frank Barlow, 2nd ed. (Oxford: Clarendon, 1992), lxvii n257.

poem on the death of William, like the Old French poetry his conquest brought to England, is composed in rhyming couplets. The differences between the poem on William's death and those recording the deaths of Anglo-Saxon rulers extends beyond form, however. In contrast to those of the Anglo-Saxon kings whose memorials precede his in the Chronicle, William's legacy is not that of the good Christian ruler; instead, the poem is a catalogue of the tribulations and sufferings he inflicted on his conquered people. For the Chronicle to characterize William as a harsh ruler is nothing new; a set of rhyming couplets s.a. 1076 D / 1075 E highlights the marriage of Earl Ralph to the daughter of William fitz Osbern, at which many of the nobles plotted to overthrow William. The prose annals of the Chronicle are likewise peppered with stories and laments about William's severity, and the annal that includes the poem on his death (1086 E) begins by describing the terrible famine of that year and blaming the people's distress on

> folces synna þet hi nellað lufian God 7 rihtwisnesse. Swa swa hit wæs þa on ðam dagum þet litel rihtwisnesse wæs on þisum lande mid ænige menn buton mid munecan ane þær þær hi wæll ferdon. Se cyng 7 þa heafodmen lufedon swiðe 7 oferswiðe gitsunge on golde 7 on seolfre 7 ne rohtan hu synlice hit wære begytan buton hit come to heom.[85]

The chronicler follows earlier models in ascribing historical hardships to the failure to obey God's law, but the West Saxon kings were never to blame for these failures in the canonical verse – Edward, recall, was specifically exonerated by being too young to prevent the anti-monastic backlash. In losing the ruler who maintained and protected both the nation and the faith, the Anglo-Saxons were sometimes prone to neglect their duties to God. In the 1086 E verse, however, William is actually the cause of these misfortunes, as his own greed and sinfulness led the people (with the notable exception of monks like our chronicler) into unrighteous behaviour. The king is no longer an object of unquestioning admiration and heroic honour; rather, he is a caretaker lax in his duties to his people and the author

---

85   MS E. 'the sins of the people, that they did not wish to love God and righteousness. Thus it was that in those days there was little righteousness in this land with any men, except with the monks who alone behaved well. The king and the nobles loved much, and overmuch, treasure in gold and in silver, and they did not care how sinfully it was acquired as long as it came to them.'

of their suffering rather than the preserver of their well-being.[86] The poem on his death reflects this attitude toward William as a ruler, in recounting the many ways in which England has suffered under his rule. In place of the catalogue of good works and noble deeds that honoured kings like Athelstan, Edmund, Edgar, and Edward, William is castigated for his hardness toward the people, for treating even wild animals with more care and concern than his own subjects. He is noted for cruelty, greed, and pride, and the poem ends with a prayer for God's forgiveness of him – a prayer that the West Saxon kings, presumably, did not need. Whereas the prose portion of the annal focuses on William and his nobles' sinfulness, the poem itself enumerates various examples of plain and simple tyranny over his subjects. Together, the two present a multifaceted, if thoroughly negative, portrayal of the king, from the points of view of both the ecclesiastical authorities and his conquered subjects. The distinct voices of church and people harmonize in their ironic memorialization of a non-heroic, because not Anglo-Saxon, king.

This poem, with its marked differences from classical Anglo-Saxon verse in both form and content, marks the literary as well as political colonization of England by the Normans; as Lerer writes, 'the lyric voice of Old English personal poetry disappears into curiosities modelled on Latin schoolroom exercises,' and 'the annal mimes the imposition of a Norman verbal world on the English linguistic landscape.'[87] With this rhyming passage, the Chronicle poetry comes full circle, once again memorializing a king in verse on the occasion of his death. But the tremendous changes that have affected historical poetry in the 150 years since *Brunanburh* are evident. The prosimetric form was introduced into the Chronicle for the purpose of creating verse memorials to the West Saxon kings; the memorials made use of an ideological connection between traditional Old English poetry and the descendants of Alfred, and the conservative rigour of their form and thematic content created poems meant to endure. But once the Chronicle began to take on the form of *prosimetrum* (however unwieldy

---

86 B.J. Whiting calls this annal the 'best contemporary estimate of William's achievement and character,' noting, however, that 'verse is, perhaps, too elegant a word' to describe the rhyming passage (but see Stanley, n74 above), in 'The Rime of King William,' in *Philologica: The Malone Anniversary Studies*, ed. Thomas A. Kirby and Henry Bosley Woolf, 89–96 (Baltimore: Johns Hopkins University Press, 1949), 89. Lerer also places this annal in the context of salvation history, citing its great debt to the Old English prose tradition, in particular Wulfstan's homilies and Bede's use of history; see 'Afterlife,' 11–18.

87 Lerer, 'Afterlife,' 8 and 18.

that form may appear at times), and as it got further away, both geographically and chronologically, from the influence of royal patronage, the text became open to the many possibilities of that form.

With the defeat of West Saxon kingship, first during Danish rule and later following the Norman Conquest, English historiography was unable to sustain itself by means of identification with the royal house. The voice of English historiography became the voice of the outsider. The distance of the later Chronicle verse from centres of court and cultural power is perhaps best illustrated by the short rhyming couplet that is the final verse entry in the Chronicle, s.a. 1104 in manuscript E. 'Nis eaðe to asecgenne þises landes earmða þe hit to þysan timan dreogende wæs þurh mistlice 7 mænigfealdlice unriht,' laments the chronicler, finally crying out that

> eall þis wæs God   mid to gremienne
> 7 þas arme leode   mid to tregienne.[88]

The text of the Chronicle still identifies with the Anglo-Saxon people, but the 1104 annal shows quite clearly that the unity between the people and their ruler has fallen away; the days of heroic Anglo-Saxon kingship are gone, and in their place are years of suffering under tyrants who despise both God and the Anglo-Saxons. The rulers of England no longer defend either the people or the faith, and the disappearance of heroic verse from the Chronicle correlates with the political disappearance of Anglo-Saxon kingship. As new types of verse materialize to augment and highlight parts of the prose narrative, the Chronicle texts take on a polyphonic quality, in which a variety of voices speak up to introduce new themes and interpretive frameworks, and, to quote Mikhail Bakhtin, 'literary language is not represented ... as a unitary, completely finished off, indubitably adequate language – it is represented precisely as a living mix of varied and opposing voices.'[89] This heteroglossia, fostered by the Chronicle's unusual position as a living, continually growing, almost organic set of texts, replaces the epic national past evoked by the classical verse with contemporary viewpoints that mirror the fragmentation of English identity following the

---

88 'It is not easy to say the miseries of this land, which it suffered at this time through various and manifold injustices'; 'all this was likewise to enrage God / and likewise to harass this poor people.'

89 Mikhail Bakhtin, quoted by Michael Holquist, 'Introduction,' in M.M. Bakhtin, *The Dialogic Imagination: Four Essays*, ed. Michael Holquist, trans. Caryl Emerson and Michael Holquist (Austin: University of Texas Press, 1981), xviii.

Conquest. As a result, the history of verse in the Anglo-Saxon Chronicle charts a transitional period in both English identity and English poetry; it registers the introduction of new forms in a conveniently chronological record across a wide geographical range, and bears out the importance of the relationship between history and poetry through the Anglo-Saxon period and across the Norman Conquest.

III. Defining Poetry, Defining the Past

The Anglo-Saxon Chronicle has always been recognized as a document of great diversity, and scholars repeatedly warn readers against the tendency to think of it as a single text. The Chronicle speaks with many voices. Its various manuscripts often exhibit profound differences, and placing the records side by side enables us to see the discrepancies among competing accounts and the politics inherent in their historical representation. The early poetry of the Anglo-Saxon Chronicle identifies it as a document rooted in the values and traditions of a royal family deeply invested in seeing its ancestral heritage enshrined as the basis of a national identity. These poems linked the *dom* of the Germanic warrior with the glory of the *miles Christi* through evocative fragments of historical verse. But the Chronicle's subsequent geographical dissemination also influences its development. As it grows beyond the influence of its originators, the prosimetric form proves both responsive and adaptable to the needs of its continuators, and the ideology underwriting the document's production shifts from royal to ecclesiastical. The England depicted in the Chronicle verse changes from being a heroic nation on the Germanic model to being a Christian nation that, like all nations, ultimately fails to fulfil its responsibilities to God's law and suffers the consequences. This transformation itself is as much historically as politically conditioned. In the course of the eleventh century, the history of Anglo-Saxon England becomes one of conquest and domination by foreign forces, and the Anglo-Saxon Chronicle reflects that change in becoming a document of mourning and lament instead of celebration and honour.

The implications of these shifts for understanding the uses and functions of historical poetry are significant, and the kinds of historical consciouness they engender vary along with their formal features. The earliest uses of verse in the Chronicle are strictly controlled, in terms of both their form – the alliterative metre – and their content – the heroic epic (sometimes with Christian overtones). These verses serve a conservative memorial function, not only because they exploit a nostalgic longing for the glories of the ancient past, but also because the formality of their structure attempts to guarantee that they will emerge more or less intact through generations of textual transmission. The generic conventions they exploit cue readers to look for heroism, glory, and triumph in the stories they tell. These verses do not spring from the impulse of the moment, but are the carefully constructed products of a historical discourse that promotes the ideal of heroic Wessex kingship as the foundation of a national identity. They give the impression of voices spontaneously raised in songs of praise for noble leaders, whereas in reality the traditional form and heroic content of these verses capitalize on popular cultural memory to foster an image of the Anglo-Saxons as not only the inheritors but the fulfilment of ancestral glory. Like *The Battle of Maldon*, the classical Chronicle verse encodes recent events using the tropes and types associated with the heroic tradition; the contemporary world is thus refracted through the ideology of the heroic past. This kind of reading, as Jameson remarks, 'presupposes the possibility that at an outer limit, the sense people have of themselves and their own moment of history may ultimately have nothing whatsoever to do with its reality: that the existential may be absolutely distinct, as some ultimate "false consciousness," from the structural and social significance of a collective phenomenon.'[90] The monolithic image of England presented in those earlier Chronicle verses does not, and cannot, represent the fullness of historical meaning in the tenth and eleventh centuries;[91] and the constructedness of this ideology emerges even more strongly in contrast to the variant ideologies and verse forms of the later, northern chronicles – as does the imbrication of poetic form and historical consciousness.[92]

As a form, the classical Chronicle verse emerges from a thematics of triumph and victory, and the history of later Anglo-Saxon England makes

---

90   Fredric Jameson, 'Nostalgia for the Present,' in *Postmodernism, or, The Cultural Logic of Late Capitalism*, 279–96 (Durham: Duke University Press, 1991), 281–2.

91   Jameson writes, 'There is, however, an even more radical possibility; namely, that period concepts finally correspond to no realities whatsoever, and that whether they are formulated in terms of generational logic, or by the names of reigning monarchs, or according to some other category or typological and classificatory system, the collective reality of the multitidinous lives encompassed by such terms is nonthinkable (or nontotalizable, to use a current expression) and can never be described, characterized, labeled, or conceptualized' ('Nostalgia,' 282).

92   As Susan Stewart puts it, 'It is not lived experience which literature describes, but the conventions for organizing and interpreting that experience, conventions which are modified and informed by each instance of the genre' (*On Longing: Narratives of the Miniature, the Gigantic, the Souvenir, the Collection* [Durham: Duke University Press, 1993], 25–6).

that form irreconcilable with the events the Chronicle needs to record, especially in the eleventh century. Almost as if in reponse to this aesthetic crisis, both the rhythmical and the rhyming verses of the northern recension, especially in their later instances, step outside the historical narrative to highlight moments of emotional impact, and their homiletic form encourages audiences to expect a providential interpretation of the events they recount. They do not employ an aesthetics of nostalgia to resurrect a glorious past or to forge links between present readers and ancient traditions. Instead, they seek to move readers spiritually, to enclose the traumatic events they recount in the safe space of the aesthetic object, and to encourage reflection on the meaning of history by distancing readers from the event rather than bringing them closer to it. The later Chronicle verse does not offer itself to its reader as a constellation awaiting the reader's apprehension and interpretation; it carries its own interpretation with it, as a part of its aesthetic form.

In addition to supporting the theory of a strong royal connection to the Chronicle in its early years, the patterns of change revealed by this distribution of verse show a decided shift in the influence of that connection as the texts progress both chronologically and geographically. As it grows, the Chronicle and its writers take on greater historiographic responsibility. In addition to recording events, the chroniclers seem to feel both free and even duty-bound to comment on them as well, and verse was one of the many techniques available for apostrophizing or heightening the emotional impact of a record. Poetry, formerly a tool of hegemonic discourse in the Chronicle, becomes in these new circumstances a voice of dissent, chronicling the misery of the English people and the wrongs their rulers inflict on them – a point of view otherwise unrepresented in contemporary historiography. The later verse passages stand as memorials not to the glory of kings, but to the suffering of a nation under foreign rule. They gaze longingly not to the heroic past, but to future salvation. In these poems, we are able to see the extent to which the Chronicle itself has become a document of Englishness, not only in its attempts to foster a sense of English identity, but in its desire to represent an English perspective through a period when little else survives of written English. The shifts in historiographic mode documented by these poems coincide with major shifts in English history itself, from vernacular historiography as a project concentrated in the royal court to history-writing that reflects the values and viewpoints of the ecclesiastical centres that eventually took over its production, and from a heroic, Germanic notion of England to a sense of the English as a conquered people.

Perhaps most important for the purposes of this study, the later Chronicle verse mines the fragments of history to assemble an image of the present, but it is not an image of redemption; rather, the present is a ruin of former Christian glory that does not, for the poets of the later Chronicle, inspire the imaginative reconstruction that the speaker in *The Ruin* undertakes. Instead, these poets seem to look on the same wreckage that horrifies Benjamin's Angel of History, without the hope that suffuses the constellations of the heroic form.[93] In the Chronicle, poetry becomes a locus for the politics of historical representation, and the struggle for discursive hegemony plays out through three centuries of annals and across the tremendous historical upheaval of the Norman Conquest. By the time of the final poetic Chronicle entry s.a. 1104, Anglo-Saxon England, as characterized by its cultural heritage and its heroic poetry, is no more; Anglo-Norman England has taken its place, both politically and poetically.

---

93 See pp. 40–1 above, and Benjamin, *Theses on the Philosophy of History*, in *Illuminations*, ed. Hannah Arendt, trans. Harry Zohn (New York: Schocken, 1968), 253–64 at 257.

Conclusion:
The Past in the Present

The truth content of artworks is the unconscious writing of history.

Theodor Adorno, *Aesthetic Theory*

... eall þis wæs God   mid to gremienne
7 þas arme leode   mid to tregienne.[1]

Anglo-Saxon Chronicle, MS E

By the time the Peterborough chronicler enters his mournful rhyme s.a. 1104 lamenting the suffering and loss that characterize, for him, post-Conquest history, both Anglo-Saxon England and the poetic tradition associated with its heroic heritage have fallen into ruins. The scop no longer sings in the hall of his lord's heroic deeds; hall, scop, and hero are all things of the past, lost along with the dominion of the island. English poetry goes into hiding for the better part of two centuries, driven out by the cultural ascendancy of Latin and Anglo-Norman literature. When it does begin to resurface during the late twelfth and early thirteenth centuries, the English language has changed a great deal from its pre-Conquest form, and verse written in early Middle English uses alliteration as a deliberately archaizing poetic technique, one evoking the glory and grandeur of Insular culture before the historical rupture of conquest and loss of dominion. But poetic form and historical grandeur alike are a part of the pre-Conquest past. Both heroic alliterative metre and the Old English in which it was

---

1 'all this was likewise to enrage God / and likewise to harass this poor people' (Susan Irvine, ed., *MS E*, The Anglo-Saxon Chronicle: A Collaborative Edition 7 [Cambridge: D.S. Brewer, 2004], s.a. 1104).

written are located firmly on the far side of that historical divide, whence they defy the nostalgic attempts of Laȝamon and other revivalists to bring them back to life.

The impossibility of bridging that historical and aesthetic gap reinforces the connection among language, form, and history that has been the governing concern of this book. Poetic forms are themselves inherently historical, as critics like Walter Benjamin and Fredric Jameson have argued; history is unconsciously written into the truth-content of each individual work, and becomes sedimented in the material form itself. The historical and the aesthetic merge in these texts, both because they are works of art concerned with the representation of history and because they are historically situated products of a temporally distant culture. The task of the critic, then, is to listen for the historical meaning of Old English poetry on two levels: what its narrative content tells us about the history it recounts, and what its aesthetic form tells us about its own historicity. The result is a double reading, that reflects on what these poems meant as history for their original audiences but that also considers how their meanings can change for modern audiences as historically situated and historically self-conscious readers.

This dual challenge, to think about how Old English historical poetry imagines history both explicitly and implicitly, must be answered with a methodology that considers form and content dialectically, for the form of Old English poetry is integral to its historical content. In part, these poems use generic expectations to cue an audience's interpretation of historical events; primed by the genre to expect heroes and bravery, readers of *The Battle of Maldon* and *The Capture of the Five Boroughs* find heroes and bravery in contemporary events. Yet the temporality embedded in the aesthetic form of alliterative poetry, with its movements of rupture, juxtaposition, and recursion, also works to shape historical consciousness. From its earliest legendary beginnings, heroic poetry gives rise to an ideology of history that connects past and present through individual people and events that are separated by both time and space. The model of the critical constellation that I have adapted from Benjamin illustrates how diverse fragments of history can coalesce meaningfully yet differently for every reader. As a critical methodology, the constellation opens up a space for difference, contradiction, and possibility and can mediate between the historically distinct moments of Anglo-Saxon England and the modern critic.

The utility of the constellation, however, extends beyond critical methodology; it functions equally as a metaphor for how Old English poetry itself imagines historical relations. Like the constellation, Anglo-Saxon alliterative verse works through techniques of juxtaposition and contradiction to create an aesthetic whole, and classical Old English poetry stages its narratives as a series of constellations for its readers to apprehend. By juxtaposing fragments of historical narrative, the constellation abstracts them from their original contexts and uses them to build a monad in the work of art. The elegiac verses of the heroic tradition, such as *Deor*, *The Ruin*, and *Widsith*, undertake philosophical reflection on individuals' relations to cultural traditions of the past. The speakers of these poems do not ignore historical distance. They dwell on separation in time and space, and on the traces left behind by the passage of time in the form of crumbling walls, toppled towers, and heroes long dead. But they also reaffirm the importance of those ruins for their own present. Figures from the biblical past or the pre-Migration heroic age appear alongside contemporary characters, and their role in constructing the poem's meaning is mediated by the critical efforts of the reader who perceives their juxtaposition. When the *Beowulf* poet evokes Beowulf, Sigemund, and Heremod in quick succession, and when Deor aligns his own suffering with that of Beadohild and Welund, and when the poet of *Genesis A* links the poem's audience directly to Cain's murder, Eve's sin, and Adam's creation all in one aesthetic gesture, they advocate for a certain interpretation of the constellations they create, but they also encourage their readers to add their own perspectives to that interpretation. They elicit a consciousness of historical distance and difference, but also of cultural and personal correspondence. What has long been identified as the ambiguity of the appositive style, then, exists in the same space of possibility created by the critical constellation, and the goal of both the appositive style and the critical constellation is to induce readers to reflect on and participate in the creation of meaning.

The juxtaposition shared by the appositive style and the critical constellation thus has important implications for how we think about historical time in Anglo-Saxon poetry. Simply put, these poems do not adhere to an absolute separation between past and present, and they do not imagine time as something unidirectional. They transcend time and space to separate elements from their original contexts and recontextualize them, and when this mode of representation is applied to history, the result is a sense that the past continues to live each time it is evoked in the present. Anglo-Saxon readers can find Hygelac's raid in Frisia to be as close and as meaningful as the Battle of Maldon; they can be present at the Creation and empathize with Adam and Eve after the Fall; and they can perceive how Athelstan and Edmund embody the valour of their Saxon ancestors, Cerdic and Cynric. History does not simply flow from the past through the present and on into the future; nor does it necessarily move in predictable cycles of sin and punishment or conquest and invasion. It is something far more amorphous and unpredictable. Put another way, the dialectics of form in the appositive style result in a dialectics of temporality as well; the past becomes a less foreign country in the poems that recount it and assert its significance for their audiences. And Old English poems make the most of this flexible temporality. They can be achingly nostalgic for days long gone by but not forgotten, or they can present Abraham in modern dress, so to speak, with thoughts and feelings familiar to contemporary audiences. They can simultaneously recognize loss and assert redemption, mediating the consciousness of historical distance by using aesthetic mechanisms that allow audiences to connect across historical and geographical distances. By virtue of the ambiguity engendered by the appositive style and its constellations, and working in tandem with the imaginative and affective capacities of their readers, these poems both reflect and reflect on their own historical consciousness. The ancient past is not irrelevant, a dead letter; it is the repository of the values, beliefs, and ambitions by which Anglo-Saxon England defines itself as a heroic Christian nation with a present and a future as glorious as its past. These poems are optimistic in their outlook, suffused with a truth-content that resides in potentiality rather than in certainty; hope rather than despair is immanent in the constellations of Anglo-Saxon poetry. Their reflections on the past rescue fragments of history from obscurity at a moment in which they resonate with the present, and their form allows for unique meditations by every reader at every present moment. Their modes of imagining the past are not monovocal, but depend on interaction with readers to reach the conclusion of interpretation.

The aesthetic form of the alliterative long line thus becomes central to how Anglo-Saxon culture imagines its relationship to the past, and recognition of that centrality impacts our understanding of identity, community, and cultural memory in Anglo-Saxon England. Secular historical poetry, like the tradition of heroic legend from which it descends, embodies certain forms of collective memory that align contemporary events with touchstone moments from the mythic past, both thematically and ideologically, as a way of establishing meaning in the present. In poems like *The Battle of Maldon* and the classical Chronicle verse, for example, the Germanic past becomes fertile ground for imagining a present ideology of lordship and loyalty. Such imaginings could easily strike a note of empty nostalgia, but the dialectical temporality of the form plays deftly on readers' desires to transform that nostalgia into the redemption of a new heroic age. As a result, the alliterative verse of the late Anglo-Saxon period works against the despair of other contemporary writings that chronicle the Viking crisis; where the Chronicle and Wulfstan forecast the downfall of Anglo-Saxon England, *The Battle of Brunanburh*, *The Capture of the Five Boroughs*, and *Maldon* see these conflicts with foreign invaders as an opportunity to enshrine new heroes in old poetic forms. Yet their optimism is double-edged; at the same time that these poems vivify the heroic tradition, they also affirm its existence as a historical and aesthetic artefact – something that does not exist in the tenth century in quite the same way it did in the fifth, but that bears the weight of centuries of historical accumulation and loss. The nostalgic form of heroic verse memorializes these events and fixes their significance for collective identity in much the same way – or so they would like readers to think – that the *carmina antiqua* did for Tacitus's pre-Migration Germanic tribes. The values of the heroic age live again, literally, in the poems of millennial England, but their resurrection is mitigated by an acknowledgment of their original loss.

When the same forms take on narratives from biblical history, they continue to adopt a dialectical notion of historical separation that works to make the ancient past of the Old Testament familiar and meaningful to Anglo-Saxon readers, who were deeply invested in their identity as a Christian nation. Although events such as the Creation, the Fall, and the Exodus are firmly located in the past, the *Genesis* and *Exodus* poems revel in their ability to overcome that historical distance and make the characters and events of biblical history fully present for their readers; and identification with Old Testament patriarchs and matriarchs contributed to readers' ability to imagine their community as a New Israel triumphing over paganism. For lay people in particular, the stories of biblical heroes and heroines, told in the familiar diction and cadences of heroic verse, blended their Christian and Germanic heritages to produce a distinctly English and remarkably personal relationship to the history of their faith. The poetic medium could have its own message, however, as the same poems that created affective bonds between audiences and their Christian history also encouraged those audiences to actively participate in the interpretive process. The difference between the ambiguity and potentiality of these constellations of Christian history and the definitive telos emphasized in homiletic literature from the same period illustrates the tension between different modes of historical consciousness in any given period, as well as the degree to which the interpretation of history depends on historiographic form.

In both secular and religious contexts, then, the aesthetic forms of heroic verse highlight a triumphant narrative of Anglo-Saxon England as the inheritor and redeemer of a long and glorious tradition, and it is not difficult to see why these poems were preserved in Anglo-Saxon manuscripts, nor why they are canonized in the literary tradition. When the story being told no longer resonates with the honour and triumph that the form embodies, however, writers turn to different forms – such as the homiletic verse of the later Anglo-Saxon Chronicle – to express different kinds of historical consciousness, and we are reminded that the writing of history in Anglo-Saxon England was far from monovocal. Although classical heroic verse in the Chronicle and in *The Battle of Maldon* may offer opportunities to recast conflict as heroism and to bolster English identity, it also limits the possibilities for identification, and the genre of historical poetry ultimately becomes monolithic itself. Far from fostering the potentiality inherent in the appositive style, the nostalgia of *Brunanburh* and its ilk turns inward, closing down the possibility for multiple interpretations as a result of the generic demands of the heroic form. And as the people writing history, and especially historical poetry, become less deeply invested in the heroic tradition, they begin to diverge from the form that has come to embody those ideals: historical poetry no longer produces an image of a heroic Anglo-Saxon England, and Anglo-Saxon England no longer produces heroic poetry. With a wide variety of historical traditions and a sprawling range of literary forms from which to draw, poets, historians, and poet-historians in the tenth and eleventh centuries produced works that continually grappled with the question of how these many strands of historical and cultural influence could be woven together into a coherent image of the present. In their engagements with various historical traditions, Anglo-Saxon poets struggle to come to grips with what those different pasts mean for their own present and for the communities that receive their texts.

Our own engagements with these texts take part in a similar struggle. Our primary goal, as scholars, is to better understand the Anglo-Saxon period through its cultural products, and our various experiences of reading these poems – the foreignness of the language, the fading pages of a manuscript, the sheer alterity of the characters and actions presented – all remind us persistently of the historical distance between ourselves and the original audiences, and of the still greater distance between us and the ancient stories the poems evoke. Yet, in the very act of reading these verses, we reanimate them for a new millennium, and reading these ancient texts in a foreign tongue is somehow most satisfying when they also speak to us of our own concerns. The themes of suffering, of longing, of honour and heroism, of despair, and of hope continue to resonate, both in Anglo-Saxon historical verse and with the people who read it in the present day. As readers, we become a part of the constellations they stage; we gaze, with our own brand of nostalgia, on a world that we recognize as lost and that we hope to somehow re-create through scholarship, criticism, and imagination.

'Longað þonne þy læs þe him con leoþa worn,' declares the poet of *Maxims I*.[2] If knowing many poems can help a person cope with longing, then the Anglo-Saxons have left us with a wide array of coping mechanisms. The verses surveyed in the chapters of this book all struggle to redeem the present, in Benjamin's sense of the term, through a confrontation with history; but they offer various avenues to that redemption, and they leave open the question of how future readers will apprehend these aesthetic objects and the layers of history sedimented in them. The challenges of studying Anglo-Saxon literature do not lessen as time goes on; modern scholars continually strive to make sense of the texts in the terms both of their time and of our own. In our own struggles to come to terms with Old English texts as a part of past and present life, it is both instructive and reassuring to note that the Anglo-Saxons themselves struggled with the problem of how best to embrace the legacies of past eras – pre-Migration Germanic, Roman Christian, classical pagan, and more – in meaningful ways. In the historical poetry of Anglo-Saxon England, we can glimpse a reflection of our own fascination with, and exile from, the distant past.

---

2 'He who knows many poems will long the less' (*Maxims I*, in *The Exeter Book*, ed. George Philip Krapp and Elliot van Kirk Dobbie, ASPR 3 [New York: Columbia University Press, 1936], 156–63 at 169).

Bibliography

Primary Sources

Abbo. *Abbon: Le Siège de Paris par les Normands*. Ed. and trans. Henri Waquet. Paris: Société d'édition 'Les Belles Lettres,' 1942.

Alcuin. *Two Alcuin Letter-Books*. Ed. Colin Chase. Toronto: PIMS, 1975.

Aldhelm. *Aldhelmi opera*. Ed. Rudolf Ehwald. MGH, Auctores antiquissimi, 15. Berlin: Weidmann, 1919.

– *Prosa de virginitate*. Ed. Scott Gwara. CCSL 124 and 124A. Turnhout: Brepols, 2001.

Assmann, Bruno, ed. *Angelsächsische Homilien und Heiligenleben*. Bibliothek der Angelsächsichen Prosa 3. Kassel: Georg H. Wigand, 1889.

Augustine. *The City of God against the Pagans*. Ed. and trans. R.W. Dyson. Cambridge: Cambridge University Press, 1998.

– *Sancti Augustini Confessionum libri XIII*. Ed. Luc Verheijen. CCSL 27. Turnhout: Brepols, 1981.

Sancti Aurelii Augustini De Civitate Dei. 2 vols. Ed. Bernard Dombart and Alphons Kalb. CCSL 47–8. Turnhout: Brepols, 1955.

Ælfric. *Ælfric's Catholic Homilies: Introduction, Commentary, and Glossary*. Ed. Malcolm Godden. EETS, s.s., 18. Oxford: Oxford University Press, 2000.

– *Ælfric's Catholic Homilies: The First Series*. Ed. Peter Clemoes. EETS, s.s., 17. Oxford: Oxford University Press, 1997.

– *Exameron Anglice or the Old English Hexameron*. Ed. S.J. Crawford. Hamburg: H. Grand, 1921. Repr. Darmstadt: Wissenschaftliche Buchgesellschaft, 1968.

– *The Homilies of Ælfric: A Supplementary Collection*. 2 vols. Ed. J.C. Pope. EETS, o.s., 259 and 260. London: Oxford University Press, 1967–8.

– *The Old English Heptateuch and Ælfric's Libellus de ueteri testamento et nouo*. Ed. Richard Marsden. EETS, o.s., 330. Oxford: Oxford University Press, 2008.

Baker, Peter S., ed. *MS F. The Anglo-Saxon Chronicle: A Collaborative Edition* 8. Cambridge: D.S. Brewer, 2000.

Barlow, Frank, ed. and trans. *Vita Ædwardi Regis qui apud Westmonasterium requiescit.* 2nd ed. Oxford: Clarendon, 1992.

Bately, Janet M., ed. *MS A. The Anglo-Saxon Chronicle: A Collaborative Edition* 3. Cambridge: D.S. Brewer, 1986.

– ed. *The Old English Orosius.* EETS, s.s., 6. London: Oxford University Press, 1980.

Bede. *Bedas metrische 'Vita Sancti Cuthberti.'* Ed. Werner Jaager. Leipzig: Mayer and Müller, 1935.

– *Bede's Ecclesiastical History of the English People.* Ed. and trans. Bertram Colgrave and R.A.B. Mynors. Oxford: Clarendon, 1969.

– *Two Lives of Saint Cuthbert: A Life by an Anonymous Monk of Lindisfarne and Bede's Prose Life.* Ed. and trans. Bertram Colgrave. Cambridge: Cambridge University Press, 1940. Repr. 1985.

Buchholz, Richard, ed. *Die Fragmente der Reden der Seele an den Leichnam in zwei Handschriften zu Worcester und Oxford.* Erlanger Beiträge zur englischen Philologie 6. Erlangen and Leipzig, 1890.

Cædmon. *Cædmon's Hymn: A Multi-media Study, Edition, and Archive.* Ed. Daniel Paul O'Donnell. Woodbridge: D.S. Brewer, 2005.

Campbell, Alistair, ed. *The Battle of Brunanburh.* London: William Heinemann, 1938.

Cubbin, G.P., ed. *MS D. The Anglo-Saxon Chronicle: A Collaborative Edition* 6. Cambridge: D.S. Brewer, 1996.

Doane, A.N., ed. *Genesis A: A New Edition.* Madison: University of Wisconsin Press, 1978.

– ed. *The Saxon Genesis: An Edition of the West Saxon* Genesis B *and the Old Saxon Vatican* Genesis. Madison: University of Wisconsin Press, 1991.

Dobbie, Elliott van Kirk, ed. *The Anglo-Saxon Minor Poems.* ASPR 6. New York: Columbia University Press, 1942.

Dodwell, C.R., and Peter Clemoes, eds. *The Old English Illustrated Hexateuch.* EEMF 18. Copenhagen: Rosenkilde and Bagger, 1974.

Dümmler, Ernst, ed. *Poetae Latini aevi Carolini.* Vol. 1. MGH, Poetarum Latinorum medii aevi, 1. Berlin, 1881.

Dumville, David, and Simon Keynes, eds. *The Anglo-Saxon Chronicle: A Collaborative Edition.* 9 vols. Cambridge: D.S. Brewer, 1983– .

Finnegan, Robert Emmett, ed. *Christ and Satan: A Critical Edition.* Waterloo, ON: Wilfrid Laurier University Press, 1977.

Gibson, Edmund. *Chronicon Saxonicum.* Oxford, 1692.

Gildas. *The Ruin of Britain and Other Works*. Ed. and trans. Michael
    Winterbottom. London: Phillimore, 1978.

Godman, Peter, ed. and trans. *Poetry of the Carolingian Renaissance*. Norman:
    University of Oklahoma Press, 1985.

Gollancz, Israel, ed. *The Cædmon Manuscript of Anglo-Saxon Biblical Poetry,
    Junius XI in the Bodleian Library*. London: Oxford University Press, 1927.

Healey, Antoinette di Paolo, ed. *Old English Corpus*. Ann Arbor: University of
    Michigan Press, 1998. http://quod.lib.umich.edu/o/oec/.

Holthausen, Ferdinand, ed. *Die ältere Genesis mit Einleitung, Anmerkungen,
    Glossar, und der lateinischen Quelle*. Heidelberg: C. Winter, 1914.

Ingram, James, ed. *The Saxon Chronicle*. London, 1823.

Irvine, Susan, ed. *MS E*. The Anglo-Saxon Chronicle: A Collaborative Edition 7.
    Cambridge: D.S. Brewer, 2004.

Irving, Edward B., Jr, ed. *The Old English Exodus*. New Haven: Yale University
    Press, 1953.

Isidore. *Isidori Hispalensis episcopi Etymologiarum sive Originum libri xx*. 2 vols.
    Ed. W.M. Lindsay. Oxford: Clarendon, 1957.

Junius, Franciscus, ed. *Caedmonis monachi paraphrasis poetica Genesios ac
    praecipuarum Sacrae pagina historiarum*. Amsterdam, 1655. Repr. and ed. Peter
    J. Lucas. Amsterdam: Rodopi, 2000.

Klaeber, Friedrich, ed. *Beowulf*. 3rd ed. Boston: D.C. Heath, 1950.

Klinck, Anne L., ed. *The Old English Elegies: A Critical Edition and Genre
    Study*. Montreal: McGill-Queens University Press, 1992.

Krapp, George Philip, ed. *The Junius Manuscript*. ASPR 1. New York: Columbia
    University Press, 1931.

Krapp, George Philip, and Elliott van Kirk Dobbie, eds. *The Anglo-Saxon Poetic
    Records*. 6 vols. New York: Columbia University Press, 1931–53.

– eds. *The Exeter Book*. ASPR 3. New York: Columbia University Press, 1936.

Lantfred of Winchester. *Translatio et miracula S. Swithuni*. In *The Cult of
    St Swithun*, ed. and trans. Michael Lapidge, Winchester Studies 4.ii, 252–333.
    Oxford: Clarendon, 2003.

Laȝamon. *Laȝamon: Brut*. Ed. G.L. Brooke and R.F. Leslie. EETS, o.s., 250 and
    277. London: Oxford University Press, 1963–78.

Leslie, R.F., ed. *Three Old English Elegies*. Rev. ed. Exeter: University of Exeter, 1988.

Liebermann, Felix, ed. *Die Gesetze der Angelsachsen*. 3 vols. Halle: Max
    Niemeyer, 1903–16. Repr. Aalen: Scientia, 1960.

Lucas, Peter J., ed. *Exodus*. London: Methuen, 1977.

Lutz, Angelika, ed. *Die Version G der angelsächsichen Chronik*. Munich:
    Wilhelm Fink, 1981.

Malone, Kemp, ed. *Deor*. Rev. ed. Exeter: University of Exeter, 1977.

– ed. *Widsith*. London: Methuen, 1936.

Miller, Thomas, ed. and trans. *The Old English Version of Bede's Ecclesiastical History of the English People*. 2 vols. EETS, o.s., 95, 96, 110, and 111. London: EETS, 1890–8.

Moffat, Douglas, ed. *The Soul's Address to the Body: The Worcester Fragments*. East Lansing, MI: Colleagues Press, 1987.

Muir, Bernard J., ed. *A Digital Facsimile of Oxford, Bodleian Library MS Junius 11*. Bodleian Library Digital Texts 1. Oxford: Bodleian Library, 2004.

– ed. *The Exeter Anthology of Old English Poetry: An Edition of Exeter Dean and Chapter MS 3501*. Rev. 2nd ed. Exeter: University of Exeter Press, 2000.

O'Brien O'Keeffe, Katherine, ed. *MS C*. The Anglo-Saxon Chronicle: A Collaborative Edition 5. Cambridge: D.S. Brewer, 2001.

Orosius, Paulus. *Pauli Orosii Historiarum aduersum paganos libri VII*. Ed. Karl Zangemeister. CSEL 5. Vienna, 1882.

– *Seven Books of History against the Pagans: The Apology of Paulus Orosius*. Trans. Irving Woodworth Raymond. New York: Columbia University Press, 1936.

Oxford Digital Library. 'Bodleian Library MS. Junius 11.' *Early Manuscripts at Oxford University*. http://image.ox.ac.uk/show?collection=bodleian& manuscript=msjunius11.

Plummer, Charles, ed. *Two of the Saxon Chronicles Parallel*. 2 vols. Oxford: Clarendon, 1892–9.

Schlosser, Horst Dieter, ed. *Althochdeutsche Literatur*. Frankfurt/Main: Fischer, 1989.

Scragg, Donald G., ed. *The Battle of Maldon*. Manchester: Manchester University Press, 1981.

– ed. *The Battle of Maldon, A.D. 991*. Oxford: Basil Blackwell, 1991.

– ed. *The Vercelli Homilies and Related Texts*. EETS, o.s., 300. Oxford: Oxford University Press, 1992.

Swanton, Michael, trans. and ed. *The Anglo-Saxon Chronicle*. New York: Routledge, 1998.

Tacitus. *The Agricola and the Germania*. Trans. Harold Mattingly. Rev. trans. S.A. Handford. Harmondsworth: Penguin, 1970.

– *Cornelii Taciti opera minora*. Ed. Michael Winterbottom and R.M. Ogilvie. Oxford: Clarendon, 1975.

Taylor, Simon, ed. *MS B*. The Anglo-Saxon Chronicle: A Collaborative Edition 4. Cambridge: D.S. Brewer, 1983.

Thorpe, Benjamin, ed. and trans. *The Anglo-Saxon Chronicle According to the Several Original Authorities*. 2 vols. London, 1861.

Waitz, Georg, ed. *Annales Bertiniani*. MGH, Scriptores rerum Germanicarum in usum scholarum, 5. Hannover, 1883.

Whitelock, Dorothy, ed. and trans. *English Historical Documents, c. 500–1042.* EHD 1. 2nd ed. London: Eyre Methuen, 1979.

– ed. *The Peterborough Chronicle*. EEMF 4. Copenhagen: Rosenkilde and Bagger, 1954.

Whitelock, Dorothy, ed., with David C. Douglas and Susie I. Tucker. *The Anglo-Saxon Chronicle: A Revised Translation*. New Brunswick: Rutgers University Press, 1961.

William of Malmesbury. *Gesta pontificum Anglorum: The History of the English Bishops*. Vol. 1. Ed and trans. Michael Winterbottom. Oxford: Clarendon, 2007.

Wulfstan. *The Homilies of Wulfstan*. Ed. Dorothy Bethurum. Oxford: Clarendon, 1957.

– *Wulfstan*. Ed. Arthur Napier. Berlin: Weidmann, 1883.

Secondary Sources

Abegg, Daniel. *Zur Entwicklung der historischen Dichtung bei den Angelsachsen*. Quellen und Forschungen zur Sprach- und Culturgeschichte der germanischen Völker 73. Strassburg: Karl J. Trübner, 1894.

Adorno, Theodor W. *Aesthetic Theory*. Ed. Gretel Adorno and Rolf Tiedemann. Trans. Robert Hullot-Kentor. Theory and History of Literature 88. Minneapolis: University of Minnesota Press, 1997.

– 'On Lyric Poetry and Society.' In *Notes to Literature I*, ed. Rolf Tiedemann, trans. Shierry Weber Nicholson, 37–54. New York: Columbia University Press, 1991.

Agamben, Giorgio. *The Time That Remains: A Commentary on the Letter to the Romans*. Trans. Patricia Dailey. Stanford: Stanford University Press, 2005.

Albu, Emily. *The Normans in Their Histories: Propaganda, Myth, and Subversion*. Woodbridge: Boydell, 2001.

Alonso, Jorge Luis Bueno. '"Less Epic Than It Seems": *Deor*'s Historical Approach as a Narrative Device for Psychological Expression.' *Revista Canaria de Estudios Ingleses* 46 (2003): 161–72.

Ames, Ruth M. 'The Old Testament Christ and the Old English *Exodus*.' *Studies in Medieval Culture* 10 (1977): 33–50.

Amodio, Mark C., and Katherine O'Brien O'Keeffe, eds. *Unlocking the Wordhord: Anglo-Saxon Studies in Memory of Edward B. Irving, Jr* Toronto: University of Toronto Press, 2003.

Amtower, Laurel. 'Some Codicological Considerations in the Interpretation of the Junius Poems.' *ELN* 30, no. 4 (1993): 1–10.

Anderson, Benedict. *Imagined Communities: Reflections on the Origin and Spread of Nationalism*. Rev. ed. London: Verso, 1991.

Anderson, Earl R. 'Style and Theme in the Old English *Daniel*.' *ES* 68 (1987): 1–23.

Andersson, Theodore M. 'The Viking Policy of Ethelred the Unready.' In Niles and Amodio, *Anglo-Scandinavian England*, 1–11.

Anlezark, Daniel. 'Connecting the Patriarchs: Noah and Abraham in the Old English *Exodus*.' *JEGP* 104 (2005): 171–88.

Auerbach, Erich. *Scenes from the Drama of European Literature*. New York: Meridian, 1959.

Bakhtin, M.M. *The Dialogic Imagination: Four Essays*. Ed. Michael Holquist. Trans. Caryl Emerson and Michael Holquist. Austin: University of Texas Press, 1981.

Bately, Janet M. *The Anglo-Saxon Chronicle: Texts and Textual Relationships*. Reading Medieval Studies Monographs 3. Reading: University of Reading, 1991.

– 'The Compilation of the Anglo-Saxon Chronicle 60 BC to AD 890: Vocabulary as Evidence.' *PBA* 64 (1980 for 1978): 93–129.

– 'The Compilation of the *Anglo-Saxon Chronicle* Once More.' *Leeds Studies in English*, n.s., 16 (1985): 7–26.

– 'Manuscript Layout and the Anglo-Saxon Chronicle.' *Bulletin of the John Rylands University Library of Manchester* 70 (1988): 21–43.

Bately, Janet M., and D.J.A. Ross. 'A Check List of Manuscripts of Orosius "Historiarum adversum paganos libri septem".' *Scriptorium* 15 (1961): 329–34.

Battles, Paul. '*Genesis A* and the Anglo-Saxon "Migration Myth".' *ASE* 29 (2000): 43–66.

Baxter, Stephen. 'MS C of the Anglo-Saxon Chronicle and the Politics of Mid-Eleventh-Century England.' *EHR* 122 (2007): 1189–1227.

Bedingfield, M. Bradford. *The Dramatic Liturgy of Anglo-Saxon England*. Woodbridge: Boydell, 2002.

Benjamin, Walter. *The Arcades Project*. Ed. Rolf Tiedemann. Trans. Howard Eiland and Kevin McLaughlin. Cambridge, MA: Harvard University Press, 1999.

– *Illuminations*. Ed. Hannah Arendt. Trans. Harry Zohn. New York: Schocken, 1968.

– *The Origin of German Tragic Drama*. Trans. John Osborne. London: Verso, 1998.

Bessinger, Jess B., Jr, ed. *A Concordance to the Anglo-Saxon Poetic Records*. Ithaca: Cornell University Press, 1978.

Bethurum, Dorothy. 'Wulfstan.' In Stanley, *Continuations and Beginnings*, 210–46.

Bhabha, Homi K. *The Location of Culture*. London: Routledge Classics, 2004.

Biddick, Kathleen. *The Shock of Medievalism*. Durham: Duke University Press, 1998.

Bjork, Robert E. 'Oppressed Hebrews and the Song of Azarias in the Old English *Daniel*.' *SP* 77 (1980): 213–26.

Blake, N.F. 'The Battle of Maldon.' *Neophilologus* 49 (1965): 332–45.

– 'The Genesis of *The Battle of Maldon*.' *ASE* 7 (1978): 119–29.

– 'Rhythmical Alliteration.' *MP* 67 (1969): 118–24.

Bliss, A.J. *An Introduction to Old English Metre*. Oxford: B. Blackwell, 1962.

– *The Metre of Beowulf*. Oxford: Blackwell, 1958.

Bloch, R. Howard. *Etymologies and Genealogies: A Literary Anthropology of the French Middle Ages*. Chicago: University of Chicago Press, 1983.

Bloomfield, Morton W. 'Beowulf, Byrhtnoth, and the Judgment of God: Trial by Combat in Anglo-Saxon England.' *Speculum* 44 (1969): 545–59.

– 'The Form of *Deor*.' *PMLA* 79 (1964): 534–41.

– 'Patristics and Old English Literature: Notes on Some Poems.' *Comparative Literature* 14 (1962): 36–43.

Blumenfeld-Kosinski, Renate. 'Moralization and History: Verse and Prose in the *Histoire ancienne jusqu'à César* (in B.N. f.fr. 20125).' *Zeitschrift für romanische Philologie* 97 (1981): 41–6.

Bonner, Gerald, ed. *Famulus Christi: Essays in Commemoration of the Thirteenth Centenary of the Birth of the Venerable Bede*. London: SPCK, 1976.

Boulton, Maureen Barry McCann. *The Song in the Story: Lyric Insertions in French Narrative Fiction, 1200–1400*. Philadelphia: University of Pennsylvania Press, 1993.

Boyd, Nina. 'Doctrine and Criticism: A Revaluation of "Genesis A".' *NM* 83 (1982): 230–8.

Boym, Svetlana. *The Future of Nostalgia*. New York: Basic, 2001.

Bredehoft, Thomas A. 'Ælfric and Late Old English Verse.' *ASE* 33 (2004): 77–107.

– 'The Boundaries between Verse and Prose in Old English Literature.' In *Old English Literature in Its Manuscript Context*, ed. Joyce Tally Lionarons, 139–72. Morgantown: West Virginia University Press, 2004.

– *Early English Metre*. Toronto: University of Toronto Press, 2005.

– 'History and Memory in the *Anglo-Saxon Chronicle*.' In Johnson and Treharne, *Readings in Medieval Texts*, 109–21.

– '*Malcolm and Margaret*: The Poem in Annal 1067D.' Forthcoming.

– 'OE *yðhengest* and an Unrecognized Passage of Old English Verse.' *N&Q*, n.s., 54 (2007): 120–2.

– *Textual Histories: Readings in the* Anglo-Saxon Chronicle. Toronto: University of Toronto Press, 2001.

Bright, J.W. 'The Relation of the Cædmonian *Exodus* to the Liturgy.' *MLN* 27 (1912): 97–103.

Britton, G.C. 'The Characterization of the Vikings in "The Battle of Maldon".' *N&Q* 210 (1965): 85–7.

– 'Repetition and Contrast in the Old English *Later Genesis*.' *Neophilologus* 58 (1974): 66–73.

Brockman, Bennett A. '"Heroic" and "Christian" in *Genesis A*: The Evidence of the Cain and Abel Episode.' *MLQ* 35 (1975): 115–28.

Brown, George Hardin. 'Old English Verse as a Medium for Christian Theology.' In *Modes of Interpretation in Old English Literature: Essays in Honour of Stanley B. Greenfield*, ed. Phyllis Rugg Brown, Georgia Ronan Crampton, and Fred C. Robinson, 15–28. Toronto: University of Toronto Press, 1986.

Brown, Ray. 'The Begging Scop and the Generous King in *Widsith*.' *Neophilologus* 73 (1989): 281–92.

Buck-Morss, Susan. *The Origin of Negative Dialectics: Theodor W. Adorno, Walter Benjamin, and the Frankfurt Institute*. New York: Free Press, 1977.

Bynum, Caroline Walker. *Fragmentation and Redemption: Essays on Gender and the Human Body in Medieval Religion*. New York: Zone, 1992.

Cable, Thomas. *The English Alliterative Tradition*. Philadelphia: University of Pennsylvania Press, 1991.

– 'Metrical Style as Evidence for the Date of *Beowulf*.' In *The Dating of Beowulf*, ed. Colin Chase, 77–82. Toronto: University of Toronto Press, 1981.

Cain, Christopher M. 'The "Fearful Symmetry" of *Maldon*: The Apocalypse, the Poet, and the Millennium.' *Comitatus* 28 (1997): 1–16.

Calder, Daniel G. 'Perspective and Movement in *The Ruin*.' *NM* 72 (1971): 442–5.

Campbell, Jackson J. 'To Hell and Back: Latin Tradition and Literary Use of the "descensus ad inferos" in Old English.' *Viator* 13 (1982): 107–58.

Campbell, James. 'England, France, and Germany: Some Comparisons and Connections.' In D. Hill, *Ethelred the Unready*, 255–70.

Cherniss, Michael D. 'Heroic Ideals and the Moral Climate of *Genesis B*.' *MLQ* 30 (1969): 479–97.

Clanchy, M.T. *From Memory to Written Record: England, 1066–1307*. 2nd ed. Oxford: Basil Blackwell, 1993.

Clark, Cecily. 'Byrhtnoth and Roland: A Contrast.' *Neophilologus* 51 (1967): 288–93.

– 'The Narrative Mode of *The Anglo-Saxon Chronicle* before the Conquest.' In Clemoes and Hughes, *England before the Conquest*, 215–35.

Clark, George. '*The Battle of Maldon*: A Heroic Poem.' *Speculum* 43 (1968): 52–71.

– 'Maldon: History, Poetry, and Truth.' In *De Gustibus: Essays for Alain Renoir*, ed. John Miles Foley, 66–84. New York: Garland, 1992.

Clemoes, Peter. 'Ælfric,' in Stanley, *Continuations and Beginnings*, 176–209.

– *Interactions of Thought and Language in Old English Poetry*. Cambridge: Cambridge University Press, 1995.

– 'Language in Context: *Her* in the 890 *Anglo-Saxon Chronicle.*' *Leeds Studies in English* 16 (1985): 27–36.

Clemoes, Peter, and Kathleen Hughes, eds. *England before the Conquest: Studies in Primary Sources Presented to Dorothy Whitelock*. Cambridge: Cambridge University Press, 1971.

Cole, Andrew. 'Jewish Apocrypha and Christian Epistemologies of the Fall: The *Dialogi* of Gregory the Great and the Old Saxon *Genesis.*' In *Rome and the North: The Early Reception of Gregory the Great in Germanic Europe*, ed. Rolf H. Bremmer, Kees Dekker, and David F. Johnson, 157–88. Paris: Peeters, 2001.

Crook, John. '"Vir optimus Wlfstanus": The Post-Conquest Commemoration of Archbishop Wulfstan of York at Ely Cathedral.' In Townend, *Wulfstan*, 501–24.

Cross, J.E. 'Oswald and Byrhtnoth: A Christian Saint and a Hero Who Is Christian.' *ES* 46 (1965): 93–109.

Cross, J.E., and Alan Brown. 'The Literary Impetus for Wulfstan's *Sermo Lupi.*' *Leeds Studies in English*, n.s., 20 (1989): 270–91.

Cross, J.E., and S.I. Tucker. 'Allegorical Tradition and the Old English Exodus.' *Neophilologus* 44 (1960): 122–7.

– 'Appendix on Exodus ll. 289–90.' *Neophilologus* 44 (1960): 38–9.

Curzan, Anne, and Kimberly Emmons, eds. *Studies in the History of the English Language II: Unfolding Conversations*. Berlin: Mouton de Gruyter, 2004.

Dailey, Patricia. 'Questions of Dwelling in Anglo-Saxon Poetry and Medieval Mysticism: Inhabiting Landscape, Body, and Mind.' *New Medieval Literatures* 8 (2006): 175–214.

Daniélou, Jean. *From Shadows to Reality: Studies in the Biblical Typology of the Fathers*. Trans. Wulstan Hibberd. London: Burns and Oates, 1960.

Davidse, Jan. 'The Sense of History in the Works of the Venerable Bede.' *SM* 23 (1982): 647–95.

Davis, Craig R. 'Cultural Historicity in *The Battle of Maldon.*' *PQ* 78 (1999): 151–69.

Davis, Kathleen. 'National Writing in the Ninth Century: A Reminder for Postcolonial Thinking about the Nation.' *JMEMS* 28 (1998): 611–37.

Day, Virginia. 'The Influence of the Catechetical *narratio* on Old English and Some Other Medieval Literature.' *ASE* 3 (1974): 51–61.

Dean, Paul. 'History versus Poetry: The Battle of *Maldon*.' *NM* 93 (1992): 99–108.

DeGregorio, Scott. 'Footsteps of His Own: Bede's Commentary on Ezra-Nehemiah.' In DeGregoio, *Innovation and Tradition*, 143–68.

– ed. *Innovation and Tradition in the Writings of the Venerable Bede*. Morgantown: West Virginia University Press, 2006.

Dix, Gregory. *The Shape of the Liturgy*. London: A and C Black, 1945.

Doane, A.N. 'Legend, History, and Artifice in "The Battle of Maldon".' *Viator* 9 (1978): 39–66.

Doubleday, James F. '*The Ruin*: Structure and Theme.' *JEGP* 71 (1972): 369–81.

Dronke, Peter. *Verse with Prose from Petronius to Dante: The Art and Scope of the Mixed Form*. Cambridge, MA: Harvard University Press, 1994.

Dumville, David N. 'The West Saxon Genealogical Regnal List and the Chronology of Early Wessex.' *Peritia* 4 (1985): 21–66.

– 'The West Saxon Genealogical Regnal List: Manuscripts and Texts.' *Anglia* 104 (1986): 1–32.

Earl, James W. 'Christian Traditions in the Old English *Exodus*.' *NM* 71 (1970): 541–70.

– 'Hisperic Style in the Old English "Rhyming Poem".' *PMLA* 102 (1987): 187–96.

Eckhardt, Caroline D. 'The Medieval *Prosimetrum* Genre (From Boethius to *Boece*).' *Genre* 16 (1983): 21–38.

Ehlert, Trude. 'Literatur und Wirklichkeit – Exegese und Politik: Zur Deutung des Ludwigsliedes.' *Saeculum* 32 (1981): 31–42.

Einenkel, Eugen. 'Der Sermo Lupi ad Anglos ein Gedicht.' *Anglia* 7 (1884): 200–3.

Elliott, Ralph W.V. 'Byrhtnoth and Hildebrand: A Study in Heroic Technique.' *Comparative Literature* 14 (1962): 53–70.

Emmerson, Richard K. '*Figura* and the Medieval Typological Imagination.' In *Typology and English Medieval Literature*, ed. Hugh T. Keenan, 7–42. New York: AMS, 1992.

Enright, Michael J. *Iona, Tara, and Soissons: The Origin of the Royal Anointing Ritual*. Berlin: Walter de Gruyter, 1985.

Ericksen, Janet S. 'Penitential Nakedness and the Junius 11 *Genesis*.' In *Naked before God: Uncovering the Body in Anglo-Saxon England*, ed. Benjamin C. Withers and Jonathan Wilcox, 257–74. Morgantown: West Virginia University Press, 2003.

– 'The Wisdom Poem at the End of MS Junius 11.' In Liuzza, *MS Junius 11*, 302–26.

Evans, J.M. '*Genesis B* and Its Background.' 2 pts. *RES*, n.s., 14 (1963): 1–16 and 113–23.

Fanning, Steven. 'Bede, *Imperium*, and the Bretwaldas.' *Speculum* 66 (1991): 1–26.

Farrell, Robert T., ed. *Daniel and Azarias.* London: Methuen, 1974.
– 'A Reading of OE. *Exodus.*' *RES*, n.s., 20 (1969): 401–17.
Fentress, James, and Chris Wickham. *Social Memory.* Oxford: Blackwell, 1992.
Ferguson, Paul F. 'Noah, Abraham, and the Crossing of the Red Sea.' *Neophilologus* 65 (1981): 282–7.
Foley, John Miles. *Immanent Art: From Structure to Meaning in Traditional Oral Epic.* Bloomington: Indiana University Press, 1991.
– 'Oral Traditional Aesthetics and Old English Poetry.' In *Medialität und mittelalterliche insulare Literatur*, ed. Hildegard L.C. Tristram, 80–103. Tübingen: G. Narr, 1992.
– 'Signs, Texts, and Oral Tradition.' *Journal of Folklore Research* 33 (1996): 21–9.
Foot, Sarah. 'The Making of *Angelcynn*: English Identity before the Norman Conquest.' *TRHS*, 6th ser., 6 (1996): 25–49.
Fox, Michael. 'Ælfric on the Creation and Fall of the Angels.' *ASE* 31 (2002): 175–200.
Frank, Roberta. 'The *Beowulf* Poet's Sense of History.' In *The Wisdom of Poetry: Essays in Early English Literature in Honor of Morton W. Bloomfield*, ed. Larry D. Benson and Siegfried Wenzel, 53–65 and 217–77. Kalamazoo, MI: Medieval Institute Publications, 1982.
– 'The Ideal of Men Dying with Their Lord in *The Battle of Maldon*: Anachronism or *Nouvelle Vague*?' In *People and Places in Northern Europe, 500–1600: Essays in Honour of Peter Hayes Sawyer*, ed. Ian Wood and Niels Lund, 95–106. Woodbridge: Boydell, 1991.
– 'Some Uses of Paranomasia in Old English Scriptural Verse.' *Speculum* 47 (1972): 207–26.
– 'What Kind of Poetry Is *Exodus*?' In *Germania: Comparative Studies in the Old Germanic Languages and Literatures*, ed. Daniel G. Calder and T. Craig Christy, 191–205. Wolfeboro, NH: D.S. Brewer, 1988.
Frantzen, Allen J. *Desire for Origins: New Language, Old English, and Teaching the Tradition.* New Brunswick: Rutgers University Press, 1990.
– ed. *Speaking Two Languages: Traditional Disciplines and Contemporary Theory in Medieval Studies.* Albany: State University of New York Press, 1991
Freud, Sigmund. *The Standard Edition of the Complete Psychological Works of Sigmund Freud.* Trans. and ed. James Strachey. 24 vols. London: Hogarth, 1953–74.
Fritzman, J.M. 'The Future of Nostalgia and the Time of the Sublime,' *Clio* 23 (1994): 167–89.
Fulk, R.D. 'Old English Poetry and the Alliterative Revival: On Geoffrey Russom's "The Evolution of Middle English Alliterative Meter".' In Curzan and Emmons, *Unfolding Conversations*, 305–12.

Fulk, R.D., and Christopher M. Cain. *A History of Old English Literature*. Malden, MA: Blackwell, 2003.

Gadamer, Hans-Georg. *Truth and Method*. 2nd rev. ed. Rev. trans. Joel Weinsheimer and Donald G. Marshall. New York: Continuum, 1995.

Garde, Judith N. *Old English Poetry in Medieval Christian Perspective: A Doctrinal Approach*. Cambridge: D.S. Brewer, 1991.

Garde, Judith N., and Bernard J. Muir. 'Patristic Influence and the Poetic Intention in Old English Religious Verse.' *Journal of Literature and Theology* 2 (1988): 49–68.

Gatch, Milton McC. *Preaching and Theology in Anglo-Saxon England: Ælfric and Wulfstan*. Toronto: University of Toronto Press, 1977.

Godden, Malcolm. 'Apocalypse and Invasion in Late Anglo-Saxon England.' In *From Anglo-Saxon to Early Middle English: Studies Presented to E.G. Stanley*, ed. Malcolm Godden, Douglas Gray, and Terry Hoad, 130–62. Oxford: Clarendon, 1994.

Godden, Malcolm, and Michael Lapidge, eds. *The Cambridge Companion to Old English Literature*. Cambridge: Cambridge University Press, 1991.

Godman, Peter. 'The Anglo-Latin *opus geminatum*: From Aldhelm to Alcuin.' *Medium Ævum* 50 (1981): 215–29.

Goetz, Hans-Werner. *Geschichtsschreibung und Geschichtsbewußtsein im hohen Mittelalter*. Berlin: Akademie Verlag, 1999.

– *Die Geschichtstheologie des Orosius*. Darmstadt: Wissenschaftliche Buchgesellschaft, 1980.

– 'Historical Consciousness and Institutional Concern in European Medieval Historiography (Eleventh and Twelfth Centuries).' In *Making Sense of Global History: The 19th International Congress of the Historical Sciences, Oslo 2000 Commemorative Volume*, ed. Sølvi Sogner, 350–65. Oslo: Universitetsforlaget, 2001.

Goffart, Walter. 'Bede's History in a Harsher Climate.' In DeGregorio, *Innovation and Tradition*, 203–26.

Goldman, Stephen H. 'The Use of Christian Belief in Old English Poems of Exile.' *Res publica litterarum* 2 (1979): 69–80.

Gransden, Antonia. *Historical Writing in England, c. 550 to c. 1307*. Ithaca: Cornell University Press, 1974.

Greenfield, Stanley B. 'Geatish History: Poetic Art and Epic Quality in *Beowulf*.' *Neophilologus* 47 (1963): 211–17.

– *Hero and Exile: The Art of Old English Poetry*. Ed. George Hardin Brown. London: Hambledon, 1989.

Greenfield, Stanley B., and Daniel G. Calder. *A New Critical History of Old English Literature*. New York: New York University Press, 1986.

Haines, Dorothy. 'Unlocking *Exodus* ll. 516–532.' *JEGP* 98 (1999): 481–98.
– 'Vacancies in Heaven: The Doctrine of Replacement and *Genesis A.*' *N&Q* 44 (1997): 150–4.
Halbrooks, John. 'Byrhtnoth's Great-Hearted Mirth, or Praise and Blame in *The Battle of Maldon.*' *PQ* 82 (2003): 235–55.
Halbwachs, Maurice. *Les cadres sociaux de la mémoire.* Paris: Presses Universitaires de France, 1952. Ed. and trans. Lewis A. Coser as *On Collective Memory.* Chicago: University of Chicago Press, 1992.
– *La mémoire collective.* Paris: Presses Universitaires de France, 1950. Trans. Francis J. Ditter, Jr, and Vida Yazdi Ditter as *The Collective Memory.* New York: Harper and Row, 1980.
Hall, J.R. 'The Old English Epic of Redemption: The Theological Unity of MS Junius 11.' In Liuzza, *MS Junius 11*, 20–52. Originally pub. *Traditio* 32 (1976): 185–208.
– 'The Old English Epic of Redemption: Twenty-five Year Retrospective.' In Liuzza, *MS Junius 11*, 53–68.
– 'On the Bibliographic Unity of Bodleian MS Junius 11.' *AN&Q* 24 (1986): 104–7.
Hanning, Robert W. '*Beowulf* as Heroic History.' *Medievalia et Humanistica*, n.s., 5 (1974): 77–102.
– *The Vision of History in Early Britain: From Gildas to Geoffrey of Monmouth.* New York: Columbia University Press, 1966.
Hansen, Jim. 'Formalism and Its Malcontents: Benjamin and de Man on the Function of Allegory.' *New Literary History* 35 (2004): 663–83.
Hanson, Kristin, and Paul Kiparsky. 'The Nature of Verse and Its Consequences for the Mixed Form,' in Harris and Reichl, *Prosimetrum*, 17–44.
Hanssen, Beatrice. *Walter Benjamin's Other History: Of Stones, Animals, Human Beings, and Angels.* Berkeley: University of California Press, 1998.
Hardison, O.B. *Christian Rite and Christian Drama in the Middle Ages: Essays in the Origin and Early History of Modern Drama.* Baltimore: Johns Hopkins University Press, 1965.
Harris, Joseph. '"Deor" and Its Refrain: Preliminaries to an Interpretation.' *Traditio* 43 (1987): 23–53.
– 'Love and Death in the *Männerbund*: An Essay with Special Reference to the *Bjarkamál* and *The Battle of Maldon.*' In *Heroic Poetry in the Anglo-Saxon Period: Studies in Honor of Jess B. Bessinger, Jr*, ed. Helen Damico and John Leyerle, 77–114. Kalamazoo, MI: Medieval Institute Publications, 1993.
– 'A Nativist Approach to *Beowulf*: The Case of Germanic Elegy.' In *Companion to Old English Poetry*, ed. Henk Aertsen and Rolf H. Bremmer, Jr, 45–62. Amsterdam: VU University Press, 1994.

Harris, Joseph, and Karl Reichl, eds. *Prosimetrum: Cross-Cultural Perspectives on Narrative in Prose and Verse*. Cambridge: D.S. Brewer, 1997.

Hart, Cyril. 'The B Text of the *Anglo-Saxon Chronicle*.' *JMH* 8 (1982): 241–99.

Hauer, Stanley R. 'The Patriarchal Digression in the Old English *Exodus*, Lines 362–446.' *SP* 78, no. 5 (1981): 77–90.

Head, Pauline E. *Representation and Design: Tracing a Hermeneutics of Old English Poetry*. Albany: State University of New York Press, 1997.

Hegel, G.W.F. *Introductory Lectures on Aesthetics*. Trans. Bernard Bosanquet. Ed. and introd. Michael Inwood. London: Penguin, 1993.

Helmling, Steven. 'Constellation and Critique: Adorno's Constellation, Benjamin's Dialectical Image.' *Postmodern Culture* 14, no. 1 (2003). http://muse.jhu.edu/journals/pmc/v014/14.1helmling.html.

Hen, Yitzhak, and Matthew Innes, eds. *The Uses of the Past in the Early Middle Ages*. Cambridge: Cambridge University Press, 2000.

Herbison, Ivan. 'The Idea of the "Christian Epic": Towards a History of an Old English Poetic Genre.' In Toswell and Tyler, *'Doubt Wisely'*, 342–61.

Hermann, John P. *Allegories of War: Language and Violence in Old English Poetry*. Ann Arbor: University of Michigan Press, 1989.

Hieatt, Constance B. 'Divisions: Theme and Structure of *Genesis A*.' *NM* 81 (1980): 243–51.

Higham, N.J. *The English Conquest: Gildas and Britain in the Fifth Century*. Manchester: Manchester University Press, 1994.

Hill, David, ed. *Ethelred the Unready: Papers from the Millenary Conference*. Oxford: British Archaeological Reports, 1978.

Hill, Joyce. 'The Benedictine Reform and Beyond.' In Pulsiano and Treharne, *Companion*, 151–69.

– 'Confronting *Germania Latina*: Changing Responses to Old English Biblical Verse.' In Liuzza, *MS Junius 11*, 1–19. Originally pub. *Latin Culture and Medieval Germanic Europe. Proceedings of the First Germania Latina Conference Held at the University of Groningen, 26 May 1989*, ed. Richard North and Tette Hofstra, 71–88. Groningen: E. Forsten, 1992.

Hill, Thomas D. 'The Fall of Angels and Man in the Old English *Genesis B*.' In *Anglo-Saxon Poetry: Essays in Appreciation for John C. McGalliard*, ed. Lewis E. Nicholson and Dolores Warwick Frese, 279–90. Notre Dame: University of Notre Dame Press, 1975.

– 'The Fall of Satan in the Old English *Christ and Satan*.' *JEGP* 76 (1977): 315–25.

– 'History and Heroic Ethic in *Maldon*.' *Neophilologus* 54 (1970): 291–6.

– 'The Measure of Hell: *Christ and Satan* 695–722.' *PQ* 60 (1982 for 1981): 409–14.

- 'The Myth of the Ark-Born Son of Noe and the West-Saxon Royal Genealogical Tables.' *Harvard Theological Review* 80, no. 3 (1987): 379–83.
- 'Pilate's Visonary Wife and the Innocence of Eve: An Old Saxon Source for the Old English *Genesis B*.' *JEGP* 101 (2002): 170–84.
- 'The "Variegated Obit" as an Historiographic Motif in Old English Poetry and Anglo-Latin Historical Literature.' *Traditio* 44 (1988): 101–24.
- '"When the Leader is Brave ...": An Old English Proverb and Its Vernacular Context.' *Anglia* 119 (2001): 232–6.

Hollis, Stephanie. 'The Thematic Structure of the *Sermo Lupi*.' *ASE* 6 (1977): 175–95.

Holsinger, Bruce. 'The Parable of Cædmon's *Hymn*: Liturgical Invention and Literary Tradition.' *JEGP* 106 (2007): 149–75.

Homann, Holger. 'Das Ludwigslied – Dichtung im Dienste der Politik?' In *Traditions and Transitions: Studies in Honor of Harold Jantz*, ed. Lieselotte E. Kurth, William H. McClain, and Holger Homann, 17–28. Munich: Delp, 1972.

Howe, Nicholas. 'The Cultural Construction of Reading in Anglo-Saxon England.' In *The Ethnography of Reading*, ed. Jonathan Boyarin, 58–79. Berkeley: University of California Press, 1993.
- 'Falling into Place: Dislocation in the Junius Book.' In Amodio and O'Brien O'Keeffe, *Unlocking the Wordhord*, 14–37.
- 'Historicist Approaches.' In *Reading Old English Texts*, ed. Katherine O'Brien O'Keeffe, 79–100. Cambridge: Cambridge University Press, 1997.
- 'The Landscape of Anglo-Saxon England: Inherited, Invented, Imagined.' In *Inventing Medieval Landscapes: Senses of Place in Western Europe*, ed. John Howe and Michael Wolfe, 91–112. Gainesville: University Press of Florida, 2002.
- *Migration and Mythmaking in Anglo-Saxon England*. New Haven: Yale University Press, 1989. Repr. Notre Dame: University of Notre Dame Press, 2001.
- 'The New Millennium.' In Pulsiano and Treharne, *Companion*, 496–505.
- *The Old English Catalogue Poems*. Anglistica 23. Copenhagen: Rosenkilde and Bagger, 1985.
- 'Rome: Capital of Anglo-Saxon England.' *JMEMS* 34 (2004): 147–72.

Howlett, D.R. 'The Theology of Cædmon's Hymn.' *Leeds Studies in English* 7 (1974): 1–12.

Huisman, Rosemary. 'Anglo-Saxon Interpretative Practices and the First Seven Lines of the Old English Poem *Exodus*: The Benefits of Close Reading.' *Parergon*, n.s., 10, no. 2 (1992): 51–7.

Hunter, Michael. 'Germanic and Roman Antiquity and the Sense of the Past in Anglo-Saxon England.' *ASE* 3 (1974): 29–50.

Huppé, Bernard F. *Doctrine and Poetry: Augustine's Influence on Old English Poetry*. New York: State University of New York Press, 1959.

Irvine, Martin. 'Medieval Textuality and the Archaeology of Textual Culture.' In Frantzen, *Speaking Two Languages*, 181–210.

Irving, Edward B., Jr. '*Exodus* Retraced.' In *Old English Studies in Honour of John C. Pope*, ed. Robert B. Burlin and Edward B. Irving, Jr, 203–23. Toronto: University of Toronto Press, 1974.

– 'The Heroic Style in *The Battle of Maldon*.' *SP* 58 (1961): 457–67.

Isaacs, Neil D. '"The Death of Edgar" (and Others).' *AN&Q* 4 (1965): 52–5.

Jameson, Fredric. *Postmodernism, or, The Cultural Logic of Late Capitalism*. Durham: Duke University Press, 1991.

Jauss, Hans Robert. *Toward an Aesthetic of Reception*. Trans. Timothy Bahti. Theory and History of Literature 2. Minneapolis: University of Minnesota Press, 1982.

Johnson, David F., and Elaine Treharne, eds. *Readings in Medieval Texts: Interpreting Old and Middle English Literature*. Oxford: Oxford University Press, 2005.

Jost, Karl. 'Einige Wulfstantexte und ihre Quellen.' *Anglia* 56 (1932), 265–315.

– 'Wulfstan und die Angelsächsiche Chronik.' *Anglia* 47 (1923): 105–23.

Joy, Eileen A. '*Beowulf* and the Floating Wreck of History.' PhD diss., University of Tennessee, Knoxville, 2001.

– 'On the Hither Side of Time: Tony Kushner's *Homebody/Kabul* and the Old English *Ruin*.' *Medieval Perspectives* 19 (2005): 175–205.

Kant, Immanuel. *Critique of Judgement*. Trans. and introd. J.H. Bernard. New York: Hafner, 1951.

Kantorowicz, Ernst H. *The King's Two Bodies: A Study in Mediaeval Political Theology*. Princeton: Princeton University Press, 1957.

Kaske, R.E. 'The Sigemund-Heremod and Hama-Hygelac Passages in *Beowulf*.' *PMLA* 74 (1959): 489–94.

Keenan, Hugh T. '*Christ and Satan*: Some Vagaries of Old English Poetic Composition.' *Studies in Medieval Culture* 5 (1975): 25–32.

Kennedy, Edward Donald, Ronald Waldron, and Joseph S. Wittig, eds. *Medieval English Studies Presented to George Kane*. Wolfeboro, NH: D.S. Brewer, 1988.

Ker, Neil R. *Catalogue of Manuscripts Containing Anglo-Saxon*. Oxford: Clarendon, 1957.

– 'The Handwriting of Archbishop Wulfstan.' In Clemoes and Hughes, *England before the Conquest*, 315–31.

Kermode, Frank. *The Sense of an Ending: Studies in the Theory of Fiction with a New Epilogue*. Oxford: Oxford University Press, 2000.

Keynes, Simon. 'Ælfheah.' In Lapidge et al., *Blackwell Encyclopaedia*, 7.

– 'Anglo-Saxon Chronicle.' In Lapidge et al., Blackwell Encyclopaedia, 35–6.
– 'The Declining Reputation of King Æthelred the Unready.' In D. Hill, Ethelred the Unready, 227–53.
– The Diplomas of King Æthelred 'The Unready', 978–1016: A Study in Their Use as Historical Evidence. Cambridge: Cambridge University Press, 1980.
– 'The Historical Context of the Battle of Maldon.' In Scragg, Maldon, A.D. 991, 81–113.
Kiernan, Kevin S. Beowulf and the Beowulf Manuscript. Rev. ed. Ann Arbor: University of Michigan Press, 1997.
– 'Deor: The Consolations of an Anglo-Saxon Boethius.' NM 79 (1978): 333–40.
– 'Reading Cædmon's "Hymn" with Someone Else's Glosses.' In Old English Literature: Critical Essays, ed. Roy M. Liuzza, 103–24. New Haven: Yale University Press, 2002. Originally pub. Representations 32 (1990): 157–74.
Klinck, Anne L. '"The Riming Poem": Design and Interpretation.' NM 89 (1988): 266–79.
Kruger, Steven F. 'Oppositions and Their Opposition in the Old English Exodus.' Neophilologus 78 (1994): 165–70.
Labov, William. 'Some Further Steps in Narrative Analysis.' Journal of Narrative and Life History 7 (1997): 395–415.
Ladner, Gerhart B. The Idea of Reform: Its Impact on Christian Thought and Action in the Age of the Fathers. Cambridge, MA: Harvard University Press, 1959.
Lapidge, Michael. 'Beowulf and Perception.' Lecture, University of Notre Dame, Notre Dame, IN, 17 February 1998.
– 'Beowulf and Perception.' Sir Israel Gollancz Memorial Lecture 2000. PBA 111 (2001): 61–97.
– ed. The Cult of St Swithun. Winchester Studies 4.ii. Oxford: Clarendon, 2003.
– 'Gildas' Education and the Latin Culture of Sub-Roman Britain.' In Gildas: New Approaches, ed. Michael Lapidge and David Dumville, 27–50. Woodbridge: Boydell, 1984.
– 'The Life of St Oswald.' In Scragg, Maldon, A.D. 991, 51–8.
– 'Versifying the Bible in the Middle Ages.' In The Text in the Community: Essays on Medieval Works, Manuscripts, Authors, and Readers, ed. Jill Mann and Maura Nolan, 11–40. Notre Dame: University of Notre Dame Press, 2006.
Lapidge, Michael, John Blair, Simon Keynes, and Donald Scragg, eds. The Blackwell Encyclopaedia of Anglo-Saxon England. Oxford: Blackwell, 1999.
Leckie, R. William, Jr The Passage of Dominion: Geoffrey of Monmouth and the Periodization of Insular History in the Twelfth Century. Toronto: University of Toronto Press, 1981.
Lee, Ann Thompson. 'The Ruin: Bath or Babylon? A Non-Archaeological Investigation.' NM 74 (1973): 443–55.

Lees, Clare. 'Actually Existing Anglo-Saxon Studies.' *New Medieval Literatures* 7 (2005): 223–52.

– *Tradition and Belief: Religious Writing in Late Anglo-Saxon England.* Minneapolis: University of Minnesota Press, 1999.

Leibniz, G.W. *Monadology.* Trans. Paul Schrecker and Anne Martin Schrecker. Indianapolis: Bobbs-Merrill, 1965.

Lendinara, Patrizia. 'The Third Book of the *Bella Parisiacae urbis* by Abbo of Saint-Germain-des-Prés and Its Old English Gloss.' *ASE* 15 (1986): 73–89.

Lerer, Seth. 'The Endurance of Formalism in Middle English Studies.' *Literature Compass* 1 (2003): 1–15. http://www.blackwellsynergy.com/doi/full/10.1111/j.1741-4113.2004.00006.x.

– *Literacy and Power in Anglo-Saxon Literature.* Lincoln: University of Nebraska Press, 1991.

– 'Old English and Its Afterlife.' In *The Cambridge History of Medieval English Literature*, ed. David Wallace, 7–34. Cambridge: Cambridge University Press, 1999.

Levinson, Marjorie. 'What Is New Formalism?' *PMLA* 122 (2007): 558–69. A longer version of the essay is available at http://sitemaker.umich.edu/pmla_article.

Leyerle, John. 'The Interlace Structure of *Beowulf.*' *University of Toronto Quarterly* 37 (1967): 1–17.

Liuzza, Roy M. '*Beowulf*: Monuments, Memory, History.' In Johnson and Treharne, *Readings in Medieval Texts*, 91–108.

– ed. *The Poems of MS Junius 11: Basic Readings.* New York: Routledge, 2002.

– 'The Tower of Babel: *The Wanderer* and the Ruins of History.' *Studies in the Literary Imagination* 36, no. 1 (Spring 2003): 1–35.

Lockett, Leslie. 'An Integrated Re-examination of the Dating of Oxford, Bodleian Library, Junius 11.' *ASE* 31 (2002): 141–73.

Lucas, Peter J. 'Loyalty and Obedience in the Old English *Genesis* and the Interpolation of *Genesis B* into *Genesis A.*' *Neophilologus* 76 (1992): 121–35.

– 'Old English Christian Poetry: The Cross in *Exodus.*' In Bonner, *Famulus Christi*, 193–209.

– 'On the Incomplete Ending of *Daniel* and the Addition of *Christ and Satan* to MS Junius 11.' *Anglia* 97 (1979): 46–59.

Lund, Niels. 'The Danish Perspective.' In Scragg, *Maldon, A.D. 991*, 114–42.

Macrae-Gibson, O.D. 'How Historical Is *The Battle of Maldon*?' *Medium Ævum* 39 (1970): 89–107.

Magennis, Hugh. *Images of Community in Old English Poetry.* Cambridge: Cambridge University Press, 1996.

Malone, Kemp. '*Widsith* and the Critic.' *ELH* 5 (1938): 49–66.

Mann, Gareth. 'The Development of Wulfstan's Alcuin Manuscript.' In Townend, *Wulfstan*, 235–78.

Markland, Murray F. 'Boethius, Alfred, and *Deor*.' *MP* 66 (1968): 1–4.

Marold, Edith. 'The Relation between Verses and Prose in *Bjarnar saga Hítælakappa*.' In Poole, *Skaldsagas*, 75–124.

Mawer, Allen. 'The Redemption of the Five Boroughs.' *EHR* 38 (1923): 551–7.

Mazzotta, Giuseppe. *Dante, Poet of the Desert: History and Allegory in the Divine Comedy*. Princeton: Princeton University Press, 1979.

McIntosh, Angus. 'Early Middle English Alliterative Verse.' In *Middle English Alliterative Poetry and Its Literary Background: Seven Essays*, ed. David Lawton, 20–33. Woodbridge: D.S. Brewer, 1982.

– 'Wulfstan's Prose.' Sir Israel Gollancz Memorial Lecture 1948. *PBA* 35 (1949): 109–42.

McKie, Michael. 'The Origins and Early Development of Rhyme in English Verse.' *MLR* 92 (1997): 817–31.

McKill, Larry. 'Patterns of the Fall: Adam and Eve in the Old English *Genesis A*.' *Florilegium* 14 (1995–6): 25–41.

McKitterick, Rosamond. *Perceptions of the Past in the Early Middle Ages*. Notre Dame: University of Notre Dame Press, 2006.

Meaney, Audrey L. 'D: An Undervalued Manuscript of the Anglo-Saxon Chronicle.' *Parergon*, n.s., 1 (1983): 13–38.

– 'St. Neots, Æthelweard, and the Compilation of the *Anglo-Saxon Chronicle*: A Survey.' In *Studies in Earlier English Prose*, ed. Paul E. Szarmach, 123–39. Albany: State University of New York Press, 1986.

Metcalf, Allan A. *Poetic Diction in the Old English Meters of Boethius*. The Hague: Mouton, 1973.

Michel, Laurence. '*Genesis A* and the *Praefatio*.' *MLN* 62 (1947): 545–50.

Middleton, Anne. 'Aelfric's Answerable Style: The Rhetoric of the Alliterative Prose.' *Studies in Medieval Culture* 4 (1973): 83–91.

Miller, Molly. 'Bede's Use of Gildas.' *EHR* 90 (1975): 241–61.

Mintz, Susannah B. 'Words Devilish and Divine: Eve as Speaker in *Genesis B*.' *Neophilologus* 81 (1997): 609–23.

Mirsky, Aaron. 'On the Sources of the Anglo-Saxon *Genesis* and *Exodus*.' *ES* 48 (1967): 385–97.

Nelson, Janet L. 'Inauguration Rituals.' In *Early Medieval Kingship*, ed. Peter H. Sawyer and Ian N. Wood, 50–71. Leeds: University of Leeds School of History, 1977.

– 'National Synods, Kingship as Office, and Royal Anointing: An Early Medieval Syndrome.' *Studies in Church History* 7 (1971): 41–59.

Neville, Jennifer. 'History, Poetry, and "National" Identity in Anglo-Saxon England and the Carolingian Empire.' In *Germanic Texts and Latin Models: Medieval Reconstructions*, ed. K.E. Olsen, A. Harbus, and T. Hofstra, 107–26. Leuven: Peeters, 2001.

– 'Making Their Own Sweet Time: The Scribes of *Anglo-Saxon Chronicle A.*' In *The Medieval Chronicle II: Proceedings of the 2nd International Conference on the Medieval Chronicle Driebergen (Utrecht 16–21 July 1999)*, ed. Erik Kooper, 166–77. Amsterdam: Rodopi, 2002.

Niles, John D. 'Maldon and Mythopoesis.' *Mediaevalia* 17 (1994): 89–121.

– *Old English Heroic Poems and the Social Life of Texts*. Turnhout: Brepols, 2007.

– '*Widsith* and the Anthropology of the Past.' *PQ* 78 (1999): 171–213.

Niles, John D., and Mark Amodio, eds. *Anglo-Scandinavian England: Norse-English Relations in the Period before the Conquest*. Lanham, MD: University Press of America, 1989.

Oakden, J.P. *Alliterative Poetry in Middle English*. 2 vols. Manchester: Manchester University Press, 1930–5.

O'Brien O'Keeffe, Katherine. 'Body and Law in Late Anglo-Saxon England.' *ASE* 27 (1998): 209–32.

– 'The Book of Genesis in Anglo-Saxon England.' PhD diss., University of Pennsylvania, 1975.

– 'Deaths and Transformations: Thinking through the "End" of Old English Verse.' In *New Directions in Oral Theory*, ed. Mark C. Amodio, 149–78. Tempe: Arizona Center for Medieval and Renaissance Studies, 2005.

– 'Heroic Values and Christian Ethics.' In Godden and Lapidge, *Cambridge Companion*, 107–25.

– 'Orality and the Developing Text of Cædmon's *Hymn*.' *Speculum* 62 (1987): 1–20.

– 'Three English Writers on Genesis: Some Observations on Aelfric's Theological Legacy.' *Ball State University Forum* 19, no. 3 (Summer 1978): 69–78.

– *Visible Song: Transitional Literacy in Old English Verse*. Cambridge: Cambridge University Press, 1990.

Orchard, A.P.McD. 'Conspicuous Heroism: Abraham, Prudentius, and the Old English Verse *Genesis.*' In Liuzza, *MS Junius 11*, 119–36. Originally pub. *Heroes and Heroines in Medieval English Literature: A Festschrift Presented to André Crépin on the Occasion of His Sixty-fifth Birthday*, ed. Leo Carruthers, 45–58. Woodbridge: D.S. Brewer, 1994.

– 'Crying Wolf: Oral Style and the *Sermones Lupi.*' *ASE* 21 (1992): 239–64.

– 'Poetic Inspiration and Prosaic Translation.' In Toswell and Tyler, '*Doubt Wisely*,' 402–22.

Otten, Kurt. *König Alfreds Boethius*. Tübingen: Niemeyer, 1964.

Overing, Gillian R. *Language, Sign, and Gender in* Beowulf. Carbondale: Southern Illinois University Press, 1990.

– 'On Reading Eve: *Genesis B* and the Readers' Desire.' In Frantzen, *Speaking Two Languages*, 35–63.

Pabst, Bernhard. *Prosimetrum: Tradition und Wandel einer Literaturform zwischen Spätantike und Spätmittelalter*. 2 vols. Cologne: Böhlau, 1994.

Parks, Ward. 'Ring Structure and Narrative Embedding in Homer and *Beowulf*.' *NM* 89 (1988): 237–51.

Partner, Nancy. *Serious Entertainments: The Writing of History in Twelfth-Century England*. Chicago: University of Chicago Press, 1977.

Patterson, Lee. *Negotiating the Past: The Historical Understanding of Medieval Literature*. Madison: University of Wisconsin Press, 1987.

Pensky, Max. *Melancholy Dialectics: Walter Benjamin and the Play of Mourning*. Amherst: University of Massachusetts Press, 1993.

Phillips, Helen. 'The Order of Words and Patterns of Opposition in the *Battle of Maldon*.' *Neophilologus* 81 (1997): 117–28.

Poole, Reginald Lane. *Chronicles and Annals: A Brief Outline of Their Origin and Growth*. Oxford: Clarendon, 1926.

Poole, Russell, ed. *Skaldsagas: Text, Vocation, and Desire in the Icelandic Sagas of Poets*. Berlin: Walter de Gruyter, 2001.

Pope, J.C. *The Rhythm of Beowulf: An Interpretation of the Normal and Hypermetric Verse-Forms in Old English Poetry*. New Haven: Yale University Press, 1942.

Portnoy, Phyllis. '"Remnant" and Ritual: The Place of *Daniel* and *Christ and Satan* in the Junius Epic.' *ES* 75 (1994): 408–22.

– 'Ring Composition and the Digressions of *Exodus*: The "Legacy" of the "Remnant".' *ES* 82 (2001): 289–307.

Pulsiano, Phillip, and Elaine Treharne, eds. *A Companion to Anglo-Saxon Literature*. Oxford: Blackwell, 2001.

Raw, Barbara. 'The Construction of Oxford, Bodleian Library, Junius 11.' *ASE* 13 (1984): 187–207.

– 'The Probable Derivation of Most of the Illustrations in Junius 11 from an Illustrated Old Saxon *Genesis*.' *ASE* 5 (1976): 133–48.

Ray, Roger D. 'Bede, the Exegete, as Historian.' In Bonner, *Famulus Christi*, 125–40.

Remley, Paul G. 'The Latin Textual Basis of *Genesis A*.' *ASE* 17 (1988): 163–89.

– *Old English Biblical Verse: Studies in Genesis, Exodus, and Daniel*. Cambridge: Cambridge University Press, 1996.

Reynolds, Susan. 'What Do We Mean by "Anglo-Saxon" and "Anglo-Saxons"?' *Journal of British Studies* 24 (1985): 395–414.

Richardson, Peter R. 'Making Thanes: Literature, Rhetoric, and State Formation in Anglo-Saxon England.' *PQ* 78 (1999): 215–32.

Richter, Gerhard. 'History's Flight, Anselm Kiefer's Angels.' *Connecticut Review* 24 (2002): 113–36.

Robinson, Fred C. Beowulf *and the Appositive Style*. Knoxville: University of Tennessee Press, 1985.

– 'God, Death, and Loyalty in *The Battle of Maldon*.' In *J.R.R. Tolkien, Scholar and Storyteller: Essays* in Memoriam, ed. Mary Salu and Robert T. Farrell, 76–98. Ithaca: Cornell University Press, 1979.

Rollinson, Phillip B. 'The Influence of Christian Doctrine and Exegesis on Old English Poetry: An Estimate of the Current State of Scholarship.' *ASE* 2 (1973): 271–84.

Rollman, David A. '*Widsith* as an Anglo-Saxon Defense of Poetry.' *Neophilologus* 66 (1982): 431–9.

Rosen, Charles. 'The Origins of Walter Benjamin.' *New York Review of Books* 24, no. 18 (10 November 1977): 30–8.

– 'The Ruins of Walter Benjamin.' *New York Review of Books* 24, no. 17 (27 October 1977): 31–40.

Russom, Geoffrey. 'A Brief Response.' In Curzan and Emmons, *Unfolding Conversations*, 313–14.

– 'The Evolution of Middle English Alliterative Meter.' In Curzan and Emmons, *Unfolding Conversations*, 279–304.

Ryner, Bradley D. 'Exchanging Battle: Subjective and Objective Conflicts in *The Battle of Maldon*.' *ES* 87 (2006): 266–76.

Savage, Anne. 'The Old English *Exodus* and the Colonization of the Promised Land.' *New Medieval Literatures* 4 (2001): 39–60.

Scattergood, John. '*The Battle of Maldon* and History.' In *Literature and Learning in Medieval and Renaissance England: Essays Presented to Fitzroy Pyle*, ed. John Scattergood, 11–24. Dublin: Irish Academic Press, 1984.

Scheil, Andrew. 'The Historiographic Dimensions of *Beowulf*.' *JEGP* 107 (2008): 281–302.

Scholem, Gershom, and Theodor W. Adorno, eds. *The Correspondence of Walter Benjamin, 1910–1940*. Trans. Manfred R. Jacobson and Evelyn M. Jacobson. Chicago: University of Chicago Press, 1994.

Scragg, Donald G., ed. *The Battle of Maldon, A.D. 991*. Oxford: Basil Blackwell, 1991.

– 'Exeter Book.' In Lapidge et al., *Blackwell Encyclopaedia*, 177–8.

– 'The Nature of Old English Verse.' In Godden and Lapidge, *Cambridge Companion*, 55–70.

– 'A Reading of *Brunanburh*.' In Amodio and O'Brien O'Keeffe, *Unlocking the Wordhord*, 109–22.

Shepherd, G. 'The Prophetic Cædmon.' *RES*, n.s., 5 (1954): 113–22.

Sheppard, Alice. *Families of the King: Writing Identity in the* Anglo-Saxon Chronicle. Toronto: University of Toronto Press, 2004.

Sievers, Eduard. *Altgermanische Metrik*. Halle: M. Niemeyer, 1893.

– *Der Heliand und die angelsächsiche Genesis*. Halle: Niemeyer, 1875.

Silvestre, Juan Camilo Conde. 'The Spaces of Medieval Intertextuality: *Deor* as a Palimpsest.' *SELIM* 5 (1996): 63–77.

Sims-Williams, Patrick. 'Gildas and the Anglo-Saxons.' *Cambridge Medieval Celtic Studies* 6 (1983): 1–30.

Sisam, Kenneth. 'Anglo-Saxon Royal Genealogies.' *PBA* 39 (1953): 287–348.

Skemp, Arthur R. 'The Transformation of Scriptural Story, Motive, and Conception in Anglo-Saxon Poetry.' *MP* 4 (1907): 423–70.

Sørensen, Preben Meulengracht. 'The Prosimetrum Form 1: Verses as the Voice of the Past.' In Poole, *Skaldsagas*, 172–90.

Spiegel, Gabrielle. *Romancing the Past: The Rise of Vernacular Prose Historiography in Thirteenth-Century France*. Berkeley: University of California Press, 1993.

Stafford, Pauline. 'The Reign of Aethelred II: A Study in the Limitations on Royal Policy and Action.' In D. Hill, *Ethelred the Unready*, 15–46.

– *Unification and Conquest: A Political and Social History of England in the Tenth and Eleventh Centuries*. London: Edward Arnold, 1989.

Stanley, E.G., ed. *Continuations and Beginnings: Studies in Old English Literature*. London: Nelson, 1966.

– '*The Judgement of the Damned* (from Cambridge, Corpus Christi College 201 and other manuscripts) and the Definition of Old English Verse.' In *Learning and Literature in Anglo-Saxon England: Studies Presented to Peter Clemoes on the Occasion of His Sixty-fifth Birthday*, ed. Michael Lapidge and Helmut Gneuss, 363–91. Cambridge: Cambridge University Press, 1985.

– 'Rhymes in English Medieval Verse: From Old English to Middle English.' In Kennedy et al., *Medieval English Studies*, 19–54.

Stenton, Frank M. *Anglo-Saxon England*. 3rd ed. Oxford: Oxford University Press, 1971.

Stévanovitch, Colette. 'Envelope Patterns and the Unity of the Old English *Christ and Satan*.' *ASNSL* 233 (1996): 260–7.

– 'Envelope Patterns in *Genesis A* and *B*.' *Neophilologus* 80 (1996): 465–78.

Stewart, Susan. *On Longing: Narratives of the Miniature, the Gigantic, the Souvenir, the Collection*. Durham: Duke University Press, 1993.

Stock, Brian. *The Implications of Literacy: Written Language and Models of Interpretation in the Eleventh and Twelfth Centuries*. Princeton: Princeton University Press, 1983.

Stodnick, Jacqueline. 'Second-rate Stories? Changing Approaches to the *Anglo-Saxon Chronicle*.' *Literature Compass* 3 (2006): 1253–65. http://www.blackwell-synergy.com/doi/full/10.1111/j.17414113.2006.00380.x.

Swietek, Francis R. 'Gunther of Pairis and the *Historia Constantinopolitana*.' *Speculum* 53 (1978): 49–79.

Szarmach, Paul E. 'Ælfric as Exegete: Approaches and Examples in the Study of the *Sermones Catholici*.' In *Hermeneutics and Medieval Culture*, ed. Patrick J. Gallacher and Helen Damico, 237–47. Albany: State University of New York Press, 1989.

– 'Ælfric Revises: The Lives of Martin and the Idea of the Author.' In Amodio and O'Brien O'Keeffe, *Unlocking the Wordhord*, 38–61.

– 'The (Sub-) Genre of *The Battle of Maldon*.' In *The Battle of Maldon: Fiction and Fact*, ed. Janet Cooper, 43–61. London: Hambledon, 1993.

Tennenhouse, Leonard. '*Beowulf* and the Sense of History.' *Bucknell Review* 19 (1971): 137–46.

Thacker, Alan. 'Bede and the Ordering of Understanding.' In DeGregorio, *Innovation and Tradition*, 37–63.

Thompson, E.A. 'Gildas and the History of Britain.' *Britannia* 10 (1979): 203–26.

– 'Gildas and the History of Britain: Corrigenda.' *Britannia* 11 (1980): 344.

Thormann, Janet. 'The *Anglo-Saxon Chronicle* Poems and the Making of the English Nation.' In *Anglo-Saxonism and the Construction of Social Identity*, ed. Allen J. Frantzen and John D. Niles, 60–85. Gainesville: University of Florida Press, 1997.

– '*The Battle of Brunanburh* and the Matter of History.' *Mediaevalia* 17 (1994): 5–13.

Thornbury, Emily V. 'Admiring the Ruined Text: The Picturesque in Editions of Old English Verse.' *New Medieval Literatures* 8 (2006): 215–44.

Tolkien, J.R.R. '*Beowulf*: The Monsters and the Critics.' *PBA* 22 (1936): 245–95.

Toswell, M.J., and E.M. Tyler, eds. *Studies in English Language and Literature: 'Doubt Wisely': Papers in Honour of E.G. Stanley*. London: Routledge, 1996.

Townend, Matthew. 'Pre-Cnut Praise-Poetry in Viking Age England.' *RES*, n.s., 51 (2000): 349–70.

– ed. *Wulfstan, Archbishop of York: The Proceedings of the Second Alcuin Conference*. Turnhout: Brepols, 2004.

Townsend, Julie. 'The Metre of the *Chronicle*-verse.' *Studia Neophilologica* 68 (1996): 143–76.

Tuggle. Thomas T. 'The Structure of *Deor*.' *SP* 74 (1977): 229–42.

Turville-Petre, Thorlac. *England the Nation: Language, Literature, and National Identity, 1290–1340*. Oxford: Clarendon, 1996.

Tyler, Elizabeth M. *Old English Poetics: The Aesthetics of the Familiar in Anglo-Saxon England*. York: York Medieval, 2006.

– 'Poetics and the Past: Making History with Old English Poetry.' In *Narrative and History in the Early Medieval West*, ed. Elizabeth M. Tyler and Ross Balzaretti, 225–50. Turnhout: Brepols, 2006.

Vickrey, John F. 'The *Micel Wundor* of *Genesis B*.' *SP* 68 (1971): 245–54.

– 'The Vision of Eve in *Genesis B*.' *Speculum* 44 (1969): 86–102.

Warren, Michelle R. *History on the Edge: Excalibur and the Borders of Britain, 1100–1300*. Minneapolis: University of Minnesota Press, 2000.

Wentersdorf, Karl P. 'Observations on *The Ruin*.' *Medium Ævum* 46 (1977): 171–80.

Wert, Ellen L. 'The Poems of the Anglo-Saxon Chronicles: Poetry of Convergence.' PhD diss., Temple University, 1989.

Whitbread, Leslie. 'The Pattern of Misfortune in *Deor* and Other Old English Poems.' *Neophilologus* 54 (1970): 167–83.

White, Hayden. *The Content of the Form: Narrative Discourse and Historical Representation*. Baltimore: Johns Hopkins University Press, 1987.

– 'Historical Emplotment and the Problem of Truth.' In *Probing the Limits of Representation: Nazism and the 'Final Solution'*, ed. Saul Friedländer, 37–53. Cambridge, MA: Harvard University Press, 1992.

Whitelock, Dorothy. 'Archbishop Wulfstan, Homilist and Statesman.' *TRHS*, 4th ser., 24 (1942): 24–45.

– *The Audience of* Beowulf. Oxford: Clarendon, 1951.

– 'Two Notes on Ælfric and Wulfstan.' *MLR* 38 (1943): 122–6.

Whiting, B.J. 'The Rime of King William.' In *Philologica: The Malone Anniversary Studies*, ed. Thomas A. Kirby and Henry Bosley Woolf, 89–96. Baltimore: Johns Hopkins University Press, 1949.

Wieland, Gernot. '*Geminus stilus*: Studies in Anglo-Latin Hagiography.' In *Insular Latin Studies*, ed. Michael Herren, 113–33. Toronto: PIMS, 1981.

Wilcox, Jonathan. '*The Battle of Maldon* and the Anglo-Saxon Chronicle, 979–1016: A Winning Combination.' *Proceedings of the Medieval Association of the Midwest* 3 (1996): 31–50.

– 'Wulfstan's *Sermo Lupi ad Anglos* as Political Performance: 16 February 1014 and Beyond.' In Townend, *Wulfstan*, 375–96.

Withers, Benjamin C. 'A "Secret and Fevered Genesis": The Prefaces of the Old English Hexateuch.' *Art Bulletin* 81, no. 1 (March 1999): 53–71.

Woolf, Rosemary. 'The Fall of Man in *Genesis B* and the *Mystère d'Adam*.' In *Studies in Old English Literature in Honor of Arthur G. Brodeur*, ed. Stanley B. Greenfield, 187–99. Eugene: University of Oregon Press, 1963.

– 'The Ideal of Men Dying with Their Lord in the *Germania* and in *The Battle of Maldon*.' *ASE* 5 (1976): 63–81.
Wormald, Patrick. 'Bede, Beowulf, and the Conversion of the Anglo-Saxon Aristocracy.' In *Bede and Anglo-Saxon England: Papers in Honour of the 1300th Anniversary of the Birth of Bede, Given at Cornell University in 1973 and 1974*, ed. Robert T. Farrell, 32–95. London: British Archaeological Reports, 1978.
– 'Bede, the *Bretwaldas*, and the Origins of the *gens Anglorum*.' In *Ideal and Reality in Frankish and Anglo-Saxon Society: Studies Presented to J.M. Wallace-Hadrill*, ed. Patrick Wormald, Donald Bullough, and Roger Collins, 99–129. Oxford: Basil Blackwell, 1983.
– '*Engla Lond*: The Making of an Allegiance.' *Journal of Historical Sociology* 7 (1994): 1–24.
– *The Making of English Law: King Alfred to the Twelfth Century*. Vol. 1. *Legislation and Its Limits*. Oxford: Blackwell, 1999.
Wright, Charles D. 'The Blood of Abel and the Branches of Sin: *Genesis A*, *Maxims I*, and Aldhelm's *Carmen de virginitate*.' *ASE* 25 (1996): 7–19.
– '*Genesis A ad litteram*.' In *Old English Literature and the Old Testament*, ed. Michael Fox and Manish Sharma. Toronto: University of Toronto Press, forthcoming.
– 'The Lion Standard in *Exodus*: Jewish Legend, Germanic Tradition, and Christian Typology.' In Liuzza, *MS Junius 11*, 188–202. Originally pub. *ASNSL* 227 (1990): 138–45.
Wright, Neil. 'Did Gildas Read Orosius?' *Cambridge Medieval Celtic Studies* 9 (1985): 31–42. Repr. as chap. 4 in *History and Literature in Late Antiquity and the Early Medieval West: Studies in Intertextuality* (Aldershot: Variorum, 1995).
Wyschogrod, Edith. *An Ethics of Remembering: History, Heterology, and the Nameless Others*. Chicago: University of Chicago Press, 1998.
Zangemeister, Karl, and Wilhelm Braune. 'Bruchstücke der altsächsichen Bibeldichtung aus der Bibliotheca Palatina.' *Neue Heidelberger Jahrbücher* 4 (1894): 205–94.
Ziolkowski, Jan. 'The Prosimetrum in the Classical Tradition.' In Harris and Reichl, *Prosimetrum*, 45–65.
Žižek, Slavoj. *The Sublime Object of Ideology*. London: Verso, 1989.

Index

TORONTO ANGLO-SAXON SERIES

General Editor: Andy Orchard

Editorial Board
Roberta Frank
Thomas N. Hall
Antonette diPaolo Healey
Michael Lapidge